Colección Támesis
SERIE A: MONOGRAFÍAS, 293

A COMPANION TO CATALAN CULTURE

Over the past three centuries, the millennium personality of Catalonia has been 'disappeared', submerged and fractured by a centralist system obsessed with the cleansing of all vestiges of national difference from a homogenized Spain. Out of this configuration has emerged a fragmented vision of Catalan culture appreciated mainly through the sporadic protagonism of such irrepressible geniuses as Gaudí, Dalí, Miró and Bigas Luna.

The present volume offers a more comprehensive understanding of Catalonia's creative contribution across a broader spectrum of achievement. Written by an international team of scholars and focusing on the modern age, this monograph privileges not only conventional areas such as history, music, language, literature and the arts, but also popular experience, with elements such as sport, cinema, festivals and cuisine.

DOMINIC KEOWN is Reader in Catalan at the University of Cambridge.

Tamesis

Founding Editors
†J. E. Varey

†Alan Deyermond

General Editor
Stephen M. Hart

Series Editor of Fuentes para la historia del teatro en España
Charles Davis

Advisory Board
Rolena Adorno
John Beverley
Efraín Kristal
Jo Labanyi
Alison Sinclair
Isabel Torres
Julian Weiss

A COMPANION TO
CATALAN CULTURE

Edited by
Dominic Keown

TAMESIS

© Contributors 2011

All Rights Reserved. Except as permitted under current legislation no part of this work may be photocopied, stored in a retrieval system, published, performed in public, adapted, broadcast, transmitted, recorded or reproduced in any form or by any means, without the prior permission of the copyright owner

First published 2011 by Tamesis, Woodbridge

ISBN 978 1 85566 227 8

Tamesis is an imprint of Boydell & Brewer Ltd
PO Box 9, Woodbridge, Suffolk IP12 3DF, UK
and of Boydell & Brewer Inc.
668 Mt Hope Avenue, Rochester, NY 14620, USA
website: www.boydellandbrewer.com

A CIP catalogue record for this book is available
from the British Library

The publisher has no responsibility for the continued existence or accuracy of URLs for external or third-party internet websites referred to in this book, and does not guarantee that any content on such websites is, or will remain, accurate or appropriate

Papers used by Boydell & Brewer Ltd are natural, recyclable products made from wood grown in sustainable forests

Printed in Great Britain by
CPI Antony Rowe, Chippenham and Eastbourne

CONTENTS

List of Illustrations	vi
Contributors	vii
Acknowledgements	ix
Introduction: Catalan Culture: Once More unto the Breach?	1
1. Contemporary Catalan Culture DOMINIC KEOWN	13
2. Medieval Catalan Culture, 801–1492 ALEXANDER IBARZ	41
3. Catalonia: From Industrialization to the Present Day ANTONI SEGURA I MAS and ELISENDA BARBÉ I POU	71
4. Barcelona: The Siege City ROBERT DAVIDSON	97
5. The Catalan Language MIQUEL STRUBELL	117
6. Sport and Catalonia LOUISE JOHNSON	143
7. The Music of Catalonia TESS KNIGHTON	163
8. Catalan Cinema: An Uncanny Transnational Performance JAUME MARTÍ-OLIVELLA	185
9. Festival and the Shaping of Catalan Community DOROTHY NOYES	207
10. What's Cooking in Catalonia? MONTSERRAT ROSER I PUIG	229
Index	253

LIST OF ILLUSTRATIONS

Plates
Between pages 150–151

1. Miquel Poveda, Catalan flamenco singer and actor
2. Christ Pantocrator, Sant Esteve de Llanars, twelfth century
3. Poster for the 1936 Workers' Games by Josep Renau
4. Poster for Las Arenas Swimming Pool by Josep Renau
5. Photograph of a *correfoc*
6. Series of famous *caganers* including Sarkozy, Bruni and Bart Simpson
7. Carrying down the *falles* on St John's Eve, Durro (Alta Ribagorça)
8. *Sardanes* at the Easter *aplec*, La Pobla de Montornès (Tarragonès)

Figures

1. 'Poema', visual poem by Joan Brossa, 1969	28
2. Counties of Catalonia/Septimania in the ninth century	43
3. Catalonia and the Midi before Muret (1213)	52
4. Catalan Federation and trade in the Mediterranean (thirteenth to fifteenth century)	66
5. Map of the Catalan-speaking areas	121

CONTRIBUTORS

Elisenda Barbé i Pou is an award-holding researcher (FPU-MICINN) at the *Centre d'Estudis Històrics Internacionals de la Universitat de Barcelona*. She is member of the *Grup de Recerca i Anàlisi del Món Actual* (GRANMA), a research group recognized by the *Generalitat de Catalunya* with its project 'El franquisme a Catalunya: institucionalització del règim i organització de l'oposició (1938–1979)', financed by the *Ministerio de Ciencia e Innovación* (Ref.: HAR2009-10979 [subprograma HIST]).

Robert Davidson is Associate Professor of Spanish and Catalan at the University of Toronto. He is the author of *Jazz Age Barcelona* (2009) and has published on different aspects of the Castilian and Catalan avant-gardes, cultural theory and film. Professor Davidson is Associate Editor of *Catalan Review* and was Book Review Editor of the *Revista Canadiense de Estudios Hispánicos* between 2003 and 2009.

Alexander Ibarz studies medieval vernacular literatures (mainly Occitan and Catalan) and Romance Philology, and has written on the Catalan Troubadours, the stylistics of Occitan verse, Troubadorian *koiné* and the idea of Spain in the Chronicle of Jaume I. He teaches Hispanic Studies at the Institute for Lifelong Learning of Sheffield University.

Louise Johnson is Senior Lecturer in Catalan and Spanish in the School of Modern Languages and Linguistics at the University of Sheffield. She specializes in modern Catalan and peninsular Spanish literature and culture, and has published widely on physical and sporting culture and on major twentieth-century writers such as Llorenç Villalonga, Manuel de Pedrolo, Maria-Aurèlia Capmany and Guillem Viladot.

Dominic Keown is a fellow of Fitzwilliam College and Reader in Catalan Studies in the Department of Spanish and Portuguese at the University of Cambridge. He has published widely on contemporary Catalan and Spanish literature and film, and is editor of the *Journal of Catalan Studies* and the Anglo-Catalan Society's Occasional Papers.

Tess Knighton holds an ICREA research chair in Music History at the Institució Milà i Fontanals, Barcelona. Recent publications include a co-edited volume, with Alvaro Torrente, on the *villancico*, which won the Robert M. Stevenson Award for Outstanding Scholarship in Iberian Music of the American Musicological Society, 2008.

Jaume Martí-Olivella is an Associate Professor of Hispanic Cultural Studies at the University of New Hampshire. He is the co-founder of CINE-LIT and also co-founder and former President of the North American Catalan Society. He has published *Basque Cinema: An Introduction* (2003) and co-authored *Spain is (Still) Different. Tourism and Discourse in Spanish Identity* (2008).

Dorothy Noyes is Associate Professor, with a joint appointment in English and Comparative Studies, at the Ohio State University, where she also directs the Center for Folklore Studies. She is author of the landmark work in ethnography, *Fire in the Plaça: Catalan Festival Politics after Franco* (2003), which won the Fellows of the American Folklore Society Book Prize in 2005.

Montserrat Roser i Puig is Senior Lecturer in Hispanic Studies at the University of Kent. She has written a monograph on the Catalan critic, poet and translator Marià Manent (1998), and edited the volumes: *La recepció de la literatura catalana a Europa* (2002), *Intertextualitat a la literatura Catalana contemporània* (2007) and *A Female Scene: Three Plays by Catalan Women* (2007).

Antoni Segura i Mas is Professor of History at the University of Barcelona where he is Director of the *Centre d'Estudis Històrics Internacionals*. He is head of the *Grup de Recerca i Anàlisi del Món Actual* (GRANMA), a research group recognized by the *Generalitat de Catalunya* with its project 'El franquisme a Catalunya: institucionalització del règim i organització de l'oposició (1938–1979)', financed by the *Ministerio de Ciencia e Innovación* (Ref.: HAR2009-10979 [subprograma HIST]).

Miquel Strubell is currently director of the Linguamón-UOC Chair in Multilingualism at the Universitat Oberta de Catalunya. He has co- ordinated several projects for the European Commission and the European Parliament in the field of languages and recently co-authored *Llengua i reivindicacions nacionals a Catalunya. Evolució de les habilitats, dels usos i de la transmissió lingüística* (1997–2008) published in 2009.

ACKNOWLEDGEMENTS

Research for this project was made possible by a generous Batista i Roca award from the *Agència de Gestió d'Ajuts Universitaris i de Recerca* (AGAUR), of the *Generalitat de Catalunya*.

Fitzwilliam College, Cambridge, kindly provided assistance for the index.

INTRODUCTION

Catalan Culture: Once More unto the Breach?

Towards the end of the last century a sea-change occurred in British and Irish Hispanism as a previously held fixation with literature gave way to interest in a broader range of creative production. The pioneering volume in this respect was *Spanish Cultural Studies: An Introduction*, compiled in 1995 by Helen Graham and Jo Labanyi; and the initiative prospered four years later with David Gies' *Cambridge Companion to Modern Spanish Culture* and a further major compendium in 2000, *Contemporary Spanish Cultural Studies*, edited by Barry Jordan and Rikki Morgan-Tamosunas. All these publications offer comprehensive accounts of the nature of this discipline and the value of the broader sweep it offers to an understanding of that country and its peculiarities. And, as such, there is no need to rehearse the merits and relevance of such a perspective here.[1]

While all these volumes make a creditable effort not to exclude the contribution of Catalonia to major features of the cultural life of the state, this area of interest never quite manages to sit comfortably within the parameters established. On occasions, for example, the Catalan experience can find its way into mainstream deliberation only to disappear from view at other moments of equal significance. Elsewhere it tends to hang like an appendage which, despite the accuracy of the study, seems to be attached almost as an afterthought, vaguely confluent with the central thrust of the argument. Quite simply – and no specific reference to these helpful overviews is intended – the subject for consideration is simply too broad to fit compactly into the Spanish experience and, as a consequence, criteria for definition can often lack the necessary precision. Here and there, for example, movements that might reject the very epithet of Spanish (like the *Nova Cançó*) may find

---

[1] We have not referred here to the helpful *Companion to Hispanic Studies* (2002), edited by Professor C. Davies, as this tends to lend itself more specifically to the remit of that particular academic discipline than to the broader area of cultural studies.

themselves considered central to the state-wide chorus whereas the response of others (like the influential Barcelona School in cinema) may be surprisingly absent from consideration.

To our way of thinking – and there is little censure intended in this criticism: in a field as understudied as Catalan any consideration of its creativity is to be applauded – such editorial discomfort and hesitancy is only natural. For it is our contention that these various items may best be assimilated within the limits of their own tradition. And it is this impression – the promotion of a distinctive vision of Catalan national culture – that constitutes the principal motive for the confection of the present volume. In this way, with this attempt to offer some sort of coherence to various strands of the creative chorus of that nation we find ourselves, at the start of the second decade of the twenty-first century, very much at the same point of an inchoate exercise as Professors Graham and Labanyi, who remarked in 1995 that despite 'the excellent work being done in individual areas, there has to date been little attempt at interdisciplinary co-ordination'.[2]

In the face of such divergent scholarship their syncretic aim was, of course, 'the establishment of Spanish cultural studies as a discipline', which was to bear real fruit not only in the numerous valuable publications and journals that have now consolidated the subject so successfully but also in the wider appreciation of that country's contemporary experience now afforded students by university departments.[3] Our starting point – the desire to provide a more coherent appreciation of things Catalan – is considerably more modest. Devoid of any visionary zeal, we seek simply to offer the English reader a first port of call for information regarding the artistic personality of that nation across as broad a spectrum as is possible in a volume of this size.

Unfortunately, our endeavour is considerably more problematic than that of the more established discipline of Spanish Studies. One of the corollaries of the secular and repressive unitarianism in Spain of the modern period has been, of course, the international projection of the language and the state as total and homogeneous entities. To this effect, ignorance of that country's distinct national cultures and their relevance to the creative art of Euskal Herria, Galicia and Catalonia has ensured that such fundamental elements have been left only partially appreciated, both at home and abroad, with the whole experience tending to be subsumed unhelpfully into the wider category of Spanish.

An established player on the world map, Spain has for long enjoyed the

---

[2] Graham & Labanyi, 1995, 'Editors' Preface', v.
[3] Graham & Labanyi, 1995, p. 1.

glories of empire, historical solidity and international recognition. On the other hand, over the past three centuries, there have been little more than four decades when Catalonia was not actively 'disappeared' and its signs of difference proscribed or overlooked by a perennially repressive, centralist unit. As a result, the assimilation of its cultural voice has been severely compromised. And the fracturing and fragmentation occasioned by this oppression will be inevitably visited upon any exercise that is, like the present, geared towards an awareness of that culture as a whole.

To this extent, the disintegration experienced historically and politically by Catalonia has occasioned an identical imbalance in the sphere of cultural production and, by extension, its appreciation. Whereas, for example, a healthy presence may be appreciated in the music, literature, cinema and art of Spain, the Catalan side of the equation is riddled with voids and lacunae. And if, in their approach to the Spanish experience, Professors Graham and Labanyi identified a whole litany of areas they felt lacking from their study, in our case – that of a marginalized, repressed minority – the list could be extended by many a country mile.

However, it is hoped that this imbalance might be rectified to some extent by the attention we have attempted to show to both conventional academic subjects and also those areas more familiar to the popular experience. In this effort to bridge the divide between both elitist and vulgar poles of the creative spectrum – following the lead of our predecessors in their volumes devoted to Spain – our purpose has also been to consider how notions of high and low culture are evaluated and manipulated. As such, our spectrum encompasses the conventionally academic perspective offered by the fields of history (contemporary and medieval), linguistics and music to the more popular areas of experience that now form such a familiar part of the agenda of cultural studies: cinema, sport, festivals, the city of Barcelona and gastronomy.

To this effect, with this more panoramic view, we aspire to redress in some way the enormous fragmentation surrounding assimilation of the Catalan experience whose uneven reception may be illustrated by the fact that when international attention has focused on that nation it has generally been attracted by figures (often eccentrics) of unquestionable quality. Top of the list are, of course, the extraordinary Antoni Gaudí and Salvador Dalí, though we should in no way forget the respective geniuses of Pau Casals, Joan Miró, Roberto Gerhard, Bigas Luna, Josep Trueta, Ricard Bofill, Ferran Adrià, Montserrat Caballé, Josep Carreras and, last but not least, the institution that is FC Barcelona.

What emerges from this splintered roll is, of course, the impression of a series of isolated voices crying in the wilderness. It is our contention, however, that despite its many fissures Catalan culture is fuller and more rounded than the appreciation of these isolated celebrities might allow. If those named here have impressed internationally it is precisely because their speciality expresses itself through a medium that is not globally restrictive: graphic art and design, music, medicine, sport and gastronomy are immediately appreciated and, unlike literature, know neither the limits of language nor frontiers. In this respect, our volume seeks to retrieve a modicum of coherence from such eccentricity by proposing that these individuals did not emerge from a vacuum but are merely distinguished exponents of a cultural choir whose fellow protagonists – through repression, inaccessibility or just plain ignorance – have been denied the opportunity of the reception they so richly deserve.

Despite these contextual difficulties, then, the general pattern we have elected to follow is largely similar to those previous works related to our topic. In his excellent overview of Catalan literature – which is in itself an inspiration to the present volume – Arthur Terry considered that an exercise of this type should 'direct the reader to the most important works, placing them in their historical and social context, commenting on their most distinctive features'.[4] Or, as Graham and Labanyi would have it: 'to fully appreciate cultural processes and forms one needs to know what are the issues of legitimization at stake in any given conjuncture'.[5] It is precisely this balance we have endeavoured to achieve amid all the environmental hazards and, to this effect, the reader will not be surprised to encounter the primacy of history, both medieval and contemporary, and its explicit interface with creativity – though we have also pointed out that such an approach is not devoid of a certain reductive peril.

In this respect, it might be apposite at this juncture to consider our essay on Medieval Culture whose inclusion might appear curious in the context of a discipline which, as the previous volumes attest, tends to focus predominantly on the contemporary period (though there is, to our way of thinking, no reason why this should exclusively be the case). The fact is that this golden age simply cannot be ignored as it stands out as a continual point of reference attesting the historic presence of Catalan identity. Indeed, this particular area is exceptional in Catalan Studies. In the academic context it is one of the most prominent – not to say 'normal' – fields of study, if by 'normal' we mean internationally appreciated and well-researched. In this respect its artistic significance and academic weight require that its importance be drawn to the attention of the foreign reader.

---

[4] Terry, 2003, 'Preface', vii.
[5] Graham & Labanyi, 1995, p. 6.

What is more – and just as is the case with other minority nations – the presence of the past, in the form of recognition of previous achievements in self-legislation, conquest overseas, music, literature and philosophy, is fundamental to the recuperation of collective consciousness and the historic legitimacy of particularity and self-governance. In this respect, a literary comparison between the case of Catalonia and Ireland is revealing and might be illustrated by the restive, engaging Romanticism of the contemporaries Thomas Moore (1780–1852) and Bonaventura Aribau (1798–1862). Both poets were wont to reflect on the contemporary cultural (and, by extension, political) insignificance of their 'disappeared' nations when contrasted with the magnificence of a previous period. 'Let Erin Remember' and 'La Pàtria', for example, capture that same recourse to collective nostalgia, the remembrance of another age filled with culture and influence, which was to act so successfully as a catalyst for the restoration of national consciousness over the course of the following centuries.

Let Erin remember the days of old,	Pláume encara parlar la llengua d'aquells [sabis
Ere her faithless sons betray'd her;	Que ompliren l'univers de llurs costums é [lleys,
When Malachi wore the collar of gold,	La llengua d'aquells forts que acatáren los [Reys,
Which he won from her proud invader;	Defenguéren llurs drets, venjáren llurs [agravis.6
When her kings, with standard of green unfurl'd,	
Led the Red-Branch Knights to danger;	
Ere the emerald gem of the western world	
Was set in the crown of a stranger.	

For this reason, an understanding of the medieval period is essential for an appreciation of the Catalan mindset of today wherein the past remains so current in terms of collective sentiment and aspiration. What is more, in line with the broadening of focus as understood by cultural studies, Alexander Ibarz does not simply privilege any one particular academic field in his chapter (Chapter 2) but offers a more integrated view of the age in an outline that combines social and political history with art, literature, religion and conquest.

The inclusion of this element, which will surprise more than one critic, might serve to indicate how objectivity in terms of selection in an enterprise like the present is ultimately impossible. Like Professor Terry, we make no attempt to disguise this and stand by our choice of material even when this

---

6 It pleases me still to speak the language of those learned men/ who filled the universe with their customs and laws./ The language of those powerful men who respected their kings/ Defended their rights, avenged their affronts.

'runs counter to received opinion'.[7] Despite the risk involved we take comfort in the hope that our contribution might be the first step on the critical road to a more prolific appreciation of Catalan culture in the English-speaking world and that our success, and/or failure, will stimulate others to do further work in this area. Little could prove more satisfying for those involved in the promotion of this subject than the appearance of other volumes that postulated broader or even alternative agendas for the assimilation of this phenomenon.

As outlined earlier, the nature of this discipline requires a strong and reliable historical contextualization. To this effect we are grateful to colleagues in Catalonia for their contribution in key areas. Antoni Segura and Elisenda Barbé (Chapter 3) provide a detailed, essential yet accessible overview of the contemporary context. Similarly, it would be unimaginable to approach this subject without an informed introduction to the historical and political condition of the language which, as its recuperation attests, is of singular importance to the Catalan mindset. This daunting task, which includes references stretching over two millennia from Roman times to internet chat rooms, is compactly and expertly delivered by Miquel Strubell in an exemplary account of both philological development and ideological manipulation (Chapter 5).

These environmental elements, of course, form the cornerstone of the appreciation of the Catalan cultural fact in universities throughout the anglophone world, and their appearance in a volume of this sort is only to be expected. Such is not the case, however, with another mainstay of academia, classical music. Despite the strength of its orchestral and choral traditions this topic is largely unappreciated both at home and abroad. Tess Knighton's essay (Chapter 7), while rectifying this anomaly, also offers the broader perspective familiar to cultural studies in its isolation of the contextual dimension to this issue from medieval times to the renaissance witnessed in the last century and a half.

After such standard academic fare, however, the rest of the volume proceeds to open up those areas of contemporary experience that were previously ignored by elitist discourse. In many cases, the perspective adopted is dependent on the largely – though not always – related pillars of the general awareness about the subject and the bibliography available in English. One of the most dynamic features of contemporary scene in Catalonia, for example, is the theatre and performing arts where troupes like the *Joglars*, *Comediants*, *Dagoll-Dagom* and *La Fura dels Baus* have gained international recognition. Happily, the scholarship on this topic available to the English speaker is particularly strong,

---

[7] Terry, 2003, 'Preface', vii.

epitomized by the volume *Catalan Theatre 1975–2006: Politics, Identity and Performance* edited by María Delgado, David George and Lourdes Orozco, and the extensive and highly reliable contribution made by those involved in this field precludes the need for a chapter on the subject in our study. The same may be said of popular music where the studies by Josep Martí and others – together with the extensive discography available on the subject – furnish a scholarly introduction to the experience to the anglophone world.

The same cannot be said, however, for another area of profound actual interest: we refer, of course, to Barcelona. Though there is much valuable literature available on the city this, while accessible and informative, tends to be written with the tourist in mind. The issue, however, is also significant academically. Unlike other peripheral minority nations, the Catalans can boast of a thoroughly modern capital, which was designed to publish their claim for international recognition. In this respect, the very shape and look of the town has been predicated on concerns of a political nature. What is more, in this particular case it is not only the equation of metropolis with nation that is immensely noteworthy but also the historical tale this city has to tell, from anarchist insurgency and revolution to republic, blitz and fascist repression, which makes it acutely relevant to the wider context of the European experience in general.

In this respect, Robert Davidson (Chapter 4) skilfully picks his way through the fascinating recent scholarship devoted specifically to this subject in an engaging overview, which not only posits the equation of Barcelona with Catalan nationhood but identifies a siege mentality as representative of the experience of its population. Literally bombed into submission by the forces of centralism over the past century and a half, the Barcelonese are now seen to suffer a similar type of captivity by the international promotion of their 'designer' city as a cool or chic place to be, seemingly tailored to meet the needs of the foreign visitor and ex-pat resident. To this effect, we are presented with the poignantly ironic picture of inhabitants, once confronted by the marginalization of a living experience imposed from without, now threatened with alienation on their own door-step by the compulsive submission of politicians and city-planners to the vagaries of commercialization and rampant marketeering.

The similarly international profile that Spanish cinema has enjoyed recently, achieved mainly by the pre-eminence of the irrepressible Pedro Almodóvar, has meant that Catalan cinematography has also received collaterally some introductory attention from scholars in the US, the UK and Ireland. It is for this reason that Jaume Martí-Olivella (Chapter 8) has been able both to continue his more general consciousness-raising endeavours on the subject and offer, at the same time, some very specific readings of prominent films. In this respect, his account of the cinematic experience over the last fifty years is particularly stimulating as the full significance of the Barcelona School to Catalan production is exemplified and elucidated. At the same time, however, the impact of this tendency – and the no less powerful voice of Ventura Pons – upon successive film-makers is also considered, which leaves us with a fascinating insight into the efforts of the contemporary generation – Guerín, Balagué, Recha, Coixet – in reaction to the defining moment of Catalan film in the 1960s and 1970s.

Unfortunately, the rest of our contributors were at a comparative disadvantage for an overview of their particular field given the lack of bibliography in English at their disposal. Nonetheless, Louise Johnson (Chapter 6) is able to offer a broad view of the sporting experience despite the predominance of 2009 FIFA world club champions FC Barcelona in the football arena. Once again the topic for discussion is set within a clear social context which, while including the condition of women in the equation, also brings out the nationalist dimension to the sporting explosion of the first third of the last century, especially in the related areas of *escoltisme* (outdoor group activities such as rambling, orienteering, etc.) in which similarities with the contemporary experience in Britain are evident. Also of fundamental political significance in this respect is the Olympic element, which, from the earliest days of the modern movement up to the crowning moment of the XXV Olympiad in the Catalan capital, is of such acute relevance to aspirations for international recognition and representation in this context.

The self-same socio-political implications are also outlined in another area comparatively new to Hispanic academic study, gastronomy. After an informative introduction to the scientific relevance of the subject, Montserrat Roser i Puig's overview (Chapter 10) isolates the same external factors of history and ideology that surround cuisine no less than the other cultural values of Catalonia that are debated throughout this collection. Though apparently a sign of national identity as obvious as the language the formula is by no means so simple; and the chapter takes us through the real political complexity of the phenomenon. If initially our attention is drawn to the repressive manipulation of this issue through the years of the dictatorship, then the no less thorny nature of the subject is exposed in the years of democracy. Far from achieving a felicitous resolution, this topic has become even more fraught in the global age with a trenchant ideological battle being fought at present – as vehement as any in the field of contemporary politics, art and literature – by world-famous Michelin chefs as to what defines the culinary authenticity of the nation.

The ideological overlay to all things cultural in Catalonia, from film to food, is also underlined quite beautifully by Dorothy Noyes in her particularly engaging exposé of festivals (Chapter 9). From an initial outline of the origins of these events of folk history we are taken on a guided tour of their development through industrialization to the present day. Once again, we witness how, at critical points in contemporary history, the initial innocence of popular celebration becomes loaded with social and political conditioning in order to reflect the particular aspirations of a specific lobby. As was the case with the chapter on Barcelona, the detrimental effect of this type of interventionism is poignantly described and shown to constitute no less of a menace to Catalan popular vitality and lifestyle than other previous attempts to manipulate national expression.

As is only to be understood, despite the obvious overlaps and consistencies, the heterogeneity of these fields and the disparity between their development in academic and bibliographic terms further exemplifies the fragmentation caused by secular repression that has so blighted Catalan culture. As a result, in such an environment there can be no overarching norm or single standard that can be applied to the various elements of this very abnormal cultural experience. In editorial terms the point at issue is quite simply that there is no level playing field – no one-size-fits-all – in Catalan Studies. The fields of history and linguistics are, for example, much over-studied when compared to, say, gastronomy, sport and festivals. To this effect, it is impossible to impose any cohesive framework or *modus operandi* across all chapters and expect it to function. It would, in essence, constitute an attempt to impose a unity in assimilation that is simply not present in the fractured and fragmented Catalan experience.

As such, our contributors were invited to offer an introduction to their chosen field in a manner appropriate to that field's level of academic discourse. Those specialities that have enjoyed greater academic longevity and scholarship will inevitably be at an advantage. However, it should not be felt that such discrepancy is necessarily a drawback and the enthusiasm with which contributors have approached their subject is both positive and engaging. Indeed, a previous effort in a related area might act as an example of this. Though devoted exclusively to the world of letters, the 'Literary History of Spain' series, published in the early 1970s, offered an invaluable first port of call to undergraduates who, schooled merely in the appreciation of one particular text, were faced with the enormity of literary production as a whole. Looking beyond the limitations of its remit, the criteria established by the General Editor, Professor R. O. Jones, might well be applied to our enterprise in Catalan Studies:

> Beyond a necessary minimum, no attempt has been made to arrive at uniform criteria; the history displays therefore the variety of approach and

opinion to be found in a good university department of literature, a variety which we hope will prove stimulating. Each section takes account of the works of scholarship in its field, but we do not offer our history as a grey consensus of received opinion; each contributor has imposed his own appreciation to the extent that this could be appreciated with solid scholarship and argument.[8]

In this respect, when faced with such variety in topics and approaches, our introductory chapter seeks to function not only as an exercise in contextualization but also as a catch-all or back-up exercise. While it is hoped that this will be beneficial in papering over, to some extent, the inevitable voids and lacunae it can never be entirely successful or wholly encyclopaedic. It is hoped, however, that our partial prioritization of material may be compensated by other external factors. Certain areas of the Catalan experience, like the performing arts and folk music, for example, which certainly warrant greater exposure than our introduction can allow, have been the subject of in-depth scholarly studies in English. As such, if these elements are under-represented this is at least compensated by much valuable scholarship on the topic unlike, say, the city of Barcelona, festivals, sport and gastronomy, where the material available, although accessible and interesting, tends to be less thoroughly academic and more readily directed for tourist consumption. To this effect, contributors were requested to provide bibliographies and include a list of suggested reading with a view to pointing the reader in the right direction for further relevant information.

It is also not without some regret that we expose, at this point, an additional deficiency in the scope of our study. In terms of language, culture and history the term Catalan is also applied more widely to the experience of the Valencian community and the Balearic Islands as our map of the Catalan-speaking territories indicates. The issue may be underlined appropriately with reference to world of letters. Without the massive contribution of these two areas – as is attested in Alexander Ibarz's chapter on the Medieval Period – Catalan literature today would be at best different and at worst unrecognisable in terms of quality, breadth and depth.

Needless to say, the equation also holds good in other related areas of artistic endeavour. Unfortunately, despite our initial aspiration to adopt a comprehensive approach of the catalanophone territories in their entirety, it soon became apparent that the immensity of such a project lay beyond the possibilities of a single volume. Our desire is, however, that this shortage be

---

[8] R. O. Jones, 'Foreword by the General Editor', in Terry, 1972, xiv.

addressed and result in the production of similar initiatives focusing on these regions, which will provide a more complete account of the richness and variety of this fascinating culture across all its constituent areas.

On the more technical level, it is for the same reason of limitation of space that it was decided not to quote at length in Catalan, and authors have been good enough to substitute original versions with their own translations into English. Similarly, all references to material available on the Web were checked as accurate in the first week of January 2011. In an attempt to facilitate reading we have also endeavoured to reduce intrusion by translating acronyms, terms and titles from the original language only when these are not clear from the context or are not – like *Barça, Generalitat, maionesa* or *sardana* – recognizable currency. Similarly, given the breadth of our focus on culture the overlap and interrelationship between all areas will be apparent and complementary. As such we have only flagged up those cases when cross-referencing is felt particularly significant.

In conclusion we would merely reiterate that it is not the intention of this volume to provide a complete and comprehensive vision of Catalan culture but rather to offer as cohesive a first step as possible to key elements relating to the rich but torrid adventure of the creative experience of that nation. One more attempt, to borrow the plaint of Moore's indignant heart, 'to show that still she lives' and how.

Works Cited and Suggested Reading

Davies, Catherine (ed.) (2002) *Companion to Hispanic Studies*. London: Arnold.
Delgado, Maria, George, David and Orozco, Lourdes (eds) (2007) *Catalan Theatre 1975–2006: Politics, Identity and Performance*, special number of *Contemporary Theatre Review*, vol. 17, issue 3.
Gies, David (ed.) (1999) *The Cambridge Companion to Modern Spanish Culture*. Cambridge: Cambridge University Press.
Graham, Helen and Labanyi, Jo (eds) (1995) *Spanish Cultural Studies: An Introduction: The Struggle for Modernity*. Oxford: Oxford University Press.
Jordan, Barry and Morgan-Tamosunas, Rikki (eds) (2000) *Contemporary Spanish Cultural Studies*. London: Arnold.
Langdon-Davies, John (1929) *Dancing Catalans*. London: Jonathan Cape.
Martí, Josep (1994) 'The Sardana as a Socio-Cultural Phenomenon in Contemporary Catalonia', *Yearbook for Traditional Music*, 26, pp. 39–46.
────── (1995) 'Katalanische Volksmusik als ethnisches Konstrukt', in Lipp, C. (ed.) *Medien populärer Kultur. Erzählung, Bild und Objekt in der volkskundlichen Forschung*. Frankfurt/New York: Campus, pp. 242–251.
────── (1997) 'Folk Music Studies and Ethnomusicology in Spain', *Yearbook for Traditional Music*, 28, pp. 107–140.
────── (2001) 'Spain, Folk Music', in Sadie, Stanley (ed.) *The New Grove*.

Dictionary of Music and Musicians. London: Macmillan Publishers, vol. 24, pp. 135–154.

———— (2001b) 'Music and Ethnicity in Barcelona', *The World of Music*, 43, pp. 181–190.

———— (2002) 'Hybridization and its Meanings in the Catalan Musical Tradition', in Steingress, Gerhard (ed.) *Songs of the Minotaur. Hybridity and Popular Music in the Era of Globalization.*

Münster/Hamburg/Berlin/London: Lit. Verlag, pp. 113–138.

Martínez, Sílvia (2001) 'Seeking Connections Through A Sea: Mediterranean Sounds in Spanish Folk and Popular Music', in Plastino, Goffredo (ed.) New York and London: Routledge, 2003.

Terry, Arthur (1972) *Catalan Literature* (in the series 'A Literary History of Spain'). London: Ernest Benn.

———— (2003) *A Companion to Catalan Literature*. London: Tamesis.

1

Contemporary Catalan Culture

DOMINIC KEOWN

For the illustrious Dr Johnson the remarkable feature of a dog walking on its hind legs was not that it was done well or badly but that it was done at all. And to some extent the analogy could be applied to the cultural experience of contemporary Catalonia. When we bear in mind that over the past three centuries there have been little more than four decades when that nation and its signs of difference were not proscribed or persecuted, its continued, dynamic presence nowadays is nothing short of astonishing. What is more, while now free to be appreciated in all its richness, centuries of ignorance on an international scale – a direct corollary of the domestic repression – have left us with only a partial awareness of the phenomenon as things Catalan are all too readily subsumed into an anonymous Spanish whole. It is precisely this deficiency that we would seek to rectify with this volume and, to that end, we begin this introductory essay by casting our gaze back briefly to the early years of the eighteenth century.

The victory of the Bourbon pretender in the War of Spanish Succession in 1714 signified a crippling blow for the status of Catalan particularity and its recognition. Along with other areas of the ancient crown of Aragon, Catalonia had supported the Habsburg candidate, Archduke Charles of Austria. Needless to say, when his rival, Philippe d'Anjou, was installed on the throne reprisals against supporters of the unsuccessful contender were only to be expected. The retaliation, however, was to be savage and annihilatory with the first decrees of the new monarch designed to exact a firm, centralist control with a view to homogenizing the realm into a single, united and artificial whole.

The policy was, of course, brutally successful and spelt disaster for the nation of Catalonia. Indeed, the repression was so pervasive that throughout the eighteenth century it is difficult to perceive any distinctive autochthonous response to the overarching supranational identity imposed by Bourbon hegemony. To all extents and purposes – in this period known as that of *decadència* – Catalonia had been assimilated.¹ The same words might well have been uttered by General Franco after his victory in 1939 when, after the breathing space offered by the democratic pluralism of the Second Republic, this ancient civilization was suppressed with indescribable cruelty by the jackboot of fascism hell-bent, as their Bourbon predecessors, on imposing their ruthless vision of homogeneity over the multicultural mosaic of the state.

Yet the fact is that the totalitarian instinct did not triumph. As such, the frequently evoked notion of a cultural wasteland in the aftermath of 1714 is clearly partial. Indeed, the bias of such a view points to one of the failings in the standard academic appreciation of Catalonia currently prevalent, a blind spot that we would do well to correct. In simple terms, modern cultural histories have tended to ignore any distinct creative voice for this nation in the decadence of the eighteenth century because the focus of cultural assimilation is habitually trained at the heights of art and learning rather than the bathos of popular experience.

The point can be made quite simply. If Catalan survived this first age of suppression it was doubtless on account of the fact that the vast majority of society, the illiterate peasants and workers, were never to desist from the use of their maternal idiom for everyday discourse or the celebration of their local customs such as the enjoyment of popular theatre and festivals in the vernacular. It just so happens that with conventional academic preference fixed so firmly on the apex of cultural sophistication this demotic element, which was to become the depository of the collective soul, has been so frequently ignored. And in order to avoid this partiality we will attempt to supplement the standard academic approach by considering not only those elitist elements usually highlighted in cultural histories but also the more popular side of the equation. In this way, it is hoped that a fuller, more consolidated picture of the Catalan cultural enterprise might be better achieved.²

---

¹ The *decadència* is generally taken as starting around 1500 lasting until the early nineteenth century. Indeed, the cultural panorama at this time is so bleak that in his seminal *Companion to Catalan Literature* of 2003 Terry can only offer six pages to cover the literary output of these 300 years. Our interest, however, lies more particularly with the eighteenth century as this period covers both the proscription of the language and wider attempt to homogenize the state, policies that will be pursued by centralist governments until the present day.

² There are many theorists who have deliberated pertinently on the ideological implications of this phenomenon, and an informed synthesis is provided by Labanyi, 2002, pp. 1–22. In this context we are, of course, more concerned with the practical application of the broadening of the assimilatory vision for a more complete appreciation of the Catalan creative voice.

La Renaixença

Cultural histories have agreed that, after the final century of decadence overseen by Bourbon hegemony, the starting point for the re-entry of Catalan culture – understood as an elite discourse – into European artistic consciousness takes place after the Napoleonic period, at the end of the first third of the nineteenth century. Curiously, this reawakening of creative particularity has been afforded the specific date of 1833. It was in this year that Bonaventura Carles Aribau (1798–1862), an ex-pat banker from Barcelona working in Madrid, penned an ode in his native language in celebration of his boss's birthday. The piece was published in a review in that year, and its significance has been enough to warrant the author's name being honoured with one of the central thoroughfares in the city of his birth. The magnitude of what might seem an innocuous event, however, should not be underestimated. In sociolinguistic terms, this was the first time since 1714 that Catalan, at the time the sole preserve of the lower classes, peasantry and the street, had been employed in the elite context of literature.

The populace, of course, had never ceased expressing themselves in the autochthonous tongue and their literature was abundant throughout the century both in popular ballads and comical theatrical pieces exemplified by the *sainet*. The point may be further elaborated by the appearance in the early 1830s of *La cuynera catalana*, a cookbook of local dishes published in the vernacular for common consumption. However, the aristocracy and upper classes in Catalonia, just as their cousins in Scotland and Ireland, had adopted the language of the invader for the corresponding social prestige and recognition it embraced. As such, in this context the sophistication implied by an ode, penned by a banker of high standing, constituted an event of extreme moment. A member of the upper echelons of the social spectrum had begun to interest himself in the very language that his class had previously subordinated. What is more, after a slow start, the initiative taken by Aribau would gain currency and the process of linguistic recovery among the elite, as evinced in Miquel Strubell's chapter on the Catalan Language, would continue exponentially as the century progressed.

There is no denying, however, that the time was right for the resurgence of the common sentiment. Romanticism, a movement fascinated by both individual and collective identity, was at its strongest throughout Europe. The influence of Sir Walter Scott in this respect was enormous. His re-presentation of the essence of Scottish character struck a peculiarly strong chord in Catalonia at a historical moment that anticipated the reconstitution of other 'disappeared' or fractured national entities: Germany, Italy and, especially, Hungary. This was also the era of the poetic apology for repressed nations as epitomized by the personal and patriotic incantations of Thomas Moore after the suppression of the Croppy Rebellion of 1798 and the ensuing Act of Union. In this context, Shelley's defence of Ireland and Byron's efforts in Italy and Greece acted as a prelude for the amalgam of verse and nation that is epitomized by Aribau's ode and which would long continue in the Catalan tradition.

The process became more formalized in 1859 with the re-establishment of the *Jocs Florals*, the annual poetic festival first instituted by the Troubadours in 1324. As Alexander Ibarz's chapter on Medieval Catalonia attests, the cultural riches of that period were to act as inspiration for the recuperation of regional pride that had for long lain dormant during the century of decadence; and the resurrection of this event illustrates the point nicely. Similar in concept to the traditional Welsh *Eisteddfod*, with ancient costume and verse, the event became a demonstration of national, lyrical sentiment as underlined by its device of *Patria, Fides, Amor*. This imitation of archaic literary practice might well have been regressive and conservative in its trappings and practice. Nonetheless, it acted as a focal point for the language and its condition of subservience; and the growing popularity of the event offers clear illustration of the burgeoning concern for linguistic recuperation first voiced a quarter of a century previously by the solitary figure of Aribau.

Once again, however, the contribution of the popular classes who lived, worked and entertained themselves within the maternal idiom should not be understated. As can be seen in Dorothy Noyes's chapter on Festivals, their efforts towards autochthonous creative cohesion never ceased to be significant. This can be exemplified by the emergence of a singular feature of Catalan particularity and one immediately recognizable and enjoyed to this day: the *castells* or human towers. The practice had developed slowly in Valls, Tarragona, at the end of the previous century where, in the final phase of the 'dance of the Valencians', participants formed a three-storied human tower. This vibrant – not to say virile – exercise caught the popular imagination and spread throughout the country to become a characteristic of collective identity as impressive and latent then as it is in the present day.

What is more, it is around the halfway point of the century that the actualization and projection of the national dance occurs. Pep Ventura (1817–1875) was to revitalize the old *sardana* in terms of length, arrangement and variety of instruments in the band. Rescued from the elementary nature of its original form, the dance became transformed into one of the most striking symbols of national peculiarity, for consumption both at home and abroad, and encompassing the entire social spectrum. The point is that the force and cohesion of these popular celebrations, along with linguistic fidelity, underlines the fact that the *Renaixença* is not so much a time of rebirth, as the name suggests and as official cultural histories attest, but a moment when the more leisured classes in Catalonia rediscovered a heritage that they had abandoned but which had been left deposited in the safe-keeping of the population at large.

This *Kulturkampf*, between demotic and elitist versions of national creativity – which will permeate the assimilation of culture from this moment to the present day – is pertinently illustrated in Tess Knighton's chapter on Music. With the accumulation of wealth the bourgeoisie, like its cousins throughout Europe, elected the opera house as the perfect locus for the ostentation of its riches. Accordingly, in 1847 the Liceu theatre became a concert hall of international prestige as the classical form eventually established itself from very hesitant beginnings. At the same time, however, under the magisterial influence of the philanthropic Josep Anselm Clavé (1824–1874), a choral movement was to spring up that would involve the inchoate urban proletariat in an attempt to offer them a salutary pastime to counter the harshness of industrial life and the dangers of alcohol. Clavé's *Societats Euterpenses* were to create a popular tradition that remained vibrant to the present time and achieved immense subscription and influence throughout Catalonia and neighbouring Valencia. They also underlined the divergence during the period between the demotic voice of the people and the elitist idiom of the *Renaixença*.

This reacquisition of an autochthonous cultural sensitivity among the upper classes, however, was underpinned by a further accompanying development of utmost significance. As is described in the chapter on Modern History by Antoni Segura i Mas and Elisabeda Barbé i Pou – which might be read in tandem with the present chapter – the year preceding the publication of Aribau's ode, 1832, had witnessed the building of the first factory in Barcelona. The process of industrialization, with its focus on the production of textiles, was to continue apace throughout the century, generating enormous wealth. The importance of this revolution was not only the prosperity created but also the emphasis it placed on the sense of being different from the rest of Spain. In the space of half a century, Catalonia had become modern and up-to-date: much more akin to the developed regions of Northern Europe than to the stagnant, agrarian backwaters of the rest of the Peninsula. Furthermore, the Catalan economy was thriving precisely at the moment when the Spanish Empire was in terminal decline with the piecemeal loss of its American colonies.

All these elements conspired to confirm the growing notion of peculiarity that impacted on the new liberal classes. As early as the 1860s a Federalist programme had been devised by Pi i Margall (1824–1901), a future president of the abortive First Spanish Republic (1873–4). This ideology, which favoured the respect and nurturing of national difference, would be continued albeit in modified form by Valentí Almirall (1841–1904). And, at the end of the century, the industrial bourgeoisie, alarmed by Spain's loss of the last American colonies in the wake of the disastrous end to of the war with America in 1898, would lend its weight to the expression of a fully fledged nationalist agenda in the philosophy of Prat de la Riba (1870–1917) and his party of wealth-creators, the *Lliga Regionalista* (Regionalist League), formed in 1901.

In this environment, popular culture continued much in the same vein as before; but the establishment of a modern economic infrastructure and the expansion of the middle classes was to bring about the elaboration of a rival and more sophisticated literary idiom as the social elite continued to interest themselves in the vernacular: Verdaguer (1845–1902) in the area of poetry, Narcís Oller (1846–1930) in prose fiction and Àngel Guimerà (1845–1924) in the theatre. These authors are generally accepted as representing the culmination of the *Renaixença*. The excellence of their prolific output meant that, contrary to Aribau's solitary nostalgic musings of half a century earlier, Catalan had now become raised into the elite level of a literary language – a status it had not enjoyed since the seventeenth century. On this point Arthur Terry has reflected how 'each of these writers, by the sheer force of his talent, had extended the range of literary Catalan beyond anything which could have been conceived in the 1860s. From this moment onwards, one can detect a new sense of urgency in the literary situation.'[3]

The 'new sense of urgency', however, was not limited to the sphere of letters but encompassed the whole spectrum of the arts. The introspection that had previously typified the movement for cultural recovery among the ranks of the middle and upper classes was now to be succeeded by an artistic xenophilia – which has come to characterize all aspects of the Catalan experience – as the creative chorus now looked out to Europe and the latest trends for inspiration. The initiative took root and prospered; and the decades of *Modernisme*, the Catalan school of the international movement, were to provide one of the most impressive periods in the creative history of the nation.

Modernisme

Every year brings millions of tourists to the Catalan capital, and one of the most salient reasons for their arrival is to view the spectacular modernist architecture on display. As is illustrated in Robert Davidson's chapter on Barcelona, the growth of the conurbation followed the design of the Cerdà plan of 1859, which posited a grid system for expansion, the *Eixample*. And, if the establishment of an industrial metropolis in Iberia were unique in itself,

---

[3] Terry, 2003, p. 73.

then the pattern of its development could only further emphasize the singularity of the project. Though the grid model was not unknown in medieval and Renaissance Europe the spectacular nature of its industrial parameters underlines the notion of difference that the reconstituted Catalan nation was so keen to promote.

Intriguingly, this aspect was to be underpinned by an implicit comparison with the transatlantic experience. The grid design was not just common in North America but was also the concept applied to the construction of Lima and Buenos Aires. In this way, the sense of being a colony of sorts, as had been the case in the seventeenth century when a viceroy had overseen domestic political life, could only emphasize the separation between central Spain and the north-eastern seaboard. Indeed, the paradox of being a first-world industrial unit yet also a colonial outpost of sorts would flag up the peculiarity of the Catalan experience, which would come to be based, in many ways, on notions of contradiction.

The phenomenon might be identified in the case of language where, unlike other resurgent areas like Scotland or Ireland, the autochthonous tongue was retrieved and not substituted for the prestige idiom of the invader. This is further underlined by the architecture commissioned by the city fathers to constitute the flagship for their aspirations. The bourgeoisie in the rest of Europe had tended to mark the permanence of their project with an elegant, consolidatory conservatism. The Victorians would be typical in this respect with the ponderous conventionality of their Gothic revival, which stands proudly, if immobile, in their buildings of government – both national and local – cathedrals, provincial universities and train stations. By way of contrast, their sister class in Catalonia were alarmingly *à la page* in their patronage and, rejecting the traditional values associated with their social group, commissioned architects of the most innovative inspiration and drew attention to the ultra-modernity of their metropolis as evinced by the international expositions hosted there in 1888 and 1929.

As is typical of the Catalan ethos in general, the world of letters was also particularly attentive to contemporary European trends. Just as Gaudí (1852–1926) and his counterparts had assimilated in their own particular fashion the aesthetics of Art Nouveau, Arts and Crafts and the Modern Style – as had painters such as Nonell (1872–1911), Casas (1866–1932) and the young Picasso (1881–1973), who arrived in Barcelona in his early teens in 1895 – authors were to take their inspiration from the same international source. The focal point of the experience was the artistic review, *L'Avenç* (1881–93), which gradually developed in stature, coherence and consistency into a persuasive periodical in terms of its promotion of the modern spirit.

In the last decade of the nineteenth century – and inspired by the confidence and cosmopolitanism of the buoyant economic environment – the artistic experience acquired a poise and self-assuredness in its creative endeavour. The exogamous nature of enquiry complimented the concern central to their project: the creation of a thoroughly *modern* voice for Catalonia but one that would also take into account the traditions and currents of their own society. Amid the celebration of festivals and exhibitions devoted to this cause, literary experimentation inspired by the continental-wide vogue for aestheticism flourished with the names of Ibsen, Maeterlinck and Nietzsche becoming the currency of everyday usage.

In keeping with their European counterparts the condition of the individual in the industrial world became paramount. The painter and playwright Santiago Rusiñol (1861–1931) exemplified this attitude. His 1894 depiction of a morphine addict ('La morfina') reveals, in a manner influenced decidedly by French symbolism, the contemporary upper-class abuse of this substance while also recalling the familiar dependence on narcotics of this end-of-century artistic age of decadence. Likewise, his most famous book, *L'auca del senyor Esteve* of 1907, evokes the same conflict of the isolated figure who, in search of an artistic career, refuses to enter the local, petty-bourgeois world of the family business.

In poetry the figure of Joan Maragall (1860–1911) stands out with his Nietzschean celebration of idealistic anarchism despite the comfort of his bourgeois background. His collection *Visions* of 1900 focuses the idea of the unfettered individual will in a Catalan context with the evocation of the ruthless, seventeenth-century bandit Serrallonga and the figure of legend, Count Arnau. Like other anti-heroes of legend this mythical nobleman is condemned, for his sins and depravity, to spend eternity astride a horrendous rushing steed with flames gushing from its eyes and mouth, pursued by a pack of diabolic hounds.

The rurality of the experience is also revealed in the emblematic novel of the period, *Solitud*, by Victor Català (the pseudonym of Caterina Albert, 1869–1966), which was published in 1905. This *Bildungsroman*, with elements of fantasy and Symbolism, describes the development of the female protagonist to maturity and involves two conflicting views of nature, as Arthur Terry describes: 'One is the Rousseauesque vision of the earlier Romantics (...) the other feeds on a sense of violence and evil, and it is this which prevails.' In this setting Mila's progression becomes 'an initiation into the darker reaches of the imagination, a recognition of the disturbing and powerful forces which lie beneath the *modernista* faith in institution'.[4] This

---

[4] Terry, 2003, p. 99.

novel was also to constitute a founding stone for a feminist tradition in the Catalan context, which, as will be seen, would become particularly dynamic in the second half of the century.

The same elements, reminiscent of the intrigue and hyperbole of a Verdi opera, are also apparent in the rural dramas of Àngel Guimerà (1845–1924). Despite the Chekhovian naturalism of the expression and setting, Terry considers that these plays exude an intensely lyrical quality, which is enhanced by the stagecraft of the author and his particularly acute sense of timing, as is especially evident in his most famous work, *Terra baixa/ Lowland*, of 1897. In this case the exaggeration of the plot, replete with the scurrilous manipulation exercised by the local power-broker, exploited innocence, thwarted love and murderous, cosmic revenge, is held together precisely through the skill of the dramatist.

The violence, rurality and intensity of such exalted sentiments, however, were to be severely challenged by the emergence of a secondary current in the experience of *Modernisme*, which was to gain prominence through the well-oiled machinery of patronage and propaganda that became such a feature of the party that dominated the political and cultural scene from 1906 to 1923, the *Lliga*.

Noucentisme

The advent of the new century witnessed the arrival of a peculiar off-shoot of *Modernisme* that was to prove enormously influential over the next two decades and beyond. The school of *Noucentisme* (literally 'art of the 1900s') shared the aestheticism of its predecessor but was to count on an additional means of support to achieve cultural hegemony during the period concerned. The Spanish disaster of 1898, which saw the loss of the last overseas colonies, forced the Catalan bourgeoisie to respond. Faced with the decadence of the sick man of Western Europe, the wealth-creators decided to play the nationalist card in an attempt to gain greater socio-political control. In 1901, big business underwrote the creation of the *Lliga*, which was to implement a policy founded on a greater respect in all ambits for Catalonia and its heritage of difference.

Its success in the elections of 1906 heralded a period of more or less complete control, which was to last until the Primo de Rivera coup of 1923. Aware of the importance of culture and popular mobilization in this arena the party's leader, Prat de la Riba – who had penned the elements of conservative nationalist programme in *La nacionalitat catalana* (1906) – instituted a massive campaign of promotion of the Catalan creative identity. In this respect the academy of the *Institut d'Estudis Catalans* was formed in 1906, with its philological section charged with the updating and standardization of the language. The cultural ethos was also raised by the subvention of art galleries and museums and, most important from our perspective, the creation and patronage of an official literary aesthetic based on the decorous virtues of the dominant bourgeoisie.

Every day, the ideologue of the tendency Eugeni d'Ors (1881–1954) wrote another instalment of his column in *La Veu de Catalunya*, the newspaper owned by Prat de la Riba, on the nature of this artistic enterprise, focusing on the primacy of form over content and the promotion of the values of an upper-class idyll that would be projected on to the new metropolis. Decency, urbanity and civility accompanied the usual gendered morality of the Establishment in flight from the impassioned rusticity of the *modernista* outpourings. In this peculiar and partial vision, the city of Barcelona became the new Athens where, in the gospel according to d'Ors, a fresh civic order was to be installed and prosper.

Verse was, of course, to triumph in this environment. Its intrinsic, formal harmony was allusive to the concord ascribed to the new society. And, what is more, in this new cosmopolitan environment, expression shied away from the emotional excesses of the previous generation, acquiring a reserved dimension that was the height of urbanity. The aesthetic was to count on institutional sponsorship, and the programmatic nature of this class-ridden idiom would provide a salutary contradiction to the celebrated dictum that 'you can't write poetry to order.'

Reams and reams of poetry were produced according to this bourgeois agenda; almost all was of clinical, schematic quality. At this time, writing Catalonia was an exercise to be taken literally, and the phenomenon came as close to an official artistic idiom as can be imagined in an environment devoid of any real structured autonomy. What is more, it is precisely at this time that the bourgeois perspective – based on the values of decency, civility and conservative respect for social order – became implanted as typical of the national character both domestically and elsewhere in the state: a condition against which, in the course of the last century, successive generations would have to define themselves.[5]

In this pre-packaged context it is difficult to recommend authors of any outstanding literary value. There is no doubt about the quality of the output of

---

[5] The anthology of *noucentista* verse compiled by Aulet, 1997, offers a fine example of the poetry/propaganda patronized by the *Lliga*. The violent reaction to this aesthetic programme by subsequent generations underlines the success of their implementation as indicators of the national character.

Josep Carner (1884–1970) whose enviable grasp of form and delicate irony exemplifies the best of this expression. His most significant contribution, however, would come in later life, long after this period, particularly while in exile from Franco's dictatorship. These years also saw the emergence of Carles Riba (1893–1959), one of the finest poets of the twentieth century writing anywhere in Europe though his obsession with form, which was first to endear him to the *noucentista* school, was in no way contrived or artificial but constituted a serious and deeply felt attempt to employ poetry as a means for ethical enquiry as would become impressively evident in his later work beginning with his exile after the Civil War.

In this way, a veritable *Kulturkampf* is appreciated at the start of the new century – not now between demotic and elitist versions of the national cultural idiom but between two rival aesthetic camps of the local bourgeoisie. While the *modernista* spirit continues in architecture the official literary voice is seen to be far more conventional and orthodox: in fact, more in keeping with the values of the dominant class elsewhere in Europe. Once again the familiar notion of paradox or contradiction is seen to lie at the heart of the artistic experience. A further complication is added, of course, by the emergence of the more acutely social and antithetical endeavour of the Avant-Garde which, contrary to the opinions expressed in many standard primers of culture, was to be voraciously assimilated in Catalonia.

The Avant-Garde

There can be no doubt that the *noucentistes*, in their creation of an artistic world far removed from the sordid and violently conflictive social reality of the early decades of the twentieth century, were living in their own idyllic cloud cuckoo land. The period concerned was fraught with insurgence and volatility. The disastrous upheaval of the Tragic Week in 1909 was followed by the constitution of the anarchist trade union (CNT) in 1911, which subsequently masterminded the revolutionary strikes of 1917. Additionally, the triennium of gun law (1920–3) saw open street warfare between workers, their representatives and employers.

With the upheavals in Russia of 1905 and 1917, the spirit of revolution was abroad all over Europe at this time and its aesthetic correlative, the Avant-Garde, was making its presence felt internationally. It is not surprising, then, that the particularly politicized ethos of Catalonia should not only be ripe for the vanguard spirit but also be responsible for one of the most significant events of the history of modern art. We refer, of course, to Picasso's ground-breaking work of 1907 'Les Demoiselles d'Avignon'. Though known universally by its title in French the painting in fact describes a brothel in the

Carrer d' Avinyó in the red-light area of Barcelona. This portrait of the five prostitutes on a flat, two-dimensional plane, was to provide a definitive break with the conventional artistic dependence on perspective and herald the new age of Cubo-Futurism and its countless sister schools of the Avant-Garde.

The significance of the location is fundamental to an understanding of the piece. In an ethos governed by an institutional sensibility that promoted Barcelona as an idyllic locus of social deportment with all the delicacy of the bourgeois ideal, Picasso offers us a stark vision of the contrary: the sordid reality of the capitalist age where human beings are bought and sold for sexual gratification. The figures in the picture jar unexpectedly as the sensuous contours of standard female depiction are replaced by the grating severity and discomfort of triangularity. The African masks worn by two of the sex workers likewise allude to the accompanying savagery of the setting, whose primitivism acts as a direct counter to the fatuous refinement of *noucentista* sensibility.

Picasso's lead was taken up by a series of impressive creative artists, none more impactful – or proletarian – than the poet Joan Salvat-Papasseit (1894– 1924). Orphaned at an early age, Salvat had spent his childhood in the poorhouse of the Barcelona docks alongside his mother. Given the poverty of this existence and the penury of his employment during his teens, it is hardly surprising that this self-taught radical should be attracted to the philosophy of anarchism. Similarly, his espousal of the revolutionary impulse of the Avant-Garde complies exactly with the militant inspiration of his political affiliation. Where Picasso destroyed perspective Salvat follows Apollinaire in the destruction of grammar as words are freed from the bonds of syntax and allowed to float on the page in the pictorial form of the calligramme.

It is not only in terms of form that the revolutionary zeal is detected. Salvat's verses evoke the simple essence of popular daily experience. In stark contrast to the delicacy and urbanity of *noucentista* invention, the locus for lyrical deliberation will be working-class life in all its banality. The port, the market, the tram, the bar, etc., are all evoked with a direct freshness and disarming simplicity. However, there is much more to Salvatian representation than an affectionate rendition of banality. Some of his best pieces reflect entirely that acute social critique so evident in his pamphleteering.

An alarming series of poems offers an oblique but harrowing consideration of such crucial topics as wife-beating, the female orgasm, prostitution and, in a particularly disturbing fashion, incestuous rape, in a cycle of social denunciation unheard of in the lyric convention. What is more, along with the incantation to the proletarian environment, Establishment values are further rejected in the explicit eroticism of much of his verse. In this way, the bourgeois idyll of *noucentista* fancy was rocked to its foundations in both content and form as Salvat-Papasseit followed Picasso's lead in presenting an alternative vision of the Catalan capital, warts and all.

If Tess Knighton's chapter on music duly outlines the strong presence of the Avant-Garde in that medium, as epitomized by the names of Gerhard (1896–1970) and Homs (1906–2006), then the presence of this innovative spirit in the graphic arts is no less pronounced. Exemplary of the belligerent revolt in sense and sensibility is the *enfant terrible* of twentieth-century art, Salvador Dalí (1904–1989). Though from Cadaqués on the Costa Brava, Barcelona was to be the *point de départ* of a creative career that was to make him infamous the world over. There is no finer paradigm of the rejection of received knowledge and other values contrary to vanguard sensitivity than this individual, who was expelled for insolence from the Fine Art Academy in Madrid. Little more needs to be said about this self-appointed 'Universal Catalan' in the pre-war period, though it is pertinent to consider his early work in the context of a rejection of the Catalan bourgeoisie and its aesthetic.

This is not only a question of format and style as the nauseous surreality of the Dalinian dreamscape complements the savage rejection of the comfortable values of a class obsessed with the procurement and ostentation of wealth. His revolutionary credentials are also evident in the films he made with his friend Luis Buñuel. The *Chien andalou* (1928) and *L'Age d'or* (1930) have now become cinematic classics combining the extravagance of the new innovative idiom with the most savage lambasting of the dominant class and capitalist repression.

No less celebrated is the case of Joan Miró (1893–1983). Though no angry young man, his consistency with the surrealist spirit is evident in the same destruction of conventional graphic syntax and ludic indulgence. The two-dimensionality initiated by Picasso becomes a standard feature in Miró, along with the splashes of bright Mediterranean colour and powerful subliminal elaborations based on memory, fantasy and the irrational, which evoke a confident and compelling dreamscape. Indeed, this type of subconscious reconstruction is particularly reminiscent of the poetry and prose of his friend, Josep Vicenç Foix (1893–1987), who was also a major figure in the production of the influential vanguard review, *L'amic de les arts* (1926–9). Had Catalan not suffered a long history of marginalization and repression, Foix would doubtless be celebrated as one of the finest wordsmiths of the twentieth century. The psychopathology of the literary experiments of this self-defined 'investigator in poetry' and the mystifying incantatory quality of his expression rank him alongside Kafka as subliminal chronicler of the collective traumas of the age and coincide spectacularly with the oneiric meanderings of Miró.

Despite the potency of the artistic voice that emerged in Catalonia around the turn of the twentieth century the whole experience was to be still-born precisely at its period of most promise: Catalonia's 'what if ...' moment, as readily identified by so many of the contributors to this volume. In 1923 the military dictatorship of Primo de Rivera not only halted all the advances made in the political arena but also, reverting to the repressive centralism of the Bourbons, stymied all possibilities of creative expression by the familiar proscription of the language. The democratic sexennium of the Second Republic was to offer a brief oasis in this respect. The Statute of Autonomy of 1932 allowed for advances in the sphere of education, culture and linguistic consolidation. The literary scene took its first halting steps to normalization with the international Pen Club conference held in Barcelona in 1935. Popularist sentiment found expression in the victory of the national soccer team over Brazil in 1934 and an impressive subscription to the *Associació Protectora de l'Ensenyança Catalona*.

The future was, however, to be bleak for the Catalans as, after the roller-coaster ride of the II Republic and Civil War, they became victims of the savage repression imposed by the tyrannic ogre and second military dictator of the century, *Generalísimo* Francisco Franco.

The Dictatorship (1939–75)

If the Bourbon victory of 1714 was disastrous for the culture of Catalonia then the victory of the Francoists in 1939 was inconceivably worse. At least the purge of Philip V was directed only against Catalan as a discourse of the elite and left the peasantry and the immense majority of the population free to live and create in the vernacular. The vengefulness of the *Generalísimo* was by far more insidious. If Franco had used the might of the Nazi war machine to inflict maximum damage against the unprotected civilian population at large, the cultural pogrom was no less severe.

The language was quite simply 'disappeared' either through proscription or environmental repression. Despite the restrictions, however, creative resistance was conducted clandestinely. Poetry became once again the major vehicle of literary dissent for obvious reasons: it is a compact, solitary activity, which can be spread unobtrusively whereas the absence of infrastructure and reading public made the novel an impossible venture. What is more, lyrical reviews like *Poesia* (1944–5) and *Ariel* (1946–51) constituted a defiant gesture from the underground and an attempted defence of high culture in the face of barbarity. These magazines also allowed poets like Carles Riba, J. V. Foix and Josep Carner to continue their impressive creative trajectory and remain in the public eye.

Other contemporaries like Salvador Espriu (1913–1985) combined the same preoccupation with literary quality with a more pronounced ideological commitment. His *Cementiri de Sinera* (1945) is a masterly reworking of Valéry's *Cimitière marin* (1922), whose elegant aestheticism is redirected into a defence of the Catalan cultural personality, a political dimension unheard of in the 'pure' tradition of verse. Similarly, the superbly satirical Pere Quart (Joan Oliver, 1899–1986) was to include the more colloquial dimension into his work as a counter to the ivory-towered aestheticism that characterized the phenomenon among higher academic circles.

This pair also wrote short plays for the theatre which, from the mid-1940s onwards, had managed to avoid linguistic proscription, though performances in the vernacular were rare indeed and limited, in general, to folkloric productions on religious themes, often nativity plays (*pastorets*). In the famine, penury and deprivation of the immediate post-war years survival rather than resistance was the prime directive though, as Dorothy Noyes's chapter on Festivals indicates, the Church and religious celebrations at least allowed the populace a site to gather *en masse* and maintain local traditions and contacts under the umbrella of this institution which, though a cornerstone of the regime, was one of the few entities to retain a notion of geo-administrative integrity.

By the turn of the 1950s the situation had improved slightly. A monthly artistic review, the *Dau al 7* (1948–54), appeared and was remarkable in its orientation and assembly of personalities. The most salient figures were the artist Antoni Tàpies (b. 1923), who was to gain international fame, and the equally gifted Joan Brossa (1919–1998). The pair were instrumental in the continuance of avant-garde practice, though Brossa was to underline the committed dimension of this aesthetic in his advocacy of Existentialist engagement. This went hand in hand with a thoroughly demotic element in his creation (both graphic and literary) which relied on such popular favourites as magic, conjuring and other commonplaces of the music hall. At no time, however, does his work fall into intellectual condescension or artistic compromise: much like the cinema of Buñuel, Brossa's poetry evinces rather a clear understanding of the full ideological potential of surrealist aesthetics and its isolation of the absurdity of capitalism, particularly in the context of Spain. This revolutionary artistic thrust was complemented in the sphere of music by the establishment of the Club 49, which was to become famous for its vanguard promotions and the long list of composers who, following in the footsteps of the internationally acclaimed Gerhard, frequented this establishment.

The occasional lapse in repression, or publication overseas, allowed for the odd appearance of fiction of real quality in Catalan. Such is the case of Pere

1. 'Poema'. Visual poem by Joan Brossa, 1978.
By permission of the Fundació Joan Brossa

Calders (1912–1994), who, from his exile in Mexico, employed *avant la lettre* traits of magical realism in his satires of the Catalans in general but the Barcelona middle classes in particular. Significantly, the humour derives from the same Existentialist deconstruction of the comforts of capitalism, advocating a militant reaction not only to the regime but the repressive nature of western society in its entirety. At this point mention should be made of the enormous contribution of Manuel de Pedrolo (1918–1990). Though largely ignored by the critics, the sheer extent of the literature produced by this prolific writer is amazing, at a moment of literary silence, from verse and drama to prose fiction.

The novel, of course, was the medium most castigated by the repressive situation although, slowly but surely, isolated examples were to appear in the course of the 1950s. The book that was to change the profile of Catalan fiction beyond all recognition, however, was the *Plaça del Diamant* by Mercè Rodoreda (1908–1983), published in 1962. Though a talented novelist in her own right, this *tour de force* was to be immensely popular at home and abroad, being translated into over thirty foreign languages. The trials and tribulations of its downtrodden protagonist, Colometa, from the years of the Republic up to the present, were to strike a chord by their correspondence with the experience of a nation crushed by repression. Despite its enormous aesthetic quality, however, the book is crucial for a number of extra-literary reasons.

In an environment of cultural defence that privileged both male hegemony and elitist practice, Rodoreda was to offer a differing female view much in the same manner as Victor Català's *Solitud*. The issue is significant as not only is gender important to the equation but also social class. Not since Salvat-Papasseit had the proletarian existence of Barcelona been so lyrically and plangently projected, acting as a critical counterweight to the hermetic, intellectual close that typified the creative apology for the nation. Moreover, the entirely open and popular medium of what appears in the first instance as a *novela rosa* – or sentimental tale (deceptively latent in Rodoreda's expert handling) – readmitted the masses into the enterprise of artistic opposition. There can be little doubt that the popular appeal of the genre and its privileging of the female experience as representative of Catalonia constituted a radical alternative to the male-dominated elitism of the literary hierarchy of resistance, an impulse that would be followed in successive decades by a series of impressive women authors.

In the 1960s, with the advent of the economic boom, a new social directive was to become pronounced in literature. This is particularly evident in the sphere of poetry with the triumph of committed verse which, with its characteristic denunciation, was to dominate the literary scene for the next two decades. Espriu was to produce a key volume in this respect with his *Pell de brau*/ Bull-hide of 1960 becoming a highly popular rallying cry as well as apology for democracy and the autochthonous culture. A particularly significant contributor in the field of creative resistance, however, was the immediate and galvanizing folk experience that has come to be known as the *Nova Cançó*/ New Song.

The social command of the 1960s

The mass mobilization experienced worldwide in the 1960s, celebrated still for its militancy in society and the arts, was echoed in Catalonia despite the watchful and repressive eye of the ageing dictator. Its presence has already been indicated with reference to Espriu and Rodoreda, though the movement was to grow dramatically. The combined effects of the anti-Vietnam struggle, May 1968 in France, Civil Rights and Northern Ireland were to impact forcefully both on the consciousness of the individual creative genius and the Catalan public at large. If it was the Basques who, with the pro-active disruption of ETA, were to imitate the militancy of the IRA more closely, there was also widespread sympathy for the resistance to the regime in Catalonia where support of the clandestine student and labour unions was strong and the mounting social and political resistance to the regime was acutely manifest.

As usual, poetry was the medium which bore most obvious witness to the phenomenon, with the development of the committed, denunciatory aesthetic of *poesia social*, which accounted for a whole series of figures of importance such as Miquel Martí i Pol (1929–2003), Francesc Vallverdú (b. 1935), Jordi Sarsanedas (1924–2006) and Francesc Parcerisas (b. 1944), though the latter was to develop along more consciously aesthetic lines along with four other outstanding poets: Gabriel Ferrater (1922–1972), the exiled Ramon Xirau (b. 1924), Narcís Comadira (b. 1942) and Pere Gimferrer (b. 1945).

Curiously, the novel in Catalan as promoted by Sarsanedas and Joan

Perucho (1920–2003) tended to avoid such immediate and overt social denunciation, though this is most certainly apparent in the fiction and historical investigations of Montserrat Roig (1946–1991). Here again the significant presence of women authors should not go without mention. The contribution of Carme Riera (b. 1948), Maria Antònia Oliver (b. 1946) and Maria Mercè Marçal (1952–1998) among others is immense and, following the lead of Victor Català and Mercè Rodoreda, their opening up of the national cultural experience to the radical alternative of the female perspective is starkly enunciated by Marçal's harrowing *cri de guerre*:

> A l'atzar agraeixo tres dons: haver nascut dona,
> de classe baixa i nació oprimida.
> I el tèrbol atzur de ser tres voltes rebel.[6]

Similarly, in this context the figure of Terenci Moix (1943–2003) is something of an innovator who was to make a real impression. As Arthur Terry indicates his embracing of the latest trends in Pop Art effects a real break with the prevailing realism of contemporary prose; but what makes his books disturbing,

> is the deliberate attempt to undermine the conventional moral values of the bourgeoisie. This is particularly evident in the stories, where episodes from the past – seen through a Hollywood version of history – are made to confuse the usual distinctions between vice and virtue by recourse to sadism, masochism and outright cruelty.[7]

The theatre was to provide some impressive pieces by Baltasar Porcel (1937–2003), Jordi Teixidor (b. 1939) and the powerfully cogent Josep Maria Benet i Jornet (b. 1940), which show a full awareness of the latest post-war trends in European drama from Brecht to the grotesque. The real dynamism, however, was eventually to be provided by a glut of impressive performance groups. Clearly, this non-verbal medium could act as a counter to the linguistic proscription experienced socially as mime could avoid Francoist censorship by being classified within variety theatre or music hall, genres in which the censor was merely concerned with the propriety of the costumes. The instigators, in this respect, were *Els Joglars*/ Minstrels who, formed in 1962 under the direction of the charismatic Albert Boadella, were to become

---

[6] I thank fate for three things: being born a woman/ working class from an oppressed nation./ And the turbid blue of being a rebel three times over.

[7] Terry, 2003, p. 137.

hugely popular as their art of mime offered a grotesque element that struck at the heart of the regime with its acute and very pointed buffoonery. Significantly, this troupe also incorporated popular culture into its shows, including elements of farce, revue and television serials, appealing to the broadest possible social spectrum.

Though frequently subjected to police investigation until the restoration of democracy, *Els Joglars* have provided an excellence in performance and production in their exquisitely crafted, hilarious satires, which remain sparkling and vital. A similar tack was to be followed by the world-famous *Comediants*, established in 1971, who George and London describe as 'the most representative group within the categories of festival theatre and open-air theatre' with their development of 'a style which combines rituals and paratheatrical manifestations with ultramodern technology'.[8] Their impressive array of talent combines the acrobatics of the circus with the revival of popular festival as evidenced by their startling display in the closing ceremony of the Olympic Games in 1992, a large-scale macro-festival that counted on the participation of 850 people in a magnificent spectacle that combined technical precision, with memorable visual and aural impact.

Another more modest but no less gifted group is *Dagoll-Dagom*, formed in 1974. Their wildy imaginative productions of that decade have given way to no less spectacular and successful reworking of such popular classics as the prose fiction of Pere Calders, the festivities of Midsummer's night, Gilbert and Sullivan's *Mikado* or Àngel Guimerà's *Cel i mar*. *La Fura del Baus* have continued this spectacular trend from their inception in 1979, and their provocative corporally dynamic reinvention of street theatre has added a rave element to the category, where the body acts as locus for the exhibition of social tensions. George and London describe their performance wherein 'a visceral kind of acting predominates' and

> the actors' bodies are exposed to audiences as gestural and phonic vehicles, designed to create fields of energy between themselves and each spectator. In such sensuous theatre, the performers' bodies act as seismographs, registering the different states of tension throughout each production (...)

---

[8] George & London, 1996, p. 113. Though we cite this useful volume to offer a necessarily brief overview of the performing arts the definitive study is *Catalan Theatre 1975–2006: Politics, Identity and Performance*, edited by Delgado, George and Orozco, and forming the special number of *Contemporary Theatre Review*, vol. 17, issue 3, of 2007.

> Bodily communication and exhibitionism form an essential part of the neo-rituals of 1980s culture. However, *La Fura dels Baus*'s style of performance can be termed 'behaviour-based', since each production displays diverse forms of human behaviour. There is also an evaluation of the destructive act as a critical reflex of an object-based society. (The best known scene from *Actions* is when the performers destroy a car with sledge-hammers.)[9]

In this respect their magnificently choreographed contribution to the Opening Ceremony of the Barcelona Olympiad was less antagonistic than the undistilled, raw aggression evident in the corporality of many of their productions, which continue to scandalize and impress in equal proportion.

Finally, the end of the 1970s also witnessed the foundation of *El Tricicle*, whose *teatre gestual*/ theatre of gesture continues to delight audiences today. Less socially confrontational than their predecessors, this trio has achieved an unparalleled degree of sophistication in their mime productions, which strongly recall the clowning performances of farce, puppet theatre and the *commedia dell'arte*. In simple terms, the Catalan contribution to the recovery of spectacle as a festival of popular culture has been remarkable and spans a spectrum from conventional drama to pyrotechnics, acrobatics, circus, sport, festivity and music. In many ways its relationship with the latter is particularly significant.

To a great extent, both phenomena were to develop concurrently as the re-emergence of folk music, as channelled politically through the medium of the *Nova Cançó*, coincided with the initial experiments of *Els Joglars*.[10] The inspiration, of course, was to be taken from the Civil Rights movement in the USA, which, inspired by The Weavers and Woody Guthrie in the late 1950s, had counted on the involvement of such monumental figures as Joan Baez, Bob Dylan, Pete Seeger, etc., in the following decade. Of immense importance also was the contribution of the contemporary *chantauteurs*, particularly Georges Brassens, Léo Ferré and Jacques Brel, whose soulful, ideological engagement was to inspire a generation of Catalan *cantautors* in the next decade. By 1959 the pressure to elaborate a musical idiom that would unite opposition to the regime through the universal appeal of folk was discernible in musical circles. Subsequently, the *Setze Jutges* were formed in 1961, and their impact was to be enormous over the next twenty years not

---

[9] George & London, 1996, p. 114.

[10] The studies by Josep Martí provide an understanding of the phenomenon in general; Boyle, 1995, and Tinnell, 1999 offer a good introduction to the nature and orientation of folk music in this mass movement.

only in terms of popularity but, as in the USA and Northern Ireland, the forging of the link between mass protest and socially orientated lyric.

The group, amorphous in terms of membership and, like The Weavers, not without dissent among its ranks, faded with the death of the dictator in 1975, as was only to be expected given the political dimension of dissidence and resistance that accompanied the experience. However, the widespread popularity enjoyed by these performers eventually brought about a corresponding professionalisation in terms of presentation, production and marketing. And the sophistication of certain of its members and other associated artists has made them household names today both at home and abroad: Raimon (b. 1940), Francesc Pi de la Serra (b. 1942), Ovidi Montllor (1942–1995), Joan Manuel Serrat (b. 1943), Maria de la Mar Bonet (b. 1947) and Lluís Llach (b. 1948). The commitment and sobriety of the ideological intention, however, frequently conveyed in a lyrical idiom of poignant denunciation, did not exclude the real quality of the music nor, indeed, humour. *La Trinca* were immensely popular in this respect, providing theatricality and spectacle to their hilarious lyrics for over two decades from the late 1960s onwards before making the transition into television with equal success.

This more militant understanding of social commitment in the spheres of both elite and popular culture, however, dovetailed into the more general air of social involvement that now characterized the dynamic opposition to the regime and its injustice. Though the forces of democracy might well have been unable to rid themselves of the dictator, their constancy, mobilization and dynamism, crystallized in committed literature, song and performance, ensured that autocratic and tyrannical government would never be permitted to blight the nation of Catalonia again.

After Franco

During the years of the Transition the overt social commitment evident in Catalan culture was to slowly dry up, although the continued presence of the established writers and songsters was very much a reminder of the recent past and the proximity of the struggle against the dictator. The phenomenon is nicely illustrated in Jaume Martí-Olivella's chapter on the Cinema, where conventional historical essays like *La ciutat cremada* (The Burnt City, 1976) and biopic, *Companys, procés a Catalunya* (Companys, Catalonia on Trial, 1979) saw directors Antoni Ribas and Josep Maria Forn offering a committed though by no means pedestrian cinematic reflection on key moments of the recent collective past.

The times were changing, however, and after the trauma of the Transition and Tejero's abortive coup in 1981 a spirit was emerging socially that offered a more vibrant alternative to the pious sobriety of the ethic of engagement that had so typified artistic resistance of the Franco period. The earnestness of the struggle against the dictator was understandably superseded by a period of profligacy and indulgence in personal, moral, sexual and social terms as the country cast off the straitjacket of repression that had pervaded the previous system.

What is more, the celebration of the return of democracy and publication of the Statute of Autonomy of 1979 was to give way eventually to a general air of disillusion and apathy. So much had been expected and, despite the advantages of a democratic format, so little was felt to be achieved as, from the committed illusion of the years of resistance, the country returned to an uncomfortably orthodox relation of subservience in the context of Spain and also to the established immobility of society in Western Europe.

In the creative world, the energy expended previously in agitation and protest gave way to a political indifference accompanied by an egocentric hedonism that typified the new age. The reaction to the serious dedication of the progressive struggle became crystallized subsequently in the desperate profligacy of post-modernity across the artistic spectrum, as might be typified by the erotic titillation of Bellmunt's *L'orgia* of 1978. Similarly, a group of young turks began to take centrestage who, with their complete rejection of established values – particularly the gospel of *noucentisme* – epitomized the frenetic wildness, or *rauxa*, of the contemporary generation. The sacrilegious brilliance of the short stories of Quim Monzó (b. 1952), for example, exude not only acute literary skill but overhaul with their vulgarity, humour and devilment, conventional narrative as much as the prized Catalan virtue of *seny*, decency, sobriety and industry. In terms of the theatre, the immensely talented Sergi Belbel (b. 1963) was to shake the local dramatic tradition to the roots with his experimental and daring productions, which seemed to offer an amalgam of post-war European theatricality with a savage depiction of domestic realities.

What is, of course, most fascinating at this moment of post-modern re-evaluation is the combination of the conventional high-cultural idiom generally ascribed to literary activity with the bathos and vulgarity of the most common of experience. For the first time since the *Renaixença*, the idiom of the elite combined freely with the unencumbered vitality of popular culture, and the effect was explosive. The formula is perhaps best typified by Monzó's hilarious *El perquè de tot plegat*/ What it's All About, of 1993 and Belbel's caustic *Carícies*/ Caresses of 1992, later adapted for cinema by Ventura Pons in 1998. Equally impressive in this respect is the volatile cocktail of Bigas Luna's conflictive trilogy, *Jamón jamón* (1992), *Huevos de oro* (Golden Balls, 1993) and *La teta i la lluna* (Tit and the Moon, 1994).

It is perhaps typical of the ill-starred fate of Catalan culture that this imaginative trilogy in defence of the autochthonous personality in the face of burgeoning Spanishness should have been so blandly assimilated. The trilogy is rarely read as such and, paradoxically, its first two elements are taken as little more than an Almodovarian celebration of the essence of Spain, which tends to miss the point of much of the speculation. It is not until the third part of the tryptich that commentators have focused on the true difference of Catalan popular culture whose validity is evoked by the attraction of local cuisine, the collective spontaneity of the *castells* and the artless virtuosity of the rip-roaring *fartiste*, an extension of the *caganer* – the defecating figurine of the Nativity scene – whose foregrounding of demotic flourish is so important to our context and is so elegantly explained in Noyes's chapter on festivals.

The phenomenon is mirrored by the ceremonies surrounding the Olympic Games of 1992. The sobriety of the opening act, for example, echoed the sophisticated classical discourse of poets like Riba and Espriu dealing with the mythical founding of Barcelona, the spectacular evocation of the labours of Hercules and a polychromatic voyage of discovery reminiscent of Jason's epic quest. Counting on the appreciable input of *La Fura dels Baus*, the spectacle was multitudinarious and magnificent. The crowning image of the lame archer igniting the torch with a flaming arrow not only underlined an ideological commitment to the greater visibility of disability but also cleverly evoked the deity of Pan in this scene of Apollonian majesty.

Conversely, despite the frequent operatic interludes, the closing ceremony privileged the more demotic element, with the hilarious posturing of the mime group *El Tricicle*, the fire festival of the *correfoc* and exquisite hot-air balloon acrobatics of the *Comediants*, followed by the popular music of *Los Manolos*. This Catalan group of Andalusian extraction had become highly successful in their development of the *Rumba catalana*, the authentically local response to the medium of flamenco, championed by the irrepressible popular performer, Peret (b. 1935), well established in the area over generations. Their songs in both Catalan and Spanish provided a further pertinent example of the nation's positive response to the inclusivity embraced by Bigas Luna, who had also highlighted the virtuosity of the Catalan flamenco singer Miquel Poveda in *La teta i la lluna*. And this affirmative amalgam of the autochthonous with the alien, along with the mass dancing of the rumba in the Olympic arena, underscored the combination of sophistication and popularism offered by both ceremonies.

However, reference to the 1992 Games in Barcelona should not pass without criticism as it involves a major crisis in the cultural experience of the city as a point of artistic reference. From its modernization in the mid-nineteenth century onwards Barcelona, as industrial centre, national symbol and site of class cohabitation, was a constant for the creative deliberation. The point is also underscored in Martí-Olivella's chapter on cinema, which isolates the stark yet imaginative deliberations on the metropolis, offering a focal point for appreciation and understanding of Catalan cinematography. The issue remains centrestage, however, precisely owing to the post-Olympic conversion of the capital into a brand name for cultural tourism, sophistication and international chic. In accordance with this design, whole quarters of the conurbation have been gentrified, which has had the most detrimental effect on the quality of life of the inhabitants, whether immigrant or native, as underlined by Davidson's chapter on the City.

Conclusion

One of the central tenets for the assimilation of Catalan culture – and one embraced by this volume – has been the provision of a detailed, historical perspective that lends solidity to an initial understanding of the phenomenon in its context. With this in mind, the Valencian intellectual Joan Fuster would often reflect that, in the case of Catalonia, language, culture and politics were inseparable and would remain so evermore. Though these criteria have worked well in the first instance for determining the most salient characteristics of the national voice – as the Valencian makes plain in his seminal *Literatura catalana contemporània* of 1972 – care must be taken to avoid a certain risk of foreclosure evident in the critic's words.

The point might be illustrated with reference to the contemporary context where, unlike Fuster's prediction, the previous fixation with things Catalan is replaced by a refreshing outgoingness on the cultural scene. A case in point would be Albert Sánchez Piñol (b. 1965) who, with his first two novels, *Pell freda/ Cold Skin* of 2002 and *Pandora al Congo/ Pandora in the Congo* of 2005, entered the best-sellers' list in a number of countries. In their focus, both works are clearly exogamous and, rather than centring specifically on the Catalan experience, are more international in orientation: the first dealing with the struggle for Irish emancipation and the second with British involvement in the Congo, particularly the role played therein by Conrad and Casement. The universality of the reference is also reflected by the creative process as the author experiments with the novel form in an ingenious reworking of previous essays in fiction to produce, firstly, an innovative, uncanny tale, followed by a hopelessly self-critical Kiplingesque adventure yarn. In this respect, deliberation has escaped the obsessive confines of domestic concern – a point accentuated by the location of the novels, sited far beyond the reaches of local geography at the South Pole or in the heart of Africa.

The same progression might be noted in the cinematic arena. Whereas previously the Catalan dimension could be explicitly isolated by such phenomena as, say, the Barcelona School, Bellmunt's version of *La Plaça del Diamant* or Bigas Luna's *Teta i la lluna*, the experience has now grown to accommodate the less introspective and more universally accessible sensibility of Marc Recha, José Luis Guerín and Isabel Coixet whose films, set in France, the USA or an oil rig in the Atlantic, involve deliberation of a more general cinematic nature far removed from the immediacy of the reference of earlier generations.

Concomitant with this creative extraversion perceived in the first decade of the new millennium, the next step on the critical road may well entail a softening of the rigidity of the historical and political criteria habitually adduced as a means of classification. Indeed, such a modification might only be expected as, after centuries of repression, the political freedom consolidated after a generation of democracy begins to provide the moment for a fuller and less qualified recognition of the cultural contribution of this marginal, minority but extremely vibrant nation.

Works Cited and Suggested Reading

Ades, Dawn (1982) *Dalí*. London: Thames & Hudson.
Arkinstall, Christine (2004) *Gender, Class, and Nation: Mercè Rodoreda and the Subjects of Modernism*. London: Associated University Press.
Aulet, Jaume (1997) *Antologia de la poesia noucentista*. Barcelona: Edicions 62.
Balcells, Albert (1996) *Catalan Nationalism: Past and Present*. Basingstoke: Macmillan.
Bilbeny, Norbert (1988) *Eugeni d'Ors i la ideologia del noucentisme*. Barcelona: La Magrana.
―――― (1999) *Política noucentista: de Maragall a d'Ors*. Catarroja, País Valencià: Editorial Afers.
Boyle, Catherine (1995) 'The Politics of Popular Music: On the Dynamics of the New Song', in Graham, H. and Labanyi, J. (eds) *Spanish Cultural Studies: An Introduction: The Struggle for Modernity*. Oxford: Oxford University Press, pp. 291–294.
Coad, Emma D. (1995) 'Modernista Architecture: Using the Past to Build the Modern', in Graham, H. and Labanyi, J. (eds) *Spanish Cultural Studies: An Introduction: The Struggle for Modernity*. Oxford: Oxford University Press, pp. 58–62.
Conversi, Daniele (1997) *The Basques, the Catalans and Spain: Alternative Routes to Nationalist Mobilisation*. London: Hurst.
Crameri, Kathryn (2000) *Language, the Novelist and National Identity in Post-Franco Catalonia*. Oxford: Legenda.
―――― (2008) *Catalonia: National Identity and Cultural Policy, 1980–2003* Cardiff: University of Wales Press.
Delgado, Maria, George, David and Orozco, Lourdes (eds) (2007) *Catalan*

Theatre 1975–2006: Politics, Identity and Performance, special number of *Contemporary Theatre Review*, vol. 17, issue 3.

Eaude, Michael (2007) *Catalonia: A Cultural History*. Oxford: Signal.

Franzke, Andreas (1992) *Tàpies*. London: Thames & Hudson.

Fuster, Joan (1972) *Literatura catalana contemporània*. Barcelona: Curial.

Gibson, Ian (1997) *The Shameful Life of Salvador Dalí*. London: Faber.

Guibernau, Montserrat (2000) 'Nationalism and Intellectuals in Nations without States: the Catalan Case', *Political Studies*, 48, pp. 929–946.

—— (2002) *Between Autonomy and Secession: The Accomodation of Catalonia within the New Democratic Spain*. Brighton: University of Sussex.

—— (2004) *Catalan Nationalism: Francoism, Transition and Democracy*. Abingdon: Routledge.

—— (2007) *The Identity of Nations*. Cambridge: Polity.

Hargreaves, John (2000) *Freedom for Catalonia? Catalan Nationalism, Spanish Identity, and the Barcelona Olympic Games*. Cambridge: Cambridge University Press.

Ishaghpour, Youssef (2006) *Antoni Tàpies: Works, Writings and Interviews*. Barcelona: Polígrafa.

Keown, D. and Larios, J. (2010) 'Contemporary Catalan Literature: Fact or Friction?', in Cabo Aseguinolaza, F., Abuín Gonzalez, A., and Domínguez, C. (eds) *A Comparative History of Literatures in the Iberian Peninsula*. Philadelphia: John Benjamins, pp. 237–252.

King, Elliott (2007) *Dalí, Surrealism and Cinema*. Harpenden: Kamera Books.

Labanyi, Jo (ed.) (2002) 'Introduction: Engaging with Ghosts; or, Theorizing Culture in Modern Spain', in *Constructing Identity in Twentieth-century Spain: Theoretical Debates and Cultural Practice*. Oxford: Oxford University Press.

Langdon-Davies, John (1929) *Dancing Catalans*. London: Jonathan Cape.

—— (1953) *Gatherings from Catalonia*. London: Cassell.

Loyer, François (1997) *Art Nouveau in Catalonia*. London: Taschen.

McRoberts, Kenneth (2001) *Catalonia: Nation Building without a State*. Oxford: Oxford University Press.

Martí, Josep (1994) 'The Sardana as a Socio-Cultural Phenomenon in Contemporary Catalonia', *Yearbook for Traditional Music*, 26, pp. 39–46.

—— (1995) 'Katalanische Volksmusik als ethnisches Konstrukt', in Lipp, C. (ed.) *Medien populärer Kultur. Erzählung, Bild und Objekt in der volkskundlichen Forschung*. Frankfurt/New York: Campus, pp. 242–251.

—— (1997) 'Folk Music Studies and Ethnomusicology in Spain', *Yearbook for Traditional Music*, 28, pp. 107–140.

—— (2001a) 'Spain, Folk Music', in Sadie, Stanley (ed.) *The New Grove. Dictionary of Music and Musicians*. London: Macmillan Publishers, vol. 24, pp. 135–154.

—— (2001b) 'Music and Ethnicity in Barcelona', *The World of Music*, 43, pp. 181–190.

—— (2002) 'Hybridization and its Meanings in the Catalan Musical Tradition', in Steingress, Gerhard (ed.) *Songs of the Minotaur. Hybridity and Popular Music in the Era of Globalization*. Münster/Hamburg/Berlin/London: Lit. Verlag, pp. 113–138.

Moure, Gloria (1995) *Tàpies: Objects of Time*. Cologne: Wienand.
Néret, Gilles (1994) *Salvador Dalí, 1904–1989*. Cologne: Benedikt Taschen.
Orwell, George (1975) *Homage to Catalonia*. Harmondsworth: Penguin.
Payne, John (1991) *Catalonia: Portrait of a Nation*. London: Century.
Penrose, Roland (1978) *Tàpies*. London: Thames & Hudson.
Pittock, Murray (ed.) (2006) *The Reception of Sir Walter Scott in Europe*. London: Continuum.
Prat de la Riba, Enric (1978) *La nacionalitat catalana*. Barcelona: Edicions 62.
Read, Jan (1978) *The Catalans*. London: Faber.
Robinson, William, Falgas, Jordi and Bellon Lord, Carmen (2006) *Barcelona and Modernity: Picasso, Gaudí, Miró, Dalí*. New Haven, CT: Yale University Press.
Terry, Arthur (1995) 'Catalan Literary *Modernisme* and *Noucentisme*: From Dissidence to Order', in Graham, H. and Labanyi, J. (eds) *Spanish Cultural Studies: An Introduction: The Struggle for Modernity*. Oxford: Oxford University Press, pp. 55–7.
—— (2003) *A Companion to Catalan Literature*. London: Tamesis.
Tinnell, Roger (1999) 'Spanish Music and Cultural Identity', in Gies, D. (ed.) *The Cambridge History of Spanish Literature*. Cambridge: Cambridge University Press, pp. 287–297.
Vilarós, Teresa (1999) 'A Cultural Mapping of Catalonia', in Gies, D. (ed.) *The Cambridge History of Spanish Literature*. Cambridge: Cambridge University Press pp. 37–53.

The following items from ACSOP, the Anglo-Catalan Society Occasional Publications, which includes translations, are freely available online at: www.anglo-catalan.org/monographs.htm

Giner, Salvador (1980) *The Social Structure of Catalonia*.
Keown, D. and Owen T. (1982) *Joan Salvat-Papasseit: Selected Poems*.
Mackay, David (1985) *Modern Architecture in Barcelona*.
Terry, Arthur (ed.) (1987) *Homage to Joan Gili. Forty Poems*.
Trench, E. and Yates, A. (1988) *Alexandre de Riquer (1856–1920): The British Connection in Catalan Modernism*.
Polack, Philip (trans.) (1989) *Salvador Espriu: Primera Història d'Esther*.
George, David and London, John (1996) *Contemporary Catalan Theatre. An Introduction*. http://www.anglo-catalan.org/op/monographs/issue09.pdf
Terry, Arthur (1998) *Readings of J. V. Foix*.
Bowen, Meirion (ed.) (2000) *Joaquim Homs: Robert Gerhard and his Music*.
Roser i Puig, M. (2008) *A Female Scene. Three Plays by Catalan Women*.

Other translations in English by authors cited

Belbel, Sergi (1990) *Deep Down*. Barcelona: Ed. 62.
—— (1996) *After the Rain*. London: Methuen.
—— (1999) 'Caresses', in Dodgson, E. and Peate, M. (eds) *Spanish Plays*. London: Nick Hern.
—— (2000) 'Fourplay', in London, J. and George, D. (eds) *Modern Catalan Plays*. London: Methuen.

—— (2004) *Blood*. New Brunswick, NJ: Estreno Contemporary Plays.
—— (2009) 'Strangers', in *Barcelona Plays: A Collection of New Plays by Catalan Playwrights*. New York: CUNY/Martin E. Segal Theatre Center.
Benet i Jornet, Josep M. (1997) *The Ship*. Barcelona: Ed. 62.
—— (2000a) 'Desire', in London, J. and George, D. (eds) *Modern Catalan Plays*. London: Methuen.
—— (2000b) *Legacy*. New Brunswick, NJ: Estreno Contemporary Plays.
—— (2009) 'Salamander', in *Barcelona Plays: A Collection of New Plays by Catalan Playwrights*. New York: CUNY/Martin E. Segal Theatre Center.
Brossa, Joan (1992) *Words are Things*. London: Riverside Studios.
—— (2000) 'The Quarrelsome Party', in London, J. and George, D. (eds) *Modern Catalan Plays*. London: Methuen.
—— (2001) *Joan Brossa or the Poetic Revolt*. Barcelona: Fundació Privada Joan Brossa.
Calders, Pere (1982) *'Brush': Story by Pere Calders*. London: Blackie.
—— (1991) *The Virgin of the Railway and Other Stories*. Warminster: Aris & Phillips.
Carner, Josep (1962) *Poems*. Oxford: Dolphin.
—— (2001) *Nabí*. London: Anvil Press Poetry.
Català, Víctor (1992) *Solitude*. Columbia: Readers International.
Espriu, Salvador (1975) *Lord of the Shadow*. Oxford: Dolphin.
—— (1978a) *The Bull-hide*. Calcutta: Indian Writers' Workshop.
—— (1978b) *Sinera Cemetery*. Barcelona: Institut d'Estudis Nord-Americans.
—— (1989) *Selected Poems of Salvador Espriu*. London: W. W. Norton.
—— (1997) *Selected Poems*. Manchester: Carcanet.
Foix, J. V. (1988) *When I Sleep, Then I See Clearly*. New York: Persea Books.
Guimerà, Àngel (1915) *Martha of the Lowlands*. New York: Double Day, Page.
—— (1916) *La Pecadora*. New York: Putnam.
Moncada, Jesús (1994) *The Towpath*. London: Harvill.
Monzó, Quim (1986) *O'Clock*. New York: Ballantine.
Oliver, Maria Antònia (1989) *Antipodes*. Seattle: The Seal Press.
—— (1989) *Study in Lilac*. London: Pandora 1989.
—— (1998) *Blue Roses for a Dead ... Lady?* New Orleans: University Press of the South.
Parcerisas, Francesc (1992) *The Golden Age and Other Poems*. Barcelona: Institut d'Estudis Nord-Americans, 1992.
Pedrolo, Manuel de (1985) *Final Trajectory*. New York: Carlton Press.
—— (1993) *Touched by Fire*. New York: P. Lang.
Riba, Carles (1970) *Poems*. Oxford: Dolphin Book.
—— (1993) *Savage Heart*. Oxford: Dolphin.
—— (1995) *Elegies of Bierville*. Oxford: Dolphin.
Riera, Carme Riera (2001) *Mirror Images*. New York: Holmes & Meier.
Rodoreda, Mercè (1967) *The Pigeon Girl*. London: André Deutsch.
—— (1983) *Two Tales*. New York: Red Ozier, 1983.
—— (1986) *The Time of the Doves*. Minneapolis: Graywolf.
—— (1993a) *My Christina and Other Stories*. Minneapolis: Graywolf.
—— (1993b) *Camellia Street*. Minneapolis: Graywolf.

2

Medieval Catalan Culture, 801–1492

ALEXANDER IBARZ

Along the borderlands of Al-Andalus

Catalan society developed from the ninth to the fifteenth centuries in circumstances that would leave a profound mark upon the region. A new sense of its own geography, its development as a hub of European and Mediterranean trade, its language and collective imaginary, its cultural difference, all emerged from a lengthy and often difficult process of collective formation. It was no coincidence that during this period there also evolved the political, economic and legal frameworks within which identities were forged. But in its origins in the ninth century Catalonia was just one of several small regions of old Spain (*Hispania*) struggling for survival along the outlying borderlands of the weakening yet still mighty empire of Al-Andalus.

'The Christian reconquest south of the Pyrenees', wrote Pierre Bonnassie, 'began with a memorable defeat.'[1] In early summer 778, Charlemagne responded to a call for help from the Muslim governor of Barcelona, who had rebelled against his overlord in Cordoba. But Charlemagne's offensive came to nothing. Then, while retreating from Saragossa, the rearguard of the Franks' army was ambushed in a Pyrenean mountain pass by Basque warriors. The epic defeat, which became the stuff of Roland's legend, had some positive after-effects for those unhappy with the status quo in the region. It was no coincidence that, seven years later, Girona and a number of other Catalan towns and fortifications opened their gates to Charlemagne's warriors and became united in a common purpose. Local support for the Franks must have been widespread, because Cerdanya (Cerdagne) and Urgell declared allegiance to them in 789. After Charlemagne's main deputy in the

---

[1] Bonnassie, 2001, p. 162. Visigothic Spain was defeated in 711 by combined Islamic forces. Over the years that followed the armies of Islam pushed northwards. After crossing the Pyrenees they were halted by the Franks at Poitiers in 732.

region, Guilhem, count of Toulouse, entered Barcelona in 801, with other local magnates under the command of Charlemagne's son, Louis the Pious, control of the region would never again pass to a Muslim governor. At the time, however, this prospect cannot have seemed like much of a certainty for the two thousand or so citizens of Barcelona.

The vast majority of people in the region stayed away from the coast. Most of it was deserted, apart from a few fortified positions like Barcelona, on account not only of the threat of *razzias* (military raids) but because of the fear of coast-hugging pirates and Viking war bands. Consequently, population was concentrated in the mountains. Safest of all were the high Pyrenean valleys of Urgell and Cerdanya. As a result, these mountains were comparatively densely populated throughout the ninth century. It has been estimated that in the 830s there were more inhabitants in the Pyrenees than in the 1860s, when rural populations were at their highest. The Catalan mountains were to remain populated for the foreseeable future, and although the pre-Pyrenean ranges were inhabited and increasingly began to come under cultivation during the ninth and tenth centuries, there was no rapid reconquest along the coast beyond Barcelona, or over the fertile valleys into Lleida, until well into the twelfth century.

So why was the reconquest in the north-eastern part of the Iberian Peninsula so slow? Part of the answer may have to do with a mindset developed over the years of mountain dwelling. Not only geographically, but culturally too, Catalonia faced in two directions. The Christian population of Asturias-Leon had been with their back against the wall of the Atlantic Ocean, and so the reconquest there, understandably, was undertaken more vigorously as there was no direction but southwards in which to advance. However, the north-eastern Pyrenees offered a different spatio-cultural landscape which allowed for close links to Septimania.

Here, for two centuries preceding the Moorish invasion of 711, Septimania, the eastern part of the Midi or Occitania, had been ruled as a unit by the Visigoths, alongside the region later to become Catalonia. The rule of the Visigoths was succeeded, after a short period of Islamic rule, by the Carolingian Franks who absorbed Septimania as they pushed south in the wake of their victory at Poitiers. When the Hispano-Romans and Goths in the north-eastern corner of Spain in turn became a part of the Frankish world they too were included within an expanding Carolingian sphere of influence. Too weak numerically to impose their will by force, the Franks negotiated with the locals, in a way that left the area enriched rather than disturbed. In his study of this process Archibald Lewis endorsed this view, envisioning a negotiated Gothic–Frankish alliance, rather than a subject Septimania–Catalonia conscripted to protect the empire in the form of a *Marca Hispanica* (borderland with Al-Andalus):

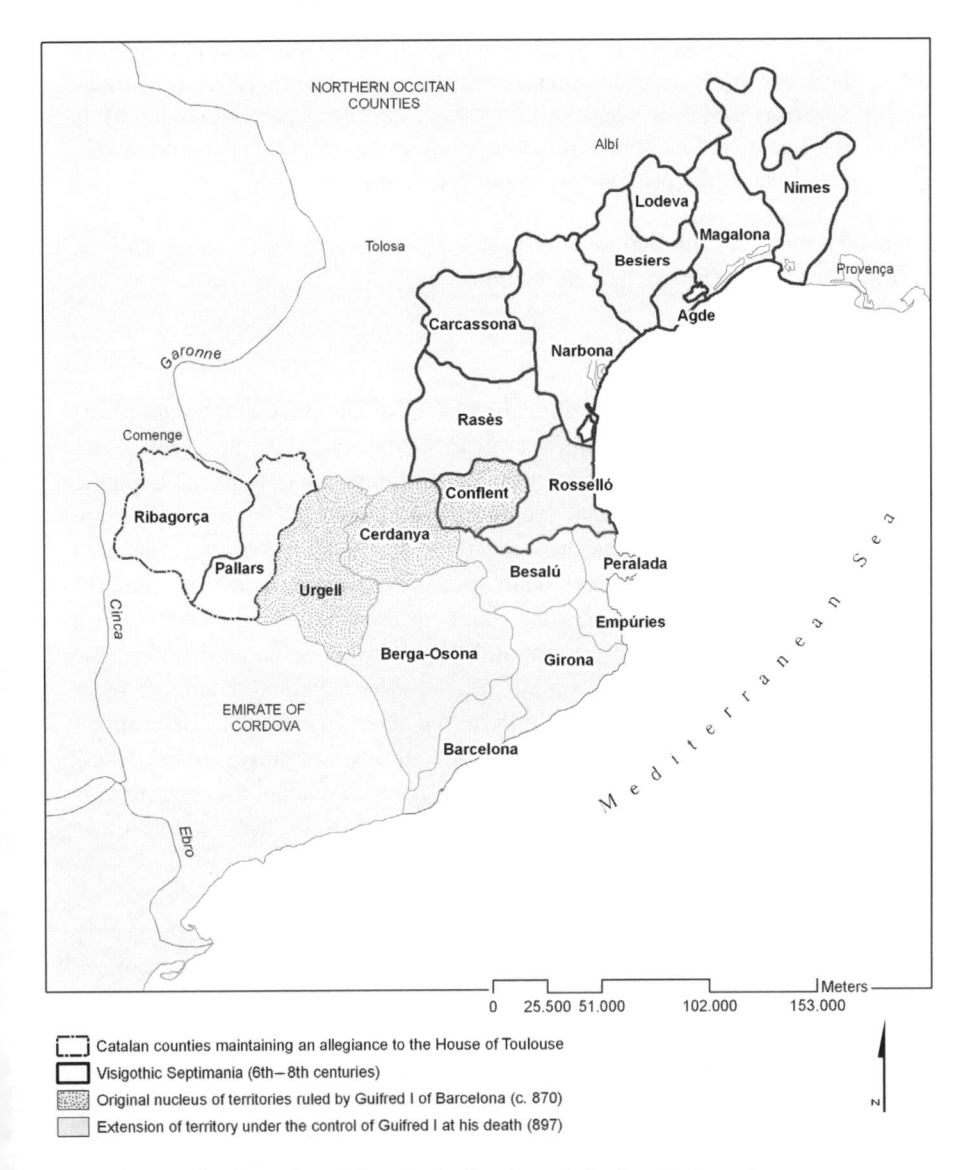

2. Counties of Catalonia-Septimania in the ninth century.
By permission of Mercè Ibarz

The Carolingian system of government after 778 stands revealed as a multinational or multi-racial one [sc. Basque, Gallo-Roman, Hispano-Gothic, Frankish] (…) the use of *aprisiones* [unihabited land taken by right of settlement] in Septimania and Catalonia is a specially good example of privileges given the non-Frankish population (…) there was a steady infiltration of non-Franks into both the Carolingian secular administration and the Church, which was resulting in a slow but inexorable modification of both toward a very different system than that envisaged by the distant emperors of Aix-la-Chapelle [Aachen]. Two forces, then, were at work in the Midi and Catalonia during this period and interacting upon one another [sc. The Carolingian and 'society of the Midi'].[2]

Broadly speaking, the Septimanians (and future Catalonians) assimilated the Franks within an already rich ethnic mix.

Land settlement

The most pressing task facing any administrative authority in the region was the apportionment of land; this was necessary because the peaceful settlement of a large influx of population in mountain areas required a public organization. Some *hispani* had sought refuge in northern Septimania during the Moorish invasion; it was they and their descendants who accompanied Charlemagne's armies to Barcelona in 801, and they were richly rewarded for their efforts. It makes sense to view south-eastern France and Catalonia as a unit during the Carolingian period, and the multi-ethnic composition of the twelve comital families of the region indicates the federated nature of power in the early period. This is one differential characteristic that determined Catalonia's outlook. According to Giuseppe Tavani, this prevented the development of a 'siege mentality', and goes some way to explain the long periods in which Catalonia did not significantly expand its borders, unlike other Christian peninsular states.

This view is not inconsistent with the idea that the existing land requiring settlement absorbed all available human and material resources. In heavily wooded, mountainous or boggy areas this process was slow and time-consuming and was a labour of generations up to and beyond the year 1000. From the start, the Carolingian counts were central to this process, administering and responding to the natural colonization of waste land, or thinly populated areas. Thus *aprisio* refers to uninhabited land, which is taken by right of settlement and which, usually after a thirty-year period, became an *allod*, land held freely without any obligation of feudal homage; other land, a much smaller percentage to begin with, was held as a *beneficium* of some sort, granted according to an agreement of *convenientia*, a forerunner of land bestowed according to feudal levies and homage. Because of this system, which responded to the ad hoc movement of colonists into areas of barren land, most settlements continued to be held by smallholders as allodial land.

[2] Lewis, 1965, p. 68.

In parallel with this movement, the count controlled land directly, and via his representatives along fortified positions. Surrounding land was cultivated by smallholders as *benefices*, on which a percentage of production went to the landowner. Just as important for the organization of settlements was the work of the monasteries. Over time, both aristocratic and ecclesiastical landowners slowly increased the size of their domains. Donations of land by the faithful in wills and testaments added to the Church's possessions. Monasteries also purchased allodial land from many smallholders who were forced to sell their property because much of it was difficult to make productive. In this way, the eleventh century saw a shift in the type of land tenure, with the aristocracy and the monasteries controlling an increasing percentage of the total land available and this prepared the way for the later rise of feudalism.

Monastic foundations transmitted the international culture of Latin Europe. As the only source of a literary education in many places, the contribution of Western monasticism to the development of culture across Europe was great. The monks of Ripoll earnt themselves a reputation both as historians and poets by composing the genealogical histories of the House of Barcelona and the *Carmina Riuipullensia*, a collection of Latin poetry, in the eleventh or twelfth century.

The documentary artefacts of the age bear comparison with the work of the architects, artisans and stonemasons who housed the churchmen and churchgoers. This architecture, together with some artwork, from either side of the tenth century, is collectively referred to as Romanesque. Enough literary and musical artefacts have survived for a picture of Catalonia to be reconstructed which, by the late tenth and early eleventh centuries, seems already to be bursting with cultural self-confidence. The region also possesses a large body of architecture, together with some artwork, from either side of the tenth century, collectively referred to as Romanesque. Viewed as a whole, these remains serve to evoke a fecund cultural phase where the link with southern France remained a strongly cohesive factor in determining the avenues along which the Romanesque style developed. Economic and military power also helped fuel the creative expansion exemplified in church building, made possible by an increased exploitation of iron deposits in the Pyrenees as evinced by the Canigó mines and the forges developed around Ripoll.

The Romanesque cultural milieu

Evidence of cultural confidence is again found in the early establishment of educational institutions. In the tenth century, teaching was imparted in two main centres: monasteries and cathedral schools. Here manuscripts could be shared and copied and students ensured knowledge circulated. The first mention of the monastery of Sant Pere de Rodes dates from 878 and Santa Maria de Ripoll was consecrated in 888. Schools were established at Barcelona, Sant Fèlix d'Urgell and Vic. A crucial figure of the period is Oliba (971–1046), count of Berga and Ripoll. He became an abbot and a bishop and proved to be a major educator, championing monasticism and its accompanying Romanesque idiom. This movement sought to combat a rise in feudal violence, by supporting the Peace and Truce of God. Thus Oliba, at Toluges (near Perpignan) in 1027, alongside Ermessenda of Carcassonne, established a peace movement that aimed to draw together different strands of society in a common cause, using religion and education to combat the rapacity of freebooters and wayward feudal lords. In the same year that the Truce of God was declared, Oliba founded Montserrat monastery. As a religious and educational centre, and the spiritual focus of Catalonia's cultural personality, it has continued to fulfil the objectives of its founder to the present day.

The prestige attained by the educational institutions is epitomized by Gerbert of Aurilhac who opted to study several years in the monasteries of the Pyrenees (967–70), because of their access to mathematical, musical and astronomical learning (including Islamic material unavailable elsewhere). His decision to study in Catalonia stands out, above all, as a testimony to the key cultural and strategic location of the Catalan counties on the borders of Al-Andalus and their status as educational centres of European renown, especially since he went on to become Pope Sylvester II in 999.

The new monasteries and churches that began to appear on the spurs of the Pyrenees in the ninth and tenth centuries constituted the first works of Catalan Romanesque architecture. At first these works were rude stone structures, over time growing more ambitious in scale and technique. Romanesque, as its name suggests, was in essence a continuation of late Roman architecture. It was a European-wide movement, with one of its main epicentres in northern Italy.

Travelling stonemasons, painters, sculptors, engineers and architects formed a significant conduit of cultural exchange during the Carolingian and later periods. For example, about the year 1000 a group of Lombard masters arrived in Catalonia and taught the local artisans to build with squared blocks and to embellish the structures they erected with decorative bands of stone, forming friezes of pilasters and blind arches along the top of walls. It is not hard to imagine the excitement in towns and villages caused by the arrival of these travelling masters.

In the higher valleys that lead down towards Sant Joan de les Abadesses and Ripoll stands the tenth-century church of Sant Jaume de Queralbs. Its simple design still lacks the square towers that are so characteristic of the twelfth-century masterpieces, such as the church of Sant Climent de Taüll

(1123), in the Boí valley in the Vall d'Aran. But it shares with more famous buildings its capacity to evoke a very different milieu from that which most immediately springs to mind when we think of medieval architecture. In contrast to the sharp Gothic that characterized European architecture from the thirteenth century onwards, the Romanesque is far more intimate, its shapes softer and more feminine.

It has been remarked that 'the Dark Age following the collapse of Rome was anything but dark', and this is certainly the impression we gain by visiting a Romanesque cloister, with the exquisite proportions of its colonnades, and the measured curves of its arches that frame the sky. Its capitols are carved with reliefs of fantastic animals from the medieval bestiary, semi-mythical figures, like the green man, saints and demons, and are replete with zoological, botanical, heraldic, mythological and scriptural stories carved in stone for the edification of a predominantly illiterate society. In a quadrangle reflecting the four elements of creation and designed for peaceful peripatetic meditation, the mixture of stone, running water and an open sky is conducive not only for silent communion with the Almighty, but also for constructing the self as a locus of transition between matter and spirit. In this atmosphere, the whole of Romanesque art can be summarized in one symbol, found in many of its paintings: Christ Pantocrator ('Ruler of All').

The Pantocrator was developed by early Christians, and the Catalans inherited it from Late Antique and Byzantine artists, who left work such as the mosaic surviving in the sixth-century monastery of Mount Sinai, which celebrates Christ risen as the source of guidance and light, in the early apostolic tradition. This figure is at once a symbol of the Divine but also of Christ as a human being (the central mystery of Christianity) and is the predominant representation in Romanesque art. From a cultural perspective, the frequent repetition of the motif introduces us to a key aspect of the medieval notion of originality, understood as the reinterpretation of received wisdom, or tradition.

In the Middle Ages, artists were skilled artisans who worked within a rigid and conventional framework. Such was the weight of tradition that at this time an artist would try to distract attention away from what is original by drawing attention to that which bears the stamp of received authority. However, in common with twelfth-century literature, it is one of the enduring attractions of Catalan Romanesque artwork that it vividly manages to express the individual uniqueness of the artist who composed it, as can be seen from the various depictions of the Pantocrator.

This is a practice that also found expression in the blossoming of troubadouresque culture, which flourished towards the second half of the Romanesque period, in the eleventh and twelfth centuries, and was to become a defining feature of the Catalan Middle Ages. From its origins this movement expressed a new approach to themes of aristocratic courtship, perhaps responding in part at least to fashions prevalent in the Muslim courts of Spain, and possibly also deriving some inspiration from renewed Muslim–Christian cultural contacts during the First Crusade.

It is commonly referred to as Courtly Love, and many scholars have long understood that the emergence of troubadour poetry coincidentally with the rise of feudalism has a logical basis. As such, in order to locate the flowering of troubadour culture in its socio-political milieu, it is useful to examine the rise of feudalism.

Feudal Catalonia

After 985, the year in which Barcelona was sacked by the armies of Al-Mansur, the relationship with Al-Andalus was not all about mutual aggression. Though periodic cross-border raids were frequent on both sides, their main aim was not conquest, but the pursuit of plunder. For many years, truces were signed and tribute agreed. Increasingly, this flowed in the direction of Barcelona and the other Catalan counties. In the eleventh century, Catalan forces were also employed by the Moors and their gold filled the coffers of Catalan treasuries. This influx of currency was central to the revitalization of the economy from the 1020s and led to a number of fruitful treaties. While the gold flowed northwards, the count of Barcelona had little incentive to pursue the conquest of his neighbours, now weakened by the break-up of the Caliphate.

By the middle of the eleventh century, the feudal restructuring of land tenure, coupled with an aristocracy deprived of its main source of revenue (plundering Arabs), created an atmosphere of violence. The pent-up aggression of a knightly class bred for war was wrought upon the peasantry, who suffered the consequences of a nobility anxious to increase its power base, which meant increasing its control of the land. For many years the monasteries had been the chief competitors for allodial land; this was all to change in the eleventh century as the nobility competed with the Church to deprive the peasantry of their free status.

The monasteries had tended to pursue their territorial expansion through peaceful means. Now, however, the increasingly feudalized nobility took more direct action. Legal documentation of the period shows many complaints about nobles forcing landowners to swear homage, thereby changing their legal status from allodial smallholders to tenant farmers obliged to return a percentage of their crop and stock, raising yields to their new feudal masters.

The high aristocracy remained unchanged but they were being challenged by the subaltern wings of their lineages, often vicecomital branches, who were no longer content to perform their traditional role and were intent on controlling their domains as private fiefs independent of public authority wielded by counts. This side effect of feudalism completely transformed society and would only be compensated for, in the long term, by the rise of cities, outside the nobility's control, which took their privileges directly from the Crown. As long as the lords of the countryside continued to expand their private powerbases at the expense of public administration, however, public authority was under threat of being undermined, and the whole country in danger of being held to ransom by lawless warlords of greater or lesser stature.

In the meantime, the eleventh and twelfth centuries were the age of feudalism proper, in which a new class, derived from the peasantry, became knights in the service of the aristocratic families. They held the castles from the overlords and, in turn, enfeoffed knights with enough land to maintain at least their horses and equipment to garrison the castle, intimidate the local peasantry into paying their dues and, when needed, served their overlord in whichever local or national conflict he or she were engaged.

To this new pattern of development, Ramon Berenguer I (1035–1076), the count whose predecessors had long exerted the most power and influence in the region, responded in kind. He took military action against each of his opponents in turn, forcing them not just to surrender but to pledge feudal homage to himself as the overlord of overlords. In this way, he turned the feudal system to his own advantage. He structured the feudalization of Catalonia and his other possessions in Languedoc. The ensuing internal political stability brought about social cohesion and cultural development. Ramon Berenguer then decided to turn the aggression of the knightly class into the conquest of land from the Moors. By the end of the twelfth century, Catalonia had grown beyond Tarragona to Tortosa, in the south, and Lleida in the west. Development of the state and consequent strengthening of nascent national identity followed.

Feudalism in Catalonia took a unique course, in that the counts responded to this new emerging social order by attempting to salvage what they could of the public authority defined by the Romano-Visigothic legal traditions. Because these traditions both *de facto* and *de iure* afforded free status to the lower echelons of society, continuity was sought between them and a new legislative system that the counts had to introduce in order to codify the changes occurring in society. A compromise was sought that ensured the continuity of law. Central state authority developed a new legal code, the *Usatges de Barcelona* (1173), one of the first in Europe, which recognized feudal violence as – within limits – legal, but which it attempted to constrain and control through the legal validation of contracts within this system. In this way, the new reality of feudal–vassalic ties was endowed with a lawful framework. Out of the feudal maelstrom conflict was counterbalanced not only by comital policies but by a newly emerging atmosphere of social mobility and, as often occurs in periods of social flux, original ideological responses emerged that found expression in the arts.

Troubadour culture

The value system of the troubadours, collectively referred to as *fin'amor* culture, fits well within this feudalized environment. This is because a central metaphor of courtly love poetry borrows from the newly legalized ceremony of feudal vassalage. Thus a troubadour lover pledged his allegiance to his lady in much the same way as a knight pledged fealty to his overlord, a devotion that required the utmost loyalty. But there was also a more complex dialectical process of both affiliation and disassociation and critique on the part of literary voices of the time. Given the indubitable prominence of this mirroring of poetic and social servanthood, it is all the more remarkable to note that literature as much reflected social practice as it critiqued, ironized, parodied and attempted to influence it through a juxtaposition of temporal with spiritual hierarchies of power. One of the earliest Catalan troubadours, Berenguer de Palou, who was already composing perhaps as early as 1150, voices the principal tenet of courtly culture as the unassailable spiritual dominance of lady over lover:

> Tant m'abelis joys et amors e chans
> et alegrier, deport e cortezia,
> que·l mon non a ricor ni manentia
> don mielhs d'aisso·m tengues per benanans;
> doncs, sai hieu ben que midons ten las claus
> de totz los bes qu'ieu aten ni esper,
> e ren d'aisso sens lieys non puesc aver.[3]

In other words, courtly love not only parallels feudalism, but even sets itself up as a rival ethical ideology, given that, according to this doctrine, all moral and material existence derives through the lady's grace. Troubadour ideology is part of the same civilizing process as the *Usatges*, intended to counteract the masculine excesses of feudalism. Like the Peace of God movement, the

---

[3] Riquer, 1975, p. 307; Beretta Spampinato, 1978, p. 147; for the melody of the song, see Anglès, 1936, p. 381. 'So pleasing to me is joy and love and song and happiness and sport and courtliness that the world cannot provide any wealth or abundance that might make me feel more content; and so, I know well that my lady holds the keys of all the good things that I might ever attain or hope for, and none of these things might I possess without her.'

development of courtly love owed much to the powerful women who took a leading part in promoting its ideals.

Thanks in part to the traditions of Roman and Visigothic law in Catalonia and the Midi, powerful women played an important role in the cultural definition of the region from the earliest period. Between 840 and 843, Dhuoda, countess of Barcelona, composed an educational treatise, the *Liber Manualis*, demonstrating the high level of literary and theological training among various women of the aristocracy and the crucial role they played in moral, political and intellectual life from the earliest period. Another example from the ninth century was Emma, to whom her father, Count Guifred I of Barcelona, granted the land to found the nunnery of Sant Joan de les Abadesses in about 885. Women who governed alongside their husbands, in spite of them or as regents for a minority, included such famous personalities as Ermessenda de Carcassonne and Almodis de la Marca in the eleventh century, and Ermengarda de Narbona in the twelfth.

When considering the troubadours, it is paramount to identify the vernacular as the linguistic medium that justifies categorizing that literary movement as among the earliest manifestations of mass secular culture in southern European tradition.[4] Up to that point Latin was privileged as the vehicle of a high culture. By contrast, the troubadours employed the vernacular and sought to transmit their message to all strata of society. So, although Catalan poets used Occitan as a vehicle of expression, we must acknowledge first of all the idiom's vernacular condition, and its usefulness as a prestigious standard with which to communicate across Catalonia–Occitania, a single cultural area in which the varieties of Romance spoken were mutually understood, thus creating the first literary Romance in Europe.

Troubadour culture – sung in the *canso* – dealt with the theme of love. However, when sung in the *sirventes*, it contained in kernel the whole of contemporary political culture. Neither was its political content determined from on high, but involved a highly dialectical component, epitomized in the genre of debate poems – *partimens* and *tensos* – in which a non-aristocratic troubadour could enter a discussion on an equal footing with a noble lord and even a king. So, while undoubtedly aristocratic in tenor, troubadour poetry is a cultural manifestation of a meritocratic ethos that created a new cultural elite based not on access to wealth, status or power so much as mastery of a linguistic–poetic idiom. This creates an interesting parallel with

---

[4] Although initially a 'courtly', and therefore an elite, phenomenon, the impact of courtly love as an ethos entered the wider social consciousness through literature and therefore justifies its status as 'mass culture' – alongside communal events such as feasts, jousts, dances, concerts, public trials and executions.

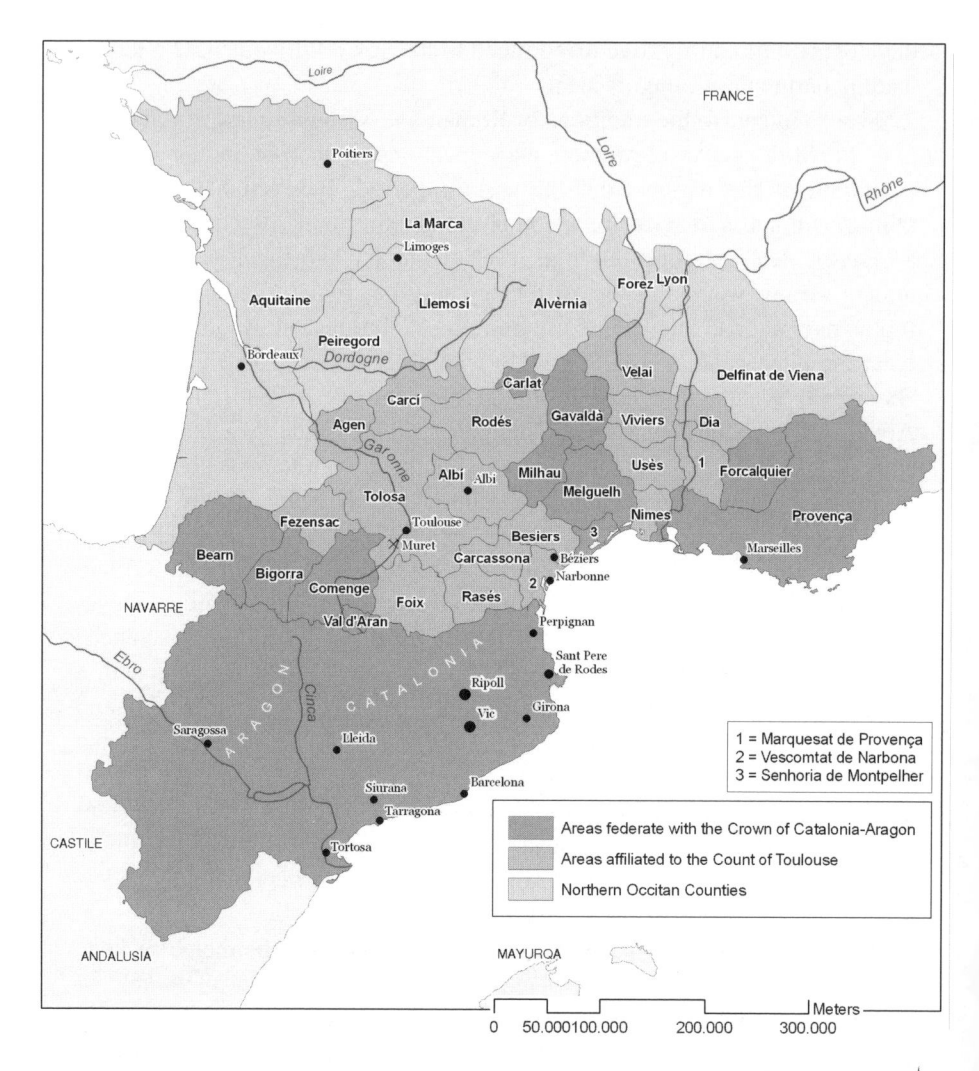

3. Catalonia and the Midi before Muret (1213).
By permission of Mercè Ibarz

the legal culture, in which high aristocrats often lost lawsuits brought against them by smallholders and in which all were equal in the eyes of the law, *de iure*, a tension remaining, *de facto*, with the feudal division of power.

Out of this civilizing process emerges a society that would witness the flowering of religious tolerance, followed rapidly by a reactionary backlash sparked, famously, by growing Papal intolerance of the Cathar heresy.

Cathars and Crusaders

In this way, Catalonia as a stable cultural unit appears to be in full existence by the twelfth century. As we have already seen, the two dominant powers, the secular and ecclesiastical authorities, functioned positively to channel cultural activity – in the form of hagiography, historiography, literature and religious worship – and they also impacted upon popular culture, for example, around the celebrations of the liturgical calendar, and in the management of the rule of law. This sometimes assumed a format that was overtly repressive, in declarations of what was and what was not acceptable to think, say and do.

Up until this point, a sign of the cultural tolerance during this period is the peaceful coexistence of Cathars (or Albigensians) and troubadours, whose religious and artistic practices were antithetical to much orthodox Christian thinking. Cathar is a word of uncertain etymology, but it was used by the Church to refer to a type of heresy that posited two creative principles rather than one: one Good, the world of the spirit, and the other Evil, the material world of satanic creation as epitomized by the materially orientated Church of Rome. The doctrine was denounced as Manichaean – habitually a theologian's hold-all used to describe heresies in general.

This term, however, was not employed by those considered to be heretics, who referred to themselves as *bons homes* and *bons crestians*. Neither did they think of themselves as heretics; instead they felt that they were the true inheritors of Christianity, claiming that the Church had been corrupted early in its history, and that its apostolic succession was interrupted. Their own rituals, which revolved predominantly around the laying on of hands, were believed to channel an alternative apostolic succession, transmitted by Christ in an unbroken chain down to their own time. Rome was viewed by *bons homes* as an evil enterprise, which they held to be under the direct influence of the Antichrist. The Papacy was, according to this view, a tool of the material domination of the World. These controversial ideas, not surprisingly, drew the Cathar sect into a direct confrontation with officialdom, one that led, eventually, to their extermination by the Inquisition (est. 1233). But first, a crusade was needed to conquer the lands in which the heretics operated.

The Cathars became so widespread in the lands of the count of Toulouse that the Papacy decided action needed to be taken against them. There were many sympathizers among the aristocracy and this meant that the society of the Midi could not be trusted to punish its own people. As a result, Rome was left no option but to enlist the help of a foreign power. It chose the closest available ally to the source of the problem and the one that had the most to gain by a reassertion of its power in the region. The monarchy of France, during the twelfth century, exercised little influence in the Occitan regions. As a result of the crusade led against the Albigensians (1208–26) by Simon de Montfort, it would not only reassert its presence there but would also remove power from the counts of Toulouse and Barcelona and their vassals, replacing them with a northern French aristocracy, thus inaugurating the creation of France as it is today.

The troubadour culture of the Midi flourished at the same time as the Cathar heresy, and alongside it. It shared with Catharism a cult of spiritual beauty and an underlying Neoplatonism. But scholars have on the whole been reluctant to pursue any direct connection between troubadour ideology and Cathar religious beliefs, not least because troubadour poetry can also be highly sensuous and celebratory of an earthy Mediterranean culture. Although there were a handful of troubadours who are also known to have been Cathars, associations remain to be shown for the majority. What is important to emphasize, however, is the coexistence of troubadours, Cathars, Catholics, Muslims and Jews in a situation of relative cultural harmony.

This leads to the conclusion that the struggle that emerged at the time of the Albigensian crusade was less of a religious conflict than a political and cultural one: an antagonism between practices of the north and south. In this sense, the many troubadours who turned their artistry into propaganda for the cause of Occitania against France during the crusade sympathized with the heretics without necessarily sharing their beliefs or practices. It was in this cultural milieu of mutual toleration that Catharism needs to be situated.

Unlike the Dominican order founded to combat them, the Cathars were not, in essence, an evangelizing sect; they taught those who came to learn, they healed those who sought their medical expertise, they received the donations of the faithful and their aristocratic patrons, they added to their wealth through the fruits of their industry. They did not, however, seek to convert through proselytization and rejected force of arms.

Indeed, their pacifism has been raised as one of the causes of their military defeat. An important cultural lesson can still be learnt from the massacre at Béziers on 22 July 1209. What shocked the chroniclers was the indiscriminate murder of thousands including not only non-Cathars, but women and children. The leader of the crusade, Simon de Montfort, eagerly decided to make an example of those who tolerated heretics. When asked 'what shall we do?' by a crusader worried about sorting out the heretics from the faithful, Arnaut Amalric, the pope's representative allegedly replied 'Kill them all! Verily, God will recognize his own!' The official report sent back to the Pope stated that 20,000 people had been slaughtered.

The war against the Cathars led to the intervention of King Pere I of Aragon (1196–1213), as the legitimate overlord and champion of lands threatened by a foreign invader. Pere I, himself, was an orthodox Catholic, as were the majority of his subjects. Why, then, did he lead his army to Muret in September 1213 in order to fight De Montfort's crusaders? This is the clearest example in Catalan history of political taking precedence over ecclesiastical loyalty. By extension therefore it is the cultural bond that proves stronger than obedience due to Rome. In this case, feudal loyalty took precedence over religious obedience. At Muret, Pere I was defending his vassals. All he had to do was take effective control of the region. He could only do this by removing De Montfort and his garrisons. Feudalism thus led Pere I to commit a cardinal sin, by fighting a man appointed to lead a crusade.

By all accounts, Pere enjoyed a large numerical superiority over his opponent at Muret. The fact that he was killed on the battlefield and de Montfort achieved a victory against all the odds caused some embarrassment for contemporary Catalan chroniclers, who did their best to skirt around the issue. The author of the *Gesta comitum Barcinonensium*, states simply: 'He chose death rather than turn his back upon the enemy,' which is at best a kind gloss on a military fiasco. In due course, Catalonia's dynastic rights in Occitania would be relinquished to the French at the Treaty of Corbeil (1258). Thenceforth, Occitano-Catalan relations would only continue in the form of the shelter received by Albigensian refugees and the dispossessed nobility of Occitania.

The survival of Pere's heir, Jaume I (1208–1276) during a troubled minority was in no small part due to the stability of the monarchy as an institution. This had been made possible because of the betrothal of Jaume's great-grandfather, count Ramon Berenguer IV (1131–1162), to Petronilla, heiress to the Kingdom of Aragon in 1137. This uniting of Aragon and Catalonia meant a new balance of power in the Peninsula was possible as both Aragon and Catalonia emerged strengthened. Jaume was only a boy of five when he succeeded to the throne; and the survival of the royal house is a testament to the solidity of the confederation, when there were powerful pretenders at hand to usurp the title. Significantly, the Aragonese–Catalan alliance kept intact the separate legal, economic, administrative and constitutional independence of the various realms. Through this mutual respect, Aragon and Catalonia were able to undertake conquests that neither would be able to achieve alone. In this way, in Jaume's reign – where the notion of confederation was continuously reiterated – their attentions turned towards the conquests of Mallorca and Valencia. Naturally, these conquests also benefited from the influx of refugees from war-torn Occitania.

Mallorca, Valencia and the frontier society

The conquest of Mallorca (1229) was an arduous and bloody undertaking. But it was also relatively straightforward, accomplished in a space of months rather than years. In Jaume's chronicle, the king's own account shows some of the gruesome and disorganized nature of medieval warfare, which was led, sometimes in an ad hoc fashion, by the leading nobles. This factionalism is nowhere more evident than in the account of the siege of Mallorca. When the city was taken by storm, the town's inhabitants were put to the sword or captured and sold as slaves. This was a common enough practice that quenched the nobility's thirst for booty and captives, but it also demonstrated that the monarch was not yet in complete control of his army.

For the young Jaume the conquest concluded his education as a warrior-king with ambitions of conquest. Politically, it secured him a kingdom in the sea and, though it was only a modest realm, the victory was a propaganda coup, restoring his relationship with the Papacy – because it was taken out of Muslim control – and enhancing his prestige with neighbouring monarchies. It paved the way for maritime and commercial expansion as it secured the safety of the sea route to the Mediterranean. It was also a preparatory exercise for the conquest of Valencia, which had long been an ambition of the count-kings.

A great deal of planning went into the invasion of Valencia, by far a larger and better-defended kingdom. Jaume and his counsel knew that it was an enormous undertaking that would last many years. After the preparatory reconnaissance, when negotiations with border chieftains ready to change allegiance were completed, the main thrust of the attack resulted in the seizure of the strategic Puig de Cebolla (1237). From there, Jaume organized the siege of the city of Valencia, which finally capitulated in 1238. Having learned from his experience in Mallorca, Jaume orchestrated this siege quite differently. To the dismay of some of his nobles, eager to savour the violent rewards of sacking the city, Jaume arranged for the inhabitants to sue for terms, organizing their safe conduct out of the city with as many of their belongings as they could carry.

Contrary to the disorganization of the Mallorca campaign, the Valencian conquest was slow and methodical, with Jaume laying special emphasis on agreeing terms with as many of the Muslim lords as possible. There was an economic advantage to this method; ensuring that large sections of Muslim population remained *in situ* was essential, as the location was a vital centre of agrarian production, and neither Aragon nor Catalonia had enough spare population to repopulate the country. With the fall of Xàtiva (1244) and Biar

(1245) the conquest was virtually complete. With such large populations of subject Muslims still in place, rebellions were frequent, and these caused Jaume to abandon some of his more enlightened policies. Nonetheless, in many parts of Valencia Muslims, with freedom to worship and live under Shariah law, remained in the majority until the seventeenth century, when they finally succumbed to the mass conversions and expulsions of a less tolerant 'Spanish' monarchy.

Viewed in historical terms, Jaume's military conquests and organizational ability can be seen to have laid the groundwork for the whole pattern of political life in the Crown of Aragon until the fifteenth century.

Culturally, a new page was turned in the thirteenth century, which is defined by the strong emergence of Catalan as a literary language, with prose-writing as a foregrounded genre. Historiography, literature and philosophy become accepted spheres in which Catalan is used, and the vernacular also becomes the official language of administration. These new directions seem to be strongly linked with decisions taken by Jaume I, who himself dictated the first chronicle not to be written in Latin. The sudden prominence given by Jaume I to the vernacular as a vehicle of literary expression should not go unnoticed, as is made clear in Miquel Strubell's chapter on the language, as it coincides with the political break with Occitania.

Though Catalan poets continued writing in flawless Occitan in the pay of the monarchy, Jaume does not seem to have been as interested in troubadour culture as were his predecessors, and the reason for this may have been political. After the separation of Occitania and Catalonia, the road was open for Catalan to become identified as a unique medium of prose expression. It was in this environment that Catalan became an official language of the Royal Chancellery. It was also in this atmosphere that Ramon Llull (1232–1316), the prominent philosopher, felt encouraged to begin a very large programme of publication of philosophical works in Catalan, the first such works to be written in a vernacular language in medieval Christendom. All of this can be put down to the cultural confidence gained during the Romanesque and troubadour periods, which finds its mature blossoming in Llull's philosophical and novelistic prose.

It may be no coincidence that Llull in the late thirteenth century, like Shakespeare in the late sixteenth, found at his disposal a mature literary language, as cultural confidence grew alongside political and commercial expansion. The conquest of the Kingdom of Mallorca, where Llull was based and where he founded a school for Arabic translators, provided a strong impetus to the growth of maritime trade. What was new about the period of Mediterranean expansion is that it did not inaugurate a new epoch of colonization by military conquest but was predominantly a time of contractual political agreements with insular Mediterranean polities (of greatest importance was Sicily, then Sardinia). Unlike some other experiments in the history of expansionism, the Catalan Federation – which cannot properly be called an 'empire' – was culturally and linguistically tolerant of the peoples it governed, and was not based as much on military conquest as on reaching a political consensus, sometimes termed a 'tradition of pactism'.

In 1282, Pere added the Kingdom of Sicily to the confederation. The acquisition of Sicily incurred the wrath of the Papacy and the French Crown, which launched an unsuccessful crusade against Catalonia in 1285, contrary to the Treaty of Corbeil. In Sicily, Pere undertook a policy of expansion according to the institutional structures of Catalonia. In this way, cultural homogeneity was largely avoided because autonomous political structures operated in all the kingdoms of the confederation. However, the contractual paradigm of government was only partly successful. If, on the whole, it worked in Sicily it almost completely failed in Sardinia. This was precisely because the contractual model, as opposed to the colonizing one, could only work with sufficient local support. In Sardinia, which resented the Papal grant of the island to the confederation, rebellion was an option supported by Pisa. Catalonia responded with a half-hearted attempt at colonization, populating only one town – Alguer – which has, surprisingly, remained Catalan-speaking to the present time (though lately the situation has been changing rapidly in favour of Italian), in spite of the fact that Catalan ceased to be an official language there in 1711.

Meanwhile, the cultural encounter with the Muslims of Valencia had opened up direct access to Andalusian technical expertise. Their know-how was also evident in other technical advancements, including astronomy, medicine and the technology for paper-making, which was a much cheaper and less labour-intensive process for the procuration of writing materials than the existing method of making vellum parchment. In combination with the harnessing of water-power in the eleventh and twelfth centuries this technology represented something akin to an industrial revolution, and it was one that was made possible upon the integration of Arab lands with paper-making technologies by the Crown of Aragon.

This new and abundant source of cheaper writing materials goes hand in hand with the rise of literacy and literary accomplishments in Catalan as a language of mass communication, which facilitated not least the dissemination of Llull's works and the rising prestige of Catalan as a literary tool in the wake of Jaume's chronicle.

It also went hand in hand with the thirteenth-century renaissance in the institutions of learning. This was the age of cathedral schools and of the aristocratic and municipal patronage of the arts, which witnessed the rise of the universities, a movement also facilitated by the incorporation of Muslim lands. Following the rapid advance of Castile–Leon and Catalonia–Aragon's frontiers, a number of Muslim scholars found themselves the object of Christian patronage, and these were welcomed by those co-religionists who had already fled the tyranny of the Almohads, by and large unfriendly to the pursuits of scholarship. While in Castile all these elements combined to produce a flowering of legal, philosophical and literary culture during the reign of Alfonso X, a similarly conducive situation was to be found in Catalonia–Aragon under the auspices of Jaume I and his successors.

In 1300, to cater for a growing demand for higher education, Jaume II authorized the foundation of the University of Lleida following the dispensation of a Papal privilege conceding to the Crown the same rights as those granted to the University of Toulouse. The town of Lleida was chosen because of its high concentration of scholars and scriptoria, and because of its strategic location halfway between Saragossa and Barcelona (the two capitals of the Kingdom of Aragon–Catalonia). Official culture, which is the most abundantly documented, was not only fostered in the institutions of higher learning, so necessary for the training of the administrative, notarial, legal and medical classes; it found special scope for transmission in the official historiography commissioned by the monarchy.

Bernat Desclot's Chronicle (written in the 1280s) has often been regarded as the most reliable of the Catalan chronicles, and contains a detailed account of the reign of Jaume's successor, Pere III (II of Barcelona) (d. 1285). More prone to exaggeration is Muntaner's Chronicle (written in the 1320s), which includes his eye-witness account of the Catalan mercenaries that fought in Greece earlier that century.[5] The Chronicle of Pere IV (III of Barcelona) (c. 1382) is a conscious imitation of Jaume's Chronicle, which dictates the king's perspective on the course of his eventful reign in order in part to justify the conflict with the Mallorcan branch of the Barcelona dynasty. In different ways, this flowering of vernacular histories shows us an appetite for vernacular works which was not confined to the genre of historiography.

Social and political decline (fourteenth and fifteenth centuries)

A rise in intolerance, cultural paranoia, xenophobia and superstitious beliefs, affecting even the highest echelons of society, marks out the fourteenth century as one of collective trauma across the whole of European society, and few places were worse affected by declining yields, droughts, earthquakes

---

[5] These mercenaries, the *almogàvers*, were footsoldiers specialised in operations behind enemy lines, where they lived off the land. As one of the most adaptable bodies of infantry of the period, these adventurers found their way to Greece under the command of Roger de Flor (1268–1305).

and plagues than Catalonia. Many people interpreted the years of poor harvest that preceded the plague as a sign of the impending apocalypse. The great plague that struck Europe in 1348 was viewed as a harbinger of worse to come and interpreted as God's vengeance upon a corrupt and unrepentant Christendom. The stench of death was everywhere, with most areas losing between a third and a half of their population, and some sections of society taking even greater losses. Such was the impact that, to this day, the *Danse Macabre* (*Dança de la Mort*) remembering the Great Plague, remains a part of Catalan popular culture and is performed every Maundy Thursday in Verges, Girona. The Black Death arrived early and spread rapidly in Catalonia, owing to its location on the Mediterranean trade routes. Though populations were hardest hit in the cities, trade and commerce did not come to a halt, and remained one of the main sources of economic dynamism during this period and into the fifteenth century.

Most characteristic of late fourteenth-century life is the rise of the towns and the more prominent emergence of a new class of townsfolk. Municipal politics were dominated during this period by the *ciutadans honrats*, the patrician class composed in large part by families grown wealthy through trade but consolidated through property. They were considered to hold noble status and lived almost entirely from the profits of their rents. In this way the *ciutadans honrats* sought to differentiate themselves from the powerful merchants, though their families may have owed the origin of their wealth to commerce. Such was their growing class consciousness, that after 1425 they even refused to be present in public ceremonies alongside representatives of the merchant class. They had years of experience in Barcelona municipal government of negotiating and trading off privileges and fiscal exemptions with the Crown. As a result, the towns had grown by now increasingly more fiscally independent, and wealthier as the fourteenth century progressed, to the detriment of the Crown.

Culturally, this was an age of interaction between nobility and the rising merchant class. Because the aristocracy could not be represented in municipal government without relinquishing its noble status, a number of aristocratic families threw in their lot with the wealthy burghers. The latter, in turn, looked to the nobility for the source of high cultural models to follow. By this time troubadour culture along with the aristocracy that patronized it had lost its momentum and was in decline. The bourgeoisie's attempt to replace their superiors, however, included also a desire to reinstate the high cultural practices inherited from them. The result was peculiar to Catalonia, but closely followed similar developments in bourgeois culture in Occitania, where the Floral Games of Toulouse (*Consistori de Tolosa*) were inaugurated in 1323. This poetry contest at which prizes – the Golden Violet, the Silver Eglantine and Marigold – were awarded by the judges for the best compositions was well attended by Catalan poets. The Games were later mirrored by the *Consistori de Barcelona*, established in 1393.

Albeit in decline, there was an aspiration to keep the troubadour tradition alive, a process made more difficult by the presence of the Inquisition, which took a dim view of secular themes. Thus it was that the troubadour lady began to fade from view. Her presence was for the most part disguised and replaced by tamer hymns to the Virgin. However, there are further socio-political processes underlying the establishment of these cultural events.

Barcelona's oligarchy, composed of the *ciutadans honrats*, fought for its supremacy over the merchants and, to a lesser extent, the guilds and artisans. The Crown, in its eternal fiscal struggle with the powerful city of Barcelona dominated by patricians who controlled municipal government, sought ways to increase the power of the merchants and guilds at the expense of the city's oligarchy. According to Tavani, the royal promotion of the Floral Games was masterminded by a group of intellectuals who in and around the court became the instruments of those social groups who were excluded from municipal government.

Behind the archaicizing veneer of the Occitano-Catalan troubadour tradition, there stood a subtle political agenda. The *Consistori* was envisaged as a forum for bestowing cultural, and therefore social, prestige upon some aspirational sections of Barcelona society, especially upon those upper middle classes excluded by the patricians from being more fairly represented in government. Therefore, we can view the *Consistori* as an attempt on the monarchy's part of acculturating and ennobling the merchant class. Many of the poets performing at these contests were from among these subaltern groups, and it was there that they polished their education in political rhetoric through the study of the arts of poetry. The monarchy used this realignment of power in its losing battle against the powerful patricians.

But the experiment was short-lived, for a major event in Catalan history was to intervene. When King Martí I was taken ill on 29 May 1410, and died two days later, he had not yet named a successor. The next in line was Jaume, count of Urgell, great grandson of Alfons III (1327–1336), who was married to Isabel, daughter of Pere III 'el Cerimoniós' (1336–1387). After a two-year interregnum, during which Jaume relinquished his right to assume the succession in favour of submitting the process to parliamentary legal arbitration, his claim was overruled in favour of a Castilian pretender, Fernando (Ferran) de Trastamara at the Compromise of Casp, in 1412.

Although his claim to the throne was unprecedented, because it derived from a female descendant, Ferran enjoyed sufficient political support, which was backed up with heavy financial investment in securing the votes of electors in the *Corts*. The success of Ferran I in usurping the Crown of Aragon – as Catalan historians often express it – had immediate and long-term consequences for the development of domestic culture because it meant that, for the first time ever, the royal house was no longer Catalan. The importation of Castilian cultural practices followed in the wake of changes to the fiscal, administrative, political and social class machinery. This process rapidly led to the political union of Catalonia with Castile, which resulted in a political subjugation of Catalonia – but only after a protracted civil war (1462–72) – with the union of Castile and Aragon being realized during the reign of Ferdinand (Ferran II) and Isabel, Queen of Castile (1479), the Catholic Monarchs.

The beginning of this process of Hispanicization has left a visible cultural imprint in the gradual but noticeable move in the fifteenth century away from poetry written in the Occitanian literary *koiné* towards a new standard language that ever more resembled the Catalan language as it was ordinarily spoken. The first poet to make the break decisively with the literary language seems to have been the Valencian Ausiàs March (1400–1459). During the early part of his career in the 1420s he had close ties with the royal court of Alfons the Magnanimous, another Trastamaran ruler. In March's substantial corpus of poetry (128 poems), there are only occasional and deliberately stylized traces of the old literary language. Though it is likely that he trained in his youth in the writing of Occitan he may be regarded, perhaps, as the paradigm of a nascent Hispanicization of Catalan courtly culture in the age of the Trastamaras.

This is the great paradox: rather than emphasizing Catalan peculiarity, it has recently been argued that the move away from Occitan towards Catalan is the first step in moving towards Hispanic acculturation. The next logical step would of course be the composition of literature directly in Castilian, which is what indeed happened increasingly as the fifteenth century progressed, and became *de rigueur* for a poet like Joan Boscà (Juan Boscán) in the sixteenth. In retrospect, the temptation to search for the roots of the sixteenth-century decline in the fifteenth-century constitutional crises is perhaps too powerful to avoid. But before we end this survey of Catalan culture in the Middle Ages by reiterating this view, we must return to the late fourteenth-century context of the towns because, apart from the Floral Games, there were other important new trends in literature arising in court and ecclesiastical circles.

The humanist and scholastic zenith

Bernat Metge's *Lo Somni/* The Dream (c. 1396) and Francesc Eiximenis's *Lo Crestià/* The Christian (begun in 1379) provide examples of two very different attempts to bring high culture to a larger audience. Viewed from the perspective of the Hispanicization of cultural activity from the sixteenth century onwards, neither Metge's humanism, nor Eiximenis's encylopaedic scholasticism, provided a sustainable cultural model for the future. This does not mean that each project, respectively, lacked the necessary innovation; simply that the cultural forces working against their approaches were to prove too powerful. Metge and Eiximenis are useful emblematic pointers of Catalan culture at its most developed and refined at the end of the Middle Ages; and so their work, naturally, ranks in their fields among the highest achievements of an era that was rapidly approaching its end.

Lo Crestià, a multi-volume encyclopaedia of scholastic wisdom, was conceived to be of some use to scientific and learned people but to speak principally to simple, lay folk. Commenting on this intention, Stefano Cingolani links the increasing 'laicization' of high culture to the same process discussed earlier in relation to the Floral Games; namely, the increasing importance of cities in the cultural life of Catalonia: it was in the cities that the bourgeoisie adapted the models of learned clerical culture to its own needs. Writers like Eiximenis were conscious of this new audience, and were eager to write for it.

So, Eiximenis enjoyed ecclesiastical backing, the patronage of the royal house and a growing lay audience for vernacular works. There is a complex dynamic in his writing between author and audience. For one thing, it manifests itself in what Sadurní Martí explains as the use of writing that mimics oral communication strategies, with edifying parables, fables, proverbs and a plain style of speech. It is also evident in the strong addressivity of his prose. We frequently find Eiximenis referring to his readers in terms of their division into social and gender roles. From the following passage from the *Dotzè del Crestià* (chapter 378), it is clear that his addressees, on the topic of leisure time, belong to the urban upper classes, whom he advises should spend it in activities of communal benefit:

> Los cavallers deuen entendre a certs dies a exercicis d'armes, e tots dies ne deuen disputar entre si mateix. (...) Los rics hòmens ciutadans així mateix deuen entendre a estudiar e a llegir en llurs cases notables llibres que sien de regiment de la comunitat e de llur vida ... deuen apendre de saviesa en guisa que puixen ben governar e consellar la cosa pública. (...) Les dones ... que són honrades e riques, tostemps deuen ésser ocupades en obrar de seda, o en filar, o en qualque bon exercici, per lo qual ajuden a la comunitat e a llurs cases e es guarden d'ociositat. (...) L'estament clerical deu entendre, en temps que és fora de l'ofici divinal, en oració o en estudi de la santa Escriptura.[6]

---

[6] Hauf, 1983, p. 211. 'Knights must spend some days in martial training, and they should not dispute among themselves on any day. (...) The great city magnates should spend their spare time studying at home and reading good books which discuss the running of the community and their lives ... they should learn wisdom so that they govern well and lend their counsel to the commonwealth. (...) Ladies ... who are honourable and wealthy, should spend their time working silk or spinning thread or in some other

While the Franciscan can, in passages like this, be seen to reflect a Utopian vision of society that would always be countered by reality, his acute pedagogical awareness led him also at times, like fellow churchmen, to apportion blame as well as encourage through exhortation. Referring to the writing profession he admonishes its practitioners for their notorious loose living: writers are ribalds, prone to drink, incapable of spelling, and when they do get down to writing what they spin is a web of lies, and, to top it all, badly spelt.[7]

Eiximenis also frowned somewhat even upon the literary tastes of his patron, the young francophile King Joan I, who had a fondness of French literary romances and music. His condemnation of the fashionable Catalan translation of Andreas Capellanus's treatise on courtly love, the *De Amore*, shows the old antagonism of the ecclesiastical and courtly cultures, but it also shows the existence of a cultural space in which debate was still operating and different voices were heard. In this sense, Eiximenis's work can be read as a good guide to Catalan society at the sunset of an epoch.

When contrasting Eiximenis's popular brand of scholasticism with the more personal and introspective vision of society described by Bernat Metge in *Lo Somni*, the plurality of Catalan literary expression comes into full view. Metge's literariness is far more prominent, and his preferred reading matter is sharply opposed to the scholastic preferences of Eiximenis. Among Metge's favourite authors were Cicero, Petrarch and Boccaccio. References to them populate his works and thus places them within a humanist tradition that has its roots in antiquity.

In contrast with Eiximenis's popularism, humanism tends towards a culturally elitist discourse, manifest not least in a highly polished style. In spite of this, Metge produced a multi-layered text, which can be mined for references, but which also maintains a fast-paced drama, is skilfully constructed as autobiographical and always eminently readable. He takes the drama of the old Boethian story and places it in a contemporary Catalan political setting: the late King Joan I visits Metge in prison as an apparition who seeks to console the author with special regard to the political crisis and court intrigues left in the wake of the monarch's unexpected death. In his use of sources, Metge's preference for classical or humanist texts portrays a desire to explore pagan learning, giving it a prominence which, as with Dante, seeks to reconcile it with Christian orthodoxy. But the context is definitively Catalan, and one of the most interesting features of the story is its

---

wholesome exercise, by which means they may help their community and their houses and prevent idleness. (…) Clerics should spend the time not employed in ministry in prayer or in the study of Holy Scripture.'

[7] *Segon del Crestià*, ch. 161; Hauf, 1983, p. 71.

close link with historical circumstances. Metge held important posts in the royal administration and, following Joan I's death, he suffered legal proceedings at the hands of his antagonists: biographical parallel and self-apology are thus never far from the surface.

Unlike the earlier phase of the troubadour movement, the humanist and scholastic cultures of the late fourteenth century reflected a society in crisis, and were far less optimistic about the possibilities of civilization. The old social order was fragmenting. The final blow to the cohesion of Catalan cultural life would be dealt by the constitutional, economic and cultural crises of the fifteenth century. So, if Eiximenis is the last author to remain a practitioner of purely medieval ideas, even Metge's type of more humanistic literary experiment would not provide a long-term paradigm for Catalan letters. There would never be another Catalan cultural commentator or author like Metge, or indeed like Eiximenis: two writers, who in their separate ways, sought to apply the categories of an ideal social organization to a society that was in fact in full crisis.

With the removal of the Trastamaran court to Naples in the reign of Alfons the Magnanimous, following its conquest in 1442, Barcelona is no longer the primary hub of intellectual and cultural activity. Even economically, Barcelona also shows signs of stagnation. This coincides with a cultural shift of dynamism to the Kingdom of Valencia, where a disparate group of intellectuals set off in a new direction. While, on the surface at least, Valencian authors like Joanot Martorell (1410–1465) and Ausiàs March, Jaume Roig (died in 1478) and Joan Roís de Corella (1435–1497) seem to be writing with a new kind of metropolitan Valencian audience in mind, their new stylistic tendencies thinly veil a very literary obsession with the past, and the passing of an age.

The theme is especially dear to March and is also found in what is perhaps the greatest cultural monument of its age, the novel *Tirant lo Blanc*, brainchild of the knight and adventurer Joanot Martorell. It is worth reading *Tirant lo Blanc* alongside the verses of Ausiàs March, because both works were the product of the same time and place – indeed, the Martorell and March families were close friends and, at times, bitter enemies.

Both these bodies of works have been appreciated for their novelty, and for being in some sense ahead of their time in their assessment of the human condition which, on more than one occasion, seems to prefigure modernity. But they also lend themselves to an inverse reading. Politically, Martorell anticipates Cervantes, his most famous admirer, for acknowledging the passing of the golden age of chivalry. Ausiàs March too, in his way, laments the passing of the golden age of Catalan–Occitan culture, embodied in the troubadour tradition, which he circumvents and returns to in his characteristically oblique manner. For Martorell, the key theme of the novel is a thinly

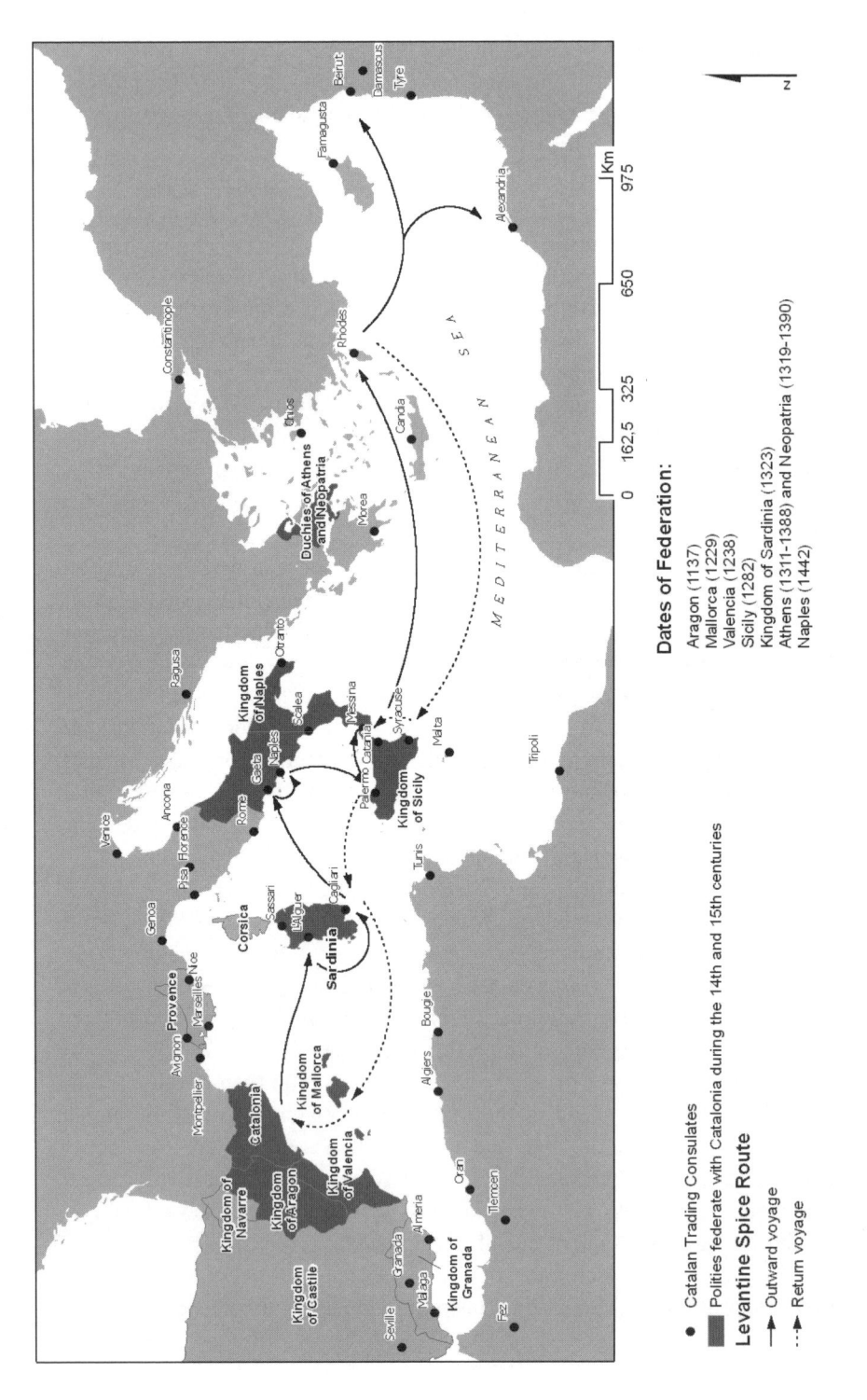

4. The Catalan Federation and Trade in the Mediterranean (13th–15th Centuries).

veiled critique of the policies of Alfons the Magnanimous who, despite his political rhetoric, failed to foresee the most calamitous event in the history of Western Christendom, the fall of Constantinople in 1453. Thus, Martorell remembers, in his hero Tirant, the flesh-and-blood adventurer, Roger de Flor, who with a rag-tag band of mercenaries, once defended Greece from the Turks in the early fourteenth century. This obsession with the past and idealization of it was also a sign of cultural stagnation.

The end of an era?

Some historians view the seeds of Catalonia's political decline in the fifteenth century as a direct result of the catastrophes of the fourteenth, though opinions remain divided on this issue, with some placing greater stress on political failures resulting in the Compromise of Casp. As discussed earlier, this event marks the moment when the ruling house of Barcelona was out-manoeuvred by the Castilian house of Trastamara which proved more dynamic and better able to react to the new circumstances, while the Catalans placed their trust in the integrity of their institutions, an error which blinded them to the contingencies of human actions.

The close of the Middle Ages witnessed the disintegration of a cohesive social ethos throughout Europe. In spite of the initial shock and lasting trauma of the ongoing and recurrent outbreaks of plague, society readjusted to the new circumstances. Indeed, for some elements, noticeably the peasantry, the reduction of the population allowed a glimmer of hope in that their scarcity gave them the prospect of better working conditions and of a relaxation of the increasingly harsher seigneurial regime of feudalism, known as the *mals usos*. But change was slow to come, and when it did, large parts of the peasantry had revolted against the nobility, taking the side of the house of Trastamara in the civil war (1462–72), which tore Catalonia in two. The Trastamaras stimulated the peasants to support their so-called usurpation of the monarchy by funding key leaders and by promising their followers a lighter feudal burden. After many years of fighting between rebellious peasant groups and the nobility, this Trastamaran promise eventually resulted in a royal decree issued by King Ferran II at Guadalupe (1486), essentially abolishing feudalism in Catalonia. But we should be wary of viewing this achievement as too transparently positive, as fiscal policy was behind the move, together with the desire of the monarchy to play the various estates of society off against each other. With the triumph of the Trastamaran dynasty, the Middle Ages in Catalonia came to an end. But what of the legacy that remained?

The achievement of Catalan culture during the Middle Ages, to paraphrase Miquel Batllori, arose from a complex intermeshing of social classes, territories and religious and economic minorities. This wealth of constituents did not develop shapelessly but was lent structure by well-defined institutions: thus from the monarchy to the *Generalitat*, reaching through the diverse organs of local power, the spontaneous elements that create cultural dynamism rested on a solid and stable political and economic basis.[8] As we have seen, Catalan society grew from the ninth to the fifteenth centuries to form a plural and diverse entity that was none the less greater than the sum of its parts, and this intangible unity was also its cultural legacy. A new sense of what made Catalonia galvanized its language and the other parts of its national consciousness into life, giving Catalans an experience of collective formation, a common purpose and a national character. It was no coincidence that during this period there also evolved the political, economic and legal frameworks within which identities were negotiated. The strength of this mesh of institutions with a popular will to cohere in a nascent national identity, could lead to such statements, in the fourteenth century as: 'Good people ... your nation is well known the world over' (Queen Elionor of Aragon to the Parliament, 21 September 1365). But this self-aggrandizing complacency could not hide the fact that Catalonia's resources were overstretched.

In fact, the monarchy harnessed nationalism as a way of engaging Catalans to work in common purpose once again, lest they rest on their oars. As the period neared what would be, in hindsight, its end, so aware had the Catalans become of this national status that references to past collective efforts are suggestive of attempts to reinvigorate waning energies. Martí I at the *Corts* of Perpignan in 1406 talked about some famous moments in Catalan history, including one reference to the participation of Roussillon in the First Crusade, alongside its leader, Godfroi de Bouillon: 'And what about when the Catalans went on the first crusade with Godfroi, were not their deeds worthy of memory?' This is the construction of national consciousness *avant la lettre*, the culmination of five centuries of cultural development. It is also the past overwhelming the present – a sure sign of a loss of dynamism.

During the following centuries, the Trastamaras, and later the Habsburgs and the Bourbons, contributed to the piecemeal dismantlement of political independence for the Catalans. The culmination of this process was the Decree of *Nueva Planta* (1715), which abolished Catalonia's institutional independence – including the suppression of the Catalan language (for the first, but not the last time) – after the Bourbon victory in the War of the Spanish Succession. However, Catalonia's political, institutional and cultural achievements provided a paradigm that endured long after the structures that fostered it had ceased to exist. Neither the vagaries of time nor the straitened

---

[8] Batllori, 1997, p. 20.

economic and political circumstances of the early modern period succeeded in undoing the legacy of medieval Catalan culture. The sense that the best was gone was a powerful internal psychological hindrance, as powerful perhaps as the adverse external political and economic environment that thwarted Catalan development during the centuries of decadence.

Eventually, the nineteenth-century cultural revival, the *Renaixença*, would see an interest in the Middle Ages as the formative period of Catalan cultural identity. Today, it remains quite impossible to explain adequately the national mentality of the Catalans without casting a glance backwards across the medieval centuries, which not only gave birth to Catalonia, but sent her out fully fledged into the world.[9]

Works Cited and Suggested Reading

Primary texts

Albert, R. and Gassiot, J. (1928) *Parlaments a les corts catalanes*. Barcelona: Barcino.
Archer, Robert (ed.) (1997) *Ausiàs March: Obra completa*. Barcelona: Barcanova.
Beretta Spampinato, Margherita (1978) *Berenguer de Palol*. Modena: Mucchi.
Di Girolamo, Costanzo (2000–) *Repertorio informatizzato dell'antica letteratura catalana* (Napoli: Università Federico II) http://www.rialc.unina.it
Hauf, Albert (1983) *Francesc Eiximenis: Lo Crestià*. Barcelona: Edicions 62.
Martí, Sadurní (2003) *Francesc Eiximenis: Angels e demonis*. Barcelona: Quaderns Crema.
Moralejo, José Luis (1986) *Carmina Riuipullensia* (MS. 74, Riuipullensis). Barcelona: Bosch.
Riquer, M. de (1975) *Los Trovadores*, 3 vols. Barcelona: Ariel.
────── (1990) (ed.) *Joanot Martorell: Tirant lo Blanc i altres escrits*. Barcelona: Ariel.
Soldevila, F. (1971) *Les quatre grans cròniques*. Barcelona: Editorial Selecta.
Thiébaux, Marcelle (1998) *Dhuoda, Handbook for her Warrior Son; Liber Manualis*. Cambridge: Cambridge University Press.

Background

Alemany i Ferrer, Rafael (1995) *Guia bibliogràfica de la literatura catalana medieval*. Alacant: Universitat d'Alacant.
Belenguer, Ernest (2007) *Jaume I i el seu regnat*. Lleida: Pagès.
Bisson, T. N. (1986) *The Medieval Crown of Aragon: A Short History*. Oxford: Clarendon Press.
Burns, Robert I. (1975) *Medieval Colonialism: Postcrusade Exploitation of Islamic Valencia*. Princeton: Princeton University Press.
Chaytor, H. J. (1933) *A History of Aragon and Catalonia*. London: Methuen.
Cingolani, Stefano (2002) *El somni d'una cultura: 'Lo Somni' de Bernat Metge*. Barcelona: Quaderns Crema.

---

[9] I would like to thank the members of the TILL Catalan class and Alan Yates for their comments and suggestions on early drafts of this chapter. Most of all I would like to thank Mercè Ibarz Roger for providing the maps.

Company, Ximo (1998) *L'Europa d'Ausiàs March: Art, Cultura, Pensament*. Gandia: Alfons el Vell.
Costen, Michael (1997) *The Cathars and the Albigensian Crusade*. Manchester: Manchester University Press.
Kosto, Adam J. (2001) *Making Agreements in Medieval Catalonia: Power, Order, and the Written Word, 1000–1200*. Cambridge: Cambridge University Press.
Lewis, Archibald (1965) *The Development of Southern French and Catalan Society, 718–1050*. Austin: University of Texas Press.
Riquer, M. de (1964) *Història de la literatura catalana*, 3 vols. Esplugues de Llobregat: Ariel.
Rossell, Antoni (2006) *Els trobadors catalans*. Barcelona: DINSIC.
Tavani, Giuseppe (1996) *Per una història de la cultura catalana medieval*. Barcelona: Curial.
Terry, A. (2003) *A Companion to Catalan Literature*. London: Tamesis.
Vinyoles Vidal, Teresa (2005) *Història de les dones a la Catalunya medieval*. Lleida & Vic: Pagès and Eumo.

Related topics
Anglès, Higini (1936) *La música a Catalunya fins al segle XIII*. Barcelona: Institut d'Estudis Catalans.
Batllori, Miquel (1997) 'Pròleg', in Pere Gabriel (ed.) *Història de la cultura catalana*, vol. 1: *l'esplendor medieval*, pp. 19–24. Barcelona: Edicions 62.
Bonnassie, Pierre *et al*. (2001) *Las Españas medievales*. Barcelona: Crítica.
────── (1975–6) *La Catalogne du Milieu du Xe Siècle à la Fin du XIe Siècle: croissance et mutations d'une société*, 2 vols. Toulouse: Publications de l'Université de Toulouse-Le Mirail.
Del Treppo, Mario (1968) *I mercanti catalani e l'espansione della corona aragonese nel secolo XV*. Napoli: Libreria scientifica editrice.
Escura i Dalmau, Xavier (2003) *Els mites de Muret i Montsergur*. Barcelona: Dalmau.
Lewis, Archibald (1980) 'The Catalan Failure in Acculturation in Frankish Greece and the Islamic World during the Fourteenth Century', *Viator: Medieval and Renaissance Studies*, 2, pp. 361–369.
Miziolek, Jerzy (1990) 'Transfiguratio Domini in the Apse at Mount Sinai and the Symbolism of Light', *Journal of the Warburg and Courtauld Institutes*, 55, pp. 42–60.
Sabaté, Flocel (2004) 'Catalunya medieval', in Albert Balcells (ed.) *Història de Catalunya*, pp. 101–334. Barcelona: L'Esfera dels Llibres.
Salrach, Josep M. (1978) *El procés de formació nacional de Catalunya (segles VIII–IX), vol. 1: El domini carolingi*. Barcelona: Edicions 62.
Soldevila, Ferrran (1965) *El compromís de Casp*. Barcelona: Dalmau.
Turró, J. (2000) 'Una cort a Barcelona per a la literatura del segle XV', www.udg.edu/ilcc/Eiximenis/narpan/documents/tirant.htm
Ventura, Jordi (1976) *Els heretges catalans*. Barcelona: Selecta.
Viera, D. J. (1996) 'Francesc Eiximenis's dissension with the Royal House of Aragon', *Journal of Medieval History*, 22, pp. 251–259.
Weis, René (2000) *The Yellow Cross: The Story of the Last Cathars 1290–1329*, London: Viking.

3

Catalonia:
From Industrialization to the Present Day

ANTONI SEGURA I MAS AND
ELISENDA BARBÉ I POU

Industrialization

In the early decades of the nineteenth century, Catalonia was the protagonist of an exceptional phenomenon in the context of the Spanish state: industrialization. This long-term, deep-rooted process had a profound effect on society, the economy and both countryside and city; and, in 1832, the opening of a factory in Barcelona to manufacture woven cotton goods on steam-driven mechanical looms marked the start of the modernization of the textile sector that would become the power house of the new industrial economy. Factories sprang up initially in Barcelona and the principal localities of the neighbouring boroughs. By the middle of the century, the availability of hydraulic power to drive the looms saw the establishing of textile colonies on river basins, especially along the Ter and Llobregat. This allowed, in turn, the closer policing of workers since these manufacturing colonies included both the factory and workers' dwellings in the same space – and, not infrequently, the Civil Guard barracks as well.

Despite its economic power, however, the Catalan industrial bourgeoisie was bereft of any political influence in the inchoate liberal configuration that emerged in Spain after the disappearance of absolutism in 1833. As elsewhere in Europe, it was the intention of these wealth-creators to participate in decision-making as fully as the other leading classes by promoting a programme based on modernization, industrialization and protectionism. This project, conceived in and fostered by Catalonia, was aimed at the state as a whole and demanded progress for Spain. The development was uneven and halting, however, with a desire to return to the old ways rearing its head in the Carlist Wars, which occurred intermittently over the next four decades.

A further complication was, of course, the condition of popular classes and proletariat. With the advent of industrialization workers had to endure long shifts with poor pay, living in overcrowded dwellings that lacked the minimum concern for hygiene or health. They would soon militate against these conditions demanding improvement in social welfare and freedom. This experience would also be dogged by violence as a series of sporadic popular uprisings and reactionary military coups made their presence felt throughout the period.

Running parallel to the economic advance was a phenomenon which, along with industrialization, would eventually change entirely the political condition of Catalonia. This was, of course, the *Renaixença*: an impulse for cultural recuperation that would grow with the century. Clearly influenced by the spirit of Romanticism and its unearthing of the collective past, the movement was centred on the recovery of the language that had been effectively proscribed by the Bourbon victory in the War of the Spanish Succession in 1714. By the end of the century, however, the *Renaixença* had become completely politicized, acting as the source of new ideologies, which developed into nationalist agendas with specific relation to Catalonia rather than to Spain.

The political system

From 1833 onwards, Liberals – Moderates and Progressives – were to alternate in power. Both parties were formed by landowners, bigwigs and local dignitaries, intellectuals, members of the liberal professions, etc., who shared a common view that was vaguely progressive. In 1849, the most radical element seceded to form the new *Partido Democrático* (Democratic Party), advocating a clean-up of political life and the setting of new democratic horizons with an extension of civil rights and universal suffrage. They also advocated the establishment of a federal republic. From that moment onwards, with the liberal political model consolidated, the debate shifted to the social arena.

In September 1868, the *Gloriosa* erupted – a popular revolution that sent Isabel II into exile and marked the beginning of period known as the Democratic Sexennium. A year later, Francesc Pi i Margall formed the *Partit Republicà Democràtic i Federal* (PRDF – Republican Democratic and Federalist Party), which proposed daring reforms in the fields of welfare and politics. With the proclamation of the First Spanish Republic in February 1873, Pi i Margall found himself with the responsibility of forming a government. However, a lack of political experience, the proliferation of internal divisions and failing public support prevented the PRDF from acting in any convincing fashion. This led, in January 1874, to a coup, which imposed an authoritarian military regime led by General Serrano, a phenomenon that was sadly to become all too familiar over the next century.

During this period (1833–74) Friendly Societies were the first forms of organization on the part of the workers when faced with desperate conditions of factory life. Slowly but surely, these would become politicized and transformed into clandestine syndicates whose first actions would be related to improvements in pay. The first Mutual Society to be legalized was the *Associació de Teixidors* (Society of Weavers) in 1840; and very soon after, attempts at unionization would be viewed with deep suspicion both by mill owners and the state. For this reason, from 1843 to 1868 the Catalan labour movement was forced to develop underground. These years were plagued by disputes as important as that of 1854, caused by wholesale lay-offs resulting from the introduction of Roberts's self-acting mule. Similarly, in 1855, there followed the first general strike in defence of the freedom of association and improvements in working conditions.

The *Gloriosa* witnessed the legalization of trade unions as workers' associations grew apace and imported new revolutionary ideas from elsewhere in Europe. Indeed, the impact was so pronounced that in June 1870 Barcelona celebrated the *I Congrés de les Societats Obreres de la Regió Espanyola* (First Congress of Workers' Societies of the Region of Spain), which witnessed the creation of the *Federació Regional Espanyola* (FRE – Spanish Regional Federation), which pledged its adherence to the International Workers' Association. In 1872, the schism at the heart of this organization between supporters of Bakunin and those of Marx saw the more extreme philosophy of libertarian communism (anarchism) win the day in the Spanish Federation.

The government of the First Republic had begun with great aspirations for democratization and social reform. The incapacity of the new system to bring these into existence alienated the masses from the political process, driving them into the arms of anarcho-syndicalism and its revolutionary policy of direct action. This inter-class belligerence was to be further exacerbated by the imposition of the authoritarian regime of General Serrano who once again suspended the right of association.

The Restoration

In 1875 the restoration of the Bourbon monarchy took place with the crowning of Alfonso XII. With a view to giving the impression of parliamentary democracy, a new system was brought into being. The two major groupings, Conservatives and Liberals, agreed to a peaceful alternation in power. Each party's 'turn' in government was guaranteed by a rigging of the electoral census, bribery and coercion carried out by the local political boss (*cacic*), or simple gerrymandering. In this way, there was no room for Republican parties, who were divided and unable to reorganize.

The Restoration drove the workers' movement back into clandestinity. The anarchists, the majority grouping in Catalonia, reconvened in 1881 as the *Federació de Treballadors de la Regió Espanyola* (FTRE – Federation of Workers from the Region of Spain) and embraced the general strike as their strategy in the struggle. However, more militant elements advocated direct action and publicized this line with the perpetration of a series of violent outrages. In the 1880s and 1890s, during the period of expansion now referred to as the age of 'Gold Fever', Barcelona became known as *La Rosa de Foc* (The Rose of Fire). Atrocities of real virulence afflicted the city such as the Liceu bombs, which murdered 22 concert-goers in 1893, or the device that exploded in 1896 at the Corpus Christi procession, killing 12.[1]

Similar incidents – such as the attempted assassination of the king – were carried out by anarchists in the rest of the state. Of more lasting political significance, however, was the founding of a rival moderate trade union, the *Unión General de Trabajadores* (UGT – General Workers' Union) in 1888 and, in the following year, the *Partido Socialista Obrero Español* (PSOE – Spanish Socialist Party). At the end of the century the syndicalization of the peasantry was also consolidated in the wake of the agrarian crises caused by the devastation inflicted on vineyards and wine production by the phyloxera infestation.

During the nineteenth century the Catalan bourgeoisie had protected its interests via a series of employers' organizations, which led to the creation of the *Foment del Treball Nacional* in 1889. It was by means of these pressure groups that entrepreneurs endeavoured to impose their political model on the Spanish state. However, while other lobbies like Castilian wheat producers and Valencian fruit dealers agitated for – and achieved – free trade and the removal of tariffs, Catalan industrialists militated for protectionist measures that would safeguard their production in the face of competition from the vastly more advanced textile industry of Great Britain.

The structural differences between Catalonia and that of the rest of the state, however, meant that no political grouping would identify with the economic proposals of the Catalan bourgeoisie. In the face of government

---

[1] For anarchists and anti-clerical republicans, the Church was not considered in religious terms but simply as another institution of the state and its repression. It was for this reason that these outrages – and the burning and ransacking of religious property – were not unusual at times of social rebellion.

immobility in this area and the impossibility of rectifying the situation under the existing framework, the first regionalist initiatives appeared on the political front. In 1885, Catalan industrialists presented Alfonso XII with the *Memorial de Greuges* (a Memorandum in defence of the moral and material interests of Catalonia), which demanded that protectionism form the basis of financial policy. However, the Cuban crisis of 1898 was the catalyst that was to turn the whole situation on its head. Defeat in the war against the United States meant the loss Spain's last overseas colonies, which represented a moral and psychological crisis for the country. This former colonizing force was now the sick man of Western Europe – an agrarian backwater – at a moment when the principal industrialized countries had launched their own colonial adventure and were busy carving up the globe between themselves.

Catalan wealth-creators now realized that the establishment of an entirely new relationship with the state was essential in order to create fresh channels through which to influence the decision-making of government in Madrid. In this way, the dominant classes began to toy with the notion of a conservative form of Catalanism and, in order to strengthen their hand, accompanied their political and economic demands with others of a more regionalist and autonomous nature. In the course of the last quarter of the nineteenth century this sense of particularity had been articulated in various quarters. Valentí Almirall was the chief apologist among the ranks of federal republicans. The conservative strain found its point of reference in the *Unió Catalanista* (UC), which published its manifesto in 1892 in the form of a declaration of principles for the Regional Constitution of Catalonia known as the *Bases de Manresa*. In 1899, as industrialists and businessmen shut up shop with the *Tancament de Caixes* in a refusal to pay new rates, which were set higher in Barcelona than Madrid, leading lights of the bourgeoisie and landowners from the interior founded the pressure group of the *Unió Regionalista* (UR).

In 1901, with the calling of parliamentary elections, the UR and the conservative *Centre Nacional Català* led by Cambó and Prat de la Riba decided to present themselves as joint candidates on a ticket that came to be known as the 'Four Presidents' in view of the distinguished public profile of the main candidates. Surprisingly, this ad hoc grouping won the election by a landslide, sweeping the board across the four provinces of Catalonia, with all four candidates being returned. For the first time in a generation, the corrupt bipartidism of the restoration system had been severely dented – and precisely by a Catalanist caucus.

The early twentieth century: *Lliga* and Lerrouxisme

Encouraged by the success in the elections, the UR and CNC decided to merge, joining forces to form the *Lliga Regionalista* (Regionalist League). This was the first political party that was specifically Catalanist, modern, reformist, conservative and bourgeois; and it counted on a solid economic basis and an impressive roll-call of public figures. The *Lliga* thus represented the aspirations of the industrial bourgeoisie and the upper and middle classes of Catalonia, with its mouthpiece the daily *La Veu de Catalunya*. Its success was so pervasive that, from 1901 onwards, the state-wide Liberal and Conservative parties disappeared completely from the Catalan political scene.

The real competition faced by the *Lliga* came from the *Partit Republicà Radical* (PRR – Radical Republican Party), created in 1908 by Alejandro Lerroux. This extrovert Andalusian orator, who had settled in Barcelona, connected perfectly with the discontent among the proletariat and came to be the champion of republicanism in Catalonia. His programme of social criticism based on anticlericalism, improvement in the conditions of the workers and, most of all, a visceral anti-Catalanism (aimed precisely at the upper and middle classes) was served up with great helpings of demagogy and articulated in pseudo-revolutionary terminology. Indeed, in the first decade of the century, the electoral force of the PRR in Barcelona could only be countered by *Solidaritat Catalana*, a broad church of pro-Catalan parties including the *Lliga*, federalist and nationalist republicans, the *Unió Catalanista* and Carlists. This coalition had been cobbled together for the elections between 1903 and 1909 as a protest against the anti-Catalanist policies imposed by central government. However, from 1911 until Primo de Rivera's military coup in 1923, the *Lliga* ruled the roost once again as the PRR was severely weakened by in-fighting and a series of scandals.

In 1907, working-class organizations grouped together to form the *Solidaritat Obrera* (Workers' Soldarity) trade union, which, in 1911, became the *Confederació Nacional del Treball* (CNT – National Confederation of Labour). This anarchist union was to become pivotal over the three decades in the area of the leadership of the working class. In this context, the glaring increase in social inequality and destitution had engendered both widespread discontent and extremism among the proletariat, which was finally to explode in a violent and uncontrolled uprising – the Tragic Week – at the end of July 1909.

Disturbances began in Barcelona over the embarcation of conscripts to the war in North Africa where the Spanish state was involved in yet another unwinnable colonial conflict. Popular outrage began to manifest itself in familiar anticlerical terms with the burning of religious buildings in the metropolis and other industrial cities. The revolt, however, lacked any real organization and was put down with great ferocity by the authorities. Over 75 people were killed during the riots; and the ensuing repression witnessed over 5,000 trials, with the execution of five insurgents.

In the wake of the disaster and the retribution visited on the working class, the *Lliga* was able to regain electoral predominance and popularity through the pursuit of its nationalist policies such as the project of the *Mancomunitat*. This initiative involved pooling the resources of the four different Catalan provinces into one single organ, which would have the capacity to take administrative decisions on behalf of Catalonia as a whole. Though functioning merely at the level of local government it was one of the first decentralizing measures accepted by the Spanish state, coming into being in April 1914 with Prat de la Riba as its first president.

The contribution of the *Mancomunitat* was particularly impressive in the field of education. It instituted the building of schools, centres of professional formation and public libraries; it also promoted the introduction of innovative pedagogical methodologies from abroad. The *Mancomunitat* also worked tirelessly in the field of communications. An adventurous road-building programme was undertaken, the telephone service was extended and post and telegraph utilities improved. This investment in infrastructure would again highlight the difference between a modern, urban Catalonia and a regressive, agrarian Spain. Finally, it also supported Catalan language and culture with the sponsorship of the *Institut d'Estudis Catalans* (IEC – Institute of Catalan Studies) and the process of linguistic standardization under the stewardship of Pompeu Fabra.

The strike at La Canadenca and gun law

In the wake of the Tragic Week the social situation in Catalonia became increasingly tense. The working class had learned from its unpreparedness during the Tragic Week and was now organized in a tighter, more cohesive manner than had been the case earlier. The CNT was of major importance in this respect, boasting over 700,000 members in 1919. As such the proletariat was now able to mobilize in a structured fashion and labour disputes proliferated. It was in this context that, between February and April 1919, a strike erupted at *La Canadenca* – the firm that provided electricity to the whole of Barcelona. The conflict soon spread to other utilities and the city was brought to a standstill. The reaction of the state was extreme and striking workers were conscripted, subjecting them to martial law. For their part, employers used the lock-out and, with the collaboration of the army, organized and armed vigilantes who patrolled the city in pursuit of workers and their leaders. Despite the repression, the conflict was to destabilize the government to such an extent as to force its resignation while achieving, in turn, the implementation of the eight-hour working day, a demand that had been voiced continuously since the last decades of the previous century.

This revolutionary dispute, however, marked the start of a savage, dirty war in Barcelona between industrialists and workers. The employers' objective was to crush the powerful CNT, an aim that was pursued in a variety of ways. Firstly, they created a rival union, the *Sindicats Lliures* (Free Unions), to compete directly with the CNT. These associations were in reality little more than lackeys of the employers. As mentioned above, the wealth creators also reverted to the lock-out, which was used systematically to avoid fresh strikes and dismiss conflictive workers. Finally, bands of gunmen were hired to assassinate key union figures. With the complicity of the civil governor, Martínez Anido, these murderers acted with total impunity. Anarchist extremists responded in the same fashion, arming themselves and killing employers or local government leaders. Between 1919 and 1923, the death toll caused by this conflict stood at 246, of which around 200 were workers or union leaders.

Open warfare on the streets of Catalonia, the institutional crisis of the corrupt political system of the Restoration, the post-war recession and disastrous defeats in the African campaign, particularly that of Annual in 1921, culminated in an appeal by the social elite for the re-establishment of law and order. In the face of the total inability of the state-wide parties to control the explosive social unrest the call to save the country was answered by the military coup of General Miguel Primo de Rivera in September 1923.

The dictatorship of Primo de Rivera

In Spain's first military dictatorship of the twentieth century, constitutional guarantees were suspended and all parties and trade unions proscribed with the aim of restoring public order. A single political grouping was imposed, the *Unión Patriótica* (Patriotic Union), along with other corporate institutions in the social and labour field in order to strictly regulate all forms of association. Furthermore, in an effort to stimulate the economy and assuage proletarian belligerence the dictator promoted a significant public works programme to alleviate temporarily the acute problem of mass unemployment.

Through censorship and the institutional machinery of his government, Primo de Rivera imposed the model of a unitary and uniform country based on the hegemonic and homogenizing notion of traditional Spain and its values. As far as Catalonia was concerned, this included the tireless repression of every sign of national difference. The various cultural expressions of singularity, such as the language and the *sardana*, the national dance, were proscribed. Hundreds of institutions were closed, from private centres of leisure and culture to the *Mancomunitat*, which was dismantled in 1925. Paradoxically, instead of eradicating the Catalan sense of peculiarity these patently repressive policies merely stimulated resistance with the emergence of new groups and tendencies that left behind the moderate regionalist sentiment typical of the *Lliga* to embrace a more radical and fully nationalist programme.

After six years of ineffectual government, the dictatorship fell into crisis having lost all credibility. In the wake of the resignation and exile of the autocrat his successors mapped out a period of transition back to the discredited Restoration system. The regressive proposal, however, managed merely to strengthen the hand of the republican movement all over the state. In August 1930, the major republican parties signed the Pact of San Sebastian in which all agreed to work together to bring the Second Spanish Republic to fruition and, in the case of Catalonia, recognize its right to self-government. In an attempt by the authorities to effect what they expected to be a smooth return to the previous constitutional monarchy, local elections were called for 12 April 1931. Those in control saw no reason why their plans should not progress without incident. A mere two days later, however, the Republican spring was to burst into flower.

The Second Republic

In simple terms, the elections of 1931 were turned into a referendum between constitutional monarchy and the alternative of a republic. In virtually all major cities in Spain the anti-monarchy vote held sway and, from the morning of 14 April, proclamations of the Republic were broadcast accompanied by mass euphoria and expressions of popular support. With the abdication of the monarch the various republican groupings set about establishing a new system. First of all, the parliament in Madrid would draw up a new constitution for the modernizing of Spain in areas such as religion, private property, labour relations, education and the armed forces. In Catalonia, the provisional government formed by the majority party, *Esquerra Republicana de Catalunya* (ERC – Republican Left of Catalonia), would initiate the urgent process of drafting a statute of autonomy that would regulate the nature of the self-government.

By December 1931, the Spanish parliament had approved a new constitution. The state would be democratic, non-confessional and 'integral' in nature, albeit compatible with the autonomy of its regions. The Statute of Núria was also drafted and recognized the right of Catalonia to constitute an autonomous state within the federal republic of Spain. The statute would award Catalans the freedom to legislate and govern themselves in matters of education, civil law, public works, justice and public order. However, it soon became apparent that the powers awarded to the state by the *magna carta* clawed back significantly those proposed by the Núria Statute. Debate for ratification began in May 1932 in a climate strained by anti-Catalan sentiment and publicity. However, the document was approved by the parliament in Madrid in the following September, albeit in a form which was substantially curtailed. In this way, a full two centuries after the War of Spanish Succession, Catalonia was to recover its capacity for self-government with the restoration of the *Generalitat*, the medieval organ of authority, which legislators felt to be a legitimate basis for the implementation of devolution. The nation's right to self-determination, however, had not been recognized.

On 20 November 1932, the first elections to the Catalan chamber were held. The results gave an absolute majority to the ERC, with 56 seats, followed in second place by the *Lliga*, with a mere 16. On 13 December, Lluís Companys was elected speaker of the chamber, and on the following day Francesc Macià was invested as the first President of the *Generalitat* in modern times.

During the biennium 1931–3, numerous reforms were carried out both on the autonomous and state levels with a view to transforming the country by making it more democratic and, above all, modern: the approval of female suffrage, the inauguration of a state school system (non-denominational and scientific), the disestablishment of religion, agrarian reform, the re-structuring of the army and the recognition of workers' rights. These were also years of social agitation caused, more than anything, by the economic depression that assaulted the country after the crash of 1929. There was also a proliferation of strikes and labour problems as the CNT became gradually more distanced from the reformist Republican Government. This social unrest, combined with the intense resistance to reform headed by traditionalist politicians, bourgeoisie and landowners, finally brought about a crisis of government. Thus, in November 1933, general elections were called, which were won by the right. It was in this fashion that the Black Biennium was to begin, when the incoming government paralyzed, suspended or annulled the reforms that had been passed in the first two years of the Republic. At the same time, the competences transferred by Madrid to the *Generalitat* were frozen, which complicated fatally the exercise of self-rule.

Agrarian reform was the issue that generated most polemic during these years. With an Act of 1932 the government had initiated a series of measures to effect a fairer distribution of land and thereby make it more accessible to a broader sector of the population, particularly the landless peasantry. These policies, however, were applied both too selectively and too slowly and merely polarized the situation. The landowners were enraged by the appropriation in itself; and the peasantry by the delay in its implementation. The ERC also attempted to deal with land reform in the *Generalitat*. Its legislation of April 1934 envisaged the possibility of converting *rabassaires* (tenant farmers) into owners of the land they worked. The objective was to turn Catalonia into a country of small and medium-sized holdings, based about the family level. The initiative caused great tension between the conservative tandem of the *Lliga* and the landowners on the one hand and, on the other, the ERC and the *rabassaires*. Nerves were also becoming frayed in the relationship between the progressive *Generalitat* and reactionary central government, which was on the point of declaring the project unconstitutional.

Just when it seemed that agreement had been reached on this issue, in early October 1934, the Prime Minister, Alejandro Lerroux, took the decision to incorporate certain ultra-conservative figures into his cabinet. All around Spain voices were raised against this action. In Catalonia the issue took on a decidedly political hue as the president of the *Generalitat* declared Catalonia a 'State of the Spanish Federal Republic'. The gesture, an attempt to reiterate republican values, was interpreted as an invitation to secessionism and a state of war was declared. The army occupied the Catalan Parliament and Barcelona Town Hall, imprisoning representatives, and there followed a *de facto* suspension of the Statute of Autonomy. The legislation on agrarian reform was also ruled invalid, which unleashed wave after wave of evictions of those peasant farmers who had signed up to a revision of their rents or an improvement in their contract.

From this moment onwards the activities of central government were based on repression and the curtailment of freedom as crystallized by the brutal suppression of the Asturian miners' strike later that year at the hands of the government's enforcer, General Francisco Franco. This, of course, led inevitably to a loss of credibility and support. In the face of this public unrest, a scandal was to precipitate Lerroux's decision to resign and elections were called for February 1936 in an atmosphere of social polarization and intense radicalization. Two antagonistic blocs faced each other in the poll. These were known as the *Frente Popular* (Popular Front or, in Catalonia, the *Front d'Esquerres de Catalunya* [Front of the Catalan Left]), headed by ERC, and the reactionary *Front Català d'Ordre* (Catalan Front for Order), which consisted of parties of the right led by the *Lliga*.

Despite the rarefied atmosphere of tension and confrontation, the elections were conducted successfully with a high participation of nearly 70 per cent of the electorate. Both in Spain and Catalonia the left-wing alternative was to prove victorious with an absolute majority. This triumph of the Popular Front brought about the reinstitution of the Statute of Autonomy; and central government endeavoured to implement the reforms, which had been paralysed for almost two years. The initiative, however, was to be complicated by the increase in workers' demands, the proliferation of strikes and a wave of social conflict. More menacing still was a series of right-wing plots and intrigues that had as their aim the annihilation of the Republic. The situation got progressively more violent, leaving the government incapable of asserting its authority until the problem was taken out of its hands with the uprising of rebel army generals determined to bury the experience of democracy.

The Civil War

Between 17 and 18 July 1936, an uprising was instigated by Generals Mola, Sanjurjo, Queipo de Llano, Goded and Franco. By 20 July, the insurgence had only proved successful in a handful of cities and provinces, not sufficient for the rebels to overthrow the government. As such, Spain became divided into two zones, one loyal to the Republic and the other under the control of the insurgents. It was in this way that the Spanish Civil War began.

In Catalonia the attempted coup was dismantled right from the start. The uprising was put down by the forces of public order and popular resistance in the hundreds of armed CNT members who took to the streets. A few days later the anarchists and parties of the left began to organize divisions of militia filled with volunteers who marched out of Barcelona in the direction of the Aragon Front in order to halt any possible rebel advance on Catalonia from the west. The stabilization of the front left Catalonia in the rearguard of the Republic for almost the entirety of the conflict.

The defeat of the military insurgents acted as catalyst for the process of revolution in Catalonia with the implementation of a series of measures that radically transformed society, economy and political life. Initially, this process was accompanied by a totally uncontrolled spiral of violence guided, in the main, by hatred and personal score-settling. In the streets of Barcelona, the most radical sector of the CNT-FAI, together with left-wing militants, imposed an alternative authority to that of the *Generalitat* with their own vigilante patrols. As such, with the government sidelined, a blood-thirsty repression was unleashed against all those suspected of having lent their support to the military coup. This extended to those connected with parties of the right or centre, who were not necessarily fascists and, above all, against Catholics. The indiscriminate violence spread to the torching of religious buildings and anything representative of the previous order. Some 6,000 people were to die in the first months of the war, either at the hands of revolutionary committees, militia patrols or maverick gunmen.

In the autumn, given the extraordinary nature of the moment, the *Generalitat* began to assume many of the competences not provided for in the Statute, such as defence, industry, finances and external commerce. One of the sectors most transformed by the conflict was, of course, the economy. Here the CNT and other leftist parties instigated collectivization as factories were appropriated. Collectivization also took place in the agrarian sector but to a much lesser extent. For its part the *Generalitat*, realizing that the workers' appropriation of manufacturing was a *fait accompli*, endeavoured to regulate and legalize the process in order to control it.

In May 1937, however, a schism emerged at the heart of the anti-fascist war effort. The lack of unity on the Republican side was again made patent as rival groups divided along familiar lines in a bloody struggle for control. On the one hand were Communists of the *Partit Socialista Unificat de Catalunya* (PSUC – United Socialist Party of Catalonia) and ERC, who advocated the defeat of fascism as a first step to the return of legitimate government. On the other were the Trotskyists of the *Partit Obrer d'Unificació Marxista* (POUM – Workers' Party of Marxist Unification) and the CNT, who considered the war as an inseparable companion to revolution. The conflict was particularly violent, taking place on the streets of various cities in Catalonia. The *Generalitat* was unable to put a halt to the confrontation, and central government attempted to regain control of public order by dispatching the elite Assault Guards to Barcelona.[2]

In political terms the PSUC's hand was much strengthened by the outcome of the hostility. Firstly, the position of the Communists as partners in government was to be reinforced. Secondly, a hysterical witch-hunt was conducted against its rival the POUM. The party was suppressed and its members persecuted. Finally, the inability of the *Generalitat* to maintain public order during the in-fighting induced central government to claw back the diverse competences that had been in the hands of the Catalans, leaving them with even less authority than stipulated in the Statute. Their influence was further compromised – with an additional reduction in autonomy – when, in early November 1937, the Government of the Republic was transferred from Valencia to Barcelona.

---

[2] The hostilities of May 1937 and the ideological reasons for this are, of course, elegantly portrayed by George Orwell, in his *Homage to Catalonia* and, more recently, by Ken Loach in his impressive filmic reconstruction, *Land and Freedom* (1995).

Life in the rearguard was by no means an easy option, and many problems had to be addressed: the scarcity of supplies – causing a spectacular rise in the price of primary produce – food rationing and the appearance of the black market. Faced with these massive shortages Catalonia also played host to a significant number of refugees from all over Spain who were billeted in municipal buildings, government offices and even in the houses of the local population. By the end of 1938 there were close on a million refugees from other Republican areas that had fallen into fascist hands. What is more, since the start of 1937 the country had been battered by constant bombings ordered by the Francoist High Command, which counted on the support of Fascist Italy and Nazi Germany's notorious Condor Legion. The air raids killed some 5,000 people and destroyed around 2,500 buildings in Catalonia. Barcelona suffered the brunt of the punishment, with a total of 384 bombing raids. The result was to demoralize and traumatize the civilian population just as would happen, in due course, elsewhere on the continent.

In early March 1938, the Aragon Front collapsed and Franco's army engaged in a brash offensive that carried it to the Mediterranean coast the following month. In this way, Republican territory on the eastern seaboard became divided into two isolated areas. It was during this campaign that the Catalan city of Lleida became the first to fall into Francoist hands. In July that same year the decisive encounter of the war took place, the Battle of the Ebro. By the end of November this bloody episode had claimed the lives of some 55,000 combatants and concluded with victory for the insurgents. The outcome was to sound the deathknell for the Republic and herald the occupation of Catalonia.

From this moment, Franco's troops advanced virtually unopposed. In January 1939 the city of Tarragona fell and was soon followed by Barcelona. The withdrawal of the defending army to the French border was already well under way. With it went the country's political and intellectual cadre in its entirety, along with thousands upon thousands of ordinary citizens. Every road to France was packed with men, women and children with nothing more than the few belongings they could carry. The harsh winter weather, the snow-filled mountain passes, the lack of food, the endless trudge and the incessant strafing from the fascist air force made the road to exile more bitter still. By mid-February this last means of escape was closed with the arrival of Franco's army. In the course of the previous weeks nearly half a million people had crossed into exile.

For the victors, the 'Third Year of Triumph' was in full swing. For the defeated, the immense majority of Catalonia, it was the beginning of Year Zero: scorched earth, the total destruction of a country, its people, its institutions, its language and its culture. The nightmare of the post-war period was about to commence.

Francoism

On 1 April 1939, an end to hostilities was declared with the occupation of the last remaining areas still under Republican control. The New State of Francisco Franco, *Caudillo* of Spain by the Grace of God, was now in force and had, as its primary aim, the destruction of all modernization and changes that the Republic had instigated. Until the end of the Second World War, the new configuration had all the vestiges of a fascist regime, showing particular sympathy towards the Axis Powers who had lent military support so generously to its cause. A one-party system came into being, a single vertical trade union and, following the lead of Mussolini, other state-wide organizations for the control of the masses.

A regime imposed by the force of arms had to consolidate itself in the same manner, with constant and calculated repression exercised by all the organs of state. The dictatorship sought to annihilate the enemy through coercion; and force was employed systematically to suppress any type of political or ideological dissidence while, at the same time, aiding the imposition of the 'new' culture of Francoist Spain. The measures taken against Catalonia were drastic. The entrance into Catalan territory of Franco's army in April 1938 was accompanied by an edict dissolving the Statute of Autonomy. On 15 January 1939, the *Generalitat* was abolished, and the very next month use of the Catalan language was proscribed. The intention was to wipe out once and for all any vestiges of national difference among the population.

The repression carried out by the army, the civil guard and the police, aided and abetted by informers, was organized and legitimized by a new legal code. These laws were created according to the needs of the moment, subverting all principles of jurisprudence and with scant consideration for human rights. Subjugation was enforced in every possible sphere: politics, the economy, labour, religion, culture, language, etc., in a wholesale institutionalization of repression. This is best seen in its crudest form after the war in the concentration camps where captured Republican troops were rounded up and detained; or the prisons, where men and women in their thousands were incarcerated and tortured in the most abject conditions imaginable.

This interventionism was also visited on public administration, with a purging of the civil service. Bureaucrats were obliged to demonstrate their faithfulness to Francoist principles; and, in Catalonia, there was an attempt to exclude as many Catalans as possible from the sector. Similarly, with regard to the economy, the state flexed its muscles with the imposition of autarky. This fascist policy advocated self-sufficiency within the framework of rigidly controlled financial planning. The consequences of this strategy were dreadful – especially for the defeated – in a country devastated by war and devoid of resources, turning the post-war experience into one long punishment visited upon the people, allegedly for the sins of the Republic.

As was to be expected, the agricultural and industrial sectors suffered important setbacks in production owing to the shortages of primary material, equipment and energy. Spain remained locked into this regressive economic cycle until 1950, which saw the concession of the first loans from the US. Indeed, Catalonia did not achieve the levels of industrial output attained in the year 1932–3 until two decades later, in 1951–2. The government also systematically marginalized industry in Catalonia by a policy of relocation to other parts of the state, chronic disinvestment and frequent restrictions in the provision of power.

Autarky also caused huge shortages of products of primary necessity and, as had happened during the war, rationing was imposed and not removed until 1952. As a result, huge fortunes were amassed by speculators dealing in the black market. Finally, the subjugation of the population was also effected by the imposition of Catholic morality. Personal freedom was abolished as the population was forced, through schooling and intimidation, to embrace unquestioningly Franco's ideals and ethics, with the repression at its most patent in the censorship of the press, cinema, theatre, television and literature.

Resistance in that Year Zero and, indeed, throughout the first decade of the post-war period could amount to little more than the struggle for survival: not to fold under the pressure of the subjection, to find something to eat for family that was locked up and starving in prison; to find an intermediary from somewhere or other to help with employment or release someone from jail; to bribe prison officers not to carry out special punishments or to improve the living conditions of interned friends and relatives. To resist was simply to carry on in the worst circumstances imaginable. Internal political opposition had been dismantled both by state machinery and the abject living conditions of the period.

The political opposition in exile remained at loggerheads and far removed from the reality of what was going on in the country. The only thorn in the regime's side of any note were the *Maquis*, guerrilla groups formed by anarchists and communists who made various incursions into Catalonia by way of the Pyrenees. They carried out acts of sabotage and attacks on the police and army, the most impressive of which saw the Vall d'Aran occupied by 5,000 men who confronted the Spanish army. In due course, the *Maquis* were to become an urban and anarchist guerrilla group, committing high-profile acts of propaganda and sabotage in the main towns of Catalonia, with protagonists of the notoriety of Facerias, Caracremada or the Sabater brothers.[3]

As developments in the Second World War began to turn in favour of the Allies the regime realized a face-lift was required if it was to survive in the new international environment. From 1943 the dictator was to remove from view the rhetoric, rituals and symbols most readily associated with fascism. By the end of the war Spain still remained an outcast, however, excluded from all international associations, especially the United Nations. Franco's regime was also condemned by the major powers and economically isolated. Despite all these tokens of rebuttal, however, no international body was willing to intervene with a view to restoring democracy.

By 1948, with the advent of the Cold War, US foreign policy was marked by a shift to radical anti-communism. The dictator was able to exploit this opportunity and turned his propaganda machine to the exaltation of his anti-Soviet credentials, crowning himself as the 'Sentinel of the West'. The gambit paid off and brought the country in from the cold. The UN lifted its veto against dealings with Spain in 1950, the US re-established relations in 1951 and, in 1953, an agreement was signed that provided military and economic support in exchange for the locating of American army bases in the Peninsula. In the same year a concordat was signed with the Vatican and, finally, in 1955 Spain entered the UN as a full member. For all this window-dressing, the country continued to be an authoritarian military dictatorship.

Recognition of the regime allowed a line to be drawn under the disastrous policy of autarky and a period of economic growth began thanks mainly to US aid. Most importantly, the Stabilization Plan of 1959 freed up the market, allowing massive inward investment from multinationals, the opening of the *costas* for the tourist boom and mass emigration of labour to the factories of Europe, all of which brought about an era of spectacular growth that spanned the 1960s. This expansion was maintained more or less continually up until 1974 but ended with the international petrol crisis, which happened to coincide with the death of Franco in 1975, and the collapse of the dictatorship. The period of industrial expansion was duly felt in Catalonia which, seen as an attractive option for the future, became one of the main centres of reception of immigration from the rural areas of southern Spain.

---

[3] The action of the *Maquis* has been emotively represented by the Oscar-winning *Pan's Labyrinth* (del Toro, 2006), and a mock-up of Faceries' exploits in Barcelona is seen in Balagué's documentary, *La casita blanca. La ciudad oculta* (2002) as is described in Martí-Olivella's chapter on the Cinema.

As far as internal opposition to the regime was concerned, workers' protests were sporadic but still occurred from 1946–7 onwards; and a demonstration of popular discontent in 1951 would mark the beginning of a new era of resistance to the dictator. The ill-named tram strike in Barcelona saw citizens refusing to use this utility in protest against the rise in fares. Support was so widespread that the increase had to be rescinded. Heads had to roll as a result of the success of this mass action and both the mayor of Barcelona and the civil governor of the province were removed from their posts.

Throughout the 1960s the forces of opposition employed this same strategy of mass mobilization – to which the authorities had no answer – to further demands for improvement in pay, working and living conditions. This was structured along three main axes, with entirely new tactics of resistance. Firstly, the workers' movement established and galvanized a clandestine yet powerful trade union, the *Comisiones Obreras* (CCOO – Workers Commissions). Secondly, the student body managed to outmanoeuvre and annul Franco's vertical closed shop, the *Sindicato Español Universitario* (SEU), and create a dynamic alternative. Finally, there was a spectacular growth in neighbourhood associations, a caucus that demanded urban improvements and satisfactory services for their respective areas. On a political level, one of the groups that carried most weight in the struggle was the PSUC, the illegal Communist party.

At the same time, as opposition to the regime was mounting there was a corresponding upsurge in the recuperation of the civic and cultural Catalanism evident in the early decades of the century. As seen in Louise Johnson's chapter on Sport, this was felt most sharply in the rambling, hiking and mountaineering movement (*escoltisme*) but also in the various Catalan Christian societies. The impulse for language-recovery was galvanized by the folk movement of the *Nova Cançó*, which, inspired by Pete Seeger, Joan Baez, Bob Dylan and the US Civil Rights movement, took advantage of mass culture to promote Catalan and protest against the regime with its own home-grown singer-songwriters. In addition, the contribution in the more elite or specialized cultural entities such as the *Institut d'Estudis Catalans* and *Omnium Cultural* was also of significance.

Despite Franco's espousal of Catholicism, with the Second Vatican Council the Church had now turned against the dictator and his values. The Abbey of Montserrat was one of the epicentres of opposition to the regime, acting as host to important anti-Franco concentrations such as the lock-in of intellectuals in 1970 in protest against the six death sentences passed by a military court in Burgos against members of ETA. In the face of a society in rapid process of evolution the regime, now run by apolitical technocrats of the *Opus Dei*, remained immobile. There was no advance attempted towards institutional democratization, and the constant repression of the opposition continued to be the chosen method to guarantee the stability of the regime.

When confronted with this incessant subjugation the opposition reverted to solidarity in the face of injustice. In this way, overarching organisms against the regime came into being, the most important of which was the *Comissió Coordinadora de Forces Polítiques de Catalunya* (Coordinating Committee of the Political Forces of Catalonia). Established in 1969, it included the PSUC, the *Front Nacional de Catalunya* (FNC – Front for the Catalan Nation), the *Moviment Socialista de Catalunya* (MSC – Socialist Movement of Catalonia), the *Unió Democràtica de Catalunya* (UDC – Democratic Union of Catalonia) and a sector of ERC. The committee considered it appropriate to convene an assembly that would bring together all entities and organizations in favour of democratic change in Catalonia. It was in this way that the *Assemblea de Catalunya* (Assembly of Catalonia) was brought into being in 1971, a unified platform of Catalan political, social and cultural pressure groups. The assembly drafted a programme based on four fundamental points: freedom, amnesty, statute of autonomy and coordination with democratic forces elsewhere in the state. The initiative was an enormous success, attracting huge publicity throughout Spain as well as numerous adherents to the cause.

It was within this context of growing unity in the anti-Franco struggle and erosion of the powers of the regime that the dictator died on 20 November 1975. The opposition had not managed to overthrow the regime but at that moment, thanks to the systematic denouncement of its illegitimacy and the incessant promotion of the cultural values of democracy, the forces of freedom had ensured that the much-loathed configuration would enjoy no continuity after the death of the autocrat. And it was thus that the transition to democracy and the recuperation of self-government in Catalonia began.

The Transition

On the death of Franco, Juan Carlos de Borbón was crowned king of Spain, as the dictator had decreed in 1969. The first government under the new monarch, led by arch-Francoist Arias Navarro, introduced minor reforms, which were clearly insufficient to bring about a move to democracy. On the street the opposition realized that now was the time to achieve political change. The divorce between the prime minister and the aspirations of the masses brought about the resignation of the former, who was substituted by the young Adolfo Suárez, who enjoyed the confidence of the king. Suárez, charged to oversee the evolution to democracy, was a skilful *apparatchik* and shrewd enough to dismantle from within the Francoist legal machinery. His

Ley de Reforma Política (LRP – Law of Political Reform) nullified the fundamental principles of the regime and created new democratic institutions. Through a series of pacts with the opposition, though always from a position of control, Suárez was able to ensure that a large number of Francoists travelled with him on this adventure.

From January 1977, the impulse was accelerated with the progressive legalization of parties and trade unions, and with official acceptance of the freedoms of speech, association and the press. The liberalizing steps taken by Suárez went hand in hand with a renunciation on the part of the opposition of any sudden break with the system. Instead of this, the opposition backed a pactist approach with a government that had emerged from the existing framework and also steered clear of calling the monarchy into question. The Transition, then, was the fruit of a generation of politicians capable of overcoming their personal and ideological differences who reached agreement in order to find a consensual and workable way out of the dictatorship.

The elections of 15 June 1977, the first of the democratic period, gave victory to Adolfo Suárez and his *Unión de Centro Democrático* (UCD – Union of the Democratic Centre), with 165 seats. The PSOE was the second most supported party, with 103 seats (plus 15 Catalan Socialist deputies). Results in Catalonia varied widely from those in the rest of the state, underlining the commitment to self-government alongside the struggle against Francoism. Approximately 80 per cent of the poll was cast in favour of groups that had explicitly demanded the restoration of the *Generalitat* and the Statute of Autonomy. These realities were confirmed by the huge demonstration on the streets of Barcelona on Catalan national day, 11 September. Around a million people participated in what was at that time the biggest gathering ever witnessed in the Catalan capital, endorsing the demands for the restitution of their national rights.

The ballot box had spoken and Suárez, as new prime minister, was given two clear messages. Firstly, he realized that the newly elected parliament was obliged to draft a new democratic constitution for post-Franco Spain. Secondly, it had become patent that the re-establishment of self-government for Catalonia was a *sine qua non*. As such, the drawing up of a *magna carta* was put into process with the text agreed by all the major parties. This constitution, approved by referendum on 6 December 1978, was based on five principles: democracy, the rule of law, the welfare state, constitutional monarchy and autonomy. In this respect, self-government was permitted for every community that requested it without any recognition of the plurinational character of the state. Also left unclear was the question of the division of competencies. Which areas, for example, were to be the responsibility of central government and which would be transferred to the autonomies?

Suárez was conscious, however, of the urgency to give a swift reply to Catalan aspirations for self-government. Ignoring political parties, he dealt directly with Josep Tarradellas, the President of the *Generalitat* in exile, who demanded recognition of the institution he presided over and its provisional return, even though its composition did not reflect the results of the recent elections. In late September the central government provisionally re-established the *Generalitat* and, subsequently, a government of national unity was formed under the Tarradellas presidency along with the parties elected in the previous June. In July 1978, a committee was formed to proceed with the drafting of the new Statute of Autonomy. The working group met later that autumn at Sau (the name given to the document) and drew up a text in a climate of consensus.

General elections in March 1979 hardly altered the composition of the state chamber but underlined, once again, the difference in voting habits between Catalonia – with a left-wing hegemony of Socialists and Communists – and elsewhere. It was this parliament that would have to approve the Statute of Autonomy; and the decision was ratified in August 1979 after highly complex negotiations. Finally, however, the new Statute was approved by referendum in Catalonia and came into practice on 17 January 1980.

The document assigned three areas of competence to Catalonia. First were those legislated exclusively by the *Generalitat*: culture, patrimony, archives and libraries, territorial organization, town planning, housing, tourism and administration. Second were those areas controlled jointly between the state and the *Generalitat*, as in policing and public order. Finally were those shared competences that are divided in that they are decided upon by the state but acted upon according to the criteria of the *Generalitat*: the economy (agriculture, livestock, industry and commerce), education, mass media (radio, television, press), health and justice (power to create a Catalan police body and control of the municipal force). In other cases, the *Generalitat* was charged simply with the implementation of state policy (labour, prisons, ports and airports).

The first elections to the Catalan parliament were called on 20 March 1980. The parties that stood had already participated in the state-wide poll, with the significant novelty of the *Convergència i Unió* (CiU – Convergence and Union) coalition, which, in 1978, grouped together the nationalist formation of Jordi Pujol and the Christian Democrat UDC. Against all forecasts, CiU romped home with 43 seats against the 33 of the *Partit dels Socialistes de Catalunya* (PSC – Socialist Party of Catalonia), which had also been constituted from disparate Socialist strands in 1978 and had become federated to the state-wide PSOE. The most significant detail, however, is that this triumph would be followed by six more. The explanation of this hegemony lies in the fact that CiU was a national rather than a nationalist party and could thus represent a broad spectrum of interests at the heart of Catalan society.

From an institutional viewpoint, the 1980 elections and the formation of Pujol's first government mark the end of the Transition in Catalonia. In Spain, however, the completion of this process is located after the suppression of the attempted coup of Colonel Antonio Tejero (23 February 1981) and with the change in power heralded by the absolute majority of the PSOE in the poll of October 1982.

Thirty years of self-government and a new Statute

The first elections to the Catalan parliament had given victory to CiU, although without an absolute majority. In view of this, CiU offered the Socialists the possibility of jointly forming government, though this was rejected by the PSC, which thought that the CiU government would be short-lived and unstable. This first legislature, which might be described as the period of consolidation of self-government, was characterized by the dynamism and capacity of the CiU executive and the spirit of anti-Francoist unity, as had been exemplified by the *Assemblea de Catalunya* and epitomized by the consensual drafting of the constitution and Statute of Autonomy.

During the first CiU government the political priorities were the process of national and institutional reconstruction centring, above all, on the demands for the devolution of competences, the consolidation of the *Generalitat*, the development of the civil service and, last but by no means least, the recuperation of the language. Aware of the need for a solid foundation to this edifice CiU agreed a pact with the other parties on major questions of self-government, such as language, health and education. Measures were adopted that were both ambitious yet also unanimously consensual, satisfying all concerned. The policies that stand out from this period relate particularly to linguistic normalization in 1983 and the launching, in 1982, of mass media local to the autonomous context.

In the 1984 elections to the Catalan parliament CiU was returned with an absolute majority. Factors that influenced this result were the party's ability to unite the interests of Catalan society as a whole and other external elements. First was the weakness and lack of political project on the part of ERC, which lost a good deal of its electoral support, and the decline of the PSUC. Secondly, in order to avoid a rupture with the PSOE in 1982, the PSC had distanced itself totally from the huge mobilization that erupted in Catalonia against the *Ley Orgánica de Armonización del Proceso Autonómico/* Law for the Harmonization of the Autonomous Process (LOAPA). This law, which had been agreed by the PSOE and UCD, was considered by Communists and Nationalists as an obvious claw-back of those powers awarded to Catalonia by the Statute of Autonomy. Their appeal against it was upheld by the *Tribunal Constitucional*, the highest court in the land, which effectively invalidated a good part of its content. All these developments were greeted by utter silence from the PSC, which brought about a fall in support in the following autonomous elections.

With its shrewd dynamism, characterized by its leader, CiU obtained political hegemony in Catalonia which it maintained until 1995. Its absolute majorities in 1984, 1988 and 1992 accompanied an additional strong showing in the state parliament in Madrid. Throughout these years the *Generalitat* consolidated the policies already initiated in the first legislature. The linguistic programme, for example, continued to count on virtually across-the-board support. This was also the case with the domestic health provision, rigorously universal but with mixed provision between public and private sectors, which implemented a policy to bring it close to the patient with the building of local hospitals. In the field of education it was also CiU's desire to court popularity in government by prioritizing global interests, encouraging a mixed system that straddled the public and private divide. An autonomous police force, the *Mossos d'Esquadra*, was also created and its members began to appear on the streets.

This decade of CiU government had a further priority: recognition of Catalan identity in Europe and, additionally, the promotion of domestic mass media as an instrument for the visualization of Catalan identity within this community as a whole. As such, the *Generalitat* worked towards the creation of a quality radio and television service within the general plan of the normalization of the language. Out of this initiative were born TV3 and *Catalunya Ràdio*, which strove to establish a clearly differentiated collective imaginary for Catalonia. In Europe, CiU insistently endeavoured to achieve Catalan participation in all institutions and its projection as a political entity distinct from Spain.

The political and parliamentary hegemony of the group was to be called to account, however, towards the second part of the 1990s as CiU lost the capacity for protagonism at the autonomous level and was incapable of interpreting the changes that had taken place at the heart of Catalan society. The new perspectives for political achievement now lay in the area of demands for a fresh Statute of Autonomy. For its part, the PSC was more attuned to these sentiments and could demonstrate that, after a period in the shadow of the PSOE, it now had its own strong vision of the future of Catalan self-government.

In the 1995 elections to the Catalan parliament CiU lost its absolute majority but still continued to govern the country thanks to a pact with the conservative *Partido Popular* (PP – Popular Party), the new party of state government after 1996. With this agreement, however, CiU was to get progressively tied down to more trenchantly reactionary positions, losing one of the keys to its previous success: the power to be a truly national force. The incapacity to represent Catalan interests across the board was made abundantly evident in 1999 when the grouping avoided the chance to open a debate on a topic of critical significance: the creation of a new system of finance.

The pact established with the Spanish nationalists of the PP, however, was to call CiU's Catalanist credentials into question. This agreement was reached in order to marginalize the rival ERC from government and avoid, in this way, any possibility of institutional change. The party's inexplicable decision, however, to extend its support for this conservative Spanish grouping to the chamber in Madrid (quite unnecessarily since the PP enjoyed an absolute majority after the 2000 elections), compromised the chances of CiU forming a government in any immediate future. It was a question of guilt by association as José María Aznar's (PP) second administration was characterized by a reduction in democracy and autonomy through the imposition of centralist and unitarian decrees that effected a claw-back of Catalan self-government.

This highly charged situation between Madrid and Barcelona, starved more and more of competences and resources to effect the necessary modernization of Catalonia, brought about a crisis. This came to a head in 2002 with the approval of the Catalan parliament (minus PP) of a motion to reform the Statute of Autonomy. CiU initially declined to support the project but was finally forced to adhere given its general support throughout the country. While this debate raged elections to the Catalan parliament were called in November 2003. CiU won the most seats (46) but not the most votes. The best-supported party was the PSC, which returned with only 42 seats. This group, however, was to form a tripartite pact of government with ERC (23 seats) and the nine seats of the coalition *Iniciativa per a Catalunya Verds* (ICV – Initiative for Catalonia and Greens), beginning a new era of left-wing, nationalist government in Catalonia, unseen since the 1930s, and leaving CiU in the opposition with the PP (15 seats).

On 16 December 2003, Pasqual Maragall, mayor of Barcelona during the Olympics, was invested as the new President of the *Generalitat*. A few months later the PP was to lose the state elections and José Luís Rodríguez Zapatero, leader of the PSOE, began a new era of socialist control.

This tripartite government, which became known as the *Tripartit*, was marked by the elaboration of the new Statute of Autonomy. Despite a period of turbulence in the political arena, with trenchant opposition from the PP, the new document would define a fresh relationship between central and autonomous administrations, especially in matters of finance. As was the case with the Statute of Sau the process was long and involved. After protracted negotiations in Catalonia, with across-the-board support (minus PP), the text was approved and sent for ratification to the chamber in Madrid. All this took place within a tense, rarified atmosphere in Spain, interspersed with diverse anti-Catalan demonstrations. In due course, a severely curtailed text was approved by the Madrid parliament in March 2006 and endorsed overwhelmingly by referendum in June 2006, albeit with a high rate of abstention (51.15 per cent).

As such the new Statute of Autonomy became law and heralded a new framework of relations between the *Generalitat* and the Spanish state. The negotiations, curtailments and conflict, however, had taken their toll not least upon the solidity of the *Tripartit* where the ERC had dissented from its partners in government, refusing to endorse the final text. The result was the calling of early elections held in November 2006, which, despite the ferocity of the internal dissidence, returned the *Tripartit* to power once again under the new leader of the PSC, José Montilla.

Works Cited and Suggested Reading

Abelló, T. (2007) *El debat estatutari del 1932*. Barcelona: Parlament de Catalunya.
Aracil, R. and Segura Mas, A. (eds) (2000–2) *Memòria de la Transició a Espanya i a Catalunya* Vols I, II and III. Barcelona: Edicions Universitat de Barcelona.
Aracil, R., Mayayo Artal, A. and Segura Mas, A. (eds) (2003) *Memòria de la Transició a Espanya i a Catalunya.* Vols IV, V and VI–VIII. Barcelona: Edicions Universitat de Barcelona.
Balcells, Albert (1995) *Catalan Nationalism: Past and Present*. New York: Macmillan.
Dueñas Iturbe, O. (2007) *Els esclaus de Franco*. Barcelona: Ara Llibres.
Fontana, J. (1989) *La Fi de l'antic règim i la industrialització: 1787–1868*. Barcelona: Edicions 62.
Guibernau, Montserrat (2000) 'Nationalism and Intellectuals in Nations without States: the Catalan Case', *Political Studies*, 48, pp. 929–946.
——— (2002) *Between Autonomy and Secession: The Accommodation of Catalonia within the New Democratic Spain*. Brighton: European Institute, University of Sussex.
——— (2004) *Catalan Nationalism: Francoism, Transition and Democracy*. London: Routledge.
——— (2007) *The Identity of Nations*. Cambridge: Polity.

Lo Cascio, P. (2008) *Nacionalisme i autogovern: Catalunya, 1980–2003*. Catarroja: Afers.
Loach, K. (dir.) (1995) *Land and Freedom*.
Mayayo, A. (1995) *De pagesos a ciutadans. Cent anys de sindicalisme i cooperativisme agraris a Catalunya (1893–1994)*. Catarroja: Afers.
―――― (2002) *La ruptura catalana. Les eleccions del 15 de juny de 1977*. Catarroja: Afers.
Muniesa, B. (1996) *Dictadura y Monarquía en España: 1939–2002*. Barcelona: Ariel.
Orwell, G. (1938). *Homage to Catalonia*. London: Secker & Warburg.
Riquer Permanyer, B. (1989). *El Franquisme i la transició democràtica: 1939–1988*. Barcelona: Edicions 62.
―――― (2003) *La Catalunya autonòmica 1975–2003*. Barcelona: Edicions 62.
Risques, M. (dir.) (2006) *Història de la Catalunya contemporània: de la guerra del Francès al nou Estatut*. Barcelona: Mina.
Rúa Fernández, J. M. (2008). *Nacionalisme i món sindical a Catalunya (1974–1990)*. Barcelona: Consell de Treball, Econòmic i Social de Catalunya.
Segura Mas, A. (2006) *Catalunya Year Zero*. 8th Joan Gili Memorial Lecture, University of Birmingham. Birmingham: Anglo-Catalan Society, available at: www.anglo-catalan.org/op/lectures/lecture08.pdf
―――― (2007a) 'Transició i memòria històrica', in *Revista del Col·legi Oficial de Doctors i Llicenciats en Filosofia i Lletres i en Ciències de Catalunya*. Barcelona, pp. 42–47.
―――― (2007b) 'Un balance del Estado de las Autonomías en España (1976–2002)', in Quirosa-Cheyrouze, R. (co-ord.) (2007) *Historia de la Transición en España. Los inicios del proceso democratizador*. Madrid: Biblioteca Nueva.
Solé, Q. (2008) *Els morts clandestins: les fosses comunes de la Guerra Civil a Catalunya*. Catarroja-Barcelona: Afers.
Solé i Sabaté, J. M. and Villarroya, J. (1989–90) *Violència i repressió a la reraguarda catalana (1936–1939)*, 2 vols. Barcelona: Publicacions de l'Abadia de Monserrat.
―――― (2004–7) *La Guerra Civil a Catalunya: 1936–1939*. Barcelona: Edicions 62.
―――― (2005–7) *El franquisme a Catalunya: 1939–1975*. Barcelona: Edicions 62.
―――― (2008) *La Transició a Catalunya (1975–1984)*. Barcelona: Edicions 62.
Termes, J. (1987) *De la revolució de setembre a la fi de la guerra civil: 1868–1939*. Barcelona: Edicions 62.
Various authors (1999) *Vint anys de l'Estatut d'Autonomia de Catalunya. Balanç i perspectives*, special number of *Idees*, October–December, no. 4.
Villarroya, J. (1981) *Bombardeigs de Barcelona durant la Guerra Civil*. Barcelona: Publicacions de l'Abadia de Monserrat.

4

Barcelona: The Siege City

ROBERT DAVIDSON

Barcelona is a metropolis for which the concept of siege has specifically modern connotations. Captive in various forms for much of its history following the comprehensive defeat of Catalonia in 1714, what was to become the economic motor of Spain would learn to live under the watchful eyes, cannon and restrictive centrist policies of the Spanish state for the bulk of its modernization. What is more, around the turn of the twentieth century, a foundational period both in cultural and political terms, this external vigilance was supplemented in the Catalan capital by periods of brutal class warfare among its own citizens. The fact that this time of growth was inflected by urban violence only heightened the city's understanding of what it meant to be under prolonged attack as both working- and ruling-class Barcelona felt besieged from without and from within.

The city persisted and survived these trials. It withstood, as well, two military dictatorships in the twentieth century totalling some 43 years. In terms of urban expansion and growth the period of transition to democracy in 1975 would come to rival the latter half of the 1800s. As had happened during the first modern Catalan renaissance, Barcelona was able to slough off its overt prison garb as it built and developed frenetically. This process of revitalization culminated in the hosting of the 1992 Olympics. The ostensible success of those Games as a performance of urban possibility and renewal has resonated around the world ever since. Even though critics are increasingly questioning the ultimate consequences of this period, urbanists now point to a 'Barcelona model' – especially in terms of waterfront revitalization – as a way of helping urban centres connect not only to their citizenry but to the built environment and their natural geographies as well.

Barcelona's arrival as a sought-out destination – an 'in' city – on the world's map, though, has been a mixed blessing. Among its valued attractions Gaudí and his contemporaries' *modernista* architecture has helped confer upon Barcelona 'must see' status for travellers to Europe. At the same time, the celebrated urban renewal has brought the holiday beach experience to within steps of the city proper. Similarly, the image of Barcelona has become one not of a specifically Catalan conurbation but rather as a cosmopolitan/sensorial experience that one consumes. As a result of these multiple dynamics, the city is a local city less and less and a 'world' metropolis more and more: a style, a surface to be admired or a brand, as Andrew Smith has suggested.[1]

The flip side of this success is that the city is also, increasingly, a difficult place to live. Mass tourism and its desirability for the potential expatriate are changing Barcelona, with the wide-ranging consequences of both having been felt in a relatively short period of time. Not surprisingly, this rapid ascension after years of repression has had unintended results; and now, as in the past, the Catalan capital is once again facing a siege. The walls and conflicts of old have been replaced by new threats to social cohesion, but the effects are just as serious. Real estate speculation, top–down urban planning and the promise of a unique urban experience projected by the postmodern brand image have all had deleterious consequences.

Perversely, the city's strong design-based foundation has contributed to the current danger. The perspective offered in this chapter engages the topic of Barcelona as a historically besieged city with its own continuing dynamic of blockade by critiquing the increasingly mainstream reading of Barcelona as a place that is a very deliberately 'designed' city on the one hand and that is a now pre-eminent 'city of design' on the other. The cleavage between these two entwined Barcelonas is becoming as increasingly patent as the Barcelona *brand* and invites an examination of the Catalan capital through the lens of what may be termed its own siege modernity.

An exploration of these facets of the urban experience and its packaging is especially appropriate now that the idea of what an urban siege entails has been literally and figuratively internalized with the advent of the postmodern global city. What is more, the insistence on *look* has also been fundamental to forced evolutions in the city's *sound*: a telling yet under-appreciated aspect of how the Catalan capital has changed through external and internal pressures such as densification, immigration and the consequences of mass tourism.

Phase 1: A city squeezed

Geography, forts and a wall

The city of Barcelona lies on a seaside plain contained by the Collserola massif and its emblematic Tibidabo peak on the west, the Besòs river to the north and, to the south, the Llobregat river and the imposing Montjuïc

[1] Smith, 2005, pp. 398–423.

mountain, which looms over the old city. This geography would come to figure prominently not only in the way that Barcelona would develop but also in how it would experience the various forms of siege that were to await it. The city has its roots in the Roman colony of Barcino, which was established in the first century BC, and this natural setting was advantageous for future development. Fortified in the third century, the city suffered subsequent conquests by Visigoths in the fifth century, Moors in 711 and then a reconquest by the Franks under Louis the Pious in 801. This last event saw Barcelona converted into a literal buffer zone or Hispanic Marchland between the Franks and the Umayyad Moors of Al-Andalus.

The urban nucleus of the city was consolidated during the Middle Ages, and it was Jaume I who moved to reinforce the existing walls, a process that took more than a hundred years to finish. With the establishment in the twelfth century of a Catalonia with similar borders to those of today, Barcelona began to flourish, reaching its apex as the capital of the western Mediterranean under the Crown of Aragon, which controlled areas such as Sardinia, Corsica, Naples and the Roussillon.

Catalonia's – and hence Barcelona's – early modern moment of 'what if?' occurred with the defeat of their forces at the end of the War of Spanish Succession in 1714, the geopolitical repercussions of which would persist into the twenty-first century. Catalonia's capital, a Mediterranean port and former centre of an important mercantile empire, would be metaphorically cut off from the openness of the sea as well as literally restricted in terms of growth and development. Rather than projecting outwards and creating its own destiny as a capital, Barcelona would be cast into second-city status by a hostile proto-state and would see the force of a centralist Spain thwart its ambitions while actively seeking to snuff out Catalan cultural difference in public discourse.[2] Thus began a period of cultural and literal siege that included various crackdowns on teaching, business and other dealings in Catalan, the banning of cultural production in the vernacular and other limitations on Catalan culture in the public sphere that stretched out until almost the end of the twentieth century.

When the Spanish military established its presence in Barcelona following the events of 1714, it used the city's own geography against it. Cannons were placed on the stronghold of Montjuïc mountain and trained not towards the sea to fend off external foes, but rather down on the city to keep the citizenry

---

[2] The effects of centralist repression are evinced in virtually every chapter in this collection. Ainaud de Lasarte's *El Llibre Negre de Catalunya*, 1996, provides a comprehensive compilation of these attacks on Catalan culture from 1714 onwards.

in line. To the north, a massive army barracks and military citadel – the *Ciutadella* – was constructed. Its location at the edge of the old city facilitated the quick response of infantry and cavalry in the event of any more local revolts against Madrid's authority. These two bases of operations – above, the always visible Montjuïc and its army-held castle; below, the bulky and ominous *Ciutadella* – anchored the first sense of siege in the modern consciousness of Barcelona.

It would be hard to underestimate the psychological impact of such twin threats on the population; even more so given the fact that on two dark junctures, first in 1842 and then again a year later, the threat of lethal force passed from potential to actual as the regents of Barcelona decided to teach their rebellious city a lesson. The second occasion was especially fierce and punishing as a barrage was ordered that saw more than 4,800 projectiles fired on the city during a military siege that lasted 81 days.

One of the prime reasons for the revolt of 1843 was the level of poverty and suffering in the city caused by sheer overcrowding. That Barcelona's old walls still stood in the middle of the nineteenth century was a primary reason for this dangerous congestion. From ancient times to the point when modern munitions rendered them obsolete, walls were cities' primary fortifications. Intended to help a populace repel invaders and control entry and egress, in the case of modern Barcelona the massive barriers came to function in precisely the opposite manner. The city did not control how they were managed and had no say in when they might be demolished so as to allow the burgeoning urban centre to expand.

That authority was held by Madrid, and because it did not serve the central government's political purposes to permit the Catalan capital to develop, the walls kept their latent military charge: that of containing Barcelona, pinning it to old dimensions even as industrial growth occurred and population density increased to hazardous and unsustainable levels. In this way, the walls became their own form of siege engine, a cordon around the populace to regulate and restrict it while maintaining the strategic capacity of the *Ciutadella* and Montjuïc to impose military authority and punishment should the need arise.

Rebirth and the designed city

Barcelona's modern rebirth was sparked by Madrid's eventual capitulation on the issue of the city's walls. The old barricade started to come down in the early 1850s and once it was demolished, the city could finally expand. Even though a radial project was preferred by the Catalans, Madrid imposed the now-famous grid system devised by Idelfons Cerdà. Cerdà's plan was to literally urbanize the rural and ruralize the urban by creating a series of octagonal blocks, with half of each being dedicated to green space. In this way, Barcelona would encroach on the meadows separating it from its closest neighbours but would still maintain an important trace of rural character by incorporating land into the city's modern expansion zone or *Eixample*.

This utopian vision along the lines of Howard's Garden City was not to be. Cerdà had not counted on the relentless power of the nascent bourgeoisie's desire to maximize space – and thereby increase profit – during the decades that would then lead to Catalonia's famous Gold Fever. Thus, rather than maintain the green spaces, the grid filled in and buildings and flats were constructed to a height of five or six floors. Given that the original idea was to have parks at every corner, with the elimination of this facet, the new district would over time find itself bereft of any substantial urban green space. What is more, the construction of buildings on all sides of the grid's octagons and the abundant spaces that Cerdà presaged for traffic usage would come to have a large impact on sound pollution in the city in the twentieth century.

Part and parcel of the architectonic dynamics at work was the fact that the *nouveaux riches* had economic power but lacked the history and tradition that gave Barcelona's old aristocrats their social and cultural pedigree. The businessmen compensated for this by relying on spectacle and design, contracting the city's architects to create buildings of increasing grandeur and style. Of course, these barons also competed among themselves through this conspicuous consumption of architecture as they jockeyed for individual standing while, at the same time, seeking as a group to consolidate the sea-change that had occurred in social terms relating to the concentration of political and economic power in Barcelona. Of course, this interest in city-building and civics was never totally philanthropic; it was also a sound investment in bricks and mortar that would appreciate even more quickly given the artistic supplement attached.

As the city's manufacturing and industrial capacity grew, new money came to trump old; the metaphorical centre of Barcelona shifted from the labyrinthine Gothic City, bastion of the old aristocratic families, to the *Eixample*'s young turks. The main artery of this new sector, the *Passeig de Gràcia*, became the grand boulevard of a city that was living a period of intense growth and change, when mercantile expansion and speculation were rife and the city was awash in new money, construction projects and the allure of getting rich quick.

Appearances are key to social status and reputation and, as such, surface appeal emerges as an important aspect of bourgeois aesthetics. This consideration is especially marked in the case of Catalan *Modernisme*, the artistic movement that coincided – and flourished – along with the rise of the new upper class in Barcelona. The issue is addressed more fully in Dominic Keown's chapter on Contemporary Catalan Culture, but the architectural phase of the experience was spearheaded by such luminaries as Domènech i Muntaner, Puig i Cadalfach and Antoni Gaudí, whose reputation would become world-renowned and whose work has come to epitomize the *modernista* architectonic strain.

The buildings are elaborate, detailed and, in many cases, spectacular. Works such as Gaudí's *Casa Milà* and *Casa Batlló*, which incorporated new building techniques while also speaking to the local vernacular architecture and Catalan natural environment, have since become globally renowned. Likewise, Domènech i Muntaner's *Simon Editorial* (now the Tàpies Foundation) and Puig i Cadafalch's *Casa Amatller* and *Edifici Terrades* (*Casa de les Punxes*) contributed to the concentration of impressive *modernista* buildings in the area. So while, on one hand, the new rational, grid-based *Eixample*, which represented Barcelona's liberty from the confinement of the old city's walls, grew according to practical concerns regarding the maximization of space and profit, an aesthetic mandate governed by *look* was also key to its development. This is the part of the *Eixample*'s foundation that would become an important basis for future tourist interest.

Catalan architectural *modernisme* occurred around the same time as other European styles of a similar mien, such as Arts and Crafts and Art Nouveau, and while it integrated vernacular models and influences the overall result was to draw Barcelona closer to the European centre that it had long admired and wanted to join. Integration into European circuits – even though state power still resided in Madrid – was also of interest to those who had contracted the building of the *Eixample*. Catalonia and its capital were looking towards Paris, backs turned on the Spanish capital, which was in full decline after undertaking disastrous military campaigns to suppress revolts in its colonial holdings in the Americas and North Africa.

One of the results of this political and cultural orientation was the decision to hold an International Exposition in 1888, some thirty years after Paris and London had set the vogue in motion and which has persisted into the twenty-first century. In terms of the siege mentality of Barcelona, the Universal Exposition was especially important because it marked the city's reclamation of the hated *Ciutadella*. The military fortifications were demolished over the course of the 1870s, and the land on which they had stood was earmarked first for a much-needed park and subsequently, for the world's fair, an event that would serve as the coming-out party not only for the bourgeoisie who sought to consolidate their power and influence but for the modern metropolis itself.

Even though the 1888 Expo failed to make a profit and sparked a firestorm of recriminations, it was an important event for the dominant class that had organized it. The international exposure it provided was a validation of the social advances made during the Renaixença, Catalonia's linguistic and cultural reawakening. For while Castile was engaged in profound soul-searching as its moribund empire disintegrated further, Catalonia found itself on the upswing both culturally and economically.

The Expo empowered the local bourgeoisie to continue to think big, served as a precursor to the *modernista* period proper and, importantly, saw the first large-scale influx of tourists to Barcelona. From an architectural perspective, the fair contributed fine new buildings to the city's stock, but the most important edifice may well be one that was demolished at the end of the event. Domènech i Muntaner's impressive – yet temporary – 1,600-room Hotel International was built in order to address the serious shortage of tourist beds in the city, and its construction took place in an astonishing 63 days, using prefabricated modular bricks set up around a massive iron frame. A hotel of such a category placed Barcelona within an international network, closer to the European centrality that it coveted. Thus, while the fair's most important legacy was arguably the city's recuperation of an urban zone that had been a centre of oppression, its subsequent transformation into a cosmopolitan space would whet the urban appetite for more engagement beyond Spain's borders.[3]

The fact that it was through a first foray into mass tourism that this revitalization marked the symbolic removal of another part of Barcelona's past as a besieged city cannot be ignored; for in eliminating the civic memory of one oppressive element, the city was unknowingly taking its first steps into a world that would see it transformed and besieged even further more than a century later.

Phase 2: From social war to dictators

A new siege: the social war

To speak only of the Catalan bourgeoisie's role in the articulation of modern Barcelona and Catalonia is to tell only part of the story. As is described in the chapter by Segura i Mas and Barbé i Pou, an intensely militant syndicalism also helped forge the modern city and the way that the citizens would relate to it. Rigged electoral processes of the Restoration period excluded huge parts of the population from the decision-making formula. This political

---

[3] For more on the cosmopolitan aspect of the fair and the temporary Hotel International in particular, see Davidson, 2005, pp. 228–43.

disenfranchisement – especially in the case of the new Catalan proletariat – led inevitably to the excesses of extra-parliamentary activity. The counterweight to non-representative government and bourgeois economic might adopted by the immensely powerful anarchist trade union, the CNT, was 'direct action'.

This taking of matters into one's own hands often took the form of bombings and the targeted assassinations of business leaders. This social war between factory owners and workers was fought mainly over working and living conditions. It was contested in the streets and claimed many lives while terrorizing the citizenry. It is perhaps epitomized by the spectacular outrage at the Liceu opera house in 1892 where, with the building full to capacity, the anarchist Santiago Salvador threw two bombs down from the gods into the expensive, bourgeois seating. Twenty-two people died in the resulting explosion. A ruthless police round-up of presumed anarchists was ordered and 400 were detained. Salvador and six others were among them and were executed for their roles in the outrage.

The spiral of violence continued into the next century with the Tragic Week of 1909 when angry mobs rioted in response to the call-up of reservists to fight in North Africa. A state of war was declared in the city after numerous churches and convents were sacked and razed, and the military ruthlessly quelled the disturbances after seven days of conflict. The event left an indelible mark on a city that continued to experience social violence, with its ferocity increasing as both sides of the ideological divide became bolder. Faced with workers' militancy, industrialists created their own *Sindicats Lliures* (Free Unions), essentially the cover for death squads, to find and eliminate trade union leaders and others sympathetic to the anarchist cause. Between 1919 and 1923, the death toll caused by this conflict stood at 246, of which around 200 were workers or union leaders, marking another phase in the escalation of a battle between two diametrically opposed classes bent on 'defending' their own visions of Barcelona's future.

The dictatorship of Miguel Primo de Rivera

By 1923, uncontrolled warfare on the streets of Catalonia, the sham political system of the Restoration, the post-war recession and military disasters in Africa created a crisis the government was unable to resolve. The 'solution' was provided by the military coup of General Primo de Rivera.While the Catalan elites appreciated the stability that military rule brought they would quickly come to realize that the General had no interest in safeguarding the cultural gains that Catalonia had made in the previous decades. Instead, Primo de Rivera followed in the footsteps of those who had come before him and clamped down on the Catalan fact. Under his seven-year dictatorship the

Catalan capital was once more an occupied city and saw such varied acts of cultural repression as a comprehensive system of press censorship, restrictions on the sardana and even the closing down for six months of FC Barcelona after supporters had dared to boo the Spanish anthem.

The Roaring Twenties came to end in spectacular style, however, as Barcelona played host once more to an International Exhibition. The 1929 edition, initially stated to have been a showcase for Catalan culture, was reorientated under the centralist dictatorship to be a platform for Spanish cultural identity. The manner in which this was accomplished left little doubt that minority cultures such as Catalan and Basque were but folkloric parts of a greater Spanish whole. From the exposition of *Spanish* art in the gaudy and neo-Baroque *Palacio Nacional*, to the architectural inscription of Spain as a diverse yet ultimately single unit in the eerie *Pueblo Español* (Spanish Village – an amalgam of reproduction buildings from all over the state that can still be visited today as a tourist attraction), the 1929 Fair sought to bring a modernizing, europhile Barcelona back within the symbolic sovereignty of Spain. And if the metaphors of unity were not clear enough, then the presence of Spanish warships in the harbour on the Expo's inaugural day served to underline the point.

While the co-option of the fair meant that it played as a specifically *Spanish* spectacle for the international audience, the fall of Primo de Rivera and the monarchy in early 1930 gave the city some breathing space after this cultural siege. An important symbolic move occurred in the wake of the dictatorship: the ceding to the city of the despised castle on Montjuïc. A story in the Catalanist journal *Mirador* attests to both the ideological importance of such a move and the peculiar social situation in which Barcelona found itself at the time: 'The handing over of Montjuïc Castle to the city represents the beginning of a new era of individual and social liberty for Barcelona. And it is natural that this process will not be realized until freedom is guaranteed.'[4] Unfortunately, for Barcelona and Catalonia at large, this new era of personal and social liberty would be still-born during the tensions of a short-lived Republic that segued directly into the Spanish Civil War and subsequently, the Francoist dictatorship.

The Spanish Civil War and the Francoist dictatorship

With the proclamation of the Second Spanish Republic in 1931, the city was once again ostensibly free. Rising political tensions in the run-up to the Spanish Civil War, however, meant that it was hardly a tranquil place; street

---

[4] *Mirador*, 1930, p. 1.

fighting and political polarization were endemic again as official endorsement for autonomy was granted, withdrawn and reconceded virtually every two years. Street fighting broke out once again during the war itself, especially in its initial phase when, after suppressing the military coup, internecine battles on the Republican side led to Barcelona being carved up by competing groups. George Orwell's *Homage to Catalonia* paints an especially clear picture of the way in which the city became a collection of separate fiefs identifiable only to the informed local:

> What the devil was happening, who was fighting whom, and who was winning, was at first very difficult to discover. The people of Barcelona are so used to street-fighting and so familiar with the local geography that they knew by a kind of instinct which political party will hold which streets and which buildings. A foreigner is at a hopeless disadvantage. Looking out from the observatory, I could grasp that the Ramblas, which is one of the principal streets of the town, formed a dividing line. To the right of the Ramblas the working-class quarters were solidly Anarchist; to the left a confused fight was going on among the tortuous by-streets, but on that side the PSUC. and the Civil Guards were more or less in control. Up at our end of the Ramblas, round the Plaza de Cataluña, the position was so complicated that it would have been quite unintelligible if every building had not flown a party flag.[5]

The Civil War dragged on and Barcelona was subject to aerial bombardments by Nationalist forces in the spring of 1938. Then, when a Republican defeat became more and more inevitable, refugees streamed towards the French border. On 26 January 1939 the city was captured by the advancing Francoist army. It would be occupied for over 36 years.

Under Franco's dictatorship – and we refer again to our chapter on Modern History – Barcelona was a militarily besieged city once more. Reprisals in the form of torture and executions were carried out against suspected Republicans and Communists. The *Modelo* prison filled up and the stronghold of Montjuïc once again became a place of death while summary executions were carried out on the outskirts of the city. Catalan culture in general was also targeted, tainted as it was with the 'separatist' brush that had so enraged Spanish nationalists. The Catalan language was prohibited and any remaining signs of Republican rule were eliminated. Strictly confined to the private realm, the Catalan fact was erased in public and the semiotics of the city were altered, most apparent in the renaming of streets so as to reflect the imposed centrist ideology.

5   Orwell, 1975, p. 126.

By the 1950s, post-war Barcelona still showed signs of the Civil War conflict as many bombed buildings had still not been fully reconstructed. Amid the post-war economic disaster the tensions of living in an occupied city that functioned poorly in conditions of rationing and electricity restrictions provided only sporadic acts of resistance. The campaign to erase Catalan difference also entailed massive immigration and Barcelona received thousands of Castilian-speaking migrants from rural areas throughout the Peninsula. The Francoist government's intention was to homologize Catalonia within Spain. And while the immediate effect was to exacerbate the acute housing shortage in the city as huge shanty towns appeared on the outskirts, this influx would have an important impact on the social make-up of the metropolis and on linguistic politics for decades to come.

Phase 3: The postmodern siege

From the Transition to the Olympics

With the death of Franco and the transition to democracy in the late 1970s, Catalonia entered a new phase. Now relieved of the weight of overt right-wing derision, Barcelona started a rapid and steady process of change and revitalization headed by architect and critic Oriol Bohigas. Even though, as Joan Ramon Resina points out, 'Bohigas favored monumentalization of open spaces through architectural design of a markedly avant-garde character [and with] his blessing, his disciples inflicted the unpopular *places dures* on a city that was starved for green space,' there is no denying the radical nature of the changes that the city was about to experience.[6]

This type of comprehensive and interventionist urbanism was not new. Urban design as policy had begun as early as 1953 with the Francoist administration's official plan for the city and continued through this scheme's revision in 1964, and the *Plan General Metropolitano* developed and approved in principle in the 1970s under Enric Massó, the last mayor to be named by the *Generalísimo*. But now multiple projects, expansions and developments occurred around the city, with all the excitement that could be expected by a new era of domestic executive planning.

It was around this time that International Olympics Committee chief Juan Antonio Samaranch announced that Barcelona had been awarded the 1992 Olympic Games, a decision that meant the Catalan capital was to enter a new phase of its history. Barcelona would now gear itself up not only for the

---

6   Resina, 2009, p. 209.

world's premier sporting event but for its largest celebration of mass spectacle and image production. The idea of city-as-image would propel Barcelona into the global imaginary, but it would do so at a great cost. If the technocratic development principles of the city planners had initiated the estrangement between citizen and city, it was this element of spectacle that would ultimately contribute to a new sense of siege as the legacy of Barcelona's modernist past combined with new endeavours to maximize the city's potential as an image of cosmopolitan urbanity and progress.

The success and panache of the 1992 Games, with their groundbreaking opening ceremony, the drama-cum-acrobatics of the *Comediants* and *Fura dels Baus* and the compelling venues, played off Barcelona's intrinsic architectural beauty and style while underlining the tremendous transformative potential (from a capitalist perspective) of such a global media event. Indeed, in addition to the spectacular choreographed theatricality of the opening ceremony one of the most suggestive – and repeated – images, as Smith observes, was that of Olympic divers in full flight while framed against the city's skyline at the Picornell complex.[7]

The ostensible subject may have been the athletes soaring freely above the metropolis; but the placement of the pool and the diving towers when combined with the ingenious camera angles ensured that more often than not Barcelona's most recognizable building and epitome of its look, the *Sagrada Familia*, would figure in the background. The fact that Gaudí's masterpiece was (and still is) unfinished and flanked by massive cranes served as an ironic reminder of the continuous construction project that Barcelona had become – both literally and in terms of how its image would continue to be built as its renown grew in the post-Olympic years.

Barcelona's Olympic transformation was so acute and so visible that ever since urbanists, architects and politicians from around the world have sought to duplicate it. While the specifically Mediterranean context of the city is often suppressed in the transfer and application of this model, it has become, nevertheless, both a powerful template for innovative change at home and a vehicle for Catalan architects and urbanists to succeed abroad. This interchange – consolidation and planning at the local level, projection and distribution of form and technique overseas – has been celebrated worldwide.

A charitable interpretation would be to read this dynamic as a natural, yet postmodern, evolution of Barcelona's status as a port and a city to and from which people, ideas and goods have long flowed – even if that exchange has

---

[7] Smith, 2005, p. 411.

often been restricted. However, the notion that the Barcelona Model has mostly served planners, political elites and property developers is one that has begun to gain greater traction. That said, in the wake of such an ostensibly successful Games and Spain's full entrance into the EU – which Catalan nationalists initially saw as a way to further escape Madrid's influence – it seemed that the siege experiences of the past were finally over.

Olympic consequences

There is no doubting that 1992 was a watershed year as Barcelona finally achieved the international prominence that it had sought when it hosted the World's Fairs of 1888 and 1929. With the Olympics Games focusing the world's attention on the city, the Catalan capital tried to make the most of its global media close-up by portraying itself as a vibrant, economic and cultural hub. Nevertheless, while Catalan was one of the official languages of the Games, the Spanish state was determined to incorporate the event into the larger 1992 celebrations going on in the country and prevent it becoming a rallying point for Catalan national sentiment.

These tactics recalled the treatment of Barcelona during the 1929 Fair. And the further emptying of the city of its political charge as a capital of a stateless nation abetted its growth as an international image while, at the same time, contributing to the alienation experienced by its citizens. The timing for the presentation of a depoliticized urban image of city-as-spectacle was propitious in that Barcelona's ascension coincided with a general shift in style and tourism trends. The 1990s saw a rise of superficial 'specificity' as travellers looked beyond traditional packaged trips and more at tailored travel experiences that would become increasingly mainstream by the 2000s.

A concurrent general gentrification and democratization of architecture and design spearheaded by star architects such as Frank Gehry, Enric Miralles and I. M. Pei also contributed to the attractiveness of Barcelona. New monumental and trophy architecture in cities around the world helped make Gaudí's early twentieth-century work even more known and immediately recognizable. Buildings such as the *Casa Batlló*, the *Pedrera* and especially the *Sagrada Familia*, helped confer 'must see' status not only on Gaudí's *modernista* oeuvre but also, through the metonymy that the built environment can engender, on the entire city itself. These dynamics contributed to the growing stream of international tourists 'doing' Barcelona by consuming the city's surface appeal – its distinctive *modernista* look – often with only the briefest of historical or cultural contexts provided by their *Lonely Planet* or *Let's Go* travel guide. With the must-sees checked off during the day, nights would be free to enjoy the city's increasingly vibrant entertainment culture.

The image production that arises from the Barcelona Model is, on the one hand, a product of technocratic desire – development, speculation, transformation, etc. – and, on the other, predicated on the promise of experience. This potential for sensation is where the look, feel and taste of the city come into play. Unfortunately for those residents of Barcelona who aspire to a normal urban existence, this focus on sensation as both a side-effect and progression of the Barcelona brand image has had deleterious effects as regards quality of life in the city.

In response to the changes that Barcelona's international success has wrought, many neighbourhood groups have sprung up in order to protest at both public and private initiatives. For these, the Barcelona model is flawed in that it privileges capital over community. Undeniably, Barcelona's ascendance to world city status has come at the expense of a further erosion of its own Catalan specificity but, that notwithstanding, the local areas, neighbourhoods and communities that make up the greater city of Barcelona have all been caught up in consequences of the city's wider move towards spectacle and image production whether they like it or not. It is here that this latest phase of the city's experience of siege comes to the fore. For while mass tourism may pour millions of euros into municipal coffers, the effects on daily life have been far from negligible.

This siege may be unlike those previously suffered, but the attention given to large-scale developments that emphasize the city's international reputation and image have come at the expense of investments in making the city a viable place to live for its citizens. Electrical blackouts, water problems, as well as chronic delays in local train services and stunted airport growth all underline the growing disjuncture between Barcelona, the imagined city of style and design and Barcelona, the city where citizens live and work.[8]

The negative perception of top–down urbanism and its triumph of style over substance have been exacerbated by the rampant property speculation of the 1990s and early 2000s. This speculation has not only affected individuals: the irony of the economics is patent too in the changes in the nature of businesses that exist in what have become prime tourist areas of the city. High

---

[8] In July 2007, Barcelona suffered a prolonged blackout that affected more than 100,000 households, a major hospital and the metro network. Three days later, some 10,000 people and businesses were still without power. Infrastructure deficiencies also caused problems for commuters as works on high-speed train links wreaked havoc on local and regional travel. During the same period, the airport had to fight to increase intercontinental flights, allowing the city to assume the mantle of European hub and permit travellers to by-pass Madrid airport.

amounts of visitor traffic have contributed to a general loss of specificity as chain stores that can afford high rents gradually push out the small family and independent businesses that contributed to the character of the Gothic Quarter or the Ramblas.

Of course, these increasing flat rents and prices have had a serious impact on the local populace across the city in that people through the age spectrum found it impossible to afford to live in the city proper. Barcelona has become too expensive for the Barcelonese. Where walls and cannons once kept citizens in, economic forces now conspire to blockade many out. The replacement of the native with an army of foreign tourists is no doubt ironic but shows no sign of abating as trips to the Catalan capital – and their nature – have been transformed by the proliferation of cheap inter-European airlines.

The Barcelona experience

The cosmopolitan Barcelona brand is made out to be part museum and part beach, with bits of discothèque and restaurant thrown in for good measure. The physical alterations to the city's seafront have reacquainted the city with the sea and are the direct result of the rehabilitation projects of the 1980s and 1990s. As a result of the massive investment in remodelling the zone from the base of the Ramblas to the Olympic Port, the holiday beach experience has been brought literally to within steps of Barcelona proper. The knock-on effect has been to make the city even more attractive for a wide range of tourists and emigrants from Northern Europe.

As in other areas, however, this development has occurred much to the chagrin of locals. In this case, those in the proletarian Barceloneta neighbourhood have seen their waterfront radically redesigned for purposes incompatible with the needs of small-scale fishers and port workers who were once the area's primary residents. What is more, property speculation has gone hand in hand with beach development and has meant that, as elsewhere in the city, flats have been priced out of reach for many locals as property is bought up to service a growing tourist trade and expatriate community. Once again, residents are faced with a future in which their children will not be able to afford to live in the area where they grew up.

The economic question is a constant and, for tourists, the Catalan capital is still a relatively affordable city. This is especially so for the British who, up until the economic crisis of 2008–9, had seen their money go much further in Catalonia than in their own cities, particularly London. The combination of easy access through cheap flights and this basic affordability has given rise to masses of invasive weekenders – among them travelling 'stag' and 'hen' parties – who treat the city as a fun park for wild outings of binge drinking.

Neighbourhoods such as the Gothic Quarter and Gràcia, where homes, bars and restaurants are often found in very close proximity, have seen a reduction in quality of life as noise and general rowdiness encroach on formerly quiet residential areas. Frustrated by inaction at the City Hall, residents have formed a variety of groups to protest and lobby the local government for more stringent laws. Here is where one sees the intersection of the effects of Barcelona's look and the changes in Barcelona's sound.

The metropolis is increasingly loud, so much so that in 1998 *L'Associació Catalana Contra la Contaminació Acústica* was founded specifically to combat noise pollution. Residents have found themselves literally besieged by noise as night-life proliferates, discothèques multiply and flats are transformed into illegal guest apartments where tourists noisily stay during their brief sojourns. This acoustic contamination tied to the tourist trade is but one example of how life is becoming more unpleasant for the local citizenry. What is more, as Espalader astutely observes, one of the more insidious consequences of a city becoming such a tourist magnet is that citizens 'lose' parts of their metropolis to the hordes (such as the Ramblas, in the case of Barcelona) and come to see it as a stereotype.[9]

Conclusion

Barcelona is different. Capital of a stateless nation, Mediterranean port city, the place where anarchism triumphed, the site of the rebirth of the Olympic movement in an orgy of spectacle and urban potential ... Barcelona is all of these things at once. When one considers the metropolis as both an aesthetic entity/experience and as a built environment – as spatial practice and geographic place with a history of enduring siege situations – its singularity becomes even more apparent. Indeed, such is the power of the image of this lived and constructed Barcelona that one now speaks of the city's brand. This process, in which meaning is collapsed into an image or a feeling that can then be managed and manipulated, relies on patent difference in order to function effectively.

As regards the possibility of urban branding, Smith points out rightly that 'city re-imaging is the deliberate (re)presentation and (re)configuration of a city's image to accrue economic, cultural and political capital'.[10] In the case of Barcelona this practice or dynamic has taken place at various levels: as a result of innovative urbanism and, most pointedly, in municipal campaigns

---

[9] Espadaler, 2009, p. 5.
[10] Smith, 2009, p. 399.

geared towards increasing tourism and promoting the city as a stylish, sensual locale.

Image and marketing are no strangers to one another in the promotion of the Catalan capital, and a recent change in labelling practices by a Catalan company reflects this most fittingly.

MANGO

BARCELONA

DES DE 1984

MANGO apparel label with Barcelona brand added.

From the company's perspective, the addition of the city's name to its apparel logo taps into the stylish aura of the place as, say, with Burberry of London. Jordi Hereu, Barcelona's mayor, explains the advantage to the city:

> the signing of this agreement is another step towards linking the Barcelona brand with international references of renowned prestige and innovation. For Barcelona, fashion is an important aspect of its economy and culture, since our city is a reference in training and development for fashion. Through this initiative, the city is delighted to institutionalize the link between the Barcelona name and a Catalan company like MANGO, which is internationally renowned for its innovative character. It is further proof of the projection and guarantees offered by the city of Barcelona, undoubtedly a valued asset.[11]

This mutually beneficial relationship is predicated on the special character of Barcelona as a 'sure bet' of quality and distinction. But, that said, how does one adequately engage with the difference exhibited by a city such as the Catalan capital if the process of branding is itself a generic process – one that literally commodifies variation and reifies the supposedly intangible elements of urban life that make the city unique and 'authentic'? If branding – or re-imaging – has become part of the modern capitalist condition and touches everything from the smallest consumer item to how cities and even nations imagine and market themselves, what sets Barcelona apart? If the

---

[11] http://news.mango.com/?p=811&lang=ca. 15 May 2009. The following reference to the comments of the Mango chairman is at the same webpage.

easy and interchangeable symbols that come to be metonyms for cities looking to proclaim their difference do not indicate distinction, where then does it lie?

Barcelona's particular difference – and thus its inherent brand, so to speak – is powered by a motor that has not received the specific attention that it deserves: the fact that Barcelona's modernity – its social practices and strategies of development – and now its postmodern period as well, have been conditioned intimately by the experience of siege. If the Barcelona brand has become so potent today, it is because inherent in its aesthetic and spatial distinction are the tensions of centuries of struggle for cultural survival as the main urban element of the Catalan fact.

If Barcelona's hook to the world has become the intoxicating *potential* or *possibility* for transformation that it represents – which MANGO president Isak Andic points to directly when he states that the link between his company and the metropolis 'is a way of not forgetting where we started and of projecting the potential of the city across all continents' – it must be recognized that this root of the city-as-brand goes even deeper and touches the concomitant potential inherent in the thing *to not be*.[12] For it is in the experience of siege, both literal and metaphoric, that Barcelona's potential *to not be* has been made patent or enforced on so many occasions. The city's brand becomes, then, more than surface appeal: it is a question of bellicose resonance, of echoes of cannon shots and of deeper meaning for the 'consumer' who is open to its message. Barcelona is different, yes. It is popular, exciting, fun. Unfortunately, for many it is also increasingly becoming a zombie – a city with 'dead' parts that still move – animated by tourist dollars and multinational leases. It has become a burden for many residents and, as a result of the negative potentiality inherent in the city's history of oppression, has contributed to the latest manifestation of the siege rubric in which Barcelona, the seemingly indomitable capital of Catalonia, has finally been drained of its authenticity.

---

[12] Agamben explains the phenomenon in the following way: 'what is potential can both be and not be'. Agamben, 1998, p. 45.

Works Cited and Suggested Reading

Barcelona and its history

Ainaud de Lasarte, Josep M. (1996) *El Llibre Negre de Catalunya*. Barcelona: Edicions La Campana.

Anonymous (1930) 'La cessió a la cituat del Castell de Motnjuïc (sic)', *Mirador*, 73, p. 1.

——— (15 May 2009) 'L'Ajuntament de Barcelona i MANGO promocionen la marca Barcelona', http://news.mango.com/?p=811andlang=en

Brotons i Segura, Ròmul (2008) *La ciutat captiva: Barcelona 1714–1860*. Barcelona: Albertí.

Busquets, Joan (2005) *Barcelona: The Urban Evolution of a Compact City*. Rovereto: Nicolodi.

Coad, Emma D. (1995) 'Catalan *Modernista* Architecture: Using the Past to Build the Modern', in Graham, H. and Labanyi, J. (eds) *Spanish Cultural Studies: An Introduction: The Struggle for Modernity*. Oxford: Oxford University Press, pp. 58–62.

Davidson, Robert (2005) 'Observing the City, Mediating the Mountain: *Mirador* and the 1929 International Exposition of Barcelona', in Larson, S. and Woods, E. (eds), *Visualizing Spanish Modernity*. Oxford: Berg, pp. 228–243.

——— (2006) 'A Periphery With a View', *Romance Quarterly*, 53.3, pp. 169–183.

——— (2009) *Jazz Age Barcelona*. Toronto and Buffalo: University of Toronto Press.

Ealham, Chris (2005) *Class, Culture, and Conflict in Barcelona, 1898–1937*. London: Routledge.

——— (2010) *Anarchism and the City: Revolution and Counter-revolution in Barcelona, 1898–1937*. Edinburgh: AK Press.

Eaude, Michael (2006) *Barcelona: the City that Re-invented Itself*. Nottingham: Fiveleaves.

Epps, Brad (ed.) (2004) 'Barcelona and Modernity', *Catalan Review: International Journal of Catalan Culture*, 18, pp. 1–2.

Espadaler, Anton M. (2 June 2009) 'La ciudad y el tópico', *La Vanguardia*. 'Vivir', p. 5.

Graham, Helen and Sánchez, Antonio (1995) 'The Politics of 1992', in *Spanish Cultural Studies: An Introduction*. Oxford: Oxford University Press, pp. 406–418.

Hernández-Cros, J. Emili, Mora, Gabriel and Pouplana, Xavier (1973) *Arquitectura de Barcelona*. Barcelona: Colegio Oficial de Arquitectos de Cataluña y Baleares.

Hughes, Robert (1992) *Barcelona*. New York: Vintage.

Kaplan, Temma (1992) *Red City, Blue Period: Social Movements in Picasso's Barcelona*. Berkeley and Los Angeles: University of California Press.

Lawlor, Teresa (1999) 'Moncloa Pacts', in Eamonn Rodgers (ed.) *The Encyclopedia of Contemporary Spanish Culture*. London: Routledge, pp. 344–345.

Mackay, David (1985) *Modern Architecture in Barcelona*. Sheffield: Sheffield Academic Press, http://www.kent.ac.uk/acsop/op/monographs/issue03.pdf

Orwell, George (1975) [1938] *Homage to Catalonia*. Harmondsworth: Penguin.

Robinson, William, Falgas, Jordi and Bellon Lord, Carmen (2006) *Barcelona and Modernity: Picasso, Gaudí, Miró, Dalí*. New Haven, CT: Yale University Press.
Roig Rosich, Josep M. (1992) *La dictadura de Primo de Rivera a Catalunya: Un assaig de repressió cultural*. Barcelona: Publicacions de l'Abadia de Montserrat.
Serrahima, Claret and Guayabero, Òscar (2 June 2009) 'Adéu a la cultura mediterrània', *Avui*, p. 44, http://paper.avui.cat/cultura/detail.php?id=165776
Simon i Tarrés, Antoni (2006) *Historia de Catalunya. Vol. III: Catalunya Moderna*. Barcelona: L'esfera dels llibres.
Toibín, Colm (1994) *Homage to Barcelona*. New York and Toronto: Simon & Schuster.
Ullman, Joan (1968) *The Tragic Week: A Study of Anti-clericalism in Spain, 1875–1912*. Cambridge: Cambridge University Press.
Various authors (1985) *Homage to Barcelona: The City and its Art, 1888–1936*. London: Arts Council.
—— (2008) *Odio Barcelona*. Barcelona: Melusina
Vázquez Montalbán, Manuel (1990) *Barcelones*. Barcelona: Empúries.

Barcelona and Urban Studies

Agamben, Giorgio (1998) *Homo Sacer: Sovereign Power and Bare Life*. Stanford, CA: Stanford University Press.
Baulenas, Lluís-Anton (7 June 2009) 'Barcelonins orfes', *Avui*, p. 45, http://paper.avui.cat/article/ciutats/166309/barcelonins/orfes.html
Delgado, Manuel (2007) *La ciudad mentirosa: fraude y miseria del 'modelo Barcelona'*. Madrid: Libros de la Catarata.
Deliri, Maia (2004) 'Les Barcelones allotjades entre luxes i desallotjaments. Apunts sobre la precarització social i les noves formes de segregació', in *Barcelona Marca Registrada: Un model per desarmar*. Barcelona: Virus Editorial, pp. 69–82, www.sants.org/biblioteca/llibres/Barcelona,%20marca %20registrada.pdf
Epps, Brad (2001) 'Modern Spaces: Building Barcelona', in *Iberian Cities*, ed. Resina, J. R. London: Routledge, pp. 148–197.
Resina, Joan Ramon (2003) 'From Rose of Fire to City of Ivory', in *After-Images of the City* ed. Resina, J. R. and Ingenschay, D. Ithaca, NY: Cornell University Press, pp. 75–122.
—— (2008) *Barcelona's Vocation of Modernity: Rise and Decline of an Urban Image*. Stanford, CA: Stanford University Press.
Rowe, Peter G. (2006) *Building Barcelona: A Second Renaixença*. Barcelona: Barcelona Regional ACTAR.
Smith, Andrew (2005) 'Conceptualizing City Image Change: The "Re-Imaging" of Barcelona', *Tourism Geographies*, 7.4, pp. 398–423.
Various authors (2004) *Barcelona Marca Registrada: Un model per desarmar*. Barcelona: Virus Editorial, www.sants.org/biblioteca/llibres/Barcelona, %20marca%20 registrada.pdf

5

The Catalan Language

MIQUEL STRUBELL

Origins and comparison

Catalan is a neo-Latin, or Romance, language alongside a number of European 'national' languages (Portuguese, Spanish, French – the so-called western group – and Italian and Romanian – the eastern group) and several other languages that have an official status at sub-state level, or are spoken only in part of a state (Galician, Occitan, Sardinian, Ladin, Rheto-Romance, Friulian, etc.) Several of these languages became the languages of worldwide empires but within Europe itself, their borders coincide, broadly speaking, with the limits of the Roman Empire. This is especially clear in western Europe, the Romance–Germanic language divide being more or less close to the line running down the borders between French- and Dutch-speaking Belgium; between France and Germany, and between French- and German-speaking Switzerland.

Badia i Margarit (2004) reminds us that Catalan and the other Romance languages are a living heritage of the active romanization that lasted for centuries across the Empire (seven centuries, in the case of Catalan, in the north-eastern corner of Hispania, the cradle of what was to be become Catalonia). However, as Roger Wright (1999) underlines, it is impossible to point to a specific date when these languages emerged as clearly separate from the Vulgar Latin spoken throughout the lands that had been part of the Roman Empire before its collapse in the fifth century. According to Moran and Rabella (2004), all the so-called Romance languages emerged in the seventh or eighth centuries, but were not used in documents until much later, as Latin continued to be the only written and taught language (with increasing traces of the new spoken languages over time).

Badia i Margarit considers the language spoken was fairly clearly differentiated by territory at the time of the Saracen invasions in the early eighth century, though nowhere were the requirements yet met to be able to regard them as minimally organized languages, supported by independent linguistic structures. These were to appear in the ninth and tenth centuries, at least in the case of Catalan, and the first attempts to write it can be traced to the eleventh century. Of special significance in this context in the promotion of the vernacular is the Third Council of Tours (813), just before the death of Charlemagne. The account given of this event in the *Encyclopaedia Britannnica* informs us that the council decreed that sermons should be delivered by bishops in the Western empire in *rusticam Romanam linguam aut Theodiscam* ('in the rustic Roman language or German') to make them intelligible to the congregation.[1]

There is, of course, no suggestion that at this early date homiliaries should be *written* in Romance or German. Nonetheless, as the centuries progressed there are signs of the vernacular's intrusion into the written mode, and there has been a fair amount of confusion as regards the oldest extant texts in Catalan. When in 1904 Joaquim Moret discovered the *Homilies d'Organyà* – an incomplete set of six Lent sermons, almost certainly translated from Occitan – he described them as the most ancient literary text published in Catalan; but some have misread his statement to be a claim that they were the oldest text of any kind. The earliest texts fully written in Catalan actually date back to the end of the eleventh century. At the start of the eleventh century more and more Catalan words and expressions appear in feudal documents written in Latin; while by the end of the same century whole documents are written in this language: the complaints, or *Greuges de Guitard Isarn, senyor de Caboet*, for example, were probably written sometime between 1080 and 1095.

The Romans had begun to turn their eyes towards the Iberian Peninsula in the late third century BC; and victory over Hannibal in 219 BC initiated the full process of romanization, except for some areas in the mountainous north (including the Pyrenees, where Basque continued to be spoken, even in the eastern part, well into the Carolingian period). Colonization proper began in Catalonia when Scipio landed at the Greek colony of Emporion (today known as Empúries) in 218 BC. The procedure, however, was a long-drawn-out affair, and the Romans did not achieve full control of the centre and west of the peninsula until crushing the dogged resistance of the Iberians in their war of resistance to the invader (154–133 BC). Indeed, the warring tribes in the north were not finally subjugated until 19 BC during the reign of Emperor Augustus. In this way, romanization occurred much sooner and more intensely in Catalonia than in the rest of the Peninsula.

---

[1] www.britannica.com/EBchecked/topic/600886/Council-of-Tours.

For years a long-standing debate among linguists focussed on whether Catalan is closer to Occitan and French, or to Spanish and Portuguese. According to Joan Roselló, romanisation in the northeast of the peninsula (the Tarraconensis province) was largely through the vulgar Latin brought in by veterans and colonists, whereas in the south and west (the Baetica and Lusitania provinces) it took place by means of an educated local bourgeoisie, whose Latin was closer to the classical standard, and more conservative. He follows Colon in holding, on lexical grounds, that Catalan should be grouped among the languages that developed north of the Pyrenees (Galloromance), not those to the south (Iberoromance).[2]

Moran (2004), for his part, bases his claim that Catalan developed in its current constitutive area, and was not brought in by Carolingian settlers from the north, on the large number of Catalan features of Latin texts from the second half of the ninth centuries and throughout the tenth and eleventh centuries, which are not shared by Occitan or French. He believes that the similarity between Catalan and Occitan is due to the vulgar Latin that each language derives from, and which suggests an unbroken Mediterranean relationship throughout the Visigothic period. A separate issue is the notion of the awareness of linguistic difference among spoken romance. Halla-aho has pointed out that

> in the 9th century, despite a great amount of variation, there was no correlation between the various features according to geographical areas, and (...) for a considerably long time, up to the 13th century, we cannot really speak of separate Romance languages in the minds of the people speaking them (with the probable exception of Rumanian). [Wright] sees the subsequent conceptual split into different languages as resulting from nationalistic ideologies and conscious language planning in the later Middle Ages.[3]

In conclusion, Romance languages gradually evolved as Latin ceased to be a unified vernacular language. Developments over time, including the influence of Arabic or Slavic languages, have led to what we today identify as the discrete Romance languages being more or less mutually comprehensible. But we should not imagine that each language has always been as it is today (linguistically or geographically), or that in the Middle Ages Romance speakers identified their precursors by specific names. The same, of course, happened to the Germanic and Slavic languages.

---

[2] Colon, 1976, p. 12.
[3] Halla-aho, 2007, pp. 140–2.

Brief history of the language

Territorial expansion (eleventh to fifteenth centuries)

The collapse of the Roman Empire in 476 was followed by the creation, in the west, of a number of kingdoms ruled by Germanic princes, the main one of which stretched from the Loire to the Tagus, and later occupied most of the Peninsula. However, the members of the ruling class were few in number and, as they were themselves Christians, their linguistic influence on the populace was extremely weak despite their hegemonic control, which lasted some two and a half centuries. The next event of major importance, however, was the invasion and occupation from 711 onwards of the whole of Iberia by Arabic-speaking Muslims, the Moors, who reached as far north as Poitiers, where they were defeated in 732 by the Franks under Charles Martel. Despite the indelible mark they left on the Peninsula, however, their social, political and linguistic impact lasted much longer in some places than in others.

Indeed, as was discussed in Alexander Ibarz's chapter on Medieval History, much of what is today Catalonia acted as a marchland, or a buffer zone, and the outpost of Carolingian Europe bordering on Muslim Spain as Charlemagne set up a number of vassal earldoms in the eastern Pyrenees. In 803, less than a century after the Moorish invasion, Barcelona was retaken by the Frankish King Louis I, with the city of Tarragona and Girona following suit some years later. Later in that century the signs of an emergent different culture are evinced by the establishment of a number of important monasteries in the north, such as Sant Pere de Rodes (878) and Santa Maria de Ripoll (879) and Sant Cugat del Vallès, close to Barcelona, during the same period. It would not be until a century later, however, following a raid by the Moors in 988 that the count of Barcelona severed the ties of feudal loyalty that bound him to his liege lord, the Frankish king, who had failed to help him to fight off the offensive. From then on, a territorial, social and political entity, centred on the ancestral house of Barcelona, grew steadily in strength.

For over two centuries the western limit of what was to become known as Catalonia (the origin of the name is unclear) bordering onto the Moorish kingdoms was fairly fixed thanks to more or less stable alliances between the leaders on both sides. The border lay along the ridge dividing the Llobregat river valley (to the east) and those of the rivers Cardoner and Segre (to the west). It is probably no coincidence that, to this day, the isoglosses between the north-western and central dialects of Catalan largely follow that same demarcation line between 'Old Catalonia' and 'New Catalonia', as may be evinced roughly from Map 5 of the linguistic territories if a line is drawn from the eastern tip of Andorra, towards the coast south of Tarragona and north of Tortosa, separating the Balearics from the rest of the mainland.

5. The Catalan-speaking areas.
By permission of The Anglo-Catalan Society

Perhaps the feature that most clearly distinguishes between the two groups is phonetic: atonic vowels are neutralized in western forms, that is, atonic a and e do not become [ə], nor does atonic o become [u]. Other features of western forms are the [w] in possessive pronouns (*meua, teua, seua*), compared to *meva, teva, seva* in central forms; and a limited number of lexical differences such as *granera* (w.) versus *escombra* (c.) (brush); *xiquet* versus *nen* (boy); *espill* versus *mirall* (mirror); *palometa/paloma* versus *papallona* (butterfly) and *corder* versus *xai* (lamb).

In 1137, the count of Barcelona became the king of Aragon through marriage. From then onwards, this Catalan–Aragonese confederation, also known as the Kingdom of Aragon, expanded to the south. His great-grandson, Jaume I, the Conqueror, was to add the Balearics and Valencia to the realm. In 1241, the same monarch inherited the Catalan-speaking county of the Rosselló, just north of the Pyrenees, as well as the island of Sardinia, which signified the start of the expansion of the Catalan–Aragonese confederation eastwards across the Mediterranean: Naples (from 1442 to 1516, when it was inherited by Emperor Charles V) and Sicily, Corsica (1297–1448, with periods of Genovese control) and even part of Greece (1319–90), were crown territories and the confederation had colonies ('consulates') in North Africa. However, given that the only significant remnants of this occupation, in linguistic terms, are to be found in the Sardinian town of l'Alguer (Alghero in Italian), we shall consider the other territories no further.

The linguistic frontier between Catalan (in the east) and Spanish (to the west) has remained remarkably stable over the centuries, except in the southernmost tip of Valencia. In some places this border does not coincide with administrative boundaries: for instance, Catalan is spoken in a strip of eastern Aragon, close to the area divide. In the region of Valencia, for the most part, the border between Catalan- and Spanish-speaking villages runs down within the region itself. This is explained by the geo-historical process of reconquest and repopulation. In their push southwards, the Catalans tended to settle along the coastal areas whereas the Aragonese occupied the interior, with their respective languages becoming predominant as the Moorish population was subjugated or expelled.

As for the southernmost tip, Casanova (2001) believes that the loss of political power of the kingdom of Aragon following the dynastic union with Castile led, from the sixteenth century onwards, to the increasing inability of local Valencians to impose their language on the continuous wave of Spanish-speaking newcomers from Murcia and Granada. These settlers had installed themselves in and around the extreme southern town of Oriola (Sp. Orihuela) to replace the expelled population of Muslim extraction (or to start up farms in land reclaimed from marshland). Through this resettlement, Catalan steadily declined in the area in question and has now been substituted in the Horta d'Oriola and Vinalopó Mitjà, which borders present-day Murcia.

In terms of the written language, a date of fundamental importance in the history of the language is 1276, the year in which Jaume I established a royal chancellery responsible for the issue of all administrative documents. From this moment onwards every piece of official business pertaining to the realm was to be written in Catalan instead of Latin. The decision is significant as throughout Catalonia, Valencia and the Balearics the drafting of every piece of legislative procedure – from the most important to the most rudimentary – became unified. This groundbreaking task was by no means straightforward. Some of the initial attempts, carried out by scribes skilled almost exclusively in producing documents in Latin, were infelicitous to say the least. This is true to such an extent that when in 1344 Pere III of Aragon ordered a Catalan translation to be made of his cousin, Jaume III of Majorca's *Leges Palatinae* (a compilation of ceremonial ordinances, written in 1337), the bureaucratic formulae of Latin were used as a template. As such, the *Ordinacions de la Casa Reial* is drafted in a style that is incomprehensible in the vernacular unless the original Latin text is consulted in tandem!

However, by the turn of the fifteenth century linguistic proficiency had become so established upon the foundation of this highly literate institutional bureaucracy as to boast a literature of international excellence. The chapter by Alexander Ibarz singles out the artistic quality of the most famous exponents over this period such as Llull, Desclot, Muntaner, Eiximenis, Metge, etc. The sophistication was so pervasive in this area, however, that commentators have even gone so far as to remark on the exquisite preparation and literary excellence of that most banal of exercises, the drafting of official documents. Martí de Riquer, for example, is quoted as commending the stylistic excellence employed to produce 'thousands of letters, drafted in a precise, elegant and very pure Catalan, which contributed, day in day out, to impose throughout the Catalan-speaking domains an exemplary and very beautiful prose'.[4]

During the whole of this period, most of the population was monolingual with only the political elite and the clergy knowing any Latin. But as mentioned earlier – and as is evidenced by our map of dialects – the interior of what is today the community of Valencia was colonized mainly by Spanish-speaking Aragonese, a linguistic presence that continues today in those areas. There is, however, no evidence to support claims from secessionist quarters in Valencia that when James the Conqueror took the region, which had been in Moorish hands for fully five hundred years, the local population still spoke a Romance language. Indeed, Roger Wright and Carmen Barceló Torres (1984), two of the most distinguished scholars working in the field, hold that following the Moorish invasion of the Iberian Peninsula in the early eighth century the pre-existing vulgar Latin, often called Mossarabic, died out no later than the mid-tenth century (though

---

4   Riquer *et al.*, 1964, p. 350.

Arabic-speaking Christians continued to live in some parts, such as the city of Valencia, thereafter). The notion, then, of an alternative Romance tongue being extant and a rival to Catalan in these parts in the thirteenth century is entirely specious.

Catalan under the Catholic Monarchs (sixteenth and seventeenth centuries)

A dynastic change in the house of Aragon took place in the early fifteenth century, when King Martin the Humane died in 1410 without heir. The Spanish-speaking candidate of the Castilian nobility, Alfonso de Trastámara, was offered the throne to the detriment of the Catalan pretender Jaume d'Urgell and this decision, which came to be known as the Compromise of Casp (1412), would eventually have fateful consequences for the language. Initially, the election had scant immediate impact on the linguistic situation, where Catalan continued to flourish in the arts. Indeed, the same century witnessed the golden age of literature in Valencia, with poets of such magnitude as Jordi de Sant Jordi, Ausiàs March and Roís de Corella. Similarly, leading works in prose of the period included two outstanding books of chivalry: the anonymous *Curial e Güelfa* and what many regard as the immediate precursor to the modern novel, *Tirant lo Blanc*, by Joanot Martorell.

The turning point in the fortunes of Catalan, however, is more readily associated with the wedding in 1469 between the heirs to the thrones of Aragon and Castile: Prince Ferran (later Ferran II) of Aragon (1452–1516) and Princess Isabel (later Isabel I) of Castile (1451–1504). They became king (in 1479) and queen (1474) of their respective realms, and the daughter of these so-called 'Catholic Monarchs', Juana la Loca, became the first ruler of the newly united kingdoms. However, despite claims of equality – and the fact these two units were to retain their full self-government until the War of Spanish Succession at the beginning of the eighteenth century – the truth is that the comparative demographic and economic weight favoured Castile, which, moreover, was soon to reap the benefits of the colonization of the New World from which Aragon was excluded. In the course of time this kingdom would exert its exclusive dominance over the entire peninsula, much to the detriment of Catalonia and its language.

Also at this time the name of the language started to become diversified. In itself this was not a central issue as the written language was sufficiently unified for it to be hard to define the geographical origin of the authors of many texts. The word 'Catalan' began to be seen mistakenly by some as referring only to Catalonia proper, and it is evident that such a fracturing could do no more than threaten the solidity and cohesion of the idiom. Such was the confusion that in the sixteenth century Valencians, among others, started referring to their language as 'llemosí', that is, Limousin, in a misguided attempt to find an overarching name for the language. The same kind of problem exists today in what we today call Occitan (also known as Provençal, Gascon, Languedocien) or Dutch (also known as Flemish): each area tends to prefer to give its own name to the way locals speak.

Evidently, the strength and presence of Catalan had been called into question immediately after the Compromise by the ascent of the Spanish-speaking Ferran I to the throne. Quite naturally, the new monarch brought other speakers of the same language into the Catalan court with him. But it was not until the end of the century that the court of Aragon withered out completely, when their successors fixed the capital of the united realm in Toledo, and then Madrid, four hundred miles from Barcelona. This had two serious consequences on the language front. Firstly, the unifying role of the Aragonese royal chancellery ceased (whose function in terms of literary quality and consistency was mentioned previously); and secondly, most of the Catalan nobles either moved to the new court in Castile or else intermarried with their Spanish-speaking counterparts.

As a result, this loss of autonomy and dynamism – the long period of stagnation between the sixteenth and the mid-nineteenth centuries – is often referred to as the time of the decadence of Catalan literature. At this time no leading literary figures shine, and the baton of creativity was transferred to the field of popular culture. The scenario, however, was not entirely bleak since the use of Catalan continued to remain supreme in the areas of legal and administrative production, at least until the debacle at the beginning of the eighteenth century with the disastrous outcome of the War of Spanish Succession. And above all, Catalan continued to be the only language most ordinary people could speak: the only people with any knowledge of Spanish in Catalonia proper were segments of the aristocracy and urban intellectual circles. Despite the gradual spread of Spanish in the larger towns, the situation was not to change substantially until compulsory primary education (exclusively in Spanish) was established by law in the second half of the nineteenth century.

The linguistic situation north of the Pyrenees, however, worsened dramatically as a result of the annexation of Rosselló and part of Cerdanya by France, as established by the Treaty of the Pyrenees in 1659. The deliberate policy to introduce French and replace Catalan began almost immediately: a decree of 1700 made the use of French compulsory in all municipal and public documents, decrees and court judgments. However, Catalan continued to be used by notaries public, for instance, until at least the mid-1740s, and nearly all the local population spoke Catalan, probably until the First World War, after which intergenerational transmission began to wane.

Consequences of the War of Spanish Succession

A dynastic conflict, the War of Spanish Succession pitted as opponents the crown of Aragon (Aragon, Catalonia, Valencia and the Balearic Islands), together with their English allies, and Castile with their support from the French. The former endorsed – and indeed crowned – the Habsburg candidate, Charles III, whereas the latter sided with the Bourbon pretender, Philip of Anjou. The Bourbon model was rejected by the Catalans as it sought to curb regional powers and impose a highly centralized rule in Spain. They were also assured that the Habsburgs offered an alternative that would be much more respectful of diversity and local autonomy. However, their chances of success were dealt a mortal blow when their candidate's brother unexpectedly died, leaving Charles to become (the last) Holy Roman Emperor. The unexpected development significantly altered the balance of power in Europe, leading to a political realignment.

The issue was resolved by the ensuing Treaty of Utrecht (1713), which led to the English withdrawing from Spain (except for the Catalan-speaking island of Menorca). By that time Philip and the French had the upper hand, having won the Battle of Almansa, thus taking control of Valencia, in 1707. The Catalan bastions, abandoned by the English despite considerable political unrest in Britain, fell one by one; and Barcelona was eventually taken on 11 September 1714, following a bloody final assault after a 14-month siege.

As a consequence of defeat, Valencia and Catalonia were subjected to 'decretos de Nueva Planta', that is, the political structure of Castile was extended to embrace them as well. Though these decrees, apart from being monolingual, make no reference to the language issue, the new regime did not waste time; and in 1716 the head (*Fiscal General*) of the Council of Castile sent secret instructions to his political appointees (*corregidores*) in the newly occupied Catalonia, which reveal the insidious intention of linguistic extirpation:

> Nature seems to have granted each Nation its specific language, and one has to be very artful to overcome this, considerable time being necessary, and especially so when the character of a Nation such as that of the Catalans is stubborn and haughty and cherishes the traits of its country, and for this reason it seems convenient to give very low-key and discreet instructions and counsel, so that the effect is achieved without the care being noticed.[5]

---

[5] Information provided by Gironés, 1986, p. 22.

Philip V's determination to homogenize the state was swift and relentless. He closed down Catalonia's universities and opened another deep in the countryside, in the 'loyal' city of Cervera. Many popular publications in Catalan were banned, as were plays, while Spanish was imposed as the only official language. Many of these proscriptions, however, proved to be impracticable at the time; and some of the measures could not be enforced until much later with the introduction of a more powerful centralized system of government, inspired by the Napoleonic model. Nonetheless, the accession of the Bourbon monarch to the throne constitutes a watershed. Apart from brief periods, the language that had served the Catalans for over nine centuries became subjected to continuous official repression.

A further example was to be the decision of King Carlos III in the *Real Cédula* of 23 June 1768. This monarch who, at the end of the eighteenth century, finally opened the American market to the Catalans, hereby imposed Spanish at all levels of the administration of justice and, moreover, banned teaching in Catalan in both public and church schools. Despite the corresponding generalized expansion of Spanish in officialdom, resistance to these measures is still evident. Many private documents (such as wills) were drafted in Catalan; and the Church continued to register births, baptisms, weddings and deaths in Catalan well into the nineteenth century, at least in Catalonia proper. As the *Fiscal General* had intimated, however, the oppression was relentless, as may be revealed by a couple of outlandish edicts. At the end of that century, for example, the government went so far as to decree that even catechism classes (and a short time later, telephone conversations!) had to be conducted in Spanish. There can be few illustrations more eloquent of the obsessive, sinister nature of this linguistic persecution.

Nevertheless, even in the darkest years, Catalan carried on being the spontaneous oral language of the people. As we shall soon see, this was not to start to change until the political, economic, demographic and technological convulsions of the twentieth century, the century in which the first fully bilingual generation was born. The detrimental effect on Catalan of the imposition of Spanish as the only official language, however, cannot be understated. As was seen in our comments on the royal chancellery, over a period of time the presence of a language in all spheres of officialdom has a powerful unifying effect, and not only on the written language. What is more, the impact of this homogenization increases in relation to the hegemonic power of institutions and authorities, and augments further in a literate society. In this way, the threat to the subordinate idiom is doubled. In this context it is not just the menace implied by the imposition of a foreign tongue that weakens the vernacular; its exclusion from these 'high' functions (the term sociolinguists tend to use) also leads inexorably to geographic and lexical differentiation and fragmentation. These are all elements that contributed to the chaotic state of Catalan as we enter the nineteenth century.

Recovery: the Renaixença

As Miquel Siguan has pointed out, in the nineteenth century,

> Coinciding with the awakening of minority cultures in Europe, a literary renaissance took place in Catalonia accompanied by the development of community awareness which, spurred on by the new middle classes that had emerged from the process of industrialization, turned into a nationalist political movement seeking self-rule.[6]

Though it is impossible to point to a single event triggering the start of what has since come to be known as the *Renaixença* (or Rebirth), it is customary for this moment to be attributed to a poem, 'Oda a la Pàtria', a lament for a sorely missed Catalonia written in Madrid by a Catalan, Bonaventura Carles Aribau, and given to his employer as a birthday present. When it was published, in 1833, it did indeed touch a popular chord. For the first time in living memory Catalan had been used as a vehicle of literature: a 'high' function from which it had long been excluded.

But, as is discussed in Dominic Keown's chapter on Contemporary Culture, in real terms the recovery in 1859 of the medieval poetry contest, the *Jocs Florals*, probably did more to stimulate young poets to develop their literary prowess and to launch them to popularity. Among them a young priest, Jacint Verdaguer, soon began to shine: his epic and his religious verse led to his being widely regarded as the national poet: and when he died, in 1911, the funeral procession in Barcelona was probably the largest on record. This clearly indicates not only the capacity of the language question still to move people but also the overwhelming popular response to the phenomenon.

As written Catalan started to be used more and more – not just in poetry and prose but also in periodicals, with the daily *La Veu de Catalunya* appearing in 1900 – it became increasingly clear that there was a need for a unification of the spelling system and grammar in general which, over the centuries of decadence, had descended into chaos owing to lack of use and regulation. Three competing options were put forward: *el català acadèmic de tradició moderna*, that is, Catalan based on the literary tradition of immediately preceding centuries (seventeenth and eighteenth); *el català acadèmic de tradició antiga*, which adopted the highly unified medieval orthography of

---

[6] Siguan, 1984, p. 107.

the thirteenth and fourteenth centuries; and a third option, not based on forms that often strayed far from the spoken language: *el català que ara's parla*. This latter was, of course, not an attempt to unify the written language since each region was encouraged to develop its own orthography based on local custom.

By the end of the nineteenth century there was a desperate need for an authoritative voice to bring this process to a conclusion. It came, in the event, from a group of young intellectuals whose proposals were published in their magazine, *L'Avenç*. In the space of under ten years the whole panorama was transformed. In 1901 a Majorcan priest, Antoni-Maria Alcover (1862–1932), made a call, the *Lletra de Convit*, for contributions for what was to become the monumental ten-volume Dictionary of the Catalan language, completed decades later by a Minorcan, Francesc de B. Moll. In 1906, at Alcover's instigation, 3,000 people (including many renowned Romance linguists) gathered for the *I Congrés Internacional de la Llengua Catalana*.

In the same year, a unitary political movement, *Solidaritat Catalana*, led by Enric Prat de la Riba (1870–1917), was founded. After winning the 1907 elections Prat became president of the county council, or Diputació de Barcelona, on a modernizing, Catalanist ticket in which the recovery of the language for official use was a priority. In the following year, Prat established the *Institut d'Estudis Catalans*, and shortly afterwards, the *Secció Filològica* was set up to propose to the authorities the grammatical and spelling rules that were needed for the expansion of the use of Catalan. It soon became apparent that Pompeu Fabra (1868–1948), a chemical engineer working at that time in Bilbao and a member of the *L'Avenç* group, was the right person to steer Catalan into the twentieth century: he was offered a post at the Institut, and from there produced a set of publications that have guided the language ever since: the *Normes Ortogràfiques* (1913), the *Diccionari Ortogràfic* (1917), the *Gramàtica Catalana* (1918) and the *Diccionari General de la Llengua Catalana* (1932). The last year also marked the adoption of these rules, as the *Normes de Castelló*, by Valencian authors.

As the language flourished in the theatre, in the press, in publishing, and in official use, it was also (re)introduced into some schools before the turn of the twentieth century. A popular movement for the promotion of education in the language, the *Associació Protectora de l'Ensenyança Catalana*, was founded in 1898 and advanced partly because it introduced modern teaching methods and retrained teachers, under the successive influence of international figures such as Maria Montessori, C. Freinet and Decroly; the latter's methods were also followed in Majorca. The *Protectora* continued to expand rapidly after 1914.

The increasing political power of the Catalanist movement achieved new levels of home rule. Firstly, Prat managed to unite the four provincial councils under a single regional administration, the *Mancomunitat* (1914–23) which, despite having no more resources than the sum of the four councils' budgets, not only reunited Catalonia administratively but also set up modern training schools and colleges, hospitals, the national library and other institutions. The main point to be made, however, is that the newly standardized language was now once again being used and indeed, actively promoted in milieux – administration, education, culture and the media – from which it had been previously excluded.

Dictatorial repression

The *Mancomunitat* was abolished following a coup d'état by the Captain-General of Catalonia, General Primo de Rivera, whose regime (1923–30) repressed the public use of Catalan, and also struck against Catalanist organizations, even closing Barcelona football club for over a year. The autocratic interlude was to be brief, however, and when the dictatorship crumbled, bringing about the collapse of the monarchy in the 1931 local elections, nationalist parties won all the main cities in Catalonia. Within the framework of the Second Spanish Republic the *Generalitat de Catalunya* was re-established after an absence of more than two hundred years, with a Statute of Autonomy following shortly afterwards. Despite limited financial resources, Catalan culture flourished during the Republic in all fields; but the process was to be short-lived. In July 1936, the plotting of Spanish right-wing elements, with strong support from the army, bore fruit in the coup of General Francisco Franco, which resulted in three savage years of civil war.

Once victory was assured on 1 April 1939, the fascist and right-wing nationalists set about the destruction of every vestige of Catalan difference established during the home rule period. Just as after the defeat of 1714, the regional government and parliament were abolished, and supporters of the centralist regime were appointed to every single post of responsibility. Solé Tura and Aja (1997) describe how Franco did not create a 'new state' but rather 'took to their final authoritarian, bureaucratic, centralist and, in a word, antidemocratic consequences, the principles which have governed the setting-up of the apparatus and institutions which make up the current Spanish State'.[7] Widespread purges led to imprisonments and expulsions from jobs. All street signs in Catalan were removed and shop signs in Catalan had to be rapidly replaced if shopkeepers wished to avoid being fined;

---

7 Solé Tura & Aja, 1997, p. 4.

Catalan-language radio stations and publications were either closed down or taken over. Catalonia suffered what amounted to a social decapitation, virtually all of its leaders having fled across the French border with the remnants of the Republican army.

Publishing in Catalan virtually disappeared for years (except in exiled circles), in conditions of strict censorship. Until then in the twentieth century, according to figures provided by Leonor Vela, Catalan editorial activity had boomed: 150 books in 1906, 400 in 1923, 750 in 1933 (after the Primo de Rivera dictatorship), and over a thousand between 1936 and 1939.[8] The regime retained its proscription throughout its existence, although periods of relaxation did occur. It was only after 1945, for example, that a very limited number of books began to appear, and the annual figure rose gradually, especially after a relaxation in the dictatorship after 1960. Any possibility of using Catalan in schools disappeared, however, with teachers still being threatened with dismissal in the 1950s if they were caught speaking the language to pupils, even in the playground.

The grim history of the repression of the Catalan during this period has been well recorded by a number of commentators. Only once Spain began to open up to international trade and tourism, and to industrial development, with the regime's *Plan de Estabilización* (1959), did it begin to allow some Catalan-language magazines and cultural organizations such as *Òmnium Cultural* to appear, and the important popular song and civil rights movement, the *Nova Cançó Catalana*.

The return of democracy (1975–)

Even before Franco died, civil society in Catalonia began to mobilize. The *Institut d'Estudis Catalans* became more active and visible, while organizations such as *Òmnium Cultural* and the *Congrés de Cultura Catalana* (1975–7) launched campaigns for the return of Catalan to schools and to official status. Under the terms of the 1978 Spanish Constitution, Catalan became official (alongside Spanish, which remained official throughout the state) in Catalonia, Valencia and the Balearics. The devolved regional authorities had and have powers to design by law and to implement language policies to govern the use of both official languages and to promote proficiency in, and the use of, Catalan. The objective of the use of Catalan becoming 'normal' explains the term used to describe the process as one of 'normalization'.

In Catalonia proper, particularly, official policies promoting the language

---

[8] The figures are cited in Parcerisas, 2001, p. 267.

centred on the education system (with special attention to adults), the public audiovisual media (TV3 and *Catalunya Ràdio*), the official use of the language by the region's authorities, and campaigns to encourage the social use of Catalan.

Catalan today in the Catalan-speaking areas

According to survey data, there are about 9 million speakers of Catalan, of whom about 6.6 million have it as their first, or main, language. More detailed figures for Catalonia are given in Table 1.

Table 1: Population aged 15 or more, according to their first language learned, their own language, and their usual language, Catalonia, 2003

Languages	Thousands of people			Percentages		
	First language learned	Their own language	Main language	First language learned	Their own language	Main language
Catalan	2,213	2,670	2,743	40.45%	48.8%	50.13%
Spanish	2,929	2,425	2,410	53.54%	44.32%	44.05%
Both	152	283	256	2.78%	5.18%	4.67%
Aranese (Occitan)	3	2	2	0.05%	0.04%	0.04%
Other languages	174	91	61	3.18%	1.66%	1.11%
Total	5,471	5,471	5,471	100%	100%	100%

Source: Institut d'Estadística de Catalunya.[9]

The figures show that in Catalonia at least, there is an intergenerational gain in Catalan-speakers, with 530,000 more regarding Catalan as their main language than had it as the first language learned at home. This is clearly a healthy sign for the future of the language (not mirrored, however, in Valencia); and whether or not this rate of recruitment will be enough to cope with recent migratory movements (see below) remains to be seen.

---

[9] Unless otherwise indicated the following information has been adduced from information provided by the *Institut d'Estadística de Catalunya* and available on the website of the Generalitat de Catalunya. Details of the references *in toto* appear in the appropriate section of the bibliography.

Table 2: Proportion of population with Catalan competence in each of the Catalan-speaking territories (percentages)

	Understand it	Speak it	Read it	Write it
Catalunya	97.4%	84.7%	90.5%	62.3%
Illes Balears	93.1%	74.6%	79.6%	46.9%
Catalunya Nord	68.9%	37.1%	31.4%	10.6%
Andorra	96.0%	78.9%	89.7%	61.1%
L'Alguer	90.1%	61.3%	46.5%	13.6%
Com. Valenciana	75.9%	53.0%	47.3%	25.2%
La Franja d'Aragó	98.5%	88.8%	72.9%	30.3%

Table 2 shows that while formal knowledge of the written language is highest in Andorra and Catalonia, it is in the *Franja d'Aragó* that the highest proportion of the population can speak Catalan (on account mainly of its relative isolation, and also because of the lower rate of incomers living there), ahead even of Catalonia. The lowest proportion of the population that can speak Catalan is to be found in northern Catalonia, where political and social pressure have long encouraged language shift, and where large numbers of monolingual French people settle on retiring.

In terms of actual language use in different sectors, the government's annual report for 2007 gives data for cultural industries: in 2006, 34.5 per cent of books published in Catalonia were in Catalan, while in the scenic arts 62.5 per cent were in Catalan and fewer than 4 per cent of cinema-goers watched films in Catalan. In Catalonia and the Balearic Islands Catalan is the main medium of instruction in schools, and the Catalan model has been commended by the Council of Europe's committee of experts for the European Charter for Regional or Minority Languages. Statistics are offered by the authorities, on the use of Catalan as a medium in schools in Catalonia, as shown in Table 3.

Table 3: Students in public and private schools, by language in which classes are taught, Catalonia: infant, primary and secondary education, 1999–2000 (percentages)

Language in which classes are taught	Primary	Secondary
In Catalan	92	49
Predominantly in Catalan	2	36
In Catalan and Castilian	2	15
No information	4	
Total	100	100

Source: School census drawn up by the Catalan Teaching Service of the Department of Education of the *Generalitat de Catalunya*.[10]

Similarly, for the Balearic Islands, statistics are also offered by the authorities, though in this case the model has changed to some extent each time the *Partido Popular* has been in power (Table 4).

Table 4: Language of teaching in infant and primary schools, Balearic Islands, 2002–3

Language of teaching	Number of Schools	%
Catalan	181	57
More Catalan than Castilian	84	26
Compulsory minimum in Catalan (50%)	55	17
Total	320	100

Source: Department of Education and Culture, Government of the Balearic Islands.

In Valencia the language is the medium for fewer than 30 per cent of schoolchildren, and the demand is apparently not fully covered (nor is it at university level in the same region) (Table 5).

---

[10] The author is grateful to Xavier Vila of the University of Barcelona for providing the data for this and the following two tables.

Table 5: Schools with programmes in Valencian and students following the PEV or PIL in Valencia, 2006–7 academic year

	Infant and Primary and 1st year compulsory secondary curriculum in primary schools)	Secondary
Schools with programmes in Valencian	724	289
Students taught in Valencian	122,241	47,612

Source: Valencian Department of Culture, Education and Sport, Valencian Teaching Service.

Significantly, and despite regular claims to the contrary made in Spanish nationalist circles, no single study has shown that proficiency in Spanish suffers as a result.

Though the budget devoted to the promotion of Catalan is not readily available in the Balearic Islands and Valencia, in Catalonia official statistics are now published every year. In the 2007 *Informe de Política Lingüística*, a total figure is given of €156,993,855, of which the greater part went to the Secretariat for Language Policy (€M34.09), the Department of Education (€M53.61) and the Department of Culture and the Media (€M47.06).

The future of Catalan, the challenge of immigration and the Internet

The Internet

Google recently launched a massive online machine translation service, in forty languages. Catalan was among them, alongside Latvian and Finnish, but not (for example) Estonian. This is a great quantitative improvement (though not in terms of quality) on existing services developed by the Catalan government (which offers two-way machine translations between Catalan and Spanish, English, French and German) or by a university in the Valencian region, in which Internostrum only works for Catalan to and from Spanish. The open source system OpenTrad offers two-way translations between Catalan and Spanish, Aranese (Occitan), Esperanto, French and English.[11] Translendium, which developed the *Generalitat*'s system, offers two-way translations between Catalan and Spanish, French and English, and a one-way experimental service from Catalan to Aranese (Occitan).

---

[11] www.opentrad.com. Also offered is a two-way service between Spanish and Galician and Portuguese; and one-way from Spanish to Basque.

The widely acclaimed voluntary organization Softcatalà has been instrumental in the adaptation to Catalan of such important initiatives as Netscape, Firefox, the GNOME environment, Open Office, early versions of the Google interface, and various versions of the GNU/Linux operating system.

Perhaps the most graphic sign of the success of the Catalan language on the Internet is the very existence of the top-level domain, .CAT. The Internet Corporation for Assigned Names and Numbers (ICANN), a California non-profit public benefit corporation, approved the very first top-level Internet domain to be devoted to a particular human language and culture on 15 September 2005. Even before this excellent step forward, the guru of the Catalan cyber-highway, Vicenç Partal, had spoken of Catalan being a success story. Indeed, the healthy position of Catalan on the Internet has been reiterated pertinently by David Block:

> Despite the initial assumptions by some that the Internet would serve to strengthen English as the international language par excellence, current research seems to be showing that matters are evolving in a far more nuanced manner. Thus, although it is true that English was the main medium of the early Internet, it is increasingly the case that the Internet is now a communication space for other language communities, both 'big' (e.g. German, French Japanese and Spanish) and 'small' (e.g. Catalan).[12]

Citing www.alltheweb.com, Mas claims that, in terms of numbers of web pages, Catalan held twenty-sixth position in October 2005, just ahead of Slovenian, Estonian and Slovak. It is unlikely that it will have been able to hold that position; but nevertheless, the fact that Catalan is in the top forty explains why Google's recently presented machine translator, http://translate.google.com, has included it in its service. As far as the presence of Catalan on the Web is concerned, the association of *Webmàsters Independents en Català, de Cultura i d'Àmbits Cívics* (WICCAC), monitors developments regularly and publishes its *Baròmetre* on its website. The latest score, at the end of November 2010, showed that 59.38 per cent of monitored websites had a Catalan version.

This figure creeps up month by month. The Barometer classifies sites by sector, and thus shows that the presence of Catalan is very high (over 80 per cent) in six sectors: universities; theatre and dance; fairs and markets; wines; the Church; and search engines and directories. Interestingly, at the other end of the scale, with under 30 per cent of sites offering a Catalan version, are six sectors: laboratories, pharmaceuticals and chemical industries; perfumes,

---

[12] Block, 2004, p. 22.

cosmetics, cleaning and hygiene industries; cars and motorbikes; and electrical appliances and photography.

Spanish nationalism
The future of Catalan undoubtedly depends to a large extent on the degree to which Spain proves to be willing to accept its multilingual nature. Increasingly virulent attacks on a language policy, which has not substantially changed in over ten years, reveal an undercurrent of hostility towards Catalonia's linguistic planning. Such attacks run parallel with the general political situation in Spain and appear opportunistically at times of right-wing disaffection with Catalan claims. An early example of this correlation between politics and language was the so-called *Manifiesto de los 2.300*, a document denouncing the growth in the use of Catalan in the field of education. This denunciation was released on 25 January 1981, less than a month before the abortive coup d'état led by Colonel Tejero.

Similarly, following the celebration of the Catalan national day on 12 September 1993 – and just after the Popular Party's unexpected defeat at the general election and precisely when the Socialist Party was negotiating a parliamentary agreement with moderate Catalan nationalists – a headline in the traditionalist Madrid daily *ABC* read: 'Igual que Franco pero al revés/ Just like Franco but the other way round.' The latest offensive, the *Manifiesto en defensa de la lengua común* (June 2008), published by the conservative *El Mundo*, was initiated yet again after the Popular Party narrowly failed to win the general election in March 2008. It received the open support even of Tele 5, one of the main private television channels in Spain (of course, any weakening of the status of Catalan, especially in the media, would be beneficial to this monolingual Spanish broadcaster).

The Balearic Islands have also periodically been subjected to such attacks, at a more subdued level, whereas the tepid language policy applied in Valencia is widely criticized by those concerned about the decline in the health of the language in the region. All in all, unlike multilingual countries such as Finland, Switzerland, Belgium or Canada, Spain still has a default language. And the widespread use of Galician, Basque or Catalan is often problematic when in competition with Spanish, or only possible in specific circumstances. Moreover, in thirty years, no Spanish government has done anything substantial to influence the perceptions of the monolingual Spanish-speaking majority as to the richness of the multilingual mosaic; and the Council of Europe's committee of experts for the European Charter for Regional or Minority Languages has called for action in this area.

Immigration

Immigration, together with an extraordinarily low fertility rate (first noted with alarm in the 1930s), is the most challenging aspect of the current situation. Over the past hundred years, and following the basically intraregional population movements from the rural areas into the industrial cities, there has been large scale in-migration from the rest of Spain, particularly from Murcia, neighbouring Aragon and the south of the Peninsula. The influx began in earnest in the 1920s, largely to work on the construction of Barcelona's underground railways and on the exhibition halls and other monumental buildings for the 1929 International Exposition in the same city.

In-migration tapered off in the wake of the Spanish Civil War (1936–9), except for those working for the apparatus of the Franco regime (the courts, the police, education) until it took off once again in the mid-1950s, as industrial and housing development occurred on a huge scale. During this period up to 60,000 or 70,000 workers and their families arrived every year, again mainly from the economically backward southern half of Spain, until the oil crisis in 1973–4, when the numbers began to tail off. It is encouraging to note, however, that nearly all the offspring of these generations of in-migrants who were born in Catalonia can speak and read Catalan, though only a proportion of them use the language as their main, or one of their main, languages.

An element of this equation that is unknown to most people is the fact that there is still, or once more, a considerable two-way movement of people between Catalonia and the rest of Spain. Thus, according to the official source, Idescat, in 2007, 60,642 people came to live in Catalonia from outside the region (0.85 per cent of the present Catalan population) while an even greater figure went in the opposite direction: 71,283 (0.99 per cent of the population). Only ten years before, these figures had been much lower: 21,227 and 24,513 respectively. Given the poor quality of information on the sociolinguistic situation in Catalonia, often distorted by the Spanish media, it is perhaps surprising that the newcomers do not make a greater negative impact on public opinion inside Catalonia.

Since the mid-1990s, these figures have been dwarfed by the scale of foreign immigration (see Table 6). In 2007 alone, Idescat records 195,663 foreign arrivals in Catalonia, compared with 8,288 in 1997 and 56,747 in 2002.[13] Of these, a third were from America (virtually all from Latin America), a quarter from the EU (with a large recent intake from Romania

---

[13] The accuracy of statistics on this issue has in the past been dubious, given the illegal status of many arrivals. In 2007, 62,518 foreigners were recorded as having left Catalonia.

Table 6: New arrivals from abroad, Catalonia, 2007

Origin (foreigners)	EU	Rest of Europe	Africa	America	Asia & Oceania	No information	Total
	48,427	8,622	29,721	66,978	17,876	24,039	**195,663**
	24.75%	4,41%	15.19%	34.23%	9.14%	12.29%	

Source: Idescat.

and other EU enlargement member states), and a seventh from Africa (both the Maghreb and West Africa). The Asian community (mainly from China, India and Pakistan) has also grown very quickly. By 2008, 15 per cent of the population of Catalonia were foreign-born.

One cannot expect new arrivals to learn Catalan immediately, but all the data suggest that Spanish is the preferred, or first, option for most groups living in the cities. Nevertheless about 15 per cent of new arrivals are aged under 16, and there is plenty of evidence that schooling is effective in helping these youngsters to learn Catalan.

Conclusion

It is impossible to make any clear statement about the future of Catalan. Throughout the world, especially in Europe, experience shows that a language needs a modern state behind it, especially in the context of the language policy of the European Union. This is only the case for Catalan in Andorra, a state far too small to have any significant influence on the prospects for the language in other parts. Closer to home, experience shows that language shifts towards Spanish, French and Italian are not just feasible but have been taking place on a large scale, outside Catalonia proper. Nevertheless, it would be rash to classify Catalan as a typical 'minority' language: in many ways it stands out as the exception rather than the rule in many other disadvantaged language communities.

The low birth rate among Catalans undoubtedly weakens the situation and obliges Catalan society to rely on in-migration, a phenomenon that obviously weakens the language and the culture, especially when it is on such a large scale. However, this is certainly no excuse for the inertial maintenance of the habits of language choice, even among some fervent supporters of the language: this clearly reduces the economic viability of media and cultural initiatives in Catalan. It is especially important for the survival of the language to eliminate those attitudes – particularly evident in the region of Valencia – that reduce the perceived value of learning and using Catalan among those who have chosen the Catalan-speaking lands to live and work in. Nevertheless, just as Mark Twain is quoted as saying that 'the reports of my death are greatly exaggerated', it is clear that doomsayers, both as regards the imminent disappearance of Catalan and the equally vociferous claim that Spanish will soon become extinct in Catalonia, try to paint in simple terms what is a unique, highly complex and captivating case.

Works Cited and Suggested Reading

Language: history and social use

Anguera, Pere (2001) 'La resposta', in Vallverdú, F. and Bañeres, J. (dirs) *Enciclopèdia de la llengua catalana*. Barcelona: Edicions 62, pp. 73–84.

Argelaguet, Jordi, Puig Salellas, J. M., and Solé Durany, J. R. (2001) 'Estatus legal i desplegament', in Vallverdú, F. and Bañeres, J. (dirs) *Enciclopèdia de la llengua catalana*. Barcelona: Edicions 62, pp. 229–236.

Badia i Margarit, Antoni (2004) 'Les Homilies d'Organyà en la història de la llengua catalana', in Dolcet, J. and Moga, A. (eds) *Les Homilies d'Organyà*. Reporteducació (Servei educatiu Baix Llobregat-6) / Organyà: Associació Cultural Tres Ponts Avall. Edició electrònica, www.xtec.cat/crp-baixllobregat6/homilies/badia.htm

Barceló Torres, Maria del Carmen (1984) *Minorías islámicas en el País Valenciano. Historia y dialecto*. Valencia: Universidad de Valencia, Instituto Hispano-Árabe de Cultura.

Casanova, Emili (2001) 'La frontera lingüística castellano-catalana en el País Valenciano', *Revista de Filología Románica*, 18, pp. 213–260.

Colon, Germà (1976) *El léxico catalán en la Romania*. Madrid: Gredos.

Ferrando, Antoni (ed.) (1986) *Invitació a la llengua catalana*. València: Gregal Ferrer.

Gatch, Milton McC. (1978) 'The Achievement of Aelfric and His Colleagues in European Perspective', in Szarmach, Paul E. and Huppé, Bernard Felix (eds) *The Old English Homily and its Backgrounds*. Albany, NY: State University of New York Press, pp. 43–74.

Gironés, Francesc (1986) *La persecució política de la llengua catalana*. Barcelona: Edicions 62.

Gonzàlez-Agàpito, J., Marquès, S., Mayordomo, A. and Sureda, B. (2002) *Tradició i renovació pedagògica, 1898–1939. Història de l'educació. Catalunya, Illes Balears, País Valencià*. Barcelona: Publicacions de l'Abadia de Montserrat.

Guinot, Enric (1999) *Els fundadors del regne de València*. València: 3 i 4.

Halla-aho, Hilla (2007) Review of Roger Wright (2002), *A Sociophilological Study of Late Latin*. Utrecht Studies in Medieval Literacy 10. Brepols: Turnhout, in *Arctos*, 41, pp. 140–142.

Moran, Josep (2004) 'El proceso de creación del catalán escrito', *Aemilianense*, I, pp. 431–455.

Moran, Josep and Rabella, Joan Anton (2004) 'Els primers textos en català. Textos anteriors a les Homilies d'Organyà', in Dolcet J., and Moga A. (eds) *Les Homilies d'Organyà*. Reporteducació (Servei educatiu Baix

Llobregat-6) / Organyà: Associació Cultural Tres Ponts Avall. Edició electrònica, www.xtec.cat/crp-baixllobregat6/homilies.htm
Nadal, Josep Maria and Prats, Modest (1993) *Història de la Llengua Catalana*, vol. 1. Barcelona: Edicions 62.
Parcerisas, Francesc (2001) 'La producció editorial', *Enciclopèdia de la Llengua Catalana*. Barcelona: Edicions 62, pp. 267–269.
Riquer, Martí, Comas Antoni de and Molas Joaquim (dirs) (1964) *Història de la Literatura Catalana*, vol. II, Barcelona: Ariel.
Roselló, Joan Pere (2003–8) *Història de la Llengua Catalana*. http://www.usefulweb.org/hallengua/.
Siguan, Miquel (1984) 'Language and Education in Catalonia', *Prospects Quarterly Review of Education*, issue 49: *Mother Tongue and Educational Attainment*, vol. 13, no. 1, pp. 107–119. Electronic sources: http://collections.infocollections.org/ukedu/uk/d/Jh1875e/3.7.html; http://unesdoc.unesco.org/images/0005/000590/059073eo.pdf#59089
Solé i Sabaté, Josep M. and Villaroya, Joan (1994) *Cronologia de la repressió de la llengua i la cultura catalanes 1936–1975*. Barcelona: Editorial Curial.
Solé Tura, Jordi and Aja, Eliseo (1997) *Constituciones y períodos constituyentes en España (1808–1936)*. Madrid: Siglo XXI de España editores.
Strubell, Michael B. (ed.) (1992) *Consideració del cas dels catalans*. Barcelona: Curial.
Vallverdú, F. (dir.) and Bañeres, J. (coord.) (2001) *Enciclopèdia de la llengua catalana*. Barcelona: Edicions 62.
Various authors (1988) *Catalunya. Europa. Una mirada pedagògica*. Vic: EUMO.
Wright, Roger (ed.) (1991) *Latin and the Romance Languages in the Early Middle Ages*. London: Routledge.

Catalan and the Internet
Block, David (2004) 'Globalization, Transnational Communication and the Internet', *International Journal on Multicultural Societies* (IJMS), vol. 6, no. 1, pp. 22–37, http://unesdoc.unesco.org/images/0013/001385/138569e.pdf
Gerrand, Peter (2006) 'A Short History of the Catalan Campaign to Win the .cat Internet Domain, with implications for other minority languages', *Digit·HVM*, 8, www.uoc.edu/digithum/8/dt/eng/gerrand.html
Mas i Hernàndez, Jordi (2005) 'La salut del català a Internet el 2005'. Softcatalà website.
http://www.softcatala.org/la_salut_del_catal%C3%A0_internet_el_2005
Partal, Vicent (19 April 2005) 'El català a la xarxa: Història i raons d'un cas d'èxit', Softcatalà website: www.softcatala.org/articles/article39.htm

Statistics and other online reference material
Institut d'Estadística de Catalunya: www.idescat.cat
Site for statistics for language use:
www.idescat.cat/cat/societat/usoslinguistics.html
Statistics for language use in Catalonia, 2003:
www.idescat.cat/cat/idescat/publicacions/cataleg/pdfdocs/eulc2003.pdf

Statistics for language use in Catalonia, 2008:
   http://www.idescat.cat/cat/idescat/publicacions/cataleg/pdfdocs/eulp2008.pdf
Survey of language use in the Balearics, 2004:
   http://www6.gencat.net/llengcat/socio/docs/EULB2004.pdf
Dept. of Education and Culture, Government of the Balearic Islands
   http://dgpoling.caib.es/www/user/menuweb/dades_sociolinguistiques.htm
Survey of language use in French Catalonia, 2004:
   http://www6.gencat.net/llengcat/socio/docs/catnord2004.pdf
Survey of language use in Andorra, 2004:
   http://www6.gencat.net/llengcat/socio/docs/EULAndorra2004.pdf
Survey of language use in Alguero, 2004:
   http://www6.gencat.net/llengcat/socio/docs/EULA2004.pdf
Survey of language use in Valencia, 2004 (Acadèmia Valenciana de la Llengua):
   http://www.avl.gva.es/img/EdicionsPublicacions/Publicacions/LLIBREBLANC.pdf
Survey of language use in la Franja d'Aragó, 2004:
   http://www6.gencat.net/llengcat/socio/docs/EULF*2004*.pdf
Report on language policies, 2007: The budget of the Generalitat for Language Policies: Chapter IV:
   http://www.parlament.cat/activitat/bopc/08b340.pdf
Cultural industries: Chapter VII:
   http://www.parlament.cat/activitat/bopc/08b340.pdf

Statistics for immigration

Site for statistics on immigration:
   http://www.idescat.cat/cat/poblacio/poblfluxos.html
For 2008 data on in-migration:
   http://www.idescat.cat/dequavi/?TC=444&V0=1&V1=4
For 2008 data on foreign immigration:
   http://www.idescat.cat/dequavi/?TC=444&V0=1&V1=5

Translation tools

http://translate.google.com
http://traductor.gencat.cat
www.internostrum.com
www.opentrad.com
www.translendium.com/
www.softcatala.cat

Other items

WICCAC (Webmàsters Independents en Català, de Cultura i d'Àmbits Cívics):
   www.wiccac.org
Application for .cat domain: www.icann.org/en/tlds/stld-apps-19mar04/cat.htm

6

Sport and Catalonia

LOUISE JOHNSON

Origins, Catalanism and the Olympic tradition

As elsewhere in Europe, the aristocracy had been the drivers of modern sport in Madrid. However, in Catalonia the industrial bourgeoisie were the prime movers and, together with foreign nationals such as Hans – later Joan – Gamper, founder of FC Barcelona, they were intrinsic to the shaping of the sporting scene. Unlike the Basques, who promoted *pelota* and the *herri kirolak* (rural sports including stone-lifting, log-chopping and skiff racing), Catalans looked more to modern sport and international practices than to their own traditions. Accordingly, English sporting custom was a powerful ideological influence on athletes at the beginning of the twentieth century. The same effect is also well documented in the arts, as illustrated in Dominic Keown's chapter on Contemporary Culture, where a graphic obsession with the Hellenic elegance of the human form in *noucentista* painting went hand in hand with a poetic fascination with tennis and its accompanying social values of refinement.

However, Catalan *associacionisme* – the readiness of individuals with a common interest to come together and formally organize into societies – ensured that the bourgeoisie did not have a monopoly over sporting initiatives. At the turn of the twentieth century *excursionisme* – a catch-all term referring to rambling, hiking and expeditions into the Catalan interior – constituted the most vibrant and widespread physical-cultural activity within the country, in part because of its classless appeal. While *excursionisme* may certainly have become more recognizably a sport as the twentieth century progressed, it had originated rather as a philosophy of life; as a cultural and scientific – as well as physical – re-engagement with the Catalan landscape, geology, flora and fauna, born out of *Renaixença* desires to rediscover Catalan identity following the centuries of so-called decadence.

Excursionisme in the 1920s and 1930s, framed by the military dictatorship of General Miguel Primo de Rivera and later by the Second Republic, became infused with the values of hygiene, regenerationism, nationalism and citizenship, and offered an alternative to mass-sporting spectacles such as football. The *Centre Excursionista de Catalunya*, however, had not admitted women to their ranks until the founding of a mountain sports section and the first female competition was held in 1911. The English tradition was also evident in the popularity of 'boy-scoutism' (*escoltisme*), promoted by Josep Maria Batista i Roca in the third decade of the century, but this movement too was severely affected after the Civil War by the restrictions placed by the regime on internal movement and a deep-seated suspicion among Francoists of all things associated with Britain and liberalism.

While it appears to be the case that the progressive left of *Esquerra Republicana de Catalunya* (ERC) in particular were very keen that state schooling in the 1930s should incorporate all-round education into the curriculum, in practice institutional and organizational support seems to have been fragmented and lacking. The daily newspaper *La Rambla* was particularly vocal in its criticisms and, together with its sister organs *La Publicitat* and *La Humanitat*, vigorously promoted a popular and nationalist agenda for sport, acting as fora for important civic youth associations such as *Palestra*, probably the most significant Catalanist cultural and sporting collective of the 1930s. *La Rambla* also championed the cultural and sporting activities and competitions of the ground-breaking *Club Femení i d'Esports*, a socially inclusive, Catalanist society that drew support from some of the most dynamic female (and male) figures of the time.

Palestra emphasized aviation and maritime sports and also had an important *excursionista* and scouting section. It welcomed members from across the political divide, confessional and secular, male and female, organizing lectures on wide-ranging subjects. It also offered Catalan language classes and – within individual delegations – even professional and vocational training. In this respect Lluís Duran has stated:

> In a movement which aspired to improve its citizens, being 'Catalanist' between 1900–1930 was not merely a political badge (although it was a badge of many colours). 'Catalanist' is also, following *Noucentista* aspirations, the will to create a model citizen: cultured, tolerant, firm of conviction, proud of the country's progress and solicitous about improvements still to be undertaken.[1]

---

[1] 'Palestra: cultura, civisme i esport per als joves' at http://webs.racocatala.cat/cat1714/d/palestra5.pdf (quote at p. 7).

An explicit political and international referent for Catalanist sport and citizenship at this time was the broad-based Czech *sokol* (falcon) movement, founded in 1862 by Miroslav Tyrš and Jindřich Fügner. While historical vicissitudes and factionalism meant that Tyrš's progressive and inclusive agenda for the movement was compromised at moments during the ensuing decades, there is a clear distinction between the *sokols* and, for example, the Hitler Youth and Italian fascist youth movements.

The increasing disquiet of liberal Catalans at the rise of Nazi Germany and the award, in 1931, of the 1936 Olympic Games to Berlin in preference to Barcelona, motivated the decision of the *Comitè Català pro-Esport Popular* (CCEP) to constitute a working party with a view to organizing a Popular Olympics. The frustrated initiative has since acquired tremendous ideological importance and so, setting aside the obvious reference point of the 1992 Barcelona Games, it is perhaps typical of the afflicted history of the Catalans that the most important sporting co-ordinate in the early decades of the twentieth century is an event that never took place. For the so-called Workers' Olympics of 1936, due to be hosted by the Catalan capital, were abandoned at the eleventh hour. Franco's uprising occurred the day before the Games were to begin, and athletes intending to compete either returned home, or in some cases fought alongside Republican troops.

It may be premature to ascertain how Spanish and Catalan history in particular have judged the 1992 spectacle, but the 'Popular Olympiad', by contrast, has tended to be re-fashioned in the intervening period. Much writing in Catalonia has played down or even omitted the already extant tradition of Workers' Olympics, of which the proposed Barcelona Games would have been a continuation. Organized in opposition to Coubertin's bourgeois/ aristocratic event, Workers' Olympics had taken place in Frankfurt am Main (1925) and Vienna (1931), with a precursor games in Prague (1921), involving far greater numbers of participants than the revivalist Greek model. These events emphasized international solidarity rather than competition between nations; for even at this early stage – and as was epitomized by Berlin, 1936 – the focus on individual participants was losing ground to national and state affiliation, despite Coubertin's vision.

In this same year, and in the shadow of the so-called 'Nazi Games', the historical moment was further heightened by the unstable political climate within Spain itself. Subsequent commentary has emphasized Catalonia's popular, leftist credentials and political protagonism in reaction specifically to the rise of fascisms in Europe at this time. In the wake of Republican defeat and the long years of Francoist oppression this emphasis is hardly surprising. And the putative Games, to be centred on the Montjuïc stadium, could be read as proposing symbolically to reclaim the arena that had been inaugurated in 1929 for the International Exposition, under the dictatorship of Primo de Rivera. The stadium had also been intended as the centrepiece of the 1936 Olympics, were they to have been awarded to the city, and its political significance lives on still. The site had been occupied by a military prison in the aftermath of the Civil War; and it was here that the President of the Catalan Government, Lluís Companys, was executed by Franco's troops in 1940. Renovated for the Games of 1992, the stadium now bears his name.

Indeed, complexity if not paradox clouds the topic in ideological terms as nineteenth-century Catalanist aspirations to build a greater Barcelona around the Expo in 1888, as explained in Robert Davidson's chapter, were brought to fruition quite perversely, in the second holding of this event in 1929, under the fundamentally anti-Catalan military dictatorship. In a similar ironic mirroring, the city's ambitions to host the modern Olympics, thwarted by Paris in 1924 and Berlin in 1936, were finally achieved through the agency of a former minister of the Franco regime: Juan Antonio Samaranch, President of the IOC from 1980 to 2001.

If there is also the suggestion that Barcelona's candidature for 1936 might have been unsuccessful because the Marqués de Lamadrid, president of the Spanish Olympic Committee, and the Baró de Güell, IOC delegate, were unwilling to place the Games in the hands of the Republicans, the 1992 application was to come under no similar suspicion. Its enabler already had a successful track record. As a member of the Spanish Olympic Committee and completely identified with the Francoist regime, Samaranch had been instrumental in securing the Second Mediterranean Games (held under the auspices of the IOC) for Barcelona in 1955. Participants at this event, however, had either to be regime sympathizers, or were sufficiently astute to appear so. The city received no financial assistance from Madrid to stage the event.

At a conference advocating 'Respect for the Olympic Ideal' in Paris, June 1936, the CCEP had called for a boycott of the Berlin Olympics, explicitly proposing the Barcelona Workers' Games as an alternative. After Franco's death, however, Barcelona's Olympic candidacy was to count on more widespread support. The *Congrés de Cultura Catalana* (1975–7) had been charged with the enormous task of conducting a full audit of Catalan cultural activities and structures in the context of almost forty years of oppression and involuntary neglect, with a view to mapping the way ahead for all areas of a 'normal' Catalan culture under democracy. In the course of this debate, the subject of an application to host the Olympics met with certain left-wing objections, which echoed the censure of the anti-Coubertin lobby of the 1930s.

The final conclusions, however, rejected this kind of negativity and urged the development of policies for popular and grass-roots sport, denouncing the regime's attempted annihilation of Catalan difference. Criticisms of sport as spectacle and elite competition – two distinguishing characteristics of the modern Olympics – were played down. And the realization that the international projection of difference could be served very effectively by such a momentous event on the world stage emerged with some urgency in 1981, following the failed military coup in Madrid. It gathered significant momentum from 1986 with the announcement of Barcelona's successful Olympic bid, especially as a part of the campaign for an IOC-recognized Catalan Olympic Committee; and it finally took shape in the manifesto of the pressure group *Acció Olímpica*.

Sport, identity and national teams

A perennial source of controversy and debate has been the determination shown by many Catalan sports to be allowed to represent their nation in international competition. This implies in most cases first obtaining the recognition and approval of international governing bodies. The process is customarily blocked at the very earliest stages by Spanish sports federations, either directly or prophylactically, via their official representation on these international bodies. Thus, for example, seemingly ignorant of the origins of the international game, FIFA, football's governing body, ruled in 2003 that only independent states should have their own football teams following a proposal tabled by Ángel María Villar, president of the Spanish Football Federation. Similarly, having been invited to participate in the World Park Tour (Czech Republic) in 2002, the Catalan orienteering team was obliged to compete as Spain following the intervention of the *Agrupación Española de Clubs de Orientación*, the overarching state association for this discipline. Once again, in spring 2003, Spain vetoed the possibility of a Catalan team participating in a roller hockey tournament in Montreux, Switzerland; and in 2004, the Catalan Skating Federation had its admission to its international governing body revoked following pressure from the Spanish Federation. There are numerous other examples of this veto on Catalan participation in events as a national unit. As might be expected, friction between state and national federations has also from time to time had negative implications for the ability of Catalan clubs and cities to host international competition.

Ernest Benach, former president of the Catalan Parliament, has pointed out that the growth of high-performance sport and the increasing competitive potential of Catalan sportsmen and women has stimulated the desire to achieve representation with which spectators can fully identify. This imperative is further heightened by the visibility of athletes afforded by the mass media. At the same time, it would seem foolish not to acknowledge that athletes are under no obligation to meet spectators' ambitions for them: if lucrative funding or a professional contract are only available via the national (Spanish) federation of any given sport, an athlete's priorities may very well not match those of his or her audience. It ought not to be forgotten that the basic rationale for national teams in an obvious sense is that they promote the name and language of Catalonia. However, the very visibility of this difference, facilitated by the communications media, is perceived – rightly or wrongly – as threatening by opponents of the idea.

In 1998 the *Plataforma Pro-Seleccions Esportives Catalanes* was founded to work towards the aim of international recognition for Catalan national teams. Their first task was to effect a change in the *Llei d'Esport*, achieved in 1999 following the presentation to the Catalan parliament of more than half a million signatures of support. But discussion in favour of national teams is often characterized by passion and jingoism rather than reason and logic. This is nowhere more apparent than in the case of hypothetical Catalonia versus Spain fixtures. In presentations of this subject, Spain is often portrayed as being scared to lose and, more important, scared to be *seen* to lose, with all the symbolic ramifications this might involve.

A more objective interpretation acknowledges that the encounter itself would reinforce a sense of (Catalan) nationhood in powerful, visual terms. The most comprehensive and certainly enthusiastic survey – more accurately, a manifesto – dedicated to the history of Catalan national teams by Josep Maria Raduà, commits a common error in this sense citing Great Britain as the model to be followed. In reality, this model can only be followed partially. While it is true that Wales, Scotland and Northern Ireland compete as separate nations in many international competitions, the crucial exception is the Olympic Games in which Great Britain absorbs temporarily the identities of its member nations. The historical importance of the Olympics as a global stage for the showcasing of sport far exceeds that of any other competition and they are accordingly prized; the British model, however, is unhelpful from the perspective of a stateless nation. Catalan Olympic aspirations, meanwhile, appear to languish in a state of suspended animation.

The Catalan Olympic Committee (COC) presented its formal request for recognition by the International Olympic Committee (IOC) in 1991. Although there was discussion subsequently of the difficulties inherent in the Catalan case, in 1996 the IOC approved a rule change according to which only states recognized by the UN were permitted their own (official) National Olympic Committee (NOC). Notwithstanding this rule change, at the time of writing (2010), more than a dozen non-UN member territories do have officially recognized NOCs.

Governing bodies and competitions of some non-Olympic sports, on the other hand, have found space for Catalan national representation; these include the World Kickboxing Network, the World Baton Twirling Federation; Full Contact World Championships; the *Union Internationale de Bodybuilding Naturel* (2004 World Championships); and from 2007, the International Bowling Federation (bowling is a recognized Olympic sport).

A constant of the interminable wrangling over state and national representations is the detriment caused to minority groups, and to those whose sporting profile is less well-established within Spain, a phenomenon by no means limited to the Iberian context. In spite of a strong showing in the 2007 FIFA Women's World Cup – and their subsequent ranking, for the first time ever, in the World's Top Ten – English women footballers were denied the opportunity to compete at the 2008 Beijing Olympics because to do so would have meant playing as Great Britain, a possibility rejected by (male) members of the Scotland and Wales governing bodies because it would supposedly set a precedent for other international competition, threatening the independence of their respective national teams. Great Britain therefore forfeited its place. This occurred despite a decision by FIFA to allow English teams to rebadge as Great Britain exceptionally for the 2012 London Games.

Such official duplicity in this area serves nobody's purpose well. In the Catalan context junior competitors have suffered similarly as a result of nationalist politics. However, Raduà provides with some satisfaction a heartening anecdote about Catalan adaptive swimmers who took part in an International Open event at Sheffield in 2000. Spain, the Balearics, Valencia and Catalonia had their own teams; and two Catalan swimmers won medals, which 'were picked up from the secretary's office in an envelope addressed to the Catalan Team, without ceremony or speeches or delays caused by politicians. Many people there were in competition for places at the Sydney Paralympics and English rectitude prioritized competitiveness over protocol.'[2]

Different levels of competition (and different sports) appear to attract different levels of political intervention and press comment; and while it might be tempting to see an absence of intervention as the ideal, at the same time it is hard not to see such inconsistency as undervaluing grass-roots and wider participation in sport. At what point does an athlete become so significant a sporting citizen that they are told whom they can and cannot represent?

A club with the international profile and reputation of FC Barcelona – a

---

[2] Raduà, 2005, p. 307.

club, moreover, that in addition to football incorporates basketball, wheelchair basketball, handball, field hockey and ice hockey, rugby, cycling, volleyball and more – gives comparatively little space in public fora to its women's teams. The club's commitment to grass-roots participation and development, both in Catalonia and internationally, reinforced by the tagline borrowed from *La Rambla* newspaper, 'sport and citizenship', may be well-intentioned but betrays a keen marketing awareness of the intrinsically sexist media agenda for sport.

It has been said of women's sport in general that finance has a greater likelihood of materializing for those sports that have traditionally admitted women; this means that football and rugby, more closely associated with a male sporting tradition, often lose out. Development is correspondingly slow and the effects of Francoist limitations on female sporting aspiration are frighteningly persistent. The political weight of football in the modern historical context, coupled with a media role that is increasingly influential in agenda-setting, appear to leave little opportunity for an across-the-board promotion of women's sport, especially now that inclusive notions of community and participation in the pre-Olympic period have subsided somewhat.

Much of the debate surrounding national teams seems to take place in relative ignorance of historical precedents within Spain itself and is clearly damaging. Even writers in *Generalitat*-sponsored publications are guilty in this respect, when they claim that the *Federació d'Entitats Excursionistes'* acceptance as a new member by the International Mountaineering and Climbing Federation in 2000 is the first case of a Catalan association being recognized by the corresponding international body.[3] In fact, the Catalan Rugby Federation had been constituted in 1922; and in 1934, together with France, Italy, Germany, the former Czechoslovakia and Romania, it established the International Amateur Rugby Federation, its co-founders recognizing the validity of the 1931 Catalan Statute of Autonomy for sporting purposes. Centralist reaction to this initiative was not long in coming and included the familiar attempt to claw back such independence. In January 1934, for example, the *Heraldo de Madrid* had commented: 'The independence of Catalan sport is now a reality, and in consequence, all national federations should automatically be constituted in Madrid, capital of the Republic, without delay and with the greatest possible urgency.'[4]

---

[3] Unsigned, 10 January 2001, 'Dossier: Una potència esportiva', *Projecció Exterior* (Generalitat de Catalunya), pp. 17–19. The *Generalitat* is the official name of the devolved government of both Catalonia and Valencia.

[4] As cited by Raduà, 2005, p. 400.

1. Miquel Poveda. Catalan flamenco singer and actor. By permission of Miquel Poveda and Arts Factory Spain

2. Christ Pantocrator, Sant Esteve de Llanars, 12th century. By permission of Alexander Ibarz

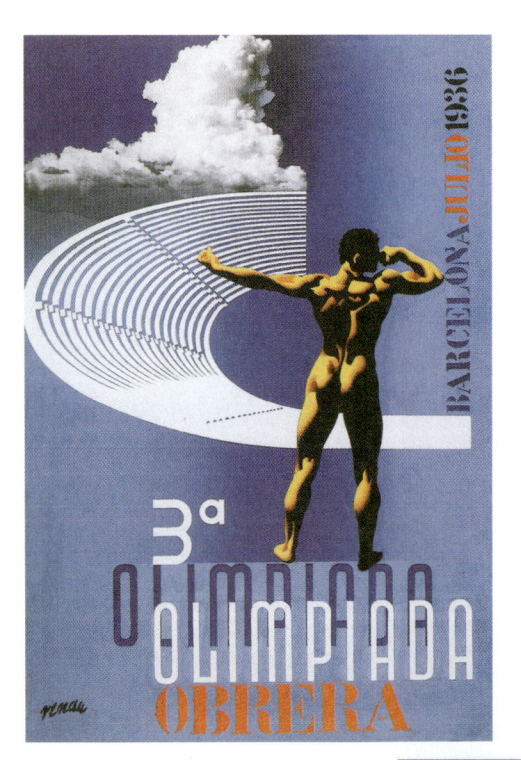

3. Joseph Renau, 'Workers' Olympiad, 1936'.
By permission of the Fundació Josep Renau and the Institut Valencià d'Art Modern

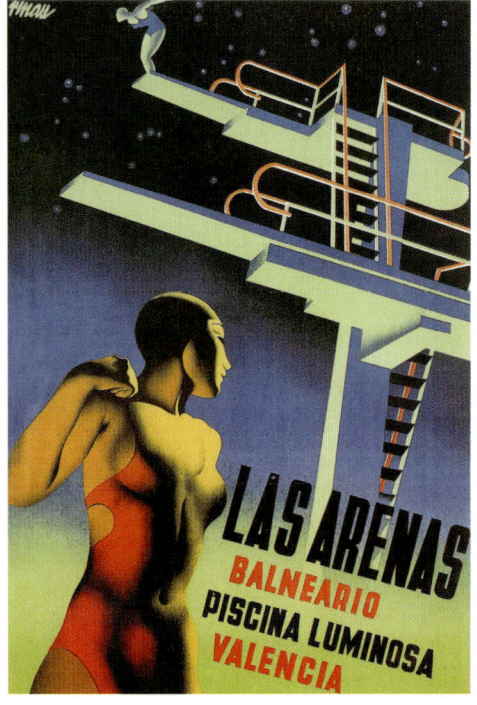

4. Joseph Renau, 'Las Arenas Swimming Pool'.
By permission of the Fundació Josep Renau and the Institut Valencià d'Art Modern

5. *Correfoc*, Festes de la Mercè, Barcelona, 2007. By permission of Manel Carrera i Escudé, director of www.festes.org

6. *Caganers* at the Christmas fair in Mataró, 2009. By permission of Manel Carrera i Escudé, director of www.festes.org

7. Carrying down the *falles* on St John's Eve, Durro (Alta Ribagorça). By permission of Manel Carrera i Escudé, director of www.festes.org

8. *Sardanes* at the Easter *aplec*, La Pobla de Montornès (Tarragonès). By permission of Manel Carrera i Escudé, director of www.festes.org

Rugby is also one of the few sports in which a Catalan women's team has been involved in international competition; and one of the few as well to have seen a united *Països Catalans* team (representing the areas of Catalonia, Valencia and the Balearics) compete internationally as against France in 1987. Similarly, camping (a leisure rather than sporting activity perhaps), *excursionisme*, skiing and aviation also formed part of their corresponding international federations in the 1930s. In 1913, the first *Comitè Olímpic de Catalunya* (COC) was authorized by the State Delegation of the IOC to participate in the 1916 Olympic Games (suspended because of the First World War), and, in 1915 and 1916, the Catalan Athletics Federation was invited to the IOC Assembly as a full member.

Catalan organizational precociousness favoured its early integration into the international sporting scene but it began to find itself marginalized as nation states, including Spain, caught up. Since the 1920s, Catalan teams have played (usually friendly) internationals in, for example, rugby, football, basketball, weightlifting and field hockey, and have taken on Spain in football, rugby, roller hockey, boxing, field hockey, canoe polo, handball and softball, among other disciplines. There had been a Catalonia versus Spain football match as early as 1924, although both before and following the Spanish Civil War the Catalan football team was more regularly pitted against Castile in games of evident high tension. From the 1950s, and particularly during the 1960s, games involving the Catalan national team became less frequent. It was – and is – not unusual, in the absence of a competing Catalan team, for the Spanish team to be constituted wholly, or by a majority, of Catalan-speaking athletes (e.g. the Spanish Davis Cup tennis team in 2000).

Given the difficulty of constituting a national team with official, wide-ranging recognition, it has often fallen to FC Barcelona to fly the flag for the Catalans, although the version of Barça's trajectory under Franco's dictatorship and beyond has tended to be romanticized in English-language publications. Even recent studies have commented, with a certain scepticism, on the uncanny uniformity of histories of the institution and suggested that re-examination of certain episodes, as a minimum, is required. The powerful, unerring presence of Barça in the collective consciousness is incontestable, however. As a socio-cultural sporting phenomenon with significant political weight, and as a social reality, the club is unique. To begin to understand its influence, we must turn to key events of the twentieth century.

Barça: Més que un club?

The celebrations following the victorious 2008–9 season when FC Barcelona won the domestic double of league and cup, the Champions League, the supercups of Europe and Spain and also the World Club Championship, with the accompanying *cri-de-guerre* 'Visca el Barça i visca Catalunya', bear incontrovertible witness to the identification between club and country. Salvador Duch has identified five essential elements in Barça's polysemic social make-up that explain the analogy between the metropolis and the nation:

- the form and design of the respective flags of the city, club and country;
- the negation of *Madridisme*;
- a *communitas* space, understood as the identification with an emblem that symbolizes opposition to centralism, counting on followers and supporters' groups (*penyes*) across the Spanish state;
- synonymy between football as a universal language and Barcelona's status (at least since 1992) as a city with a global outlook: as seen in other chapters, the metropolis is taken as a gateway open to European rather than Spanish culture;
- the centralizing and vertebrating character of Barcelona within Catalonia through the 'national' character of the club, so that local footballing identities are nearly always compatible with affection for Barça.[5]

Curiously enough, founded in 1899 by the Swiss national Hans Gamper, Barça became known as the foreigners' team. RCD Espanyol, on the other hand, was founded in the following year as the *Sociedad Española de Football*, in clear opposition to the 'foreign' character of FC Barcelona. Espanyol adopted blue and white for its kit and shield, which had been the colours of the Catalano-Aragonese fleet commanded by Roger de Llúria in the fourteenth century. Thus it was Espanyol that first associated itself with the symbols of Catalan tradition. However, in 1912 – and again in counter-position to the anti-centralist feeling current among many Barcelona residents at the time – Espanyol sought the concession of the title *Real* (royal) from King Alfonso XIII; and, once granted, the king became honorary president of the club.

While FC Barcelona publicly and officially aligned itself with the aspirations to autonomy of Catalan town and city halls in 1918, Espanyol's unpopularity continued to grow. Stereotypes surrounding the two clubs finally developed in the 1920s under the monarchy-backed dictatorship of Primo de Rivera as Barcelona went from being the team of foreigners to the team symbolizing the nation. In practical terms, this meant that the club supported

---

[5] Salvador Duch, 2005, p. 14.

teaching in Catalan and even organized courses for Catalan teachers. General Milans del Bosch had closed Barça's Les Corts stadium in 1925 when the crowd booed the Spanish national anthem played by a visiting Royal Marines band (the crowd had applauded 'God Save the King' immediately afterwards); and a similar expression of disenchantment with the centralist status quo occurred before the 2009 Cup Final between Barça and Athletic Bilbao at the Mestalla stadium, Valencia, when members of both sets of supporters drowned out the Spanish anthem in the presence of the king himself.

The Civil War marked the beginning of the myth-making period for FC Barcelona. The club's president, Josep Sunyol i Garriga, was killed by Franco's troops in August 1936. Players who refused to swear allegiance to the regime were sanctioned and many team members did not return from abroad, leaving the club decimated. Not all players, then as now, assimilated the symbolic charge of the shirt, however, and some – notably Samitier and Zamora, two of the most charismatic figures in Spanish football – were regime sympathizers. Political influence decided the result of key matches against Real Madrid (in Madrid's favour, of course), and even during the long years of the post-war dictatorship, when the club's directors were stooges appointed by the regime, Barça was gradually transformed into what Duch refers to as 'one of the only contexts that allowed a timid Catalanist and anti-Francoist revindication, with the particularity that as an indirect, ambiguous and hyperbolic protest, and at the same time, a space of authorized permissiveness, the regime could do nothing except tolerate it as a minor evil'.[6]

Attendance at matches facilitated the mobilization of popular support for civil campaigns, such as the tram 'strike', or more accurately, boycott, of 1951. On this occasion, a chain letter was circulated urging citizens to walk to the match rather than take the tram until such a time as the recent fare increase, which controversially had not been implemented in Madrid, was revoked. These became rare moments of dissidence in Franco's Spain.

The Di Stéfano affair that unfolded in the summer of 1953 has become symptomatic of the regime's political interference in sport, especially as regards its promotion of Real Madrid as the emblem of the Spanish regime. Barcelona had agreed terms with the Argentine international and obtained the rights to sign him from the club to which he contractually belonged at the time, River Plate. Di Stéfano, however, had reneged on his contract and was playing for Millonarios of Bogotá. In the meantime, having learned of the

---

6   Salvador Duch, 2005, p. 87.

move and in an attempt to hijack the transfer, Real Madrid held discussions with Millonarios. Di Stéfano's signing for FC Barcelona was made public on 16 August 1953; but on 22 August, the Francoist organ overseeing sport, the *Delegación Nacional de Deportes*, banned the signing of foreign players. Despite the timing, which would appear to have favoured Barcelona's case (according to which the signing had taken place before the ban came into force), the club were aware that the announcement was almost certainly designed officially to invalidate the move.

A compromise solution was tabled by the Spanish Football Federation to further complicate the Catalans' acquisition of the player: Di Stéfano would play for Barcelona for two years, and then for Madrid for two years. This ridiculous proposal was, of course, rejected out of hand by Barcelona. They correspondingly opened negotiations with Turin, who offered to cover the transfer fee already paid. But Di Stéfano had begun talks with Santiago Bernabéu, president of Real Madrid, and an approach was made to the federation for permission to sign the player, citing an agreement of their own with Millonarios that pre-dated the ban. Madrid had taken advantage of the Gordian contractual complexities and, with regime backing, the signing was completed. In the wake of the affair and in protest against the scandalous handling of the transfer, vice-president Martí Carreto and other members of the Barcelona management resigned and, as a result of a legal loophole, democratic elections were held to choose a successor. Much has been made of the fact that these were the only democratic elections to take place in Spain under the Franco regime.[7]

At the beginning of the twenty-first century, it has been argued somewhat optimistically that RCD Espanyol (who played their home games at the totemic Montjuïc stadium from 1997, before moving in August 2009 to a new stadium in Cornellà – El Prat) have quite as much right to consider themselves standard bearers, since they generally field more Catalan players than their city rivals. As Sid Lowe points out, turning around Barça's motto, Catalonia is 'more than just *one* club'.[8] On the other hand, Barça undoubtedly have the financial means to buy almost any player on the international scene and yet often they turn instead to gifted Catalan athletes. The treble-winning team of 2009 started and finished with seven players who had

---

[7] A fuller account of the intrusive, labyrinthine episode can be found in Barnils, 1999 and Salvador Duch, 2005. They also indicate how these elections, a would-be act of resistance to the dictatorship, were not conducted without certain irregularities.

[8] Lowe, 2007, http:// blogs.guardian.co.uk/ sport/2007/ 12/03/ espanyol_hold_barca_to_claim_a.html

come through the youth ranks – proof enough of the success of their investment in young athletes from Catalonia and further afield.

Sport and language

In the Catalonia of the 1920s and 1930s, sport became synonymous with modernity, and with certain bourgeois pretensions to European chic and Hollywood glamour. Sport was recruited into the service of sometimes mutually incompatible social, cultural and political causes. But in different manifestations, its increasing popularity crossed the social spectrum: football and cycling tended to enjoy greater popular appeal, while tennis and skiing attracted the middle and upper classes. Boxing drew pan-social support. Active participation was a facet of this popularization, but the main driver was perhaps the buoyancy of the news and sports media, which were given powerful momentum by certain high-profile sportsmen and women who captured the public's imagination: FC Barcelona forward Josep Samitier, boxers Josep Gironès and Paulino Uzcudún, and swimmer Carmen Soriano were just such figures.

At this time, anglicisms and borrowings from English entered the language where the Catalan lexicon lacked equivalent terminology, or simply because they were perceived to be more convenient, or more fashionable, alternatives. Words such as *xut, córner, penalty* (or *penal*), *dribbling* and *crol* were and remain frequent. According to renowned sports commentator Joaquim Maria Puyal, the majority of footballing terms occurring in 1920s' publications such as *La Veu de Catalunya* and *Xut!*, fell into this category: examples are *matx, orsai* (offside), *refri* or *refli* (referee), *linesman, quicof, flèquic* (free kick) and *haut* (out). Where Catalonia, and by extension, Catalan, has lacked the tradition of a certain sport, foreign vocabulary has often been adopted, or copied slavishly from Castilian where available. In recent years this has been the case of baseball before *TERMCAT*, the official body constituted expressly to resolve such issues, was enlisted into the process of normalization of sports terminology.[9]

In pre-Civil War years, receptiveness to foreign linguistic influence often answered to necessity, but among some people and in certain publications (notably the third series of *D'Ací i D'Allà*, 1932–6), English sporting vocabulary became a badge of fashion, a linguistic marker which, through the use of italics, indicated awareness and conscious recourse to the 'foreign', and

---

[9] *TERMCAT: Centre de Terminologia* was founded in 1985. It can be accessed at www.termcat.cat

denoted a kind of self-ironizing adherence to latest trends. This knowingness tempers to a degree the accusations of snobbery levelled – particularly in retrospect – at *D'Ací i D'Allà*. The growing presence of sports reporting on the radio in the 1930s, especially of football, provided an additional source for the diffusion of specialized vocabulary, and a further influence on the evolution of spoken Catalan. *Ràdio Associació de Catalunya* became the first monolingual Catalan-language broadcaster in 1930, provoking *Ràdio Barcelona* and *Ràdio Catalana* to begin broadcasting in Catalan too, though neither renounced Castilian.[10]

Franco's almost pathological dislike of words associated with (French and English) democracy resulted in a law proscribing such terms, and FC Barcelona was forced to change its name to *Club de Fútbol* (thus C de F as opposed to FC); and anglicisms were replaced with their corresponding Castilian terms, such as *saque de esquina* (corner) and *fuera de juego* (offside). Not until 1974 was the club permitted to revert to its original name in recognition of its seventy-fifth anniversary.

In the aftermath of the Spanish Civil War, both spoken and written sporting media were severely curtailed. According to Neus Faura, the immense significance of the spoken word within the Catalan-language sporting media at the end of the twentieth century is a fact explained not merely by the sheer quantity of sports coverage and, therefore, the relative predominance of this modality but also, and notably in the case of football, by the

> absence, from 1939 onwards, of an exclusively Catalan-language sporting press, meaning that in Catalan, unlike other languages which have enjoyed an uninterrupted sports-press tradition, the oral medium has been at the fore in creating and diffusing the different forms that language adopts in the transmission of sporting content.[11]

Only in 2002, with the appearance of *El 9 Esportiu*, could Catalonia count on a dedicated Catalan-language sports paper. *El 9* emphasizes its commitment to a Catalan 'vision of our own', beyond simply publishing in Catalan and its articles are Catalan originals rather than translations. The industry, with sales figures in mind, had previously shown itself to be understandably cautious about the possibilities for a Catalan sporting press, even after the language was formally showcased at the 1992 Olympics. Josep Maria Casanovas, for

---

10 See http://recursos.cnice.mec.es/media/radio/bloque1/pag3.html
11 Faura i Pujol, 1998, p. 6.

example, at the time director of the Castilian-language paper *Sport*, was quoted as saying that it was only a matter of time before Catalan attained parity with Castilian in the sports press: for when (and if) *La Vanguardia*, the flagship daily printed in Barcelona and rival of the state-wide *El País,* were published in Catalan, *Sport* would also make the transition. Even though the electronic versions of both papers became available in translation from November 2008, the reference to hard copy in Catalan was tantamount to suggesting pigs might fly (though they still might!).

In September 1976, a landmark in sporting coverage was reached as *Radio Barcelona* broadcast the FC Barcelona versus UD Las Palmas match, live and in Catalan: it was the first broadcast of a major sporting event in the vernacular since the Republic. Broadcaster Puyal and linguist Jordi Mir worked to recover the heavily anglicized football terminology that had been current before the Civil War, recognizing its richness and import in contrast to the Castilian model that had come to dominate the airwaves. It would require updating and, in the context of linguistic repression and lack of expertise, this was a fraught and complex task. Over thirty years on, the shortage of Catalan-language specialists continues to affect the linguistic quality of sports broadcasts, although the enthusiasm and dedication of commentators, linguists and scholars in this area seems manifest. The audiovisual and electronic media are nevertheless recognized as displaying much more entrepreneurial initiative in linguistic matters than their print counterparts.

The elevated public profile of the Catalan language, made possible by the naming of Barcelona as host city for the 1992 Olympic Games, was attained with a great deal of diplomatic and political effort. Even so, particularly in the international context, these efforts were not always and are still not understood. What might be intended as a display of pride in Catalan, an expression of national exuberance and vitality, was often viewed as anti-Spanish sentiment as outlined by *El català i els Jocs Olímpics*, a collection of press articles published in 1993 on the use of language at the Barcelona Games. This tension would not be resolved.

As established by the Olympic Charter, Catalan – co-official with Castilian Spanish in Catalonia – was confirmed as one of the four official languages of the Games (along with French, English and Spanish). The recognition of Catalan was facilitated by Coubertin's term 'sport country' (*país esportiu*), in which the word 'country' was defined in the Olympic Charter at the time – and we translate from the Catalan version – as 'any country, state, territory or portion of territory that the IOC might consider, at its absolute discretion, as the zone of jurisdiction of a recognized national Olympic committee'. An agreement to promote the Catalan language through the Games was signed by the *Generalitat* and the *Comitè Organitzador*

Olímpic de Barcelona-92 (COOB) in April 1989, and a further agreement between the *Direcció General de Política Lingüística* and the *Secretari General de l'Esport* catalyzed linguistic normalization via the compilation of a series of 29 dictionaries and rules of the game dedicated to the Olympic sports. *TERMCAT* was central to this undertaking. In addition, the Andorran Government published a skiing glossary, and the Valencian *Generalitat*, a *pilota* lexicon. Such initiatives continue in the twenty-first century, benefiting from the greater access afforded by Web-based communication.

As the Games approached, so internal pressure increased to ensure that they reflected 'Catalan-ness' to the most visible extent possible. *Òmnium Cultural*, an entity created for the promotion of national culture, launched *Acció Olímpica*, a campaign that called for the maximum presence of the Catalan language and signs of identity (principally the flag), both in Olympic venues and as worn by Catalan athletes and the huge body of volunteers. Similar initiatives were adopted by the COC, the third party in the Catalan Parliament at the time, ERC, and other institutions of linguistic defence. These were countered variously state-wide by conservative and socialist politicians, sectors of the press, and academics such as Manuel Alvar, former director of the Spanish Royal Academy. Reactions in the foreign media ranged from enthusiasm and cheerful objectivity, bewilderment founded on historical ignorance, and outright aggression: Henri Haget wrote in the French magazine *Express* of Barcelona and the Catalan nationalists 'snubbing' Spain. The promotion of minority languages, as advocated by the Declaration of Linguistic Rights, was clearly anathema to this francophone apologist for monolingualism.[12]

Sporting culture

As in Britain, sport and its values make a contribution to the cultural milieu of the country and its constituent nations. In Catalonia, creative engagement with sport has been more readily visual, in the form of sculpture (e.g. Josep Clarà, Rosa Serra), photography, poster art, cartoons and other drawings. In the 1930s often short-lived graphical publications constituted hugely ambitious initiatives within a still relatively small Catalan publishing industry. Contemporary references to the clichés – both visual and textual – that had become an intrinsic part of depicting sport and leisure culture, such as female legs, Hellenic grace and the charms of mermaids, allow us to isolate the persistent problem of literature's relationship with sport.

---

[12] Haget, 1993, 'La flamme catalane', in *El català i els Jocs Olímpics*, p. 90.

Visual representation permits a vividness and theatricality that literary forms often do not; or at least, attempts at literary recreations of sport shrink back when compared with the experience of the real thing.[13] Clichés are symptomatic of this failure, and the dearth of good writing about sport, outside of journalism (good or bad), regularly gave rise to complaints on the part of both writers and scholars in the last century. Prominent authors and poets have flirted with sport; and the avant-garde years in Catalonia were particularly fruitful in this respect. In almost any portrayal of Catalonia in 1920s and 1930s, sport could be expected to feature as an ingredient of cosmopolitan modernity. In more recent years, it is football, and almost inevitably, FC Barcelona, that inspires most literature. Barça or some part thereof is favoured as cover art on books: no matter that it may play but a minor role in a single short story, the visual impact and attraction of the *blaugrana* is compelling.

The first specialized sporting press in Catalonia emerged in the final decade of the nineteenth century, and photographic coverage was tremendously influential in the popularization of cycling in particular. The graphic depiction enabled by photography also provoked consternation and calls for editorial censorship as women's involvement in sporting activities increased, and sports clothing becoming more specialized, fitted and revealing. Literary frivolity on sporting subjects, either of a wry tone or decidedly snobbish, was complemented by graphical humour on an impressive scale. Notable were *Xut!* (1922–36; and post-war, *El Once*, in Castilian), edited by Valentí Castanys, which brought together talented writers, illustrators and caricaturists in a self-proclaimed innovative approach to the sporting phenomenon.[14]

Most striking of all graphic representations of sport during the twentieth century is the tradition of poster art, be it celebratory, informative, appellative or propagandistic. One of the most significant exponents, the Valencian Josep Segrelles, was FC Barcelona's official poster artist, who went on to earn international acclaim for his work on a diversity of subject matter. Also Valencian, Josep Renau produced outstanding pieces for the putative 1936 Workers' Olympics and for the Las Arenas illuminated swimming pool in

---

[13] Baddiel, 2008, p. 3, makes a related point along national lines when he questions why 'no-one [has] ever written a great novel about football' while so many novels exist on or around the subject of baseball. He concludes that football – for fans – 'is just too dramatic, too genuinely exciting, too completely involving to fictionalize'. Thus any attempt to recreate sport in prose or on celluloid, suggests Baddiel, will be of limited success.

[14] Information provided by Suñé Ysamat and Porter Moix, 1988, p. 38.

Valencia. The latter is Art Deco in style and depicts a markedly androgynous female figure in a skin-tight bathing suit looking away from the foreground and to the (viewer's) right; framing her to the right and above are the stantion and lower board of a two-stage diving board, which extend almost to the top of the poster, skyscraper-like, silhouetted against a star-filled sky. On the top-most board, leaning forward and poised to dive, is another female figure. Her only limitation, it would seem, is the poster border, which almost appears to squash her into a position of readiness.

Poster art presents a most effective and economical conjunction of the sporting theme with other cultural, and here artistic, modes. As part of Coubertin's Olympic project, every host city was (and is) required to organize the Cultural Olympiad, an Olympic Festival of the Arts, to encompass the four years prior to, and including, the Games themselves. In Barcelona's case,

> it included spectacular projects, but it was also intended to provide an impulse for the creative energy of the city and to encourage contact between the cultures and peoples that were to take part in the Games. The Cultural Olympiad, then, was to carry on with the mission of the Olympic Games of the modern era to strengthen the ties between culture and sport in the framework of the Olympic ideals.[15]

Nothing in this generic statement betrays the irony intrinsic to Coubertin's desire: that while it is not difficult to bring people together and stage culture utilizing the Games in effect as a backdrop – or pretext – it is a considerably greater challenge to strengthen the ties between culture and sport in any sustainable way. The sport–art dichotomy remains peculiarly resistant to dissolution in many of its modalities, as prologuists of sports literature anthologies (for example) have repeated with a wearying regularity since the inception of the modern Games.

Barcelona's Cultural Olympiad included, among many more prominent events, the organization of the Third International Biennial of Sportsmen [sic] in Art, which brought together works by sportsmen and women who were also amateur artists. Other publications included booklets and catalogues on sport and the Catalan avant-garde, sport in the fine arts, and so on. In this light it is hard not to see the Olympic Cultural contract as little more than a purveyor of superficial cultural contacts whose relevance to the rest of the world (and possibly to the rest of the nation) outside the period of the Olympiad is minimal.

---

[15] COOB'92, 1992, p. 345.

Language and culture were ideologically exploited in 1992, of course, and the broader context of every-day, *blaugrana* reality dimmed, briefly. The history of Catalonia's (and Spain's) cultural engagement with sport, the tradition that retroactively and symbolically validated the hosting of the Games in the varied discourses of the Cultural Olympiad, fades from view upon the return to the lens of football. FC Barcelona Foundation's agreement with UNESCO, for example, clarifies that its aims are global and through this unique partnership it seeks to franchise its vision and propagate its identity as 'more than a club'. Surely, therefore, we have to ask: has the UNESCO/ Barça conception of the relationship between culture and sport definitively dethroned Coubertin's lofty if unworkable ideal for the Olympics? The sponsorship deal with the Qatar Foundation would suggest that this is the case.

Works Cited and Suggested Reading

The Olympics
Hargreaves, J. E. R. (2000) *Freedom for Catalonia? Catalan Nationalism, Spanish Identity and the Barcelona Olympic Games*. Cambridge: Cambridge University Press.
Institut de Sociolingüística Catalana Centre de Documentació (1993) *El català i els Jocs Olímpics*. Barcelona: Centre de Documentació de la Direcció General de Política Lingüística.
Pujadas, Xavier (ed.) (2006) *Catalunya i l'olimpisme: esport, identitat i jocs olímpics (1896–2006)*. Barcelona: COC Catalunya.
The following chapters in this collection are of particular interest:
Casanoves, J., 'Els orígens de l'olimpisme a Catalunya (1896–1914)', pp. 19–41; Finestres i Martínez, J., 'El naixement d'una consciència olímpica ciutadana (1989–2006)', pp. 114–132; Santacana i Torres, C., 'L'olimpisme català durant la dictadura franquista (1939–1975)', pp. 95–105; Soler Prat, S. and Zapata Vila, M., 'Olimpisme i gènere: l'olimpisme català i la participació femenina', pp. 154–165; Santacana i Torres, C., 'L'esport i l'olimpisme a Catalunya durant la transició a la democràcia (1975–1989)', pp. 107–113; Torrebadella, X., 'Renovació del discurs olímpic català en una conjuntura d'expansió del sistema esportiu (1930–1939)', pp. 69–93.
Pujadas, X. and Santacana C. (1990) *L'altra olimpíada. Barcelona '36: esport, societat i política a Catalunya (1900–1936)*. Barcelona: Llibres de l'Índex.
Raduà i Domènech, J. M. (2006) *Història de totes les seleccions esportives catalanes (1904–2005)*. Barcelona: [removed from list by publisher].
COOB'92 (1992) *Official Report of the XXV Olympiad Barcelona 1992*, 4 vols. Vol. II: *The Means: Objectives, Resources and Venues*. Barcelona: COOB'92.

Football
Baddiel, D. (7 June 2008) 'Why has no-one ever written a great novel about football?', *The Times*, 'Books', p. 3.
Barnils, R., Finestres, J., López A., Sabartés, J. S. and Torrecilla, F. (1999) *Història crítica del Futbol Club Barcelona 1899–1999*. Barcelona: Empúries.

Burns, J. (1999) *Barça: A People's Passion*. London: Bloomsbury.
Casals, D., Faura, N. and Torrent, A. M. (2007) 'Trenta anys de futbol en català', *Serra d'Or*, 573, pp. 25–7.
Lowe, S. (3 December 2007) 'Espanyol hold Barça to claim a share in Catalanism', http://blogs.guardian.co.uk/sport/2007/12/03/espanyol_hold_barca_to_claim_a.html
Salvador Duch, J. (2005) *Futbol, metàfora d'una guerra freda: estudi antropològic del Barça*. Barcelona: Proa.

Sport, culture, language and the media
Arenas, C. (2001) 'Carles Sindreu, caçador d'imatges poètiques', in *Carles Sindreu, centenari: 1900–2000*. Cadenas, J. M. and Arenas, C. (eds) Barcelona: Institució de les Lletres Catalanes, pp. 11–17.
Duran, L. (no date provided) '*Palestra*: cultura, civisme i esport per als joves', http://webs.racocatala.cat/cat1714/palestra.htm
Espinet i Burunat, F. (no date provided) 'La ràdio com oralitat a l'estiu del 1936 a Catalunya', http://republica-republicanisme.uab.es/docs/8e98d81f8217304975ccb23337bb5761.pdf
Faura, E. (2006) 'L'excursionisme del segle XXI', *Serra d'Or*, 554, pp. 18–21.
Faura i Pujol, N. (1998) *Futbol i llenguatge: la innovació lèxica a les cròniques i a les retransmissions futbolístiques*. Barcelona: Publicacions de l'Abadia de Montserrat.
González Aja, T. and Stumm, P. (2001) 'Spain', in *European Cultures in Sport: Examining the Nations and Regions*. Riordan, J. and Krüger R. (eds) Bristol: Intellect, pp. 123–138.
Haget, H. (7 August 1992) 'La flamme catalane', *L'Express*. Collected in *El català i els Jocs Olímpics*, pp. 90–2.
Real Mercadal, N. (1998) *El Club Femení i d'Esports de Barcelona: plataforma d'acció cultural*. Barcelona: Publicacions de l'Abadia de Montserrat.
Suñé Ysamat, A. and Porter Moix, J. (1988) *100 anys d'esport català*. Barcelona. Diari Avui.
Torrebadella, X. (2000) *L'esport català durant la Segona República: el Comissariat d'Educació Física i Esports de la Generalitat de Catalunya*. Barcelona: Col·legi de Llicenciats en Educació Física i Ciències de l'Activitat Física i de l'Esport de Catalunya.

Studies produced by official bodies or societies
Congrés de l'esport català (1995) *Educació i formació en l'esport. Novembre 1993–Febrer 1994*, 5 vols. Barcelona: Generalitat de Catalunya.
Generalitat de Catalunya (2001) 'Dossier: una potència esportiva', *Projecció Exterior*, 10, pp. 17–19.
Josep Renau: cartelismo (2008) Catalogue of the exhibition of Renau's poster art held from 6 February to 10 April 2001 (Alicante: Biblioteca Virtual Miguel de Cervantes, 2003), Ministerio de Educación y Ciencia, 'Media: Radio', http://recursos.cnice.mec.es/media/radio/bloque1/pag3.html#top
Simposi Llengua i Esport. Barcelona, 5 i 6 de novembre de 1992. Barcelona: Unió de Federacions Esportives Catalanes [UFEC], 1993.

7

The Music of Catalonia

TESS KNIGHTON

Most visitors to Catalonia will be familiar with the sight and sound of the *sardana*, the simple round dance performed to the distinctive accompaniment of the *cobla* throughout the country. Yet while a Catalan folk music tradition can be readily identified it is more problematic to define a Catalan school of composition even at the high point of musical activity in the first third of the twentieth century. Clearly, the disruption of the Civil War and Franco dictatorship and the resulting diaspora of many of the protagonists, notably Roberto Gerhard, Jaume Pahissa and Pau Casals, had a deleterious effect on the consolidation of any such school. This chapter will explore the increase in musical activity from the time of the Universal Exhibition in 1888 until 1936 as well as developments later in the twentieth century.

Cultural heritage and contexts for music-making are central to this study; but music and language are also inevitably intertwined. The extent to which both the flourishing of a distinctive musical culture and its subsequent disruption is inextricably linked to the history of the language has yet to be thoroughly explored but is, nonetheless, immediately evident. Once again, in this respect as in so many others, we are faced with the notion of the history of Catalonia repeating itself as the cultural situation in the early decades of the twentieth century has a precedent in a much earlier period, as is readily apparent in the chapters by Alexander Ibarz and Miquel Strubell.

From the second half of the fourteenth century, the Catalan–Aragonese court witnessed intense musical activity that coincided with a flowering of literature in the vernacular. This, too, was largely disrupted by political circumstances. When the ambitions of the first non-Catalan-speaking king, Alfons el Magnànim (1396–1458), focused on expansion in the Mediterranean and, in particular on taking Naples (which he entered in triumph in 1443), the royal court in Barcelona ceased to be the focal point for musical activity. Furthermore, with Castilian correspondingly established as the language of the court in Naples, surviving musical settings of Catalan verse dwindle and display few distinctive stylistic traits.

The suggestion that a language equals an identifiable musical culture is too simplistic to be entirely meaningful in isolation. For the fact is that in musical terms Catalonia was always far from isolated. In the fourteenth century, with the proximity of the papal court at Avignon until 1417 during the Great Western Schism, French musical culture – just as was the case with the Troubadours and verse – prevailed at court, with Joan I (r. 1387–96) himself attempting to compose *rondeaux* and *ballades*. During the same period, court minstrels travelled each year during Lent to the gatherings of instrumentalists in northern Europe to learn new repertory and new techniques from France, Flanders and Germany.

In the fifteenth century, musical exchange extended to Italy so that the repertory performed at the royal and other courts was strikingly international in profile. As such, composers born and reared locally were decidedly open to international influence and their works characterized by a high degree of eclecticism. The *ensaladas* of Mateu Fletxa (1481–1553) afford a good example of this fusion of international awareness and more local cultural heritage. Elements of French, Italian and indigenous Hispanic musical traditions are to be found in these compositions which, though a genre by no means exclusively cultivated by him, have a strongly individualistic stamp. Catalan and Castilian folksong (generally in simple chordal harmonizations) is cited in the context of a musical idiom that displays elements of the Franco-Netherlandish motet, French chanson and Italian madrigal.

This eclectic mix of musical styles and a striking openness to pan-European trends is, arguably, a feature of Catalan culture in general and music in particular. It is also later reflected in the works of composers of the decades around the turn of the twentieth century, influenced by the diverse and vibrant creative developments of their age even though their responses to these new directions remained decidedly individual. As Xosé Aviñoa, the single most important historian of Catalan music, has so aptly remarked:

> To talk of schools in this context is not to refer to groups conscious of a distinctive compositional task, but to isolated individuals who formed part of generations differentiated by cultural perspectives in a given moment, and who consequently maintained closer relations with those involved with literature, painting or theatre than with their musical colleagues.[1]

As in the fields of literature and art, Catalan composers show themselves to be fixated with the enigma of their own condition and yet also tend to look

---

[1] Aviñoa, 1991, p. 291.

outwards, away from Spain, for their inspiration. Richard Paine has identified 'an obsession with northern cultures and a tradition of eclecticism' as central to the experience.[2] And indeed heterogeneity is perhaps the single main feature that unites these musicians. We will attempt to isolate the amalgam of disparate threads of international musical developments with local cultural heritage in a broadly chronological survey; but it must be said that despite sterling efforts by Catalan music historians much remains to be studied in this fascinatingly diverse and complex field.

The Universal Exhibition in Barcelona and the musical *Renaixença*

At the time of the Universal Exhibition in 1888 musical activity was based largely on the strong operatic tradition at the *Teatre del Liceu* and *Teatre de la Santa Creu*. Traditionally given over to the Italian repertory, during the 1880s these theatres had begun to give performances of some of Wagner's operas, and *Lohengrin* was staged on the eve of the Universal Exhibition. The enthusiasm with which Wagner's music was received in Catalonia – leading to the foundation of the *Associació Wagneriana de Barcelona* in 1901 (which, remarkably, published all his libretti in Catalan) – was indicative of the region's openness to prevailing European trends; but it also chimed with the by then well established cultural ideals of the *Renaixença* as outlined in Dominic Keown's chapter on Contemporary Culture. Wagner's realization of a national operatic tradition based on German folklore appealed strongly to the spirit of collective rebirth and to composers such as Felip Pedrell (1841–1922) who, in the year after the Universal Exhibition, began work on his trilogy of Wagnerian-inspired operas, *Els Pirineus*.

Yet it was not only the consolidation of admiration for Wagner's operas that was reflected in the Universal Exhibition; it also occasioned the growing awareness of the lack of sustained musical activity outside the opera house. As elsewhere in the Iberian Peninsula, there was an absence of a symphonic tradition in Catalonia. Attempts at establishing a Philharmonic Society in the 1840s produced some orchestral concerts which, later in the 1880s, were held sporadically in the Liceu. The 1888 exhibition opened with a concert that offered the typical programme of the time: the overture to *Tannhäuser* and symphonic movements by Beethoven and Mendelssohn, including the Wedding March from *A Midsummer Night's Dream*. In this context, the limitations of presenting incomplete works to the public and the lack of opportunity for Catalan composers to have their works heard are evident.

---

[2] Paine, 1989, p. 9.

As such, although internal divisions and outside pressures were to limit its lifespan, the formation of the *Societat Catalana de Concerts* (1892–7) was to revolutionize concert programming with symphonies by Beethoven performed complete. There was, in turn, a widening of the orchestral repertory from Bach to Berlioz and even Grieg. Similarly, a close collaborative association was established with the leading figures of the Franco-Belgian school of Vincent d'Indy, Ernest Chausson and Matthieu Crickboom, who was to become musical director of the *Societat Filharmònica* concert seasons that took place in Barcelona from 1897 to 1905. A series of *Concerts Històrics* in 1895 brought works by Mozart, Haydn, Weber, Schumann and Bizet to the attention of concert-goers; and the call for opportunities for Catalan composers was also heeded. Works by Bonaventura Frígola (1829–1901), José García Robles (1835–1910), Antoni Nicolau (1858–1933), Enric Morera (1865–1942) and Lluís Millet (1867–1941) were heard in the series of the 1890s. Of these, perhaps the most important was Morera, who had studied in Brussels, and whose symphonic poem based on Verdaguer's epic, *L'Atlàntida*, which also inspired Falla, met with great success.

Morera and Millet were key figures in the other major musical development stemming from the Universal Exhibition: the emergence of a strong choral tradition in Catalonia. Various groups had flourished in the mid-nineteenth century, largely thanks to Josep Anselm Clavé (1824–1874), whose philanthropic initiatives to bring music to the working classes through choral singing had brought about the creation of *La Fraternidad* in 1850 and the *Associació Euterpense* ten years later. Choral societies spread throughout the region and other initiatives sprang up, notably the *Orfeó Barcelonès*, founded in 1854 and funded by the Town Hall. By the time of the 1888 exhibition the *Associació Euterpense* had itself divided into two branches, and choral singing in Catalonia had lost its way.

This was confirmed in the two choir-based competitions held during the Universal Exhibition in Barcelona. Of the five mixed choirs competing only one, the *Societat Coral Barcino*, was Catalan; and that was knocked into third place by choirs from Bilbao and Limoges. The society prize went to a choir from Corunna, even though most of the thirty or so societies that had entered were Catalan. The poor standard of Catalan choirs in comparison with their competitors galvanized Millet and his colleague Amadeu Vives (1871–1932) into action. A few years later, in September 1891, they founded the *Orfeó Català*, originally a male-voice choir, to which a female-voice section was added in 1897.

In contrast to Clavé's choirs, the *Orfeó Català* was essentially a middle-class organization that found eager support from the rapidly burgeoning bourgeoisie at the turn of the twentieth century. Not only did the choir become the natural partner to the newly invigorated symphonic presence in Barcelona, performing in the great works of Beethoven and Wagner, it also functioned as an effective conduit for the expression of Catalan nationalism. While Clavé had regularly performed the hymn '¡Gloria a España!' and his own translation of the Marseillaise, Millet produced a harmonized version of the Catalan folksong 'Els Segadors'/ The Reapers and his own setting of the poet Maragall's 'El cant de la senyera'/ Song of the Flag (1896), which became veritable national anthems.

Other composers followed suit: García Robles, for example, composed a national hymn, 'La bandera catalana'/ The Catalan Flag, for the *Orfeó Català*. Together with the fostering of works by contemporary Catalan composers, the recuperation and performance of Catalan folksongs formed a central plank of the *Orfeó Català*'s activities and would later result in the vast project entitled *Obra del Cançoner Popular de Catalunya*/ Popular Songbook of Catalonia (from 1922). As Millet wrote in an open letter published in *La Renaixença* in 1897:

> With the ferment of popular song, we can see how all Catalan musicians, old and new, are rejuvenated and, re-baptized in the baptism of the art of their lands, they burn the garb of the stifling round of Italianism and 'Gounod-ism' that has so harmed the style of many of our more talented musicians.[3]

Millet was not only a nationalist, but also deeply religious and responsible for the programming of large-scale sacred works by Bach, Mozart and Beethoven, as well as the sacred polyphony of the Renaissance. As editor of the *Revista Musical Catalana* (1904–36), he further encouraged research and debate, though his essentially conservative stance left him increasingly peripheral to more modern and forward-looking developments.

This was also true of the polymath Felip Pedrell; and yet these same developments could not have occurred without his contribution, particularly as a teacher of composition. Pedrell was trained as a choirboy at Tortosa Cathedral by Joan Antoni Nin i Serra (d. 1867), a member of the Caecilian movement with a strong interest in early polyphony. Pedrell moved to Barcelona in 1873, where he heard the première of his first opera, *L'ultimo Abenzaraggio*, the following year. In the mid-to-late 1870s he studied in Rome and Paris, before settling in Barcelona in 1882, where he quickly became involved in all aspects of the city's musical life. The interest in

---

[3] As cited in the *Diccionario de la Música Española e Hispanoamericana* (*DMEH*), 1999–2002, vol. 7, 2000, p. 579.

musical heritage instilled by Nin i Serra led him to explore historical as well as folk traditions. Products of this were the popular songbook *Cancionero Musical Popular Español* and an essay on ancient and modern Spanish musicians (1888).

This was followed by a speech in the *Ateneu de Barcelona* as part of a series entitled 'The State of Spanish Culture – particularly Catalan – in the Fifteenth Century' (at which an ad hoc choir performed works by Juan del Encina) and the eight volumes of the *Hispaniae Schola Musica Sacra* (1894–6), which included editions of works by Morales, Guerrero and Cabezón, as well as the *opera omnia* of Tomás Luis de Victoria (1902–13). Pedrell also published a series of articles on sixteenth- and seventeenth- century Catalan musicians entitled 'Músichs vells de la terra/ Ancient musicians of this land' for the *Revista Musical Catalana* in 1904–10; and in 1908–9 he produced his catalogue of the collection of rare music books belonging to the musician and bibliophile Joan Carreras i Dagas (1828–1900), which formed the basis of the music section at the *Biblioteca de Catalunya*.

The pan-Hispanic profile of Pedrell's prolific contribution to both ethnomusicology and historical musicology is apparent also in the nationalist ideology underlying his compositions, an ideology expressed most clearly in his compositional manifesto, *Por nuestra música/* For our music (1891). Pedrell sought not only to create a national opera tradition along Wagnerian lines but also to develop a genuinely Spanish (i.e. not simply Catalan) musical idiom that would be rooted in folk tradition but go beyond it to reflect historical and contemporary developments in art music (looking to Wagner in the first instance). As he was to elucidate: 'The common heritage of a truly national musical idiom is found not only in folksong, or in the primitive period, but also in the time and creations of art music.'[4]

Despite the success of *Els Pirineus* (premièred at the Liceu in 1902), Pedrell's nationalist trilogy failed to establish a national operatic tradition. The opera was based on a Catalan text by Victor Balaguer (1824–1901) who had done so much to promote Catalan culture in the mid-nineteenth century, including the restoration of the *Jocs Florals* in 1859. Thus, both the choice of poet and the subject of *Els Pirineus* (the Catalans' successful struggle to secure freedom from papal rule in the thirteenth century, as mentioned in the chapter by Alexander Ibarz) resonated with the nationalist ideals of the late *Renaixença*. *El Comte Arnau* (1904) is likewise steeped in Catalan heritage, being based on an old Catalan ballad whose melody is woven into the fabric of the opera. Yet the intervening opera, *La Celestina* (1902), draws on a

---

[4] Cited in Paine, 1989, p. 14. My translation of this passage differs slightly from his.

Castilian text with no specific reference to Catalonia. And in all these works, as well as others, popular melodies from all the regions of Spain are introduced in an overarching desire to create a national (i.e. state-wide) musical idiom.

Pedrell's influence in creating a nationalist musical agenda that was essentially Spanish rather than Catalan can also be seen in the works of two renowned Catalan pianist-composers: Isaac Albéniz (1860–1909) and Enrique Granados (1867–1916). Albéniz, a child prodigy who travelled to all the major centres of music-making and who studied in Brussels at the age of sixteen, met Pedrell in 1883. A series of piano pieces based on the folk melodies and rhythmic patterns of various regions followed, resulting in the *Suite Española* (opus 47 and 97) and *Iberia*, a set of twelve pieces of Andalusian inspiration. While he did write a piece entitled *Catalonia* (1899) and a Catalan *curranda* forms one of the regional miniatures in the *Suite Española*, it would be problematic to consider him an exclusively Catalan composer.

In the same way Granados, born in Lleida, studied with Pedrell and others in Barcelona as well as in Paris. He was likewise inspired to draw on a cultural heritage that was more Spanish than specifically Catalan. His imagination, for example, was captured by the Castilian art tradition as in his *Tonadillas* for voice and piano (1910), and his most renowned work for piano, the *Goyescas* (1911). All three composers reflect a clear mentality of the late *Renaixença*. Despite their regenerative devotion to Catalonia they still considered their overarching nation to be Spain and reflected this sentiment in their compositions. Subsequent generations of musicians, while acknowledging their creative debt to the trio, would be much more emphatic in the expression of their *Catalan* national consciousness.

From *modernista* to *noucentista*[5]

In this way, Pedrell's pan-Hispanic approach to the musical heritage of Spain was linked more closely to the mentality of the *Renaixença* than to *Modernisme*. With Barcelona's musical life completely transformed by the early twentieth century – not least by the building of Domènech i Montaner's *Palau de la Música* (1905–8), home of the *Orfeó Català* and with a concert season of international reach – a new generation of composers and musicians

---

[5] *Noucentisme*: literally a school of the nineteen-hundreds (1906–23) emerging from *Modernisme*, which, rejecting the decadent individualism of its progenitor, privileged a more conservative, civic and classical articulation of aestheticism. It counted on considerable patronage and promotion from official institutions. See the chapter on Contemporary Culture by Dominic Keown for more detailed information.

began to look not only to Catalan heritage but also to the wider world outside Bayreuth. While Pedrell had championed the music of Wagner, helping to establish a more serious concert-going tradition along the lines of the major European musical centres, composers such as Millet and Enric Morera, along with their counterparts in art, architecture and literature, deliberately sought to extend Catalan creative horizons to the latest compositional trends in Europe.

The *modernista* mindset sought to create a thoroughly *national* cultural identity for Catalonia (i.e. not Spanish) that was entirely actual and in keeping with the latest developments elsewhere on the continent. As such, musicians and composers sought to clear the way for these new and more universal tendencies by rejecting Pedrell's double-edged sword of traditional Catalan music and the Wagnerian ideal of a national opera. As regards folk music, Manuel de Montaliu threw down the gauntlet for Catalan composers in *El poble català/ The Catalan People*, the organ of the *Centre Nacionalista Republicà* (published 1904–18):

> Enough! We've abused the folkloric tradition for too long now. Instead of harmonizations and variations (*glossas*), let's create something new. Instead of nice little Catalan songs, let's write European-style symphonies and tone poems; these, too, will be Catalan, since our ethnic origins will never desert us.[6]

However, liberation from Pedrell's influence took many years. Writing in *La Noche* in 1929, the composer Manuel Blancafort (1897–1987) expressed the views circulating among *modernistes* in the trenchant manner that earned him the reputation of an *enfant terrible*:

> In my opinion, a rejection of Wagner is the first of the commandments that modern Catalan music needs to obey (…) Some of us here in Catalonia are more inclined towards Paris than Berlin. It's not a question of gallicising our music, but I do believe that if Berlin comes via Paris, this is the right direction for it to reach Catalonia, where it must be definitively established. Our music must be truly Catalan, but we must reject the Catalan of folk tradition (…) There is more to Catalonia today than shepherds, peasant girls and wild thyme. The Catalan should not appear to the foreigner as a curious, picturesque person, as in nineteenth-century comedies of manners. Our music has to be something more than *sardanas* and folksongs; it must tell of Catalan heritage in a European idiom.[7]

---

[6] *DMEH*, vol. 8, 2001, p. 354.
[7] *DMEH*, vol. 2, 1999, p. 494.

An emphasis on post-Wagnerian international trends rather than regional concerns and on new compositional directions, whether from Brussels or Paris (or, some years later, Vienna), was thus the hallmark of the composers active in Catalonia from Morera to Gerhard (1896–1970), though *sardanas* continued to be composed and melodic motifs and rhythmic patterns from folksong still inflected their works.

In the early 1880s, Morera, who had spent his childhood in Argentina, studied violin and piano in Barcelona as well as, on Albéniz's advice, harmony with Pedrell. Following a brief visit to Argentina in 1885, he travelled to Brussels where he established strong connections with the Franco-Belgian school of composers formed by d'Indy, Chausson, Ysaÿe and Crickboom. D'Indy was subsequently to visit Barcelona several times, including for the *Concerts Històrics* series of 1895 and to attend the *Festes Modernistes* organized by Santiago Rusiñol in Sitges. Crickboom also became a regular conductor of the *Societat Filharmònica* concerts and a leading figure in Catalan musical life.

On Morera's return to Barcelona in 1890 to play in the Liceu orchestra, he was quickly and warmly welcomed in *modernista* circles. Rusiñol painted his portrait conducting the *Societat Coral Catalunya Nova*, which the composer founded in 1896 to continue the tradition of workers' choral societies and, in part, to counterbalance the more bourgeois and conservative *Orfeó Català*. As early as 1893 he had works performed by the *Associació Musical de Barcelona* ('Danse de gnomes') and the *Societat Catalana de Concerts* ('Introducció a l'Atlàntida'); these recently formed promoters afforded younger Catalan composers such as Morera opportunities for their works to be heard.

Perhaps the composer's most ambitious project, however, was to attempt to create a school of Catalan opera, both through his own compositions of the later 1890s (*Jesús de Natzareth*; *Les monges de Sant Aimau/* The Nuns of Saint Aimau; *La fada/* The Fairy; and *L'alegria que passa/* Happiness which passes) and the establishment of the *Teatre Líric Català* at the Tívoli. The first season of Catalan light opera took place in February 1901 and included works by Morera himself, Granados, La Peyra, Bartolí and Bal i Gay; but the venture, supported financially by Morera's father, was a complete failure. He enjoyed considerable success, however, with works such as *El Comte Arnau/* Count Arnau (1905–6; text by Carner) and *La santa espina/* The Holy Thorn (1907; text by Guimerà) performed in the context of the *Audicions Graner*, the forum for modern music in Barcelona of which he was musical director from 1905 to 1908.

In that year Morera left Barcelona once again to travel to Argentina. But on his return he continued to write operas, including *La font d'albera/*The

Fountain of Oliana (1922; text by Josep Sebastià Pons) and *Don Joan de Serrallonga* (1922; text by Víctor Balaguer). His approximately fifty stage works in Catalan have been described as including some of the 'most representative of the *modernista* and *noucentista* aesthetic'.[8] Yet, despite his links with the leading figures of the *modernista* movement and his attempts to establish a popular genre capable of transcending the local (*género chico*), Morera's star began to fade. Appointed deputy director of the *Escola Municipal de Música* on his return from Argentina, his pupils included some of the leading figures of the next generation, such as Jaume Pahissa (1880–1969) and Montsalvatge (1912–2002); yet when the directorship fell vacant in 1930 the post was given not to Morera but to Millet. Not a single work by Morera was programmed for the meeting of the International Society for Contemporary Music in Barcelona in 1936; and he spent his retirement composing *sardanes*. A revival of *La fada* in Barcelona in 1992 met with considerable success, indicating that Morera's role in developing Catalan music theatre from Pedrell's Wagnerian forays to a more modern, symbolist approach to the text remains largely to be explored.

By 1920, Barcelona offered a flourishing environment for musicians and composers, a situation that was to persist until the Civil War. Performances of chamber and symphonic music had been transformed with the foundation in 1910 of the *Orquestra Sinfònica de Barcelona* by Joan Lamote de Grignon (1872–1949) and the *Orquestra de l'Associació d'Amics de la Música* in 1916, directed by Francesc Pujol. The string sections of this orchestra were led by the four members of the *Quartet Renaixement*, which had been formed in 1911 by the violinist, conductor and composer Eduard Toldrà (1895–1962).

This quartet had led the 1912 *Cicle Històric del Quartet de Corda*/ Historic Cycle of the String Quartet, which presented works from Haydn and Mozart to Smetana and Borodin; and in April 1916 it performed the complete Beethoven quartets for the first time in Catalonia. Toldrà's one-act opera, *El giravolt de maig*/ The Somersault of May (1928: text by Josep Carner, décor by the painter Xavier Nogués) was a landmark of musical *Noucentisme*. With its eighteenth-century setting the work fell easily into the fashionable neo-classical mould and broke with Wagnerian and earlier *verismo* tendencies to plant a new cornerstone for Catalan opera. Into the midst of this burgeoning musical activity the cellist Pau Casals (1876–1973), who had already done much to promote chamber music by playing in Crickboom's

---

[8] *DMEH*, vol. 7, 2000, p. 818.

quartet and in the concerts of the *Societat Filharmónica*, returned from touring the world with an established international reputation.

Although Casals collaborated with Lamote de Grignon and Pujol in their orchestral endeavours, he determined to set up his own orchestra, with two concert seasons a year and with the intention of covering the core orchestral repertory from Bach to Stravinsky as well as promoting new works by international and local composers. In the seventeen years of its existence, the *Orquestra Pau Casals* performed well over three hundred concerts with guest conductors and soloists of international renown (including Schoenberg, Webern, Strauss, Zemlinsky and Stravinsky); its local repertory included works by Albéniz, Granados, Falla, Lamote de Grignon, Morera, Pahissa and Toldrà.

Casals strove constantly to broaden the reach of classical music beyond the middle classes. Following the spirit of Clavé, he formed the *Associació Obrera de Concerts*/ Workers' Concert Association, which was run by its own committee and had its own periodical, *Fruicions*. Their first concert season took place in 1925–6, and their last performance, held in the Liceu on 13 September 1936 during the first months of the Civil War, openly proclaimed their Republican sympathies. The programme began with the Funeral March from *Twilight of the Gods* and ended with Beethoven's *Eroica* Symphony. Casals continued to fight the cause of freedom for the rest of his life. Indeed, his oratorio *El pessebre*/ The Crib, set to a text by Joan Alavedra (1896–1981), was begun in 1943 with the intention that it would be performed with the restoration of democracy. Finally completed in 1960, it was in fact performed in December 1967 in the *Palau de la Música*.

While Lamote de Grignon's *Orquestra Simfònica de Barcelona* declined with the establishment of the *Orquestra de Pau Casals*, he nevertheless continued to be a key figure in the musical life of Barcelona. From 1914 he converted the *Banda Municipal* into a symphonic wind band that incorporated the unique sounds of the Catalan *cobla* (the treble and tenor shawms or *chirimías*). He also continued to conduct and make arrangements mainly of Catalan and European contemporary composers for this ensemble until the end of the Civil War. When Richard Strauss was in Barcelona in 1925 he conducted the *Banda Municipal* in an arrangement of his *Tod und Verklärung*, which he liked so much that two years later he toured with it in Germany.

Lamote de Grignon played an important role at the 1929 Barcelona Universal Exhibition – on this occasion a celebration of a flourishing musical environment far removed from the limited events held in 1888 – conducting the first of his *Concerts Sinfònics Populars* at the opening. His *Banda Municipal* also inaugurated the proceedings of the XIVth Festival of the International Society for Contemporary Music (ISCM) held, together with the IIIrd Conference of the International Musicological Society (ISM), in Barcelona in April 1936. Indeed, Lamote de Grignon formed part of the committee for the ISCM, together with the composers Anton Webern and Bloeslaw Wotowicz, the musicologist Edward Dent (first Professor of Music at the University of Cambridge) and the conductor Ernst Ansermet.

Civil War and the diaspora

These prestigious international events marked the apogee of musical activity in Barcelona; the outbreak of Civil War disrupted almost every aspect of its advanced, internationally based and forward-looking musical scene. In the years of the Republic the city had witnessed an extraordinary level of musical activity. Home-grown institutions and ensembles mixed with international visitors of the calibre of Schoenberg (1931), Diaghilev's *Ballets Russes* (1933) and Stravinsky who, in 1936, conducted a programme of his own works, including *Apollon Musagète*, the *Capriccio* for piano and orchestra, the *Symphony of Psalms* and *The Firebird*. The XIVth Festival of the ISCM (April 1936) witnessed the première of Alban Berg's Violin Concerto. Also performed for the first time in Spain were fragments of *Wozzeck*, Ernst Krenek's cantata *Karl V* and Gerhard's ballet *Ariel*. The programme included in turn new works by Jacques Ibert, Walter Piston, Frank Martin and Albert Roussel; and Benjamin Britten was among the many performers at the festival.

Sadly, this has to be the 'what if' moment in Catalan music history: all was to vanish during the Civil War. The Fascist victory in 1939 inevitably resulted in a diaspora of performers and composers. Some of them, like Lamote de Grignon, Frederic Mompou (1893–1987) and Joaquim Homs (1906–2003), returned to settle in Barcelona in the 1940s; but many others, such as Pau Casals, Jaume Pahissa and Roberto Gerhard, remained in exile. Casals was able to maintain an international career as a cellist living in southern France. Lamote de Grignon spent some years in Valencia as conductor of the newly founded *Orquestra Municipal* (1943–7). He returned to Barcelona in 1948 to conduct the *Orquestra Filharmònica* in a repertory with a strong Catalan emphasis, including works by Vives, Albéniz, Granados, Garreta and Toldrà and orchestral arrangements of Catalan folksongs. While this represented a way to keep the Catalan pre-war tradition alive in Francoist Spain, Pahissa was one of the first composers to draw closer to expressionism and to experiment with twelve-tone techniques; though – as was the case with Gerhard – this was more an inevitable consequence of post-Wagnerian writing than a deliberate study of Schoenberg's theories.

Pahissa's earlier works, such as the opera *Gala Placidia* (1913; text by Guimerà) and his setting of Verdaguer's *Canigó* – as well as orchestral pieces such as the *Overture on a popular Catalan theme* (1917) – refract the influence of Strauss and Mahler through a Catalan optic. By the mid-1920s, however, he was experimenting with different tonalities. This included polytonality, atonality and intertonality, a creation of his own, which first found expression in his *Sinfonía para cuerda sola/* Symphony for One String and *Suite intertonal*. In his explanation of intertonality Pahissa wrote: 'Remember that *dissonance* does not mean "to sound bad" but "to sound twice", and in fact dissonant harmony is much richer than consonance.'[9]

In February 1928 Pahissa's opera *La princesa Margarida* (based on *La presó de Lleida* and with a libretto by Adrià Gual) was premièred at the Liceu; and his importance had been recognized the previous year by a concert in his honour organized by the *Associació de Música de Cámera* in the *Palau de la Música*. With the outbreak of Civil War Pahissa moved to Argentina and, like Falla, lived the rest of his life in Buenos Aires, composing relatively little and with limited influence on developments back home.

Roberto Gerhard was in many ways the leading light of the so-called 'Generation of the Republic' or 'Barcelona group', which also included Mompou, Toldrá and Baltasar Samper (1888–1966).[10] Born in Valls in 1896 to a Swiss father and a German mother, Gerhard studied in Munich until the outbreak of the First World War. On his return to Barcelona, he studied piano with Granados and Frank Marshall, and became Pedrell's last pupil, though his earliest works display little if any Wagnerian influence. The song cycle *El alumbramiento maravilloso de Schaharazada* (1916–17; texts by J. M. López-Picó), for example, is in the German *Lied* tradition, while elements of Debussy, Ravel and Falla are prominent in pieces such as the Trio for violin, cello and piano. By 1921, however, his *Dos Apuntes/* Two Notes for piano reveals the clear influence of Schoenberg's *Sechs kleine Klavierstücke*, op. 19; and Gerhard sent this and his *Siete Haiku* on poems by Josep Maria Junoy (1922) to the Austrian composer with whom he subsequently studied from 1923 to 1928. Gerhard embraced Schoenberg's ideas on serialism (expounded in the *Harmonielhere* [1922]) and began to experiment with the technique, notably in the *Wind Quintet* of 1928, although this was combined with the contrasts of textures and oblique references to folk melodies characteristic of many of his works.

The Catalan was responsible for the concert of Schonberg's music in the *Palau de la Música* in 1928 at which *Pierrot Lunaire* was performed, a work

---

[9] *DMEH*, vol. 8, 2001, p. 356.
[10] Samper also went into exile at the end of the Civil War, first to Toulouse and then to Mexico, along with Spanish musicians such as Rodolfo Haelffter, Adolfo Salazar and Jesús Bal i Gay.

that Blancafort considered to be 'inhuman music'.[11] Gerhard's own works caused a scandal in a concert in Barcelona the following year, but he gradually won over at least the more progressive composers. His *Sis Cançons Populars Catalanes*/ Six Popular Songs (1928), the première of which was conducted by Webern at the ISCM Festival in Vienna in 1932, did much to make his music more widely acceptable at home. His role as Pedrell's successor as head of the music section of the *Biblioteca de Catalunya* drew him in the direction of musicological research, evinced by his recuperation of *La Merope* (1743) by the eighteenth-century Catalan composer Domènec Terradelles, and Soler's quintets for harpsichord and strings. Of the works he composed before the Civil War, the cantata *L'alta naixença del rei en Jaume*/ The High Birth of King James I (1931), his ballet *Ariel* (1934) in collaboration with Miró and Foix, and the *Albada, interludi i dansa*/ Song at Dawn, Interlude and Dance (1936) are important contributions that point to the innovative and original directions he would follow in exile, first in France and then in Cambridge.

Montsalvatge remembers being particularly impressed by *Ariel* at its first performance in 1936. Yet after the Civil War Gerhard's works, published in England, were heard only sporadically in Catalonia and his influence was felt mainly in the works of his only pupil from the early 1930s, Joaquim Homs. It is impossible to know whether, had Gerhard been able to remain in Barcelona, his development as a composer would have followed a totally different course. Many of the essential features of his music were established by the time he left Catalonia; and regional connections continued to inspire him, notably in his *Cancionero de Pedrell*/ Songbook of Pedrell (1941), although inevitably his works were increasingly open to other influences such as developments in electronic music.

The disruption of musical activity in Barcelona – and the disappearance of both Gerhard and Pahissa from the scene – profoundly affected progression even with the return of Mompou, Blancafort and Homs in the 1940s. Despite the continuity represented by their settings of Catalan poets, it proved impossible to recapture the sense of openness and experimentation of the Republican years.

Picking up the threads: the Liceu, Mompou, Blancafort and Homs

At the heart of musical life in Barcelona both before and after the Civil War was the *Gran Teatre del Liceu*. The artistic policy forged by the first post-war

[11] *DMEH*, vol. 2, 1999, p. 495.

intendant, Joan Antoni Pàmias, established the Liceu as a major international house, with a correspondingly wide range of repertory, from Handel to Kurt Weill. Interspersed between the staples of the operatic world, however, were performances of the works of Catalan composers, including Toldrà's *El giravolt de maig* (1948), Lamote de Grignon's *Cabeza de dragón/ Dragon Head* (1960) and Montsalvatge's *El gato con botas/ Puss in Boots* (1948) and *Una voz en off/ Voice Off* (1962). As in the 1920s and 1930s, post-war productions at the Liceu brought the great operatic performers of the world to Barcelona, and also witnessed the emergence of a strong tradition for locally trained opera singers, several of whom would achieve international renown. Victòria dels Angels (1923–2005) was born in Barcelona and studied at the Conservatory there, making her debut (as Mimi in Puccini's *La bohème*) at the Liceu in 1941 while still an eighteen-year-old student; four years later she made her professional debut as the Countess in Mozart's *The Marriage of Figaro*. The tenor Josep Carreras (b. 1946) was still more of a prodigy, making his debut aged 11, as the Trujamán in Falla's *El retablo de maese Pedro*. Carreras's first principal role as an adult was in 1970 as Gennaro in Donizetti's *Lucrezia Borgia*, with his compatriot Montserrat Caballé (b. 1933) in the title role. Following her studies at the Liceu Conservatory, Caballé joined the opera house in Basel in the later 1950s, and it was only in 1962 that she made her début at the Liceu, in the title role of Strauss's *Arabella*. Her 1988 recording of 'Barcelona' with Queen's Freddie Mercury became the anthem of the 1992 Olympic Games and, in its own peculiarly international-rock way, a successor to the Catalan hymns of the late nineteenth century.

The post-war period is characterized in compositional terms by three composers who experienced the Civil War but whose careers all developed on individual lines as a result. The sense of picking up the threads broken by war marked their creativity and enforced a strictly peculiar creative progression through the cultural Hades of Francoist Spain. This may explain the apparent paradox of the failure of their compositions to gel into a school despite the weight of their individual influence. Encouraged by Granados, Mompou studied in Paris from 1911 until his return to Barcelona to fulfil his military service. He returned to Paris in 1920 where his former teacher, Ferdinand Motte-Lacroix, organized a concert of his music that met with considerable success.

Although reserved by nature, Mompou became an established figure in Paris where he knew the Catalan pianist Ricardo Viñes (1875–1943), Falla, Ravel, Poulenc, Milhaud and Roussel, and became familiar with the music of Villa-Lobos, Bartók and Stravinsky. Back in Barcelona in 1931, Mompou was one of the members of the short-lived association of *Compositors*

Independents de Catalunya, alongside Lamote de Grignon, Blancafort and Samper. In 1936 Mompou left again for Paris and did not return to Barcelona until 1941, when César de Mendoza Lassalle's newly formed *Orquesta Filharmónica de Barcelona* performed his *Suburbis* (1916–17, originally for piano), which immediately brought him recognition within Spain.

Mompou struck up a friendship with the poet and editor Josep Janés (1913–1939) and set a number of his poems to music in the cycle *Combat del somni*/ Combat of the Dream (1942–51). Yet Mompou's career has been described as one of continual *recomençament* with several long-term compositional projects interrupted and renewed over a number of years. Perhaps the most clear examples are his *Preludis* (1927–44), *Música Callada*/ Silent Music (1959–67: inspired by the verse of San Juan de la Cruz), and the *Cançons i danses* (1921–72), which were begun in his years in Paris, continued in the 1950s and picked up again towards the end of his life. These works represent the symbiosis between his essentially European (mainly French) musical language and Catalan melodic and rhythmic elements that were absorbed into his works.

Mompou had a decisive influence on Blancafort at an early stage in his career, introducing him to works by Debussy, Ravel and Stravinsky – as well as *Les Six* – and sharing the ideal of creating a new universal Catalan music that would be free of Wagnerian domination and superficial Catalan colour. Yet Blancafort, unlike Gerhard, was not enticed by the developments of the Second Viennese School, preferring the humour and irony of the works of *Les Six*, especially those of Eric Satie and Jean Cocteau; Stravinsky's *Pulcinella* made its mark, as is clear from his *El parc d'atraccions*/ Funfare (1920–4). Neoclassical elements are also present in Blancafort's *Pastoral* (1926), *Les ombres perennes* (1934), performed at the ISCM Festival, and even in *Preludi, ària i giga* (1944).

Blancafort did not leave Barcelona during the Civil War but was forced to keep a low profile and to work in isolation. This period resulted in a shift away from the ironic tone of his pre-war works to a more sober and conceptual approach in a more concise yet dense idiom. This is perhaps best represented by the *Simfonia en tres temps* and *Rapsodia catalana* for cello and orchestra (both 1953), the *Solemne cantata Virgo Maria* (1965) and *Evocaciones* (1969). As with Mompou, reference to traditional Catalan music is deeply embedded in a largely French-inspired musical language; in his *Matí de festa a Puiggraciós*/ Morning Fair at Puiggraciós (1929), Blancafort cites the popular *Cançó d'Isabel* but in a manner far removed from the nationalist spirit of Pedrell.

French music initially fascinated Joaquim Homs, although his period of study with Gerhard in the early 1930s also introduced him to Schoenberg's twelve-tone techniques. This led him to experiment with serialism, notably in his *String Quartet no. 1* (1938), but he too began to forge his own path. Homs was to take the neutralization of the tonal system by the use of a series as a starting-point rather than a strictly adhered to procedure. Even symphonic works like his *Homenatge a Webern* (1959) take a single basic series as the source for thematic nuclei and contrast such serially derived themes with others of a modal nature. Similar techniques are developed in his *Wind Quintet no. 2* (1971), dedicated to his teacher Gerhard. Like other Catalan composers whose lives straddled the Civil War, Homs's settings of Catalan poets inevitably tended to be concentrated in the earlier part of his career when, in the 1920s and 1930s, he set poems by Sánchez-Juan, Salvat-Papasseit and Carner. Espriu's verse was a source of inspiration after the war, though his setting of *Cementiri de Sinera* (1952) was not premièred until 1961 in Hamburg; and he only returned to the poet in 1975 for his *Tríptic de Setmana Santa*.

Homs was also an important figure in picking up the threads of Barcelona's musical life. Before the Civil War he had been actively involved in the contemporary music concerts – the *Estudis de Música Contemporánea* – organized by Ramón Sastre from 1927 to 1936; indeed, one of these sessions had been dedicated to his music. After the war, he was involved in the cycles of concerts organized by Josep Bartomeu in *El Jardí dels Taronges*/ Orange Garden in Pedralbes between 1948 and 1958. In 1967 he founded the *Conjunt Català de Música Contemporània* and became the first president of the *Associació Catalana de Compositors*, legally approved a mere nine months before Franco's death in 1975. Despite his involvement in the promotion of new Catalan music Homs tended to work alone apart from discernible trends and contact with other groups. His idiom is highly distinctive although his work can be considered characteristically Catalan in its eclecticism, sharing the tendency to extract the maximum from minimal forces and forms already noted in the compositions of Mompou and Blancafort.

Montsalvatge and the Avant-Garde

Like Homs, Montsalvatge was an important figure for the avant-garde composers of the second half of the twentieth century. At the *Escola Municipal de Música* he studied with Millet, Morera and Pahissa, winning a composition prize in 1933 that enabled him to travel, like so many Catalans before him, to Paris where he became well acquainted with the works of Ravel, Satie, Milhaud, Poulenc and Borodin. Like others of his generation, he rejected Wagner to compose works in a French or Stravinskian vein: echoes of Stravinsky's *The Soldier's Tale* can be heard in an early work, the *Petita suite burlesca* (1936). Similarly, the Civil War interrupted his burgeoning career – he won a prize at the ISCM Festival in 1936 – and he resumed by following a rather different path.

In Montsalvatge's case, an initial experiment with polytonality (*Tres divertimentos* for piano, 1941) gave way to his West Indian-inspired works: first *Ritmos* for piano (1942) then the *Cinco canciones negras* (1945–6) followed by his *Cuarteto Indiano* of 1952. This strand of Caribbean exoticism can also be observed in the works of painters and architects who returned from America in the years after the Civil War; and Mompou was to collaborate with writer Néstor Luján and painter Josep María Prim on the *Álbum de havaneres* published in 1948. This collection gathered together some of the many *havaneres* that had reached Spain following the loss of Cuba in 1898 – a colony that had counted on a notable Catalan presence. Luján described their arrival and popularity:

> these [*havaneres*] are sung above all by the fishermen who inherited them from the sailors on tall ships from the end of the last [nineteenth] century. They spread to the workers in the cork factories and at the beginning of this [twentieth] century the passionately rhetorical and amorous style of these songs enjoyed a sustained vogue.

Luján elucidates how the imported Cuban rhythms were adapted by the fishermen's musical sense so that the: 'evanescent, languid and sensual *havaneres*, with their ecstatic and milky sensuality of the shake of a mulatto-woman's breasts, fall within the fixed, precise and luminous canon of the *sardana*'.[12] In this way, Montsalvatge's West Indian works should not be seen as merely exotic but more as a further individual way of responding to his situation as a Catalan composer at a time when overt expression of Catalan identity was problematic.

Montsalvatge developed further collaborations in the 1950s with the writing of film music for directors such as Julio Coll, Rafael Gil and Isasi Isamendi. Other works from these years include his *Partita 1958/* 1958 Score and his setting of Maragall's *Cant espiritual* (1960). With his *Desintegración morfológica de la Chacona de Bach* (1962–3), however, his West Indian phase came definitively to an end. Henceforth his music became increasingly oriented towards the western European tradition, experimenting with the spirit of the eighteenth century but also developing a free polytonality under the influence of French composers such as Olivier Messiaen and Georges Auric. In the 1970s and 1980s a series of concertos for renowned Spanish

---

[12] Cited in Cureses, 2003, pp. 195–6.

performers (Narciso Yepes, Nicanor Zabaleta and Rafael Puyana) was complemented by further settings of Catalan poets: Verdaguer in his cantata *Sum vernis* (1973) and Carner in his *Quatre rimes breus* (1985). Montsalvatge's influence on younger Catalan composers has been marked and, although he claimed never to have been a teacher by vocation, his appointment at the *Conservatorio Superior Municipal* in Barcelona in 1970 was a significant impulse in this direction.

Another important initiative for the regeneration of music in Barcelona after the Civil War was the formation in 1947 of the *Cercle Manuel de Falla* under the auspices of the *Institut Français*. This brought together a group of Catalan composers that included in the first instance Joan Comellas (1913–2000), Manuel Valls (1920–1984), Ángel Cerdà (b. 1924) and Juan Eduardo Cirlot (1916–1973). Also included, a little later, were Josep Casanovas (b. 1924), Antonio Ruiz-Pipó (b. 1933) and Josep Maria Mestres Quadreny (b. 1929). Of these, perhaps the most important is Mestres Quadreny, who joined the *Cercle* in 1952 and whose friendship with the artist Joan Prats also introduced him to the avant-garde cultural centre, the Club 49. While the *Cercle Manuel de Falla* afforded him the opportunity to hear Messiaen speak and the *musique concrète* developed by the *Groupe de Recherche Musicale*, the Club 49 brought Mestres Quadreny into contact with leading figures in the plastic arts such as the painters Antoni Tàpies, Joan Ponç and Joan Miró as well as the poet Joan Brossa.

A direct result of this was the pioneering interdisciplinary project *Cop de Poma/ Blow from an Apple* (1961) with Tàpies, Miró and Brossa. Other collaboratively inspired works from this period include the *Tríade per a Joan Miró* (1960–1), *Tramesa a Tàpies/ Consignment for Tàpies* (1962) and *Homenatge a Joan Prats* (1972); while in 1991 his opera *Cap de mirar* is a setting of Brossa. Mestres Quadreny was actively involved in the *Associació Catalana de Compositors* and the *Conjunt Català de Música Contemporànea*, and in 1970 set up *Phonos*, an electro-acoustic laboratory. His reputation extends beyond Catalonia, and he has taught in Darmstadt and Brazil. He has experimented with electronic and aleatoric music and broken with established performance conventions in works like *Self-service* (1973; to be performed by the audience) and *Tocatina* (1975; to be performed by a group of friends on bottles of *anis* of different levels).

Mestres Quadreny's works of the 1980s illustrate the persistent Catalan tendency to eclecticism: *Sonades sobre fons negre/ Sounds on a Black Background* (1982) introduces fragments from J. S. Bach and the Catalan folksong *El mariner*, while the *Quintet de la nit i del dia/ Night and Day Quintet* (1985) is written for five clarinets with fragments of *El cant dels ocells/ The Song of the Birds* dispersed between them. Similarly, the slow movement of the 1983 *Simfonia en Mi Bemoll/* Symphony in E minor elaborates the melody of the medieval *Cant de la Sibil·la* in the slow movement. Although perhaps the most well known, this composer is not a lone figure: Josep Soler (b. 1935), Xavier Benguerel (b. 1931), Joan Guinjoan (b. 1931), Francesc Taverna-Bech (b. 1932), Salvador Pueyo (b. 1935) and Jordi Cervelló (b. 1935) have all made major contributions both within Catalonia and internationally.

It is, of course, more difficult still to assess the trends and tendencies of the younger generations of Catalan composers. Simplistic labels such as 'eclectic' have even less value in an era when all composers internationally demonstrate this feature in their influences, ideas and inspirations in a global context. The establishment of *Phonos* has encouraged the composition of electro-acoustic works by, among others, Àlex Martínez Figuerola (b. 1957) and Jep Nuix (1955–1998). The *Associació Catalana de Compositors* has successfully supported the emergence of several generations of Catalan composers, from Manuel García Morante (b. 1937), Josep Lluís Berenguer (b. 1940), Carles Guinovart (b. 1941), David Padrós (b. 1942), Jordi Alcaraz (b. 1943) and Anna Bofill (b. 1945) to Fernando Reyes (1951–1989), Lluís Gasser (b. 1951), Miquel Roger (b. 1954), Albert Llanas (b. 1957), Agustí Carles (b. 1960) and many others. Even a quick glance at the works of these composers reveals an extraordinary range of inspiration though many continue to set Catalan texts. Roger, for example, has set poems by Espriu, Foix and Anglada.

While the post-Franco era has brought freedom of linguistic choice, it is not clear to what extent more recent generations of Catalan composers working in a democratic context and writing against a global backdrop are concerned with issues of Catalan heritage. It is too soon to judge whether they look to a single city such as Paris for all that is cosmopolitan, exotic and Wagner-free, or to Vienna or to Darmstadt for groundbreaking compositional techniques. Possibly this role will simply prove less relevant to composers of contemporary music whose works tend to appeal to and reach only a specialist audience. In any case, the wide diffusion of new works realized by the efforts of a Clavé, a Morera or a Casals had already faltered in the pre-war period, with the arrival of the 'inhuman music' of Schoenberg's *Pierrot Lunaire* in 1928.

The insistence on the interaction between music and literature, however, underlines that same commitment to the language that has permeated the musical experience from the earliest times onwards. Modern Catalan composers have responded to political circumstances in different ways though always in symbiosis with broader cultural contexts both at home and abroad. As regards their musical idiom, no single strand emerged other than an eclectic approach that resulted in a fusion of styles unique to each individual composer. This brief introduction has only touched on some of the issues raised by study of music in Catalonia over the last century and a half. This offers a rich seam to be mined by future scholars.

Works Cited and Suggested Reading

General overview

Alier, R. (1985) 'Musical Life in Barcelona, 1888–1936', in *Homage to Barcelona. The City and its Art, 1888–1936*, Catalogue for the Hayward Gallery Exhibition, 14 November 1985–23 February 1986. London: Arts Council of Great Britain, pp. 277–283.

Aviñoa, Xavier (dir.) (1999–2003) *Historia de la música catalana, valenciana i balear*. 10 vols. Barcelona: Edicions 62. The main elements of interest are as follows:
    Aviñoa, X. (1999) *Del modernisme a la Guerra Civil (1900–1939)*, vol. 4; Carbonell, J. (2000) 'El cant coral', vol. 3, pp. 147–186; Cureses, M. (2003) 'La creació musical. Escoles i tendències', vol. 5, pp. 160–255.

——— (1985) *La música i el modernisme*. Barcelona: Curial.

Casares, Emilio (dir.) (1999–2002) *Diccionario de la Música Española e Hispanoamericana*.
    10 vols. Madrid: Sociedad General de Autores y Editores. The main entries of interest are as follows:
    Avinoa Perez, X. (2001) 'Morera Viura, Enric', vol. 7, pp. 817–819;
    Bonastre, F. (2000) 'Lamote de Grignon i Boquet, Joan', vol. 6, pp. 726–729.

——— (2001) 'Mompou, Frederic', vol. 7, pp. 654–660; 'Montsalvatge, Xavier', vol. 7, pp. 739–744; Calmell, C. (2002) 'Toldrà, Eduard', vol. 10, pp. 318–321; Casares Rodicio, E. (2001) 'Pahissa, Jaime', vol. 8, pp. 353–359; (1999) 'Blancafort de Rosello, Manuel', vol. 1, pp. 493–498; Gásser, Ll. (2001) 'Mestres Quadreny, Josep María', vol. 7, pp. 480–494; Marta Cureses, E. (2000) 'Homs i Oller, Joaquim', vol. 6, pp. 332–338; Millet i Loras, Ll. (2001) 'Millet i Pàges, Lluís', vol. 7, pp. 576–581.

Gómez Muntané, M. (1979) *Música en la Casa Real catalano-aragonesa durante los años 1336–1432*. Barcelona: Antoni Bosch.

Valls, M. (1960) *Música catalana contemporània: visió de conjunt*. Barcelona: Selecta.

——— (1969) *Història de la música catalana*. Barcelona: Taber.

Specific composers and movements

Anglès, H. (1955) *Mateo Flecha: Las Ensaladas (Praga, 1581)*. Barcelona: Diputación.

Artís, P. (1980) *El cant coral a Catalunya (1891–1979)*. Barcelona: Barcino.

Aviñoa, X. (1985) *Enric Morera*. Barcelona: Edicions de Nou Art Thor.

——— (1996) *Jaume Pahissa, un estudi biogàfic i crític*. Barcelona: Biblioteca de Catalunya.

Capdevila, M. (1964) *Eduard Toldrà, músic*. Barcelona: Aedos.
Carreras, J. J. (2001) 'Hijos de Pedrell. La historiografía musical española y sus orígenes nacionalistas 1780–1980', *Il Saggiatore musicale*, VIII, pp. 153–162.
Casanovas, J. and Llanas, A. (1996) *Joaquim Homs*. Barcelona: Proa.
Casares, E. (1986) 'Manuel Blancafort o la afirmación de la nueva música catalana', in *La música en la generación del 27. Homenaje a Lorca*. Madrid: Ministerio de Cultura.
Clark, W. A. (1999) *Isaac Albéniz: Portrait of a Romantic*. New York: Oxford University Press.
——— (2005) *Enrique Granados: Poet of the Piano*. New York: Oxford University Press.
Codina, J. (1992) *Xavier Montsalvatge*. Barcelona: Labor.
Fernández-Cid, A. (1977) *Eduard Toldrà*. Bilbao: (no details of publisher).
Gómez Muntané, M. (2008) *Las ensaladas (Praga, 1581)*, 6 vols. Valencia: Generalitat Valenciana.
Hess, C. A. (2001) *Manuel de Falla and Modernism in Spain*. Chicago: University of Chicago Press.
Homs, J. (2000) (ed. Meiron Bowen) *Robert Gerhard and his work*. Sheffield: Sheffield Academic Press.
Montsalvatge, X. (1988) *Papeles autobiográficos: al alcance del recuerdo*. Madrid: Fundación Banco Exterior.
Paine, R. (1989) *Hispanic Traditions in Twentieth-Century Catalan Music. With Particular Reference to Gerhard, Mompou and Montsalvatge*. New York and London: Garland Publishing.
Pedrell, F. (1908) *Catàlech de la Bibliotech Musical de la Diputació de Barcelona: ab notes històriques, biogràfiques y critiques*, 2 vols. Barcelona: Palau de la Diputació.
Planes, R. (1972) *El mestre Morera i el seu món*. Barcelona: EP.
Taverna-Bech, F., Guinovart, C., Bonastre, F. and Codina, J. (1994) *Xavier Montsalvatge*. Barcelona: Boileau.
Tinnell, Roger (1999) 'Spanish Music and Cultural Identity', in Gies, D. (ed.) *The Cambridge Companion to Modern Spanish Culture*. Cambridge: Cambridge University Press, pp. 287–297.
Various authors (1973) *London Sinfonietta Schoenberg/Gerhard Series: The Complete Instrumental and Chamber Music of Arnold Schoenberg and Roberto Gerhard, October and November 1973*. London: London Sinfonietta.
Zalkind, A. (2002) *Study of Catalan Composer Federico Mompou's (1893–1987) Música Callada*. Lewiston, NY: Mellen.

8

Catalan Cinema:
An Uncanny Transnational Performance

JAUME MARTÍ-OLIVELLA

The coming of age of Catalan cinema?

In terms of international visibility, Catalan cinema has often been obscured by the towering figures of its famous painters, architects or musicians. As was the case with literature, during the Franco years cinema suffered from the double restriction of extreme censorship and linguistic proscription. In this way it thus could never achieve international recognition as its distinct voice was thoughtlessly subsumed into a wider 'official' national identity. However, 2007 may well have marked the end of such anonymity.

In that year the Lincoln Center in New York ran a series entitled 'Film in Catalunya. 1906–2006'. The programme included twenty-five feature films plus two special sessions: 'The Beginnings of Filmmaking in Catalunya' and 'Films of the Spanish Civil War', with documentary works on that conflict by Mateo Santos, Félix Marquet and Adrián Porchet. As such, the series covered the entire span of Catalan cinema in the last century; and although its emphasis was placed in the production of recent decades, it managed to strike a wonderful balance between landmark films, such as Francisco Rovira Beleta's *Los Tarantos* (1962), the splendid recreation of the Romeo and Juliet story amid the squalor of the gypsy community of the *Barceloneta* (later demolished to make way for the Olympic village) or Llorenç Llobet Gràcia's *Vida en sombras* (Life in Shadows, 1948), the extraordinary tale of a man obsessed with cinema, which anticipates many film-within-a-film experiments to come. Also relevant was Juli Salvador's *Apartado de Correos, 1001* (Post Box 1001, 1950), one of the first important thrillers to transpose *film noir* onto Catalan and Spanish screens.

The series also paid due tribute to the Barcelona School – a heterogeneous group of film-makers and artists who emerged during the 1960s and early 1970s with a characteristically cosmopolitan flair that set them apart from the 'official' idiom of the contemporary 'New Spanish Cinema'. Their films were experimental in both script and structure and were largely influenced by Pop Art, fashion imagery and New Wave cinemas. Three films were chosen to represent this school which, despite its commercial shortcomings, still looms large in some of the young Catalan film-makers today: Vicente Aranda's futuristically dystopic pseudo-thriller *Fata Morgana* (Mirage, 1966); Jacinto Esteva's and Joaquim Jordà's *Dante no es únicamente severo* (Dante is not Simply Harsh, 1967), a labyrinthine reinvention of an improbable couple amid musical and poetic urban images; and Gonzalo Suárez's *Ditirambo*, the Borgesian detective dream of an investigator trapped in someone else's plot.

The programme also incorporated a representation of the first post-Franco films that could deal directly with history once the fierce censorship of the dictator disappeared in 1975. Antoni Ribas' *La ciutat cremada* (The Burnt City, 1976), shot in Catalan, offers a chronicle of the events of the Tragic Week of 1909, when the streets of Barcelona witnessed a popular uprising against the conscription of reservists for yet another futile colonial war in North Africa. Similarly, Jaime Camino's *La vieja memoria* (The Old Memory, 1978) is a powerful documentary that combines archival footage with real-life interviews with some of the most prominent survivors of the Civil War. Besides constituting a remarkable historical document this film, according to Richard Peña in his notes to the programme of the Lincoln Center, 'reveals the gaps and contradictions that emerge between the records of history and our memories of them'. In fact, many of the most recent documentaries in Catalonia will continue to explore the tensions involved in such a gap.

Francesc Betriu's *La plaça del Diamant* (Diamond Square, 1982), also shot in Catalan, was another landmark film chosen to represent the drive towards historical self-representation in Catalan cinema. The story of *Colometa* (little pigeon), the remarkable protagonist of Rodoreda's eponymous novel, found in Sílvia Munt a perfect vehicle to portray the vulnerability and resilience of a young woman whose personal predicament became the emblem of the endurance of the entire country. The series also included Ventura Pons' *Ocaña, retrat intermitent* (Ocaña, Intermittent Portrait, 1978), a groundbreaking documentary on the social margins of Barcelona, as illustrated by the figure of a transvestite Andalusian performance artist who became an emblem of the homosexual community in the Barcelona of the early years of the transition to democracy.

2007 was also the year when, for the first time, the Venice International Film Festival invited four Catalan films to be shown in its different sections. Last but certainly not least, a further retrospective of recent Catalan cinema was presented at the *Deutsches Filminstitut* in Frankfurt, in recognition of the presence of Catalan literature as that year's guest of honour in the International Book Fair. If we have dwelt on this seemingly exhaustive list of titles it is for a simple reason: within the fractured experience of Catalan cinema these films may be considered a *canon* of sorts, within and against which we will be able to assess the *oeuvre* of the various directors.

What these events suggest *in toto*, however, is that Catalan cinema is no longer the ugly duckling of the nation's cultural panorama and that it is currently receiving some special attention, both official and popular. Two contemporary news items help illustrate this point. The first is Bernat Salvà's short chronicle in the Barcelona daily *Avui*, where he writes:

> The number of spectators of feature films produced in Catalonia increased a 29.6% during 2006. (...) The increase in Catalan productions is more valuable if one considers that the whole number of cinema spectators has continued its decreasing tendency: a total of 25.3 million people in 2006, which means 2% less than in 2005 and 17% less than in 2002.[1]

What these figures show is that at the moment of a general – perhaps irreversible – tendency to stop going to film theatres there is a growth in audiences for Catalan products. In a subsequent article, Salvà offers a different take on the same topic:

> 'We have to find a different means of distribution. We cannot distribute Catalan films as if they were *Spider Man* or *Harry Potter*, but we have an audience and we need to find it.' Catalan filmmaker Josep Maria Forn defends this thesis with numbers. *Coronel Macià* was premiered using alternative means last February and it has already had an audience of 40,000 people, quite a significant number if one considers its low production cost of 2 million euros.[2]

Two important lessons are to be learned from these words. First, there is a growing audience for Catalan films despite the very small overall portion of the total market (7 per cent), which is still completely dominated by Hollywood productions (68 per cent). Second, there are film-makers like Josep Maria Forn who, after more than fifty years in the profession, are not only making important films but remain completely engaged in finding alternative

---

[1] Salvà, *Avui*, 3 March 2007.
[2] Salvà, *Avui*, 2 July 2007.

ways of distributing them. In fact, Forn has always maintained that Catalan cinema could and should strike a balance between being industrially feasible and socially responsible without giving up its own markers of identity.

Ultimately, the fact that not only this director but also Vicente Aranda, Jaime Camino, Pere Portabella, Joaquim Jordà, Bigas Luna or Ventura Pons have continued to be extremely active while, at the same time, Catalan cinema has witnessed an exponential growth in the number of young film-makers – José Luis Guerín, Isabel Coixet, Marta Balletbò-Coll, Agustí Villaronga, Marc Recha, Cesc Gay or Jaume Balagueró, to name only a few – gives reason to perceive the international coming of age of a local cinematography that is clearly thinking and filming globally.

In this chapter, I will concentrate on the last fifteen years of Catalan film-making and the four major tendencies that have (re)established themselves in this period: the urban comedy in (post-) Olympic Barcelona; the new documentary and the search for historical memory; the importance of literary adaptations; and, finally, the new (female/experimental) gaze. A further element of the local/global interplay is its multilingual approach, which has crossed movements and generations. Isabel Coixet's last three films, for instance, were shot directly in English, and Joaquim Jordà's *Mones com la Becky* (Monkeys Like Becky, 1999) employed four different languages. This facet may be taken as indicative of how the Catalan creative personality attempts to negotiate its presence within the framework of the contemporary international experience.

Refashioning Barcelona: The post-Olympic vision

In many ways Barcelona is the prime focus of Catalan national sentiment. This is not just because the development of the city and its representation have commonly been determined by the ruling political classes but also – and virtually unique among minority cultures – this urban centre is a thriving metropolis that offers a *de facto* recognition of the presence of Catalonia in the modern world. As such, across the artistic spectrum the city becomes in itself an important theme for artistic speculation, being represented by three overarching metaphors: as a *ciutat de pas* (crossroads), as a *ciudad de ferias y congresos* (a city of trade fairs) and as a friendly *rendezvous*, a hospitable meeting point. I have used Catalan, Spanish and French in naming each one of these figurations not only to point to the obvious geopolitical location of Barcelona and Catalonia whose history, past and present, could be summarized by the effort to articulate its own voice amid such overpowering neighbours as France and Spain, but also to reflect the most immediate use of such extended metaphors.

Indeed – and as is evident in Robert Davidson's chapter on the capital – at the heart of the Catalan imaginary one constantly finds the real definition of Catalonia and Barcelona as the capacity to relate to many crossing cultures without losing themselves in transit. With the rise to power of the Catalan bourgeoisie in the early decades of the twentieth century and its connivance with the Franco regime during and after the Spanish Civil War, Barcelona became mostly represented as a trade fair centre, a configuration that obscured not only the city's cultural heritage but its own claim to historical singularity. With Spain's insertion in the European Community and the celebration of the 1992 Olympics in Barcelona, the metropolis underwent an iconic overhaul in order to receive the new global gaze cast on her. Allegedly, the city was to bring together those three leading images in order to become a highly visible crossroads, a business hub and a meeting point of sports and culture, in an exhibition that was conceived as immediately local and very universal at the same time.

In the collective cultural imaginary, the most obvious effect of such global marketing is that Barcelona has taken the place of Catalonia itself. And the question repeatedly posited is: what has been the role of Catalan cinema in (de)constructing this touristic version of history that has become the official story in post-Franco Catalonia? To what extent has local cinematic production embraced the master narratives of Barcelona/Catalonia as the hospitable meeting point and/or the hybrid crossroads between Europe and Spain?

None of the films that will be mentioned from now on, for instance, follows the path of Catalan official cinema, with its traditional epic reconstructions, such as Antoni Ribas' *La ciutat cremada* (The Burnt City, 1976) or Josep Maria Forn's *Companys, procés a Catalunya* (Companys, Catalonia on Trial, 1979), which offered uncritical explorations of two pivotal moments in history: the social upheaval during the Tragic Week of 1909 and the show trial of the exiled president of the *Generalitat*, handed over to Franco by the Gestapo. In fairness to both films, however, the historical context of the political transition in 1975 provided a pressing need for an alternative history to that offered by Francoism and its obliteration of Catalan identity.

This desire to create alternatives was exemplified by the *Nous Directors Catalans/* New Catalan Directors, the collective of young film-makers who used mostly the urban comedy as their cinematic vehicle. As Ferran Llagostera put it: 'the idea was to make films about here and now. We wanted to contact Catalan writers and musicians.'[3] And yet, films such as Llagostera's *Bar-cel-ona* (1986) or Ferré's *Un submarí a les estovalles*

---

[3] Llagostera, 1997, p. 7.

(A Submarine in the Tablecloth, 1991), ultimately illustrate the same touristic version of the Catalan capital as the hospitable meeting point. In fact, both films are structured as a collection of postcard-like vignettes and are totally uncritical of the vision they purport.

However, the new cinematic gaze on the city never completely abandons its critical dialogue with the official narrative. Marta Balletbò-Coll's first feature film, *Costa Brava. Family Album* (1995), for example, becomes a true parody of the tourist consumption of Barcelona with an interesting glimpse into Catalonia's Jewish historical roots. Rosa Vergés' *Souvenir* (1995), on the other hand, is a transnational comedy where Barcelona ceases to be a profitable trade centre in order to become almost an anonymous urban maze where a Japanese acts out his own game of cultural amnesia. Even the cinema of Ventura Pons, previously a series of conventional urban comedies, was to turn its attention to literary revisions of the city where human encounter becomes almost an impossibility.

This unachievable encounter receives a radical reading in Soler's docudrama *Saïd* (1999), which oscillates between urban comedy and social document in its portrayal of an interracial love affair between a Catalan student and an illegal Moroccan immigrant. In this courageous film, Soler manages to give his immigrant subject substantial historical and diegetic agency while achieving one of the clearest distortions of the official Olympic Gypsy Queen metaphor used to forecast Barcelona's global allure around the Olympic Games, as epitomized by the protagonism afforded to Cristina Hoyos' Flamenco troupe during the opening ceremony.

An indicator of the immense pressure of Barcelona on the Catalan creative psyche is the recent flight of directors from the city. Isabel Coixet's *La vida secreta de las palabras* (The Secret Life of Words, 2006), for instance, was filmed on an Atlantic oil platform; Marc Recha's *Dies d'agost* (Some Days in August, 2006) explored the eerie calmed waters of a reservoir in Tarragona; and Cesc Gay's *Ficció* (Fiction, 2006) placed its urban characters in the Pyrenees where they had to face the fiction of their true selves.

(De)Constructing Barcelona and the glocal gaze: The new documentary school

Similarly, the evident goal of the new documentary films of post-Olympic Barcelona seems to be the deconstruction of the legitimacy of the three metaphors described. José Luis Guerín's *En construcción* (Work in Progress, 2000) constitutes the harshest though most poetic rebuke of this fabrication as it is played out in the refashioning of Barcelona's *Raval*, the city's red-light district, now the densest conglomerate of foreign immigrants. Guerín's gaze is especially glocal in his marvellous capacity to merge the immediate and the universal in a film that extends the possibilities of the documentary genre to become an elegiac meditation on a way of life that no longer exists. As Imma Merino aptly summarizes it:

> 'No to demolition, yes to renovation,' what is evident in *En construcción* is the questioning of an urban redevelopment plan that, rather than improving the living conditions of the population of a district that should have been renovated, brought about the demolition of buildings that led to the inhabitants being moved out to other areas.[4]

In fact, Guerín's work bears witness to one of the clearest examples of gentrification in post-Olympic Barcelona. By placing his cameras steadily and uninterruptedly for almost a year in front of the bulldozers and workers tearing apart a sizeable portion of the Raval the director managed to denounce yet another inhuman redevelopment in the city. He reveals figuratively what the machines, and later the archaeologists, uncovered literally: the skeletons hidden in the closet of a body politic whose *raison d'être* had been to keep things quiet so not to disturb the smooth 'touristization' of geo-specific history.

Most films discussed in this section, moreover, offer a variation of the same extended visual metaphor, best summarized by the Catalan popular idiom: *no treure els draps bruts al sol* (don't hang your dirty washing out in public). Appropriately, Guerín's camera dwells lovingly on these neighbourhood balconies with their laundry both dried and sullied by the dust and the detritus of the ongoing construction all around them. And yet, it is also on those balconies that we experience the film's capacity to capture true life unfolding in the spontaneous exchanges passed from one social actor to another. Particularly emotive is the courtship involving the young worker and maid hanging out her washing nearby, whose lyricism captures the Romeo and Juliet original acted out in all its proletarian simplicity by a scaffolder and a laundress.

The emphasis, however, is not on love and life but on decay and death, both figuratively and literally, since the second overarching visual metaphor that structures the film is that of the city/country as a cemetery. At the very centre of *En construcción*, cinemagoers, together with the astonished bystanders, are offered an unmediated encounter with a Roman necropolis whose skeletons appear piecemeal for the awed consumption of all. Needless to say, it will be this utmost form of the uncanny, or as one of the most expres-

---

[4] Merino, 2006, pp. 132–3.

sive onlookers will put it, the strangest of familiar realizations – 'Quite something, isn't it? To see that we live on top of all these dead people without even noticing it!' – that turns Guerín's film into an extraordinary example of cinematic invention and explains the title of this chapter: the uncanny transnational performance of Catalan cinema.

Indeed, thanks to some imaginative editing, the series of montages that constitute the long encounter with the dead becomes a true theatrical performance, a collective acting out of the private and public ghosts confronting not only the inhabitants of the *Raval* district but those of the entire city and, by implication, those of the country and its role in the larger project of (de)constructing Europe. In this sense, the *Raval* project may be seen as an extension of the general process of gentrification started with the preparations for the Olympic Games of 1992.

It is in this way that the bulging eyes painted on a ruined wall facing a hoarding advertising the City Hall's project to redevelop the Raval is best understood. Using extreme close-up, Guerín's camera will force us to read the legend at the bottom of the poster, which informs us that 85 per cent of the costs is provided by the European Fund for Economic Cohesion. In other words, at the very moment when NATO forces were bombing positions in and around the former Yugoslavia in the last Balkans War, as we are informed by television announcers throughout the film, post-Olympic Barcelona is using transnational European funds to carry out one of the largest domestic 'cleansings' in recent memory.

As such, the failure to build a European Union where historical Others could live side by side is both rehearsed and denounced in a film that shows us, somewhat perversely, that such co-existence is already happening in the *Raval*, despite the efforts of the City Hall to drive the immigrant population – mostly Muslim – out of the district with its redevelopment. And yet, much like the failure in the Balkans, the gentrification of the Raval has also become a social failure inasmuch as the economic circumstances and living conditions of those surrounding this 'sad rambla' have continued to deteriorate.

Guerín's film is deeply self-referential, thus placing itself at the opposite end of Hollywood continuity editing. Yet, its performative nature rings true because its documentary format allows it to capture people's reactions in an unmediated way. The lyrical close-up of the first uncovered skull, an artistic topos in itself, with the sockets of its empty eyes returning an abject gaze to the camera, acts as a metaphor for the cinematic experience in itself, which develops with the appearance of a screen-like fence, a long piece of green plastic, which becomes a backdrop creating an impossible boundary between archaeological excavation and fascinated audience whose voices and shadows are projected back upon it.

In this way, the self-conscious camera records the shadowy and marginal existences of bystanders as they are cast onto the green drape and become the ghostly history of the district and of the city. Their dialogue, beautifully juxtaposed in the editing, contains all the fundamentals of Guerín's entire project: to create a cinematic and animated still-life portrait of a group of people that emerge from their ghost-like, stereotypical existence into fully fledged performances as truly actual human beings. Ultimately, they are the carriers of the historical memory that no urban redevelopment plan will ever completely obliterate or which will continually return to haunt the perpetrators.

Another remarkable documentary dealing with the recovery of popular historical memory is Carles Balagué's *La casita blanca. La ciudad oculta* (The Little White House. The Hidden City, 2002). The film chronicles the existence of a famous *meublé* (bordello) and its significance in the hidden life of the Franco years. The house got its name from the white sheets often hanging out to dry on its roof and, crucially, this image becomes a visual metaphor that inscribes verbally and visually the invisible boundary between private and public realms. A boundary that becomes the locus of a double standard inevitably predicated on the basis of washing dirty linen in private, of keeping the skeletons in the closet. In this way Balagué's film offers an uncanny glimpse of the hidden practices that constituted the other side of the official story of Franco's pious National Catholicism.

The official chronicle is elicited by the insertion of many newsreels. In these, the spectator can see how Franco came to Barcelona to preside over the celebrations of the International Eucharistic Congress of 1952. Most of the personal testimonies in the film refer to the social context in which the event took place. And yet, with the *mise-en-abyme* of the story of the elusive *maquis* anarchist, Facerias, and the direct testimony of several oppositional figures, the film ultimately effects a complete deconstruction of Francoist historiography.

The authorized version is represented by the privileging of the family metaphor – a moral ideal embraced by Franco and his Catalan bourgeois supporters. This allusion is quickly established with the first cut from the initial tracking shot of the house into an edited montage where we see archival footage of Franco's troops entering victoriously into Barcelona. This reportage continues with more images of Franco in 1946, addressing the adoring masses from the balcony of the Royal Palace in Madrid. The doublet of unauthorized political entry (occupation of Catalonia) and the crossing the threshold into moral illicitude (bordello) – is thus equated under the indulgent vision of patriarchal authority.

After this initial historical and poetic double frame, a series of talking heads offer a direct testimony of the times. Historian Rafael Abella locates the whole issue within a background of collective moral crisis. His words act as a kind of cautionary tale that tells the story in a nutshell: virtually everybody was implicated in this turpitude and its corollary of a socially accepted double standard. The next interviewee is Felio A. Vilarubias, who recalls how Eva Perón kept the Caudillo waiting for over two hours in the Palace of Montjüic where Franco was offering her a state banquet. With Evita's accompanying ode to Spain as the most exalted, noble and Catholic matriarch (*Madre Patria*) Balagué exposes the concept of *Hispanidad*, the neo-imperialist projection of the family metaphor with respect to the former American colonies. Here, Franco's family encompasses the hundred millions of Spanish Americans whose cultural and geopolitical 'mother' is supposed to be the same imperial power that first colonized them and that nostalgically reclaims them now.

Evita epitomizes the double standard that the film denounces, embodying the public/private divide with her initial bordello persona and her ulterior role as populist saint. Nowhere is that dramatic social and moral double standard more significantly and blatantly exposed then in the newsreel footage where we witness Franco's solemn arrival into Barcelona on the occasion of the Eucharistic Congress.

> The Eucharistic Congress was like the third games of the city. The first was the Expo in 1888, then the Expo in 1929 and, finally, the Eucharistic Congress in 1952 (...) It was turned by 'national-catholicism' into an extraordinary spectacle of the 'confirmation of our faith' and into a public 'blessing' of Franco's regime.

It is quite appropriate that journalist Jaume Boix refers here to three very public performances as the city's 'games', in an obvious reference to the Olympics. As in 1992, Barcelona had to 'get pretty', had to cover up in a more pragmatic and business-like manner and reconvert its 'hidden' city exposed earlier by Guerín. Again, Rafael Abella gives us a perfect account of the issue:

> The Eucharistic Congress presented the problem of where to put the large amount of pilgrims (...) Then, they decreed the takeover of the *meublés* in order to reconvert them into hotels during this time. In fact, they went through a process of disinfection and exorcism so that they could be used as regular hotels, only for sleeping!

This early gentrification of the Raval is, however, not the only cover-up that Balagué exposes. In fact, a fictional recreation emerges surprisingly – a brief film-within-a-film in cinema noir style – of the story of Facerias, the anti-Francoist urban guerrilla, who decided to storm the luxurious Pedralbes *meublé* on 21 October 1951. One man will resist Facerias and his gunmen,

Antonio Masana, and the industrialist's ensuing death sparked a huge police operation followed by a military trial that sentenced Facerias, in his absence, and two other members of the group to death. The fact that the woman found in the mogul's arms when Facerias stormed the locale was the industrialist's own niece, returns us to the family metaphor and the dirty laundry, which the official hushing up of the identity of the victims could not hide from the public eye.

In this sense, the testimony of the two nephews of Angel Oset, garrotted for his involvement in the raid, is crucial. Both are interviewed in the Eastern Cemetery, perched over the sea on the hidden side of the mountain of Montjüic. Besides reinforcing the overarching graveyard metaphor Balagué is also paying public homage to all the Catalan fighters buried anonymously and, more explicitly, to the figure of Lluís Companys, President of the *Generalitat*, whose 'military trial' and immediate execution also took place under the shadows of the Montjuïc castle, as was shown in Forn's *Companys, procés a Catalunya*.

Under Franco, Balagué is clearly saying, Catalonia was still on trial. And yet, to avoid any partisan whitewash or reductivist reading, *La casita blanca* ends over more NO-DO archival footage. Here we see Franco entering the basilica in Montserrat, Catalonia's national shrine, side by side with the Catalan prelate Abbot Escarré. It would be hard to imagine a more eloquent image of collaboration with the Franco regime among the more influential social groups in Catalonia.

Another important contributor to documentary film-making in Catalonia is Joaquim Jordà whose *Mones com la Becky* (Monkeys Like Becky, 1999) is a remarkable genre-bender that encompasses the three metaphors under consideration. The film is doubly uncanny since it shows not only Jordà's own process of self-discovery amid mental patients but also his strangely familiar way of performing his own self-exposure. Here he plays himself undergoing psychiatric treatment and, later, as participant in a therapy group in a drama dealing with the attempted murder of Egas Moniz.

Moniz, Portugal's first Nobel laureate in science, had earned worldwide recognition and criticism for his early experiments with human lobotomies. The Portuguese connection underlines the transnational relevance of the movie as does its blend of four languages, monochrome, colour and variety of formats such as video, super-eight and 35 millimetre, which continues the trend towards polyglossia and multimedia that is current today in Catalan cinema.[5]

Still faithful to the ludic experimentalism of the Barcelona School, *Mones*

---

[5] These points are made in Manresa, 2006, p. 67.

com la Becky includes two symbolic locations in the city: the labyrinth in the Horta neighbourhood and the zoological gardens in the *Parc de la Ciutadella*. In due course, we will witness the peripathetic 'lessons' of a group of meandering academics whose ruminations end in a stuttering clamour that gets lost in the shifting small picture, which zooms into a television screen, where we will see archival images of Franco receiving a degree of doctor *honoris causa* from the University of Coimbra, where Egas Moniz had imparted his own lessons. As Laia Manresa has aptly interpreted:

> The labyrinth as metaphor of the human brain may also represent a therapy understood as a way out of chaos, pain and crisis. Thus, while the intellectuals walk through the lanes of cypresses, they are seen not only as engaged in search of answers but actually performing the mechanisms of a mental cure.[6]

The entire film is thus structured as a series of juxtaposed performances, a game of textual and visual mirrors that represent 'madness' and its therapy at the same time. And, more importantly, they tell of the narrow boundary between them. By showing Franco's presence in Coimbra, Jordà is obviously adding the layer of a historical crime for whose 'madness' many still seek therapy and/or reparation. The second location takes place in the Barcelona zoo and it recalls one of the longest and most outlandish sequences in Vicente Aranda's *Fata Morgana* (Mirage, 1965), where we see a pseudo-scientist, a would-be serial killer (Antonio Ferrandis), driving a children's go-cart with Gim (Teresa Gimpera), a fashion model. Her gaze seems to have cast a spell over the semi-abandoned city. In retrospect, the empty glances exchanged between Gim and the animals they pass by seem an accurate metaphor for Jordà's own inscription of the *zoos/bios* divide at the heart of the social and medical dilemma presented in his film.

The final strand is the therapeutic staging by a group of schizophrenics of the attempted murder of Egas Moniz by one of his patients. The televised broadcast of that very performance, which we watch at the same time as the social actors, locates us also as participants in the therapy experience that is the movie. As such, the film is structured by a constant *mise-en-abyme* of these three textual mirrors. This comes to a climax in the sequence where we see João Maria Pinto (who plays four roles in the film) and hear his voiceover narrative as the film changes to colour.

At this point, in a circular panning the camera almost caresses the washing hanging out on top of the small trees of the inner courtyard of the Portuguese

---

[6] Manresa, 2006, p. 68.

mental clinic where he was treated as a patient, Pinto's final words tell us that being an actor has saved his life. Given the collective catharsis of the theatrical experience, this is but a verbal rejoinder of what the camerawork had already told us in images: the need to overcome the public/private divide in a social and/or artistic performance that encompasses both aspects at the same time. In the context of this chapter, moreover, Pinto's confession stands out as a perfect poetic synthesis of the close proximity between social 'madness' and personal secrets, and the profound need to stage them as public exorcisms.

Ultimately, that is why *Mones com la Becky* becomes one of the best illustrations of Catalan cinema's uncanny transnational performances to date. And why Joaquim Jordà has managed, like Susan Sontag, to turn the private discourse of illness into the public dimension of social metaphors for a society only partly ill at ease with its lack of a historical memory and collective consciousness. The point is made patent in a later Jordà documentary, *De nens* (About Children, 2005), a powerful indictment of the way our society vilifies and prejudges those considered to be sick and guilty of unspeakable crimes.

Moving into feature film, Manuel Huerga's *Salvador Puig Antich* (Salvador, 2006) is another important contribution in the recovery of Catalonia's historical memory and its corollary of reclaiming that justice be served to those dishonoured by Francoism. The director of this biopic is quite clear about his intentions and about the polemic awakened by his film about the anarchist executed in 1974:

> The friends and inheritors of the MIL (*Movimiento Ibérico de Liberación*) ideology criticize the film as a commercial commodity made to make money, which is precisely what Salvador was fighting against (…) Others claim that we have made an apology for terrorism or, at least of a given terrorist. This reassures me that the positioning of the film is correct (…) Our film is about Salvador Puig Antich, who was an anarchist. Leaving the two extremes aside, most people in the middle have enjoyed the film. They have watched it with an open mind and have been grateful for it. I even consider it a kind of cinematic therapy. It is a film that can help to exorcize many things and to confront many ghosts by forcing us to see face to face some things that had been hidden from us or that people were afraid to confront. These things are a part of our past and we must know our past in order to see where we are going. I insist that my film allows our youth to interpret their present. Thus, when the PP (Popular Party) speaks of Francoism without a word of condemnation, they may know what Franco and Francoism truly meant.[7]

---

7   Camí-Vela, 2006, pp. 12–13.

The fact that Huerga also uses the terms 'therapy' and 'exorcism' to characterize his aim reinforces the cathartic value he hopes to achieve by forcing contemporary audiences to face and/or (re)discover their own historical ghosts. More importantly, he hopes that those ghosts may be publicly exposed if not entirely exorcized: a case of more dirty washing to be aired in public. In order to do so, the director aimed at turning the story of a young Catalan anarchist into an action film of broad appeal. This objective was clearly achieved as the Barcelona daily *Avui* estimates the film had been seen by some 600,000 people by the end of the year; a remarkable figure by all standards, let alone considering that the movie was shot using both Catalan and Castilian.

This bilingualism also responds to the film's transnational character. In this respect, the casting of Daniel Brühl, *Good Bye, Lenin* (Becker, 2003), was an obvious glocal ploy to attract an international audience while exploiting internally the actor's linguistic ability since his mother is from Catalonia. Once again, therefore, Catalan cinema would be able to create an uncanny performance of a historical reality that was both familiar and unfamiliar to most.

The new Catalan cine-lit: The case of Ventura Pons

Since the great public and critical success of *La plaça del Diamant* (Diamond Square, 1982) many new and veteran film-makers have attempted filmic adaptations of literary texts. The list is considerable but there is no other Catalan director who has better reclaimed this cine-lit tradition in order to subvert it from within than Ventura Pons. In 1994, for example, Pons culminated the visual prologue to his filmic version of Monzó's *El perquè de tot plegat* (What It's All About, 1994) by sending a stone flying from a location vaguely resembling Montserrat into the city of Barcelona. This stone, a kind of symbolic meteorite, landed gently in front of the *Sagrada Familia*, the most iconic of Barcelona's pile of stones. With this irreverent gesture, Pons was seemingly announcing his own critique of the ongoing process of transforming Barcelona into a universal visual icon. What is more, with his amalgam of the lettered and filmed version of the city Pons not only evoked a biblical stoning but also the hypocrisy of the double visions of the reality of the Glass House of the metropolis exposed so far.[8]

Quite apart from turning Quim Monzó's sharp-edged text into a visual

---

[8] This image is central to the article by Pujol, 2010, 'Ventura Pons's *Barcelona (Un mapa)*: Trapped in the Crystal'.

meteorite, Ventura Pons has also turned much literature into film: three plays by the internationally acclaimed playwright Sergi Belbel: *Carícies/* Caresses (1997), *Morir o no/* To Die Or Not (1999) and *Forasters/* Foreigners (2008); a further two by Josep Maria Benet i Jornet: *Actrius/*Actresses (1996) and *Amic/ Amat/* Friend/ Beloved (1998); one by female dramatist Lluïsa Cunillé, *Barcelona, un mapa/* Barcelona. A Map (2007); three novels: one by Ferran Torrent: *La vida abismal/* Abysmal Life (2006) and two by Lluís-Anton Baulenas: *Anita no perd el tren/* Anita Takes a Chance (2000) and *Amor idiota/* Crazy Love (2004).

Like in many of the above, with *Food of Love* (2001) Ventura Pons succeeds once again in performing Barcelona on screen by merging the lettered and the filmed city. And this time, the gesture is even more remarkable since the written word comes not from a Catalan but the American, David Leavitt, and his novel, *The Page Turner*. What is more, Pons demonstrates the capacity to transform the other's text into his own vision and to do this while being remarkably faithful to the original. *Food of Love* is also especially significant because the meeting with the other does not occur on screen but in the personal encounter between Ventura Pons's cinematic vision and David Leavitt's written text.

There is no international or interracial encounter in *Food of Love* outside that of tourism, which indeed permeates the narrative. However, as Alberto Bermejo remarked in the film's press package, even this touristic gaze is reappropriated by the director's own:

> Ventura Pons (...) manages to convey a convincing and believable story, thanks to a perfect balance between distancing and passion. This suggestive formula becomes especially ironic as the story happens in Barcelona since it allows Ventura Pons to adopt the topical tourist gaze while superimposing his own gaze onto it. That is, the gaze of someone who is deeply knowledgeable of the spirit and beauty of Barcelona, his native city. This remarkable filmmaker is able to turn somebody else's story into his own and to do it by satisfying not only his own individual and creative needs but by stimulating the intelligence of his intended spectatorship as well.[9]

Indeed, when the camera finally takes us and Pamela on the tourist bus to share her iconic satisfaction of Gaudí's *Sagrada Familia*, we have already been taken to two additional tours. Paul, for example, introduces his mother to Catalonia's own colonial history by explaining the meaning of the Santa

---

[9] The information is available at www.venturapons.com

Maria del Mar church to her. It is a wasted effort since Pamela's reaction conflates the Catalan colonies with the colonization of America by Spain a century and a half later. This first itinerary culminates in the *Carrer de Montcada*, where the Picasso museum is located, and ends poignantly in the attempted robbery of Pamela's wallet by a group of gypsy women.

This incident constitutes the only interaction with any local people and, because of its very marginality in the diegetic framework of the film, it might be regarded as almost a parodic reminder of that other 'robbery': the gypsy stereotyping and cultural reappropriation that surrounded Barcelona with the Olympic Games of 1992. Be this as it may, the present 'encounter' occurs close to the Picasso museum and brings to an end a tour that had visually started with Paul's walking over Miró's ceramic tiles, in the very midst of the Ramblas, in yet another crucial iconic rendering of Barcelona's cultural location as an international crossroads.

The second tourist itinerary takes the three protagonists to Gaudí's second most iconic building, *La Pedrera*, in the *Passeig de Gràcia* – the hermaphroditic building upon whose totemic roof Jack Nicholson and Maria Schneider, Antonioni's strange voyagers, had played their own game of hide and seek in *The Passenger* of 1975; and in front of which Yoshio, the Japanese tourist of Rosa Vergés' *Souvenir* (1995), had both lost and regained his memory and his identity. This nocturnal voyage is filmed exquisitely, almost in slow motion, with tracking and low-angle panning shots that literally caress the façades of the art nouveau buildings. Such a gentle cinematic touch goes beyond any traditional tourist gaze and betrays the superposition that Bermejo talks about. They constitute, in Pons's own personal cinematic idiom, a visual counterpoint to those frenzied subjective shots of flashing and zig-zagging lines of flight that offered not only continuity but also the central visual metaphor of his film *Carícies* (Caresses, 1997), arguably his most radical performance of Barcelona on screen to date.

This seems to confirm that Ventura Pons is perhaps the only film-maker who has established a personal cinematic idiom about the city, his own city. It is an idiom in no way similar to that of Almodóvar, as the late Terenci Moix so aptly indicated, in his comments that: 'while becoming a sort of anomaly in the midst of current Spanish cinema, he [Pons] proves that it is possible to turn the city nights into a dramatic myth without having recourse to Almodovarian aesthetics'.[10]

In fact, Pons's visual aesthetics not only show no debt to the pervasive

---

[10] Moix at http://www.venturapons.com/Castella/peli%20caricies%20cast.html.

Almodóvar model; rather the inner strength of his *mise-en-scène* is radically opposed to it. After the Almodóvar-effect reached Hollywood foreign critics seem to have expectations of Spanish cinema of being *outrageous* or *flamboyant*, as might be recalled, for instance, in a statement on Pons by Roger Moore: 'This is a mild-mannered, been-there material given a pedestrian spin by a director who needed a touch of the flamboyant, the outrageous.' Obviously, there can be no way of describing Ventura Pons's cinematic idiom as 'pedestrian' unless, of course, literally: as someone who is close to the ground, who knows the territory he is stepping on. The fact that *Food of Love* received a divided reception in the American press is often explained as due to a lack of passion, of being too cold a film to portray the maturing of a teenage homosexual. In this respect, Pons is clearly a victim of preconceptions about Spanish film in the ambiguous assimilation of the movie's delicate balance between passion and distance which, rather than flamboyant, is both credible and convincing.

In this respect, the director's dramatic take may be on occasions misunderstood as simply 'posing'; that is, as foregrounding its own theatricality. In fact, as is extremely clear in his adaptation, *Barcelona, un mapa* (Barcelona. A Map, 2007), Pons manages to transform a play into a visual territory, and his cinematic 'territorialization' of Barcelona acquires the density that Deleuze would term a 'discursive practice'.[11] Neither distanced or dispassionate, Pons's cinematic idiom achieves the kind of political performativity that Judith Butler was describing when she encouraged the public assertion of queerness 'for the purpose of re-signifying the abjection of homosexuality into defiance and legitimacy'.[12]

What we find in *Food of Love*, however, is not so much the defiant gesture called for by Butler but the cinematic inscription of an already resignified and legitimate homosexual subject position. And it is upon this predicated normality that Pons's film rearticulates the same desiring fantasy that we saw in Balletbò-Coll's *Costa Brava. Family Album*, namely, that of the American other: a migrant desire that has reached Manhattan without having entirely left the streets of Barcelona in yet another figuration of Catalan's cinema uncanny transnational performance.

---

[11] For a detailed discussion of Ventura Pons's 'posing', see my essay of 2000, 'Ventura Pons o la teatralització de la impostura'. An extended analysis of his cinematic Barcelona as a Deleuzian territory is provided by Pujol in his article of 2009, 'Ventura Pons y la crónica de un territorio llamado Barcelona'. I would like to thank Profesor Pujol for allowing me to read his as then unpublished manuscripts.

[12] Butler, 1993, p. 21.

Epilogue: Catalan cinema's new experimental voices

As previously intimated some of the most interesting new Catalan filmmakers have moved their cameras away not only from Barcelona but also from any major urban centres.[13] Isabel Coixet's *La vida secreta de las palabras* (The Secret Life of Words, 2005), which received four Goya awards in 2006, expands one of the director's most personal motifs, the healing power of love, to create a profoundly touching visual metaphor of universal proportions.

Thanks to the memorable performances by Sarah Polley (Hanna) and Tim Robbins (Josef), Coixet manages to create an emotional tour-de-force on an oil platform in the Northern Atlantic that ends up encompassing three crucial aspects of contemporary experience: the horror of war, profound alienation in a global world, and the folly of our uninterrupted aggression against nature. The aptness of the oil platform as an extended metaphor for a remote, closed-in and cold world where men persist in injuring the Earth and themselves is all the more powerful when juxtaposed with the protagonist's own story: Hanna was repeatedly and brutally gang-raped by soldiers from her own nation during the Balkans war and now there is no place where she can escape that most uncanny and harrowing memory.

In his *Dies d'agost* (Some Days in August, 2006), Marc Recha brings cinematic minimalism a step further by turning a summer vacation into an almost unmediated interrogation of nature as the repository of man's history. Again, the director lets nature speak of the past violence that lurks under the quiet surfaces of the eerie reservoir in Mequinensa where he and his brother David have gone on vacation. In fact, this is no true vacation. It is rather another example of the uncanny performativity of recent Catalan cinema. It is also additional proof of Recha's ability to invoke the richness of an entire literary world in an extremely succinct cinematic discourse. In this case, the world is that of novelist Jesús Moncada who turned his native Mequinensa into a literary myth of enormous density. And what March Recha sets in motion under the guise of a familiar road movie is an intimate exploration of the spectral persistence of our historical memory and its process of inscription in the natural landscape where traumatic events of the past took place.

---

[13] This tendency is also present in the remarkable work produced so far by two of the youngest Catalan directors, Isaki Lacuesta and Albert Serra. Lacuesta's *La leyenda del tiempo* (The Legend of Time, 2006) was shot in the marshlands of the San Fernando island in Cadiz, and Albert Serra's latest film, *El cant dels ocells* (The Birds' Song, 2008) was filmed in an unspecified desert-like territory of the Canary Islands.

That is why, after a failed attempt to produce a documentary film about Ramon Barnils, an influential journalist whose anarchist lineage and vivid memories of the Civil War had always fascinated the young Recha, Marc and David set out to visit the places in areas surrounding the Ebro where Barnils spent the last days of his life and where the infamous front line of the Civil War was located. Beyond the oral testimonies, Recha's film seems to say, there is another space where we can reclaim our collective memory, and this place is no other than the very landscape where our spectral past remains inscribed.

The landscape of the Catalan Pyrenees will be the background of Cesc Gay's *Ficció* (Fiction, 2006), a film that shares not only a rural landscape but an initial self-referential starting point with Recha's *Dies d'agost*. Like Recha, Cesc Gay was also encountering problems in finishing a screenplay when he decided to turn that failed experience into the driving point of his film *Ficció*. Here, the metafictional exploration does not delve into the spectral presence of the past in nature. On the contrary, it uses nature as a blank mirror where the protagonist, an ironic alter ego of Gay himself, is forced to confront the fiction of his own self. Or, the fact that he is unable to articulate his true feelings beyond the impositions of his social self.

Much less ambitious in scope and range than Coixet's and Recha's films, Gay's *Ficció* becomes, nevertheless, another remarkable example of a new experimental wave in Catalan cinema that uses minimalist cinematic idiom and returns to nature in order to chart the territories of the unspoken and the uncanny. Taken separately, these films become a clear illustration of the three leading principles in this chapter. Coixet's *The Secret Life of Words* reinforces the transnational reality of Catalan cinema; Recha's *Dies d'agost* turns the most familiar landscape into an uncanny repository of both individual and collective memories; and Gay's *Ficció* becomes an almost silent performance of a character confronted with the entrapment of his own fictional self. Considered together, these films tell the story of a new Catalan cinematic idiom, conceived as a micro-cinema, whose existence on the global screen seems to depend on its capacity to recreate Catalan culture's own in-between and transnational location.

Works Cited and Suggested Reading

Angulo, Jesús (2006) 'La mirada poliédrica de Joaquín Jordá', *Nosferatu. Revista de Cine*, 52, pp. 11–30.

Bermejo, Alberto (no date provided) 'Descubrir y descubrirse', from *Food of Love* press package, www.venturapons.com

Butler, Judith (1993) *Bodies That Matter. On the Discursive Limits of 'Sex'*. New York and London: Routledge.

Camí-Vela, María (2007) 'Manuel Huerga y Salvador Puig Antich (2006). Entrevista', *Arizona Journal of Hispanic Cultural Studies*, 2, pp. 181–207.

Graham, Helen and Sánchez, Antonio (1995) 'The Politics of 1992', in Graham, H. and Labanyi, J. (eds) *Spanish Cultural Studies. An Introduction*. Oxford and New York: Oxford University Press, pp. 406–428.

Llagostera, Ferran (1987) 'A New Film Director' in 'Bar-cel-ona. The Film'. Barcelona: Centre Promotor de la Imatge.

Manresa, Laia (2006) *Joaquín Jordá. La mirada libre*. Barcelona: Filmoteca de Catalunya.

Martí-Olivella, Jaume (2000) 'Ventura Pons o la teatralització de la impostura', in Fernández, J.-A. (ed.) *El gai saber: introducció als estudis gais i lèsbics*. Barcelona: Llibres de l'Índex, pp. 373–392.

Merino, Imma (2006) 'From the Xino to the Raval. Cinema and the Construction of a New Reality', *Transfer. Journal of Contemporary Culture*, I, pp. 131–137.

Moix, Terenci (1998) 'Camino de perfección', http://www.venturapons.com/English/peli%20caricies%20eng.html

Moore, Roger (2002) 'Food of Love: A Review', http://uk.rottentomatoes.com/m/food_of_love/

Peña, Richard (2007) 'Another Spanish Cinema: Film in Catalunya 1906–2006', program handout. New York: Film Society of the Lincoln Center.

Pujol, Anton, (2009) 'Ventura Pons y la crónica de un territorio llamado Barcelona', *Arizona Journal of Hispanic Cultural Studies*, 13, pp. 61–81.

——— (2010) 'Ventura Pons' *Barcelona (un mapa)*: Trapped in the Crystal', *Studies in Hispanic Cinemas*, 6 (1), pp. 65–76.

Salvà, Bernat (26 March 2007) 'El cine català guanya pes', *Avui*.

——— (23 July 2007) 'Redistribució del cinema', *Avui*.

Films cited and further viewing

Antonioni, Michelangelo, *Professione Reporter* (The Passenger, 1975).
Aranda, Vicente, *Fata Morgana* (Mirage, 1966).
Balagué, Carles, *La casita blanca. La ciudad oculta* (The Little White House. The Hidden City, 2002).
Balletbò-Coll, Marta, *Costa Brava. A Family Album* (1995).
Becker, Wolfgang, *Good Bye Lenin* (2003).
Betriu, Francesc, *La plaça del Diamant* (Diamond Square, 1982).
Camino, Jaime, *La vieja memoria* (The Old Memory, 1978).
Coixet, Isabel, *La vida secreta de las palabras* (The Secret Life of Words, 2006).

Ferré, Ignasi P., *Un submarí a les estovalles* (A Submarine on the Tablecloth, 1991).
Forn, Josep Maria, *Companys, procés a Catalunya* (Companys. Catalonia on Trial, 1979).
—— *El coronel Macià* (Colonel Macià, 2006).
Gay, Cesc, *Ficció* (Fiction, 2006).
Guerín, José Luis, *En construcción* (Work in Progress, 2000).
Huerga, Manuel, *Salvador Puig Antich* (Salvador, 2006).
Jordà, Joaquim and Jacinto Esteva, *Dante no es únicamente severo* (Dante is not Simply Harsh, 1967).
—— and Núria Villazán, *Mones com la Becky* (Monkeys Like Becky, 1999).
—— *De nens* (About Children, 2003).
Lacuesta, Isaki, *La leyenda del tiempo* (The Legend of Time, 2006).
Llagostera, Ferran, *Bar-cel-ona* (1986).
Llobet Gràcia, Llorenç, *Vida en sombras* (Life in Shadows, 1948).
Pons, Ventura, *Ocaña, retrat intermitent* (Ocaña, Intermittent Portrait, 1978).
—— *El perquè de tot plegat* (What is it All About, 1994).
—— *Actrius* (Actresses, 1996).
—— *Carícies* (Caresses, 1997).
—— *Amic/Amat* (Friend/Lover, 1998).
—— *Morir (o no)* (To Die (Or Not)), 1999).
—— *Anita no perd el tren* (Anita Takes a Chance, 2000).
—— *Food of Love* (2001).
—— *Amor idiota* (Crazy Love, 2004).
—— *La vida abismal* (Abysmal Life, 2006).
—— *Barcelona. Un mapa* (Barcelona. A Map, 2007).
—— *Forasters* (Foreigners, 2008).
Recha, Marc, *Dies d'agost* (Some Days in August, 2006).
Ribas, Antoni, *La ciutat cremada* (The Burned City, 1976).
Rovira Beleta, Francisco, *Los Tarantos* (1962).
Salvador, Juli, *Apartado de correos 1001* (Post Box 1001, 1950).
Serra, Albert, *El cant dels ocells* (The Birds' Song, 2008).
Soler, Llorenç, *Saïd* (1999).
Suárez, Gonzalo, *Ditirambo* (1967).
Vergés, Rosa, *Souvenir* (1995).

9

Festival and the Shaping of Catalan Community

DOROTHY NOYES

Participation and coordination

In an aside to Catalan nationalism, every guidebook will send you to the *Plaça Sant Jaume* in Barcelona on Sunday morning to see the *sardana*, the national dance. You are instructed to observe the opening of the ring to admit all comers, young and old, known and unknown. The newcomers take up the nearest hands on either side and join the dance, an energetic 'pointing' of feet to the rhythms of a *cobla*, a dark-voiced but strident wind band. The best primers add that the dance was persecuted under the Franco regime, that the sober footwork bespeaks a classical spirit of order and *seny* (level-headedness) derived from the first Greek settlers, that the expansive ring indicates commitment to equality and openness and that the intricacy of its timekeeping marks the national aptitude for business: 'Catalans count even when they're dancing.'

No tradition has been as thoroughly mythologized as the *sardana*. Nationalist youth today are likely to wince at the mention of it and direct the outsider's attention rather to the *castells*, human towers erected with dizzying speed and structural complexity. Both traditions were invoked in the opening ceremonies of the 1992 Olympic Games. If the *sardana* was made an emblem of Catalan tenacity from the *Renaixença* through the post-Franco Transition, the *castell*, drawn historically not from Old Catalonia but from the southern towns of New Catalonia, became from the 1980s a sign of the nation's power to renew itself.

Both forms had less idealistic beginnings in the dances held during *festes majors* (municipal patronal festivals) as a diversion and occasion of courtship. Each split off in the late eighteenth century from a dance of which it was the final, fastest, and most aggressive figure, becoming a vehicle for male display. The young men of Valls (Tarragona) became known for their increasingly daring reworkings of the athletic conclusion to the 'dance of the Valencians'. They created 'pillars' of single men stacked up on one another's shoulders, becoming 'towers' of two, and 'castles' of three or four interlocked. As they rose skywards they diminished to a single small boy standing at the top, supported from below by an intricately ordered *pinya* (pinecone) of men, hands to backs, dissolving ultimately into the surrounding crowd. By the mid-nineteenth century, teams of men toured the summer festivals to make money, spreading knowledge of the practice. Soon *colles* (gangs) representing municipal factions or rivalries between towns would compete to construct the most elaborate castles, often through the full course of a summer festival season.

The North had instead the *sardana*, the fast finale to the sober dance of the *contrapàs*. In the nineteenth century it became popular with young men who vied to control the ring's movements and an avenue for ambitious local musicians, who incorporated cosmopolitan elements from opera, military bands and French salon balls into their *cobles*. Initially associated with liberal politics, the *sardana* was the favourite dance in the heartland of the *Renaixença*, the cultural revival of the nineteenth century as described in Dominic Keown's chapter on Contemporary Culture. Catholic Catalanist writers laboriously reconstructed this urban fashion as an ancestral peasant ritual. Equally important, the *sardana* could easily be assimilated to bourgeois disciplines of the body and generalized in participation, as the *castells* could not; once tamed and codified, the *sardana* encouraged the presence of women and the upper classes. Its structure lent itself to calculation, its movements to formalization. The dance became the standard participatory component of Catalanist public ceremony, embodying the inclusion and the consent of the people.

In their different fashions, *sardanes* and *castells* distil the general challenge of collective life: participation and coordination. Festival is distinctive as a cultural form because there is no divide between the representation, its subject, and its author. It is an operation upon the body, conferring a position and a stance, instilling gestures in memory, teaching individuals both their place and their room for manoeuvre. A festival is beneath all else a configuration of co-present bodies, whose mutual orientation is alone sufficient to frame off festival time and space from the everyday surround.

Contemporary cosmopolitans imagine traditional festival as a space of relaxation and voluntary coming together as a community. Catalans, with their conflictive history, know better. Festival is a labour and participation is obligatory: a small culture cannot sustain itself through the quiet identification of individuals in private space. There is no *sardana* until dancers step forward.

The *castell* requires much wider, diverse participation: the *anxaneta* at the top must be supported by physiques of all dimensions in the lower layers, with burly men at the base. But the *pinya* does not end with members of the *colla*: they must be supported in turn by the crowd around them if the castle is to stay up. Passive spectatorship is not an option. Indeed, *fer pinya* is a basic idiom of unity in diversity: a community makes a pinecone around a crisis or a person in need, while its members remain distinct, sticky, and prickly. The *castell* dramatizes the challenge of this coordination. Participants must be minutely sensitive not only to their interlocking positions but to one another's breathing and slightest shifts in body weight if a difficult *castell* is to be raised; its undoing must be managed with equal care and mutual attention to avoid serious hurt. It is pedagogy in the possibility and the fragility of social formations.

Qui perd els origins ...

In the late 1960s, Catalanist intellectuals in search of the primitive betook themselves to the Pyrenees to see the descent of the *falles*: torches rolled from mountain grasses, lit with pitch, and paraded down from multiple mountainsides to the village of Isil in the Pallars Sobirà. They went to Centelles in Osona, where at the end of December a giant pine tree is cut in the woods and borne into the church to be hung upside down before the altar. They went to Berga, where the vine-laden, firecracker-wearing horned devils of the *Patum* set themselves alight in what Fàbregas tellingly described as 'a *happening* straight from prehistory'.[1]

For the young of the period, *Sant Joan* – Midsummer night – became the key national festival. Activists ran torches down from the peak of Mount Canigó, on the French side of the border, to towns all over Catalonia, Valencia and the Balearics to articulate the primordial unity of the Catalan-speaking areas. The traditional bonfires of *Sant Joan* promised a resurgence of all the sexual and political energies repressed by Franco's regime, and were described accordingly as a survival of summer solstice rites of fertility. The more immediate and, in those days, unspeakable significance of fire was its communicability and resistance to containment.

Why should these nineteenth-century anthropological fantasies acquire such sudden currency among sophisticated Barcelonese and the university-educated young? In fact, our knowledge of pre-Christian ritual in the Pyrenees is almost wholly speculation. But origins are always a metaphor. Community members will often tell you that their festival is primitive, ancestral, 'in the blood'. They talk of it as deep in history because it is deep in biography. Catalan infants are danced on their fathers' backs during a *cercavila*, the musical prelude to the festivities, taken to touch the hand of the

---

[1] Fàbregas & Barceló, 1976, p. 153.

giantess before the *festa major* or given an exploded firecracker to handle after *Sant Joan*. They learn how to dance like the *capgrossos* (dwarves with huge heads) as they learn to walk. They grow up inside the festival: it is never experienced as a first time, always as a recurrence.

In the 1960s, this capacity to create shared bodily experience made festival a primary vehicle of civic pedagogy in a context of censorship, bilingualism, political division, and social mistrust. Festival had to be prehistoric so that it would precede all divisive names, all languages, all political formations. Catalan festivals were not of a single tendency but for everyone; so too then, Catalonia. This political necessity has continued into the present, for neither recent history nor present diversity are comfortable topics for communal discussion.

Conservative Catalanism at the turn of the twentieth century generated innumerable and elaborate tales placing festivals in the High Middle Ages, a time when Catalonia was powerful and independent. As part of the paternalism christened 'industrial feudalism' by Prat de la Riba, local working classes were encouraged to participate in folk performance explained as popular tributes of affection to the local lord. Origin narratives and explicit festival interpretation are also used to create political cover for risky performances. Suspicious bishops, civil governors, Catalanist leaders, potential tourists and other important outsiders were provided from the mid-eighteenth century to the end of the Franco regime with a series of allegories to account for the mysterious wordless danced combats of the *Patum* of Berga. One says what is necessary for the festival to be permitted to continue, and multiple explanations persist for any festival of a certain historicity.

'Qui perd els orígens perd la identitat' sang Raimon in the 1960s, quoting Salvador Espriu; since the Transition he has been quoted in turn by conceivably every Catalan mayor who has ever composed a festival welcome. 'If you lose your origins you lose your identity.' It is taken for granted by all sides that this matters. The division of opinion about festival origins expresses an enduring ambivalence about the communal past. It is sought as a documented, legitimate, and recognized possession but also stored in the inarticulate body, knowledge 'in the blood'.

History

Although a complete history of Catalan festivals remains to be written, we can say something of the mixed social, economic, political and, of course, religious and ludic factors that brought them into being. For the Middle Ages we know primarily about court, church, and urban celebrations. These sometimes incorporated earlier ritual practices, but popular observances also emerged in contestation with institutional celebrations in a noisy dialogue that has continued to the present.

The best-known early Catalan festivals are the elaborate Corpus Christi celebrations that began in the early fourteenth century. Initially a show of theological orthodoxy, they quickly became an occasion for competitive civic display. The *Corpus Mysticum* of which Christ was the head articulated itself in a great procession of the consecrated Host. The various corporations and elements of the local community lined up in much-contested hierarchical order of proximity to the Sacrament. This assembly of Christ's kingdom on Earth was complemented by representations of allegorical figures or tableaux of biblical figures, saints, and all the company of heaven.

Interactions among the theological programme, guild energies, and courtly and plebeian traditions to assemble the procession produced the characteristic Catalan festival vocabulary of *entremesos* (interludes), today more commonly called *comparses* or troupes of performers. This label encompasses masked dances, mimed combats, and large mobile figures of humans and animals, moulded from reinforced plaster over wooden frames with one or more carriers underneath. Some performances were supported by music and many called upon noisemakers and pyrotechnia of various kinds to attract attention.

The most popular *comparses* persisted alongside the procession or relocated themselves to the *festa major* in many Catalan towns. A full ensemble of them can be seen today in the *Patum*, a celebration that gradually detached itself from the procession in the city of Berga to become an autonomous series of dances: a combat of Turks and Christians; one of angels and devils; the *guites*, a pair of aggressive, long-necked mules; the elegant crowned eagle; majestic giants and the dwarves that joined them in the nineteenth century as emblems of middle-class emulation; and the *plens* or 'full devils', a fierce final dance of devils laden with firecrackers.

In the Counter Reformation, the Church suppressed many of these representations and promoted new cults and confraternities to foster popular devotion. Many pilgrimages to local sanctuaries date from this period, as does the *Festa del Roser*, the devotion to the rosary brought by migrants from Languedoc to become deeply rooted in much of the countryside. In the same period, as plebeian communal customs became more assertive, the aristocracy and merchant bourgeoisie of the cities began to distance themselves from the intimacies of collective performance. This 'retreat to the balcony' intensified a growing identification between festival, the street, and the common people.[2]

---

[2] Amelang, 1986, p. 195.

In the modern period urban festival became increasingly plural and commercial. Elites celebrated carnival in private balls held in theatres, while working people had dancehalls such as Barcelona's notorious *La Patacada*. More institutionalized sociability took shape with the liberal regime of 1833 and the growth of industrialization. The middle and upper classes founded intellectual *ateneus* (Athenaeum Clubs) and ludic *casinos*, increasingly divided along political lines. Workers' *ateneus* and mutual aid societies, many allied to labour unions others born in conservative reaction, pursued recreational, educational, and social agendas. Best known for their musical activities, the popular choirs founded by Clavé joined with the *Societat del Born* to revive Carnival in Barcelona as a street event, which soon had more than one hundred competing costume balls, a massively attended parade and a strong, though regulated, satirical component.

Until late in the century, social formations and competition rather than traditional performances were the focus of attention at festivals. The state began to join the Church in providing occasions. Military and political victories, coronations and royal births; and local triumphs such as the electrification of a town, the construction of an industrial canal or, later, the canonical coronation of a local religious image all called for celebration. Neighbourhood associations, which had replaced guilds as primary mobilizers, raised money to rival one another in elaborate street decorations of branches, hangings, arches, and lights.

As the traditionalist–liberal conflicts of mid-century modulated into the acute class tensions that held sway from the Restoration to the Civil War, festival became increasingly divided between paternalist folklore and ritualized riot. As described in the chapter by Antoni Segura i Mas and Elisenda Barbé i Pou on Modern History, the new fortunes of the Restoration put money into celebratory display events, expressions of a new Catalanist sensibility as the need to incorporate the new proletariat into the national project fostered renewed attention to popular forms of celebration. In 1902, Cambó's *Lliga* reconstructed Barcelona's *Festa de la Mercè* (Our Lady of Mercy) as a national holiday. Giants were invited from all over the region to a massive gathering, the *sardana* was propounded as a symbol of national brotherhood, and the first formal competition of *castells* was held: local tradition was henceforth definitively conscripted into national service. However contestatory, urban, or outright liberal they might be, popular observances were also appropriated by municipal governments and the employer class. They were reclothed as Catalan, as medieval and/or rural in origin, and respectful of hierarchy: in short, as folklore.

New ceremonial elements, dances and dramas, and festival figures – particularly the giants and dwarves that gave compelling visual testimony to supposedly natural class distinctions – enriched *festes majors* everywhere. Teachers organized folk dance groups; *literati* fabricated poetic local legends or composed paeans to Catalan festival as a spiritual contrast to the brutality of the bullfight. Social conflict spelled itself out in ritual spaces. As evident in our chapters on modern history and the city, anarchists attacked the Corpus Christi procession and the bourgeois temple of the Liceu; popular revolt of many stripes expressed itself in the burning of churches and the profanation of images and relics. The powerful ritual dimension of the Tragic Week of 1909 was recognized by the bourgeois Joan Maragall, who saw the church burners as restoring the sacred to circulation after its long stagnation in institutional enclosures.

Such explicit politicization continued. Primo de Rivera outlawed the *sardana*. Under the Second Republic and during the war, town halls privileged the popular elements of Corpus Christi and the *festa major* while condemning the clerical and 'feudal' ones. The crowns of giants were replaced with workers' caps. Purely religious festivals were often suppressed, while the worker liturgies of May Day and republican anniversaries were made official.

After his victory, Franco immediately Castilianized and re-Catholicized festival. Names were translated and new origins invoked. Traditional religious festivals were inflected with the heavy ceremonial of national-Catholicism, including outdoor masses and military parades. Carnival was banned outright or made unrecognizable: in 1939, a month after the Republican defeat, Igualada's carnival was celebrated with special daily masses and the town's patron saint was observed to have been martyred by 'the antecedents of the present hordes without God or Country'.[3]

Festivals became an occasion to rub the nose of the defeated in the new order. New Catholic observances were promoted, such as Barcelona's massive Eucharistic Congress of 1952, designed as a cautious reopening of Spain towards the world. While fear and self-interest spurred much submission to state-sponsored Catholic devotion, popular religiosity burgeoned for a variety of reasons. Many Catholics had experienced persecution during the Republic, not least with the widespread assassination of priests. The trauma of the war had to be processed. Furthermore, in a period when autonomous initiatives were repressed and gatherings of more than a handful of people had to have permission from the civil governor, the Church provided a sheltering institution for collective assembly and sociability. As early as

---

[3] Torelló, 1999, p. 8.

1940, church events might make limited use of the Catalan language; they could find funding from local employers, and they could draw upon symbols shared by clergy and nationalists.

Thus the 1947 Enthronement of the Virgin of Montserrat was attended by 70,000 people. The formation of the organizing commission allowed the establishment of a network across Catalonia in a period when no other organizational expression was permitted to the region. The Catalan flag and language were present. Not surprisingly, the *Virolai* sung to the Madonna became from that moment a substitute for the outlawed national anthem 'Els Segadors'/ The Reapers.[4]

Festes majors did not recover immediately. Town halls struggled to find enough able-bodied men to enact the *entremesos* despite the usual payment of a pair of espadrilles, a good dinner, and occasionally cash; by the 1950s participation was often encouraged with prizes and plaques. Depressed, hungry, fearful of repression, suspicious of their neighbours, reluctant to celebrate the glories of the regime and increasingly caught up with mass culture, many Catalans were not eager for communal celebration. The regime, however, needed displays of collective submission and contentment. Local authorities promoted the beauty, harmony, and morality of traditional festival against 'degenerate exotic modernity'. In the 1950s, competitions of giants were organized and a new designation of *Fiesta de Interés Turístico* (Festival of Tourist Interest) was invented for those celebrations judged most traditional, distinctive, and aesthetically impressive. Economically and politically, it was necessary to perform the new official tourist slogan, 'España es diferente'.

In the late 1960s, the young discovered traditional festival as a channel for their energies that offered at once a release for the body, a recovery of the indigenous, and a safely ambiguous form of political expression. They had been socialized under three dispensations: the regime schooling, which separated the sexes and condemned the body; the clandestine Catalanist education, which took place in scout troops, church groups, and private university-prep academies; and the proximity of Europe's political agitations and sexual revolution, visible on the beaches of the Costa Brava and across the border in Perpignan. Singing full-voiced in choirs, dancing the burning devils, and extreme mountaineering all provided kinetic release from the regime's frustrations, an expiation of felt historical cowardice through risk-taking, and most importantly an apprenticeship in cooperation.

---

[4] Frigolé, 1980, pp. 21–5.

The double meanings of festival symbolism were exploited and the transgressive potential of gestures pushed to its limits. Participation increased dramatically: bourgeois youth came down from the balconies, women concealed their difference inside the devils' suits, and the square became crowded. Artists took inspiration from traditional forms. In the 1970s, rock musicians drew on festival music and theatre groups like *Els Comediants* constructed their happenings out of the giants, dragons, and devils of local tradition. Fireworks grew more intense, dances faster and more physical, drinking heavier. The primitive energies of festival were sought to shunt off alienation and to build collective strength. The most participatory festivals, such as the *Patum* of Berga, began to attract attendance from all over Catalonia, becoming spaces of rehearsal for the massive street demonstrations in Barcelona.

Most who were young at the time remember the Transition less for specific acts of political contestation than for 'the public occupation of the street, cultural effervescence, sexual tolerance, the appearance of a series of leisure spaces, the everyday practice of newfound liberty'.[5] The Transition was itself a festival. The routinization of democratic charisma after 1979 posed a challenge. A dramatic rise in drug and alcohol abuse fostered a distancing from collective expression for many, while some of the most dedicated Transition activists rued their own 'addiction' to political agitation, now counterproductive given the real need for mundane institution-building to sustain everyday cohabitation.

In the *comarques* (counties), however, a critical mass of young people kept their focus on traditional festival as a key medium to *fer país*, to build Catalonia. They found support from municipal governments seeing a low-cost avenue to popularity, small business-owners seeking to maintain the viability of their high street, the cultural foundations of the savings banks, and the new Department of Culture of the *Generalitat*, eager to create public cultural forms that would appeal to immigrants and foster national identification. Voluntary associations dedicated to festival were created in cities like Tarragona, Reus, and Manresa in the early 1980s. Neighbourhood associations were also important creators of festival, striving to revitalize the old quarters where apartments had been left empty or occupied by new immigrants.

Activists delved through the town archives to see what kinds of festivals their community had had in the past. The 'recuperation' of scantily docu-

---

[5] Feixa, 2003, p. 28.

mented dances, bestiary, and entire festivals necessitated much imaginative reconstruction and in fact much outright invention. Throughout Catalonia, fire festivals were inspired by traditional models, but transformed the centripetal festival of the square into a *correfoc*, a 'run-through-the-fire' that filled the streets with devils and pyrotechnical constructions, ever more spectacular and at ever closer range.

Seny i rauxa: order and transgression

The tension of order and energy is basic to all festival: a community requires both to prosper, but the balance between them is ever tenuous. Vicens Vives's famous description of the Catalan character as oscillating between *seny i rauxa* (level-headedness and wildness) finds an echo in festival's distillation of social relations. Repetitive dances with prescribed movements in a delineated space often alternate with *salts*, the riotous disruptions effected by masked figures and effigies laden with pyrotechnia.

Typically a clear equation is made between style and status. Festival giants move with bourgeois decorum, while the *mulassa*, the mule associated with its human fellow-labourers, crazily transgresses both metrical and spatial boundaries. The fine clothes and clear identities of the giants stand above the crowd, echoing those of the 'orderly' classes in the balconies around them. Below in the square, the *comparses* and the common people intermingle in a sweaty, smoky mass of motion. Festivals of inclusion such as the *festa major* and Corpus Christi offer multiple points of entry to accommodate the variety of social actors in the community: some align themselves with the dwarves, some with the devils, some with the eagle.

There is an inherent dynamic of dissolution in the gathering of a crowd under a rhythmic discipline. It is encapsulated in the structure of the dances, which begin in a slow waltz, turn to a faster duple metre, and end in a rapid spin that leaves the *geganters* dizzy. Festival's techniques of the body – crowding, drinking, sleep deprivation, constant motion, strong rhythms, loud noise, and the smoke and confusion of firecrackers at close range – gradually disable the critical faculties associated with the upper body and release the energies of the lower one. Festivals fold inwards from representation to vertigo.

The festival calendar, nonetheless, retains two ideal types, popularly represented in the polarity of Corpus Christi and Carnival.[6] From its institution in the fourteenth century, the Corpus procession strove to incarnate the fullness

---

6   Marfany, 1997, p. 45.

and the clarity of the divine order. Still in the nineteenth, it embodied this order and its exclusions, becoming a focus of an anarchist attack in 1896. At the same time, the procession also attracted the aspiring classes, who imagined *ordre* as a principle of practice that would foster social mobility. Santiago Rusiñol in his 1907 *L'Auca del Senyor Esteve*, a wry epic of the Barcelona *menestralia* (petty bourgeoisie), treats the procession as the sacral matrix of a fully ritualized life in which church and shop, rosary and account books echo one another.

The Franco regime reasserted the principle of the procession as hierarchical control. 'The revolutionary masses were and meant nothing in the city,' declared the new president of the *Junta Provincial de Cultura* at the reopening of the *Ateneu de Barcelona* in 1939. 'The authentic and traditional Barcelona was that (...) which scattered flowering broom before the Sacrament during the Corpus Christi procession.'[7] But the full Corpus celebration in communities such as Berga evolved to allow the expression of all three tendencies – submission, rebellion, and aspiration – their delicate balance an acknowledgment of their irreconcilable tension in everyday life.

Celebrated by some scholars as a fulcrum of individual freedom and by others as one of collective revolution, Carnival as practised in Catalonia has plausible connections with each. *Carnaval* or *Carnestoltes* was almost wholly repressed by Franco as well as in other periods of social anxiety when the presence of maskers in the streets made power fearful of disorder – even during the 1993 outbreak of the first Gulf War. The political order is overturned on the first day by the entry of King Carnestoltes, who declares a new regime. At the other end of the celebration the sacred is made profane: Good Friday rituals are anticipated on the morning of Ash Wednesday by the burial of the King, surrounded by noisy female mourners, although the erect penis of the papier-mâché effigy promises resurrection.

Songs, parade floats in the street, and the sermon or trial or testament of the King criticize the year's misdeeds, with an emphasis on the abuses of the powerful. Costuming provides a more ambiguous blend of self-loss and self-expression. The traditional cross-dressing in which men took on grotesquely implausible feminine attributes often gave way historically to displays of wealth and sexuality that hardly challenge the social order. In other cases cross-dressing allows the assertion of an identity long silenced, as in Sitges with its large gay community.

More recently, with sensitivities high as a result of both Islamist terrorism

---

[7] Various authors, 1973, vol. 1, p. 287.

and heavy rates of Muslim immigration, traditional festival play with figures of the Other has been called into question. The image of the Moor is ambiguous, for Moors are origin figures in many Catalan legends, their dark skin associated with that of the local invocations of the Madonna, the dark-skinned Virgin of Montserrat. The blackness represented in official interpretations as alien is often popularly understood as a mark of autochthony. In any case, the Moors and the devils in Catalan *entremesos* are typically appreciated – and performed – by community members with little sympathy for the established order of the moment. Carnival cross-dressing, however, is more topical and more realistic, invoking the Arab sheiks who buy property in Spain, Saddam Hussein or, today, Osama bin Laden.

These representations and more traditional ones such as the *Moro Manani*, whose giant head once vomited candy for children on Christmas day in Vilanova i la Geltrú, have become the object of social anxiety and frequent self-censorship. But concern over racist representations, while demonstrating new sensitivity to the position of immigrants, also marks a continuing social distance, for teasing is a strategy of intimacy and evidence that the butt of the joke is understood to belong to the community.[8] Overwhelmingly reclaimed in the democratic period, Carnival now forces Catalans to question themselves instead of challenging the regime.

The sharing of food and drink unites the Catholic sacrament of communion, its civic transformation into Corpus Christi, and its travesty as Carnival. Festival drinking from shared *porrons* or wineskins incorporates individuals into the community by incorporating the community into individuals. Carnival shows up the device by bursting the boundaries of inside and outside. From Christmas through Carnival, the body is indulged for the coming privations of Lent. On St Sylvester's Day, *l'Home dels Nassos* (Man of Noses) distributes his 365 noses; Carnival will extend the phallic intimations in an endless variety of sausages and eggs, obscenely arranged, and these will return at Easter as less aggressive affirmations when the season of courtship begins. Sexual and social opponents become gradually indistinguishable in combats such as the flour war between Carlists (men) and Liberals (women) in Berga. The social world of Carnival is not sleek and defined, like that of the Corpus procession, but sticky with mud and excremental symbolism or with commodities that similarly bring fertility and collective wealth, such as the Cuban sugar that features in the *Guerra Dolça* (Sweet War) of Vilanova i la Geltrú.

---

[8] Erickson, 2008, p. 116.

Rites of collective immersion have recently invaded other festivals also. Water is often used when there is a traditional motive: thus the bringing of the miraculous water of *Sant Magí* to Tarragona is followed by a *revetlla remullada* (soaked revelry) in which participants inundate one another. In *correfocs* it is the thickness of falling sparks: scars on arms and 'jerseys more holes than jersey' become badges of honour. You have only to place yourself in harm's way to join the fun, but a hierarchy of commitment nonetheless emerges; by the end of the event, the most active, the most loved, are the filthiest: soaked in community.

To be sure, not everyone enjoys the filth, and what today is valued as inclusion was often historically feared as contamination. The forms themselves are labile; they can be pushed or restrained by performers. Festival forms configure bodies into arrangements – advancing lines, tight masses, dispersed clusters, face-to-face confrontations – that suggest but do not determine social formations. Festival genres assemble bodies in space; bodies work out the meanings of such assembly in time. The ever-present tension of order and disorder in festival is that of communities drawn together not from choice but from necessity.

The cosmopolitan and the local

Festivals oscillate between the cosmopolitan and the local. They have always been occasions of exchange with the outside world, when the prestige of metropolitan forms descended for a day or two upon the town. As Catalonia has globalized, however, its festivals have become more dedicated to reconnecting residents with their place or telling outsiders its story. As elsewhere in the Catholic world, the mountain sanctuary and the town parish incarnate the tension between local devotions and the universal Church. In the town, the priest controlled access to the sacred. In the mountains, it belonged to the humblest. Throughout the country a story is told of a child who loses one of the cows he is herding on a mountainside. He finds it kneeling in front of a statue of the Mother of God and it refuses to move from its place at the mouth of a cave or a grotto or the foot of a tree, so that the authorities are forced to build a sanctuary around it.

Individuals seek out the sanctuaries of local Madonnas – Núria, Vinyet, Tura and innumerable others – both for private reasons, such as seeking to have a child, and in community pilgrimages, typically celebrated on the feast of the 'found Madonnas' on 8 September, the nativity of Our Lady. In the past there was a procession from the parish church out to the sanctuary. Today it is more usual for hikers to make the climb for fun or for families to drive up with a picnic. After mass, the community sings the *goigs*, a hymn to the local

Madonna, while individuals circle up behind the altar to touch the Virgin's hand with no priest intervening. In the afternoon, after a longish interval of grilled *botifarres* and wine on the grass, the ring of sound and pilgrims in the sanctuary is echoed by a ring of dancers outside. The dance takes hundreds of local variations, but until well into the twentieth century the purpose was always the same. Slow, with long opportunities for conversation between partners and for physical display, it has been described as 'a machine for making marriages'.

In a more secular key, the dances of urban and seaside *festes majors* served the same purpose. There the scene was the *envelat*, a tent built on the seaside promenade or simply a rooftop of ribbons and paper flowers raised over the square. Both mountain gatherings and *festes majors* were occasions when young men travelled to neighbouring towns in search of mates, when summer people from Barcelona met local elites, when urban workers found one another, when the place and the people settled on it came together.

In the late nineteenth century, this coming together became the subject of national allegory. City people began to go to the mountains in search not just of mates but of the national soul, and mountain communities eager for urban tourists and industrial investors began to imagine origin narratives for their dances. The dances might have been wholly folklorized as cafés and recorded music reached the villages had it not been for the Franco regime. The increased repression of contact between the sexes kept the mountain dances alive as occasions for contact, sometimes occasioning clerical denunciations of 'Lucifer's yeast' profaning the festivals of the Mother of God.

Of course sex was not the only festival currency; the literal kind was also important in fostering exchange. Festivals brought in country buyers for town goods and, conversely, vendors of urban goods into villages; today immigrants sell both cheap mass-produced toys and exotic specialties such as Andean sweaters. Other emissaries of modernity come to the *festa major* in the form of urban entertainments – the travelling cinema on a truck in former days, the dance band and more recently the theatrical troupe.

A further connection to the metropolis is made by inviting politicians and personalities to visit the *festa major*. The celebrity – who often acts as *pregoner* in declaring the start to the festivities with a comic or nationalist invocation – provides glamour or entertainment. The politician will, it is hoped, bring the water of patronage to dry local wells in exchange for a homage that promises votes. The hunger for metropolitan recognition, and the less metaphorical hunger for jobs and investment, pushes local actors to seek ever more far-flung connections via their *festa major*, ranging from sister cities in foreign countries to UNESCO.

The old giants of the *festes majors* and Corpus Christi are dressed as kings and queens. Their height, weight, hard-surfaced beauty, unresponsiveness and general uselessness make them a convenient metaphor for the upper classes and even the state. At the same time, giants provide a vein of erotic fantasy in relation to unattainable objects of desire, and in the nineteenth century they served, not coincidentally, as emissaries of metropolitan fashion: the coiffure of the giantess announced the new mode for the summer.

With the restoration of municipal autonomy the giants took on a new aspect, their importance as local possession outweighing their traditional symbolic associations. Their numbers exploded, with ten times as many in 1996 as in 1980.[9] Some new giants were modelled on local personalities. Most often, new giants in rural communities are dressed as generic peasants and carry the tools of the town's former local industry. Such festivals often include demonstrations of the old skill, reaping and threshing, towing barges along the Ebro, or animal husbandry, maintaining local knowledge but also marking its archaism. The festival becomes archive.

Sant Sadurní d'Anoia, home to the sparkling wine *cava* industry, created a completely new festival creature in 1982: *Fil·loxera*, the beetle that ravaged the vineyards and ultimately transformed wine production in the late nineteenth century. More than that, they created an entire drama around the figure. Unlike traditional ensembles of *comparses*, in which indices of local social relations were abundant but not scripted and in which there is no explicit narrative thread, the series of dances in the *Festa de la Fil·loxera* (Feast of Philoxera) constitutes a local historical drama, representing the creature's invasion, the damage to the vines, the intervention of the town fathers, and the defeat of the plague. The dance of the vines is an ingenious adaptation of the *salt de plens* of the *Patum*, with its devils wreathed in greenery. The vineyards of Sant Sadurní are brown *capgrossos* shaped like the knotted trunks of old vines, with green leaves sprouting on top and metal rods to support firecrackers, said to represent the unhealthy redness caused by the disease.

The newer festivals, like the older ones, are still instruments for reproducing the local community and obtaining outside resources. By traditional standards, they are unusually expository, highly produced, and aesthetically impressive. Where once they dealt intensively, in coded ways, with such structural challenges as negotiating marriages, apportioning prestige, and criticizing deviance both high and low, today organizers concentrate on the

---

[9] Grau i Martí, 1996, p. 7.

representation of collective identities, hoping both to keep local people engaged and to create a distinctive brand for the town.

The order of time

The scent of wild thyme wafts over the *Carrer de l'Hospital* in Barcelona's *Raval*, normally dank with dust and old drains. The street is closed to traffic, filled with vendors of packaged herbs, caramels, and an impressive variety of honeys. Stands are piled high with aromatic scrub from the Catalan hillsides: rosemary, scratchy lavender, even gorse in hot yellow flower. On every 11 May, the *Fira de Sant Pons* brings the Mediterranean spring into the stone streets of the old city.

Old festivals are built upon seasonal transitions. This springtime shock of freshness and colour meets its antithesis at the start of November with All Saints' Day, the festival of the dead and the death of the year. The All Saints sensorium emphasizes desiccation, maturity, the brown and golden: the traditional foods are roast chestnuts, sweet potatoes, and *panellets*, cookies made from almonds and pinenuts, accompanied with oxidized *vi ranci*, allowed to dehydrate and concentrate as it ferments.

The festival calendar is structured around seasonal poles that shape conceptual polarities. *Sant Joan* is the summer festival when everyone is outside: rural couples once went off into the meadows, urbanites go up on the roof to throw firecrackers at their neighbours; and the domestic detritus of the year is burned off in a grand bonfire. It is countered by Christmas, the festival of ingathering, when the shepherds come down the mountainsides to the parish church and the woods are brought into the house with the *tió*, the yule log. The log is domesticated and gradually converted from nature to culture.

Decorated with a face and limbs like a kind of animal, the *tió* is fed by the children, who stuff straw or dry locust pods and water into its hollow. On Christmas Eve, the feeding pays off: they beat it with a stick and sing, demanding it to defecate 'nougat and white wine'. After the bottles of *cava*, the delicious yuletide treat of the *torrons*, and individual presents emerge from beneath the log, it excretes something properly pungent – a salted herring, garlic, coals, or suspiciously shaped dark brown sweets.

This is not the only scatological feature of the Catalan Christmas. As elsewhere in Catholic Europe, the fabrication of elaborate manger scenes is a popular hobby and the hobbyist's attention centres on the surrounding village and landscape. But the viewer is always looking for one figurine hidden in the crowded tableau: the *caganer*. Traditionally a squatting peasant in a *barretina*, smoking a pipe with his trousers lowered in the act of defecation, the *caganer* has taken on in the democratic period an infinite number of more topical identities, the latest versions of which can be found every 13 December at the Fair of *Santa Llúcia* in front of Barcelona's cathedral.

Catalan politicians and world figures as diverse as Osama Bin Laden, Pope John Paul II, Sarkozy, and Barack Obama have been portrayed in this pose. The *caganer* fertilizes the earth for the coming spring, so the crib enthusiast will tell you; at the same time, Catalan folk poetry celebrates the act of excretion as the common necessity that levels king, pope, and peasant. In contrast to the ethereal body of the consecrated Host, borne in a gleaming silver sun-shaped monstrance in the Corpus Christi procession at the brilliant early break of summer, the Christ of a Catalan Christmas, when the days are dark, is tied to the humblest aspects of his humanity.

Commensality is as basic as co-presence in Catalan festival's insistence on the levelling effect of corporeality. No Catalan festival, including Lent, is without its characteristic food, and during festivals everyone gets to eat: major festivals were the occasions of charitable distributions from the municipality, the parish, the factory owners, and the wealthy. Catalan domestic life has always been punctuated by seasonal feasts, which exist today also as communal and commercial celebrations: the *calçotada* of spring onions in Valls, the gathering of autumn mushrooms in the Berguedà, and especially the great *matança del porc*, the winter pig-killing. The distributed labour of an extended family and its neighbours dismembers the pig into hams and extravagantly named sausages that once extended and enriched the daily diet of legumes, bread, and vegetables for the coming year. This provision against everyday scarcity concluded with a celebration of momentary abundance, a feast of fresh meat shared among all who had done the work.

But the rhythms of the seasons are only the bottom layer. Next comes the Catholic liturgical calendar, which evolved in tense intimacy with those of Rome, Judaism, and Islam. In the nineteenth century and particularly after the Restoration of 1875, state politics added a further layer, imposing victory celebrations and other national holidays. By the early twentieth century the calendar was a constant focus of political tension, with republican and labour movements proposing competing commemorations.

Catalanist movements sought their own representation, notably with the 1901 institution of the *Diada de Catalunya*. This commemoration of 11 September, the surrender of Barcelona to the Bourbon pretender in 1714, was intended to show a united front and remains today an occasion to demonstrate nationalist strength and solidarity. Successive political shifts transformed the calendar along with the names of streets: the Republic abolished saints' days, while Franco restored them. Franco replaced the worker's May Day with 18 July (anniversary of his uprising) as a new paternalist *Fiesta del Trabajo*

(Labour Day); as the new author of national being, he replaced the Catalanist 11 September with his own name day, 1 October.

The feast of Saint George has undergone several reframings to become a major patriotic holiday. Patron of the Catalan military nobility, the saint has a chapel in the Gothic palace of the *Generalitat*. By the late eighteenth century, the archaic celebration of his day had given way to a popular fair of roses for those in love. In the late nineteenth century, Catalanists adopted this Barcelona custom in an attempt to promote St George as joint national patron along with the Virgin of Montserrat. Independently, in 1926, a Barcelona publisher convinced the Spanish government to institute a book festival to support the industry. In 1930 this street fair for books was translated to 23 April, not as St George's Day but as the date of the death of Cervantes.

Under Franco, the official book festival provided cover for Catalanists quietly to revive the unofficial *Festa de Sant Jordi*. In 1959 several stands of Catalan-language books appeared and, from that point on, the fair was increasingly focused on linguistic and cultural revival. Since then the publishing industry has organized its calendar and promotional activities around Sant Jordi, when half of annual sales are made, while the roses are sold to raise money for organizations, charities, and causes, often of a nationalist character. Today Sant Jordi and 11 September have become a contrasting pair of national holidays. Sant Jordi is affirmative, familial, consumerist, rather banal; the *diada* is militant and confrontational, bringing out young and old activists of all stripes to exchange exhortations and recriminations.

In the democratic period, the need to limit non-working days and bring the calendar in line with the rest of Europe compromised the abundant official holidays of the Franco era. Meanwhile, workers began to find new, consumerist uses for their days off with both commercial entertainments and tourism. The Spanish state also came to terms with the plural loyalties of its citizens, creating an official calendar jointly determined by the church, the state, the regional governments, and municipalities.

In a world of consumer choice the survival of festivals depends on the pleasures and emotional identification they can provide. Civil liberties and the private car have robbed many town festivals of participants while making it easier for outsiders to attend the most famous ones. Locals have recognized the importance of creating festivals interesting enough to keep people at home on the holiday: the necessary voluntarism has resulted in both unusual festival innovations and a strengthening of everyday social networks.

Festival futures

The traditional festival, grounded in the everyday life-world of a community, is hybridizing more than ever with modern forms of public event assembling anonymous individuals: organized sport (most notably FC Barcelona), music and arts festivals, discos and raves, amusement parks and expositions. Less important to individuals but with a complex impact on the urban fabric and regional economy are such government-driven international events as the 1992 Olympic Games and the 2004 *Fòrum Universal de les Cultures*.

From a different perspective, social movements and the *tribus urbans* of youth culture, while drawing on a mostly international vocabulary of expression, rely on the same face-to-face immediacy and everyday energies as traditional festival. In times of felt collective emergency, such as in the lead-up to the second Iraq war in 2003 or following the Madrid train bombings of 2004, collective protest achieves the effervescence of local festival on a truly national scale, just as it did during the Transition.

The famous Catalan *associacionisme*, as described in Louise Johnson's chapter on Sport, has long been associated with a weak and oppressive state. After the Transition, those who had once come out to the street to protest were now also charged with the construction of autonomous institutions. So at the same time that they 'recuperated' festivals through voluntary associations, as individuals they entered public administration, ran for office, taught at schools and universities, and began to replace the authorities they had once challenged.

Other things changed in the 1990s. There was a generational transition in festival personnel. The memory of Franco dissipated and an inevitable dissatisfaction with autonomous government loosened the connection between Catalanism and local concerns. The economic boom and real estate development, with new residential estates of single-family homes, dissipated the workplace and neighbourhood sociability on which festival had drawn. That same boom gave Catalonia the highest rate of immigration in Europe.

As a result festival organizers are at once more localist and more broadly networked. Their concerns are with their community of residence: how to keep its economy going, how to integrate the immigrant population, how to keep the young in town and the old involved. But they draw on the resources of the *Generalitat*, notably the *Centre de Promoció de Cultura Popular i Tradicional Catalana* (CPCPTC), which supports research, publication, exhibitions, teacher courses, and the annual summer school '*Festcat*' in the Pyrenees. They rely extensively on their own networking and fundraising skills, greatly aided by new media.

Today the extraordinary website (www.festes.org) exemplifies the mix of activist, entrepreneurial and scholarly talent being dedicated to traditional festival. The pace of local festival creation only continues to intensify. What is more, the network can mobilize rapidly when a need is perceived, as happened in the spring of 2009 when a European directive regarding firework safety seemed to threaten the participatory character of devils and *correfocs*.

National, European, and international dynamics have transformed traditional festival: it is no longer simply reproduced, but managed. In some communities, local governments and entrepreneurs have taken the route of representing festival as heritage, entailing formal 'safeguarding'. Since 2001, the *Patum* of Berga has been governed by a steering committee of city officials, *comparsa* members, and businesspeople. After a lengthy campaign, the *Patum* was proclaimed in 2003 by UNESCO to be a Masterpiece of the Oral and Intangible Heritage of Humanity. The effigies must now be repaired by restorers with advanced degrees, not by locals. Managed commercialization is taking place. The right to participate, traditionally negotiated through personal networks, is becoming codified, with debates over entitlement becoming more acute as immigrants, women, and non-churchgoers find both challengers and advocates. Meanings once left open and silent are now being spelled out in ways that make practical consensus a challenge.

The CPCPTC has turned its efforts strongly toward the construction of heritage institutions and the preparation of a national inventory of festivals. As of 2006 there is a hierarchy of festival designations, with those of longest tradition and most apparent 'ritual' and 'identitarian' content meriting the highest rank of *Festa Patrimonial*. The emphasis on origins and authenticity goes hand-in-hand with touristification: the *Generalitat* is creating Centres of Documentation across the *comarques* devoted to explaining various aspects of the national heritage to visitors.

Many Catalan festivals, however, have pursued a different strategy, defining themselves as 'world culture' rather than as heritage. Barcelona's *Festes de la Mercè* have won both plaudits and condemnation for their celebration of Mediterranean cultural mixing. In 1997 the city of Manresa instituted a 'traditional roots' trade fair to serve as an international commercial showcase for Catalan festival impresarios who now view their own work as 'artistic creation within tradition'. Called *Mediterrània*, it was charged by the *Generalitat* in 2009 with the integration of 'roots culture' into institutions and festivals formerly focused on high culture as part of a general modernization of the Catalan culture industries.

Whether as heritage or as art, festival is thus recognized by the *Generalitat* as a resource for economic development. But on the ground festival has not stopped serving the older purpose of mediating *convivència* (social coexistence). Some rural communities have promoted sociability by throwing off the charged notion of 'culture' altogether. Mieres in the Garrotxa and Avià in the Bergueda have created 'festivals of exchange' based in the swapping of goods and knowledge, intended explicitly to counter the social estrangement created by immigration and the building boom that transformed many old towns into empty shells of 'second residences'.

Older festival forms can still be effective across social boundaries, now as they were during the Franco regime and the Transition. In the prosperous coastal town of Vilanova i la Geltrú, the contribution of immigrants to economic vitality has made many residents open to their social presence. The town's important carnival, *festa major*, and band of *castellers* offer various points of access where new participants are needed. The festivals combine stable non-verbal genres, demanding no competence in Catalan, with improvisatory dramas in which new ideas and languages can enter. Creating shared memories, the intense encounters of festival can speed up the process of building familiarity among neighbours.[10]

Since 1968, middle-class people around the world have sought out the 'authenticity' of traditional celebrations. Catalans are no exception, and their festivals celebrate the bodily participation that seems to evoke deep identity. But festival organizers know what the general public, in its new prosperity and freedom of movement, is forgetting. The surge of joy felt in a *correfoc* or the successful downing of a *castell* is earned by the prior labour of preparation and the more taxing labour of pulling off collaboration among partners of necessity, not choice. Festival effervescence grows out of mundane, everyday interaction. The traditional Catalan *comparses* have their future institutionally guaranteed as art or as heritage; they may or may not persist as festival. Whether festival remains central to Catalan culture depends on how neighbours decide to live together.

---

[10] Further information on these issues is provided by Robertson, 2008 and Erickson, 2008.

Works Cited and Suggested Reading

Amelang, James (1986) *Honored Citizens of Barcelona: Patrician Culture and Class Relations, 1490–1714*. Princeton: Princeton University Press.

Ayats, Jaume (ed.) (2006) *Córrer la sardana: balls, joves i conflictes*. Barcelona: Dalmau.

Capdevila, Joaquim and Garcia Larios, Agustí (eds) (1997) *La festa a Catalunya. La festa com a vehicle de sociabilitat i expressió política*. Barcelona: Abadia de Montserrat. Other chapters of interest in this volume are: Gavaldà i Torrents, Antoni, 'Consideracions entorn de les festes franquistes a l'Alt Camp', pp. 221–232; Marfany, Joan Lluís, 'Notes per a l'estudi de la festa a les terres catalanes', pp. 19–50; Nagel, Klaus-Jurgen, 'Festes i costums, el seu ús polític: exemples de la Catalunya del començament del segle XX', pp. 211–220.

Erickson, Brad (2008) 'Sensory Politics: Catalan Ritual and the New Immigration', Ph.D. thesis, Department of Anthropology, University of California-Berkeley.

Fàbregas, Xavier and Barceló, Pau (1976) *Cavallers, dracs, i dimonis. Itinerari a través de les festes populars*. Barcelona: Abadia de Montserrat.

Feixa, Carles (1999) *De jóvenes, bandas y tribus*. Barcelona: Ariel.

——— (2003) 'La joventut com a metàfora de la Transició', in Aracil, R., Mayayo, A. and Segura, A. (eds) *Memòria de la Transició a Espanya i a Catalunya. Els joves de la Transició*. Barcelona: Universitat de Barcelona, vol. 4, pp. 15–44.

Frigolé Reixach, Joan (1980) 'Inversió simbòlica i identitat ètnica: una aproximació al cas de Catalunya', *Quaderns de l'Institut Català d'Antropologia*, 1, pp. 3–27.

Grau i Martí, Joan (1996) *Gegants*. Barcelona: Columna.

Noyes, Dorothy (2003) *Fire in the Plaça: Catalan Festival Politics after Franco*. Philadelphia: University of Pennsylvania Press.

Palomar, Salvador and Sugranyes Ferran (2003) 'Sant Jordi: de la llegenda a la festa', Reus: Carrutxa Biblioteca Digital, http://www.carrutxa.org/biblioteca

Prat i Carós, Joan and Contreras, Jesús (1979) *La festa a Catalunya*. Barcelona: Dopesa.

Robertson, Alexander F. (2008) 'Regeneration in Rural Catalonia', *European Journal of Sociology*, 49, pp. 147–172.

Various authors (1973) *Catalunya sòta el règim franquista. Informe sobre la persecució de la llengua i la cultura de Catalunya pel règim del General Franco*. Paris: Edicions Catalanes de París.

——— (1989) *Calendari de festes de Catalunya, Andorra i la Franja*. Barcelona: Alta Fulla / Fundació Serveis de Cultura Popular.

——— (2011) Festes.org: l'espai on comença la festa. www.festes.org

10

What's Cooking in Catalonia?

MONTSERRAT ROSER I PUIG

The association between what we eat and what we are is hardly questionable in the minds of the general public even though theorists on the subject have shown the equation to be extremely complex. Food consumption is no mere case of alimentation but also acts as a differentiating and cohesive element in a particular community, and it may be helpful for those with no grounding on food studies to offer a brief overview of the various ways of considering the phenomenon in academic terms. In the field of anthropology at the start of the last century Bronislaw Malinowski was among the first to underscore its pre-eminence in his observation that:

> In all activities we find that the use of an object as a part of technically, legally, or ritually determined behaviour leads human beings to the satisfaction of some need. (...) It is commonplace to say that humanity advances on its belly, that you can keep the multitude satisfied by providing bread as well as circuses, and that the materialistic factor of satisfactory food supply is one of the determinants of human history and evolution. (...) The integral function of all the processes which constitute the cultural commissariat of a community is the satisfaction of the primary biological need of nutrition.[1]

Following this line, the preparation of food, as later understood by Claude Lévi-Strauss, becomes a collective and distinctive feature unique to a nation as cooking 'is with language a truly universal form of human activity: if there is no society without a language, nor is there any which does not cook in some manner at least some of its food'; and 'behind the opposition between roasted and boiled, then, we do in fact find (...) the opposition between nature and culture'.[2]

---

[1] Malinowski, 2006, p. 155.
[2] Lévi-Strauss, 1997, pp. 28–35.

Similarly, more contemporary scholars like Uma Narayan see how food has much to reveal about how we understand our personal and collective identities as the seemingly simple acts of eating are flavoured with complicated and sometimes contradictory cultural meanings. As a consequence, 'Thinking about food can help reveal the rich and messy textures of our attempts at self-understanding, as well as our interesting and problematic understanding of our relationship to social Others.'[3]

Evidently all these ideas are particularly relevant to the cultural identity of Catalonia for, in the context of Spain – and following the same trend as all other historic regions –, Catalans have used both their language and their cooking as attributes of differentiation. The formula is not unfamiliar to scholars, as Thrift explains: 'the region is a product both human and physical processes: a natural landscape and a peopled landscape and, consequently, a powerful way of thinking about both place and identity', which are in turn similarly echoed through the scale of the nation.[4] Or as Bell and Valentine declare simply: 'food consumption can be regarded as one of the ways in which national identity is expressed'.[5]

The topic is outlined more politically by Roland Barthes who, referring to the specifics of several European countries, explains the mechanics of the national dimension illustrating the symbolic function acquired by individual foodstuffs: 'Wine is felt by the French to be a possession which is its very own, just like its three hundred and sixty types of cheese and its culture. It is a totem drink, corresponding to the milk of the Dutch cow or the tea ceremonially taken by the British Royal family.'[6] And in this context, the Catalans are no exception.

Popular discourses, food and the nation are almost impossible to disentangle; and this is so because, like a language, food articulates notions of inclusion and exclusion, of national pride and xenophobia. Care should be taken, nonetheless, as the issue is riddled with paradoxes that render any facile association with overt natural signifiers such as language peculiarly brittle. Time and again in this survey we will be faced with inconsistencies as the experts themselves follow gut feelings as regards the question of nationality rather than proceed in any objective and coherent fashion. Further complications arise when, as in the cases of the UK or the USA, Bell and Valentine advise us of threatened invasions of 'filthy foreign food', which are

---

[3] Narayan, 1995, p. 64.
[4] Thrift, 1991, p. 460.
[5] Bell & Valentine, 1997, p. 18.
[6] Barthes, 1973, p. 65.

seen as dangerous to the whole fabric of national identity. In the context of Catalonia, a well-known retirement and tourist area, one should also consider this phenomenon from the other side, in the problematic presence of English settlers and tourists who, by insisting on their right to eat 'proper English meals' have generated a sustained demand for fish and chips, full English breakfasts and Sunday roasts, creating real culinary ghettos in many resorts along the Costa Brava, Costa Blanca and Balearic Islands. The same commentators articulate this paradox in the following way:

> The history of a nation's diet is the history of the nation itself, with food fashions, fads and fancies mapping episodes of colonialism and migration, trade and exploration, cultural exchange and boundary-marking. And yet here begins one of the fundamental contradictions of the food-nationalism equation: there is no essential *national* food; the food which we think of as characterising a particular place always tells stories of movement and mixing, as 'deconstructions' of individual food histories show. (...) Furthermore, the foodstuffs we think of as definitionally part of a particular nation's sense of identity often hide complex histories of trade links, cultural exchange, and especially colonialism.[7]

Consequently, the symbolic importance of keeping a distinct, traditional cuisine (often made up by dishes that are unappetising to outsiders but appetising to community members) is central to what Raspa calls the *nostalgic enactment* of identity through which the consumption of particular foods proves to be a powerful statement of identity and difference.[8]

In terms of history and politics, however, the Catalan case differs considerably from the American and British models. During the Francoist dictatorship, for instance, the regime's enforced tendency towards unity, with its fixation on national (i.e. Spanish) homogeneity, produced gastronomic studies where Catalan cookery and the rest of the highly varied cuisine of Iberia were clearly subsumed into a collective whole. On the surface one does not notice much resistance to the official line in the publications of that time and could be led to believe that Franco's imposition of the unitary nation was,

---

[7] Bell & Valentine, 1997, pp. 168–9.
[8] Raspa, 1984, p. 185. On this same point Bell & Valentine, 1997 p. 147, reflect that 'As mobility and hybridity become watchdogs of the way the world now works, tradition-bound, defensive articulations of the region may start to look untenable, but the continuing appeal of regionalism, which speaks to us all from the bottom of a bottle of Bordeaux, suggests otherwise, even if – as is often the case – regional traditions are exposed as mere inventions.'

in culinary terms, certainly not questioned. Indeed, this stance seems to have been cemented by the two key Catalan gastronomes of the time, Néstor Luján and Juan Perucho. In the section on 'Old Catalonia' of *El Libro de la cocina española* / Book of Spanish Cuisine (1970) they describe Catalan cooking as extensive, varied, rural, peasant, half lard and half olive oil-based, owing a fair amount to the Mediterranean, France and central Spain because 'Barcelona is the mixture of all those cuisines, given that the *Ciudad Condal* is a big city inhabited by natives of all the Catalan regions and all the other regions of Spain.'[9]

However, reading between the lines it is interesting to note how the authors concede that, 'like the cooking of all the other historic regions of Spain, Catalan cooking seems indestructible', thus vindicating the resilient, long-standing and distinctive identities not only of Catalan but of all Spanish regional cuisines. This paradoxical attitude is echoed in the structure of their book. On the one hand its polyfacetic 'Introduction to the theory of taste' includes sections on gastronomy as art, taste, table manners, pleasure sharing, menus and guests but also a section on ancient peoples and their distinctive cooking. This is then contrasted with a single monothematic account of the 'Historical evolution of Spanish cookery', a full chapter on the *cocido* (stew), arguing that each Spanish region has its own version of the same dish and then, surprisingly, fifteen further chapters each providing the most outstandingly distinct recipes from as many Spanish regions.

This ambivalent attitude, however, was to change when, with the death of the dictator, Catalans became more empowered and much more forthright in recovering ownership of their cuisine. From that point onwards not only did they document their gastronomic peculiarities at length but they also managed, in the words of Miguel Sen, to 'discover that Catalonia possessed recipes for every landscape, more or less distinct from those of the next-door village'. Indeed, they went so far as to conclude that the geographic medium in which we exist (i.e. the climate and the constitution of the soil) conditions the produce of the land and the animals we rear, which in turn constitute the framework for our diet.[10]

Temperature dictates how we preserve, condiment and consume our food and drink as well as the places we choose for our eating and the times in which preparation and consumption take place. In this way successful methods of cooking and adoption of the most amenable influences from the outside are passed on as a distinctive tradition, and inventiveness and talent

---

[9] Luján & Perucho, 1970, p. 249. The following quotation is on the same page.
[10] Sen, 2007, p. 10.

give dishes the enjoyable characteristics that we identify as home. As a result, continuity ensures the survival of our eating habits as well as that of our people and, while disruption can wreck our eating patterns, a home-cooked meal will work the magic of restoring us (even if momentarily) to sanity.

With the success of this recovery came reassurance and, by 1986, in his *Tiempo para la mesa* / Time for the Table, the novelist and gourmet Manuel Vázquez-Montalbán already felt capable of addressing without difficulty the once-big question: does Spanish cooking exist? And indeed, after due analysis, he reached the conclusion that, unlike France where the gastronomic capital was Paris and the rest of gastronomic outputs could be classed as regional cuisine, it was 'more legitimate to see Spain as a country of many cuisines'.[11] However, it is also important to note – as has been seen in the many areas covered by this volume – that: 'Like Catalonia itself, Catalan cuisine looks outward, towards Europe and the Mediterranean, rather than back into the Iberian interior.'[12] In this respect, one could say that the rediscovery of difference has exposed a change in the public image of Catalan gastronomy (a most visceral and popular activity), to one of disassociation from the rest of Spain and of fully-fledged alignment with the culture of the Mediterranean and Europe. From this perspective, therefore, it was thought that:

> Pyrenean and Mediterranean, Catalan culture conjugates its continental and maritime vocation, fruit of diverse civilizations and of contacts with continental and Mediterranean peoples – something that over the centuries has produced equilibrium in their attitudes as well as in their artistic expression.[13]

Bell and Valentine may correctly remind us that 'a glossing of regional differences into the diet of a single international region – the Mediterranean – runs contrary to the strong tradition of classifying a number of distinct culinary regions within any one country'.[14] However, within the context of the Francoist dictatorship, this preference for the Mediterranean can also be perceived as a subtle way of sabotaging the official unifying view of Spanish gastronomy and of defending Catalan difference in yet another area of collective experience.

---

[11] Vázquez Montalbán, 1986, p. 236.
[12] Andrews, 1988, p. 4.
[13] Roque, 1993, p. 42.
[14] Bell & Valentine, 1997, p. 156.

The historical panorama

In the wider Mediterranean context, historical analyses of Catalan cooking have tended to emphasize how the area is something of a two-way street. Both Greek and Roman crops and foodstuffs reached Spain through Catalonia. Catalonia was additionally the place through which Arab culinary and horticultural influence reached continental Europe. Similarly, the Catalano-Aragonese kingdom created a two-way trading network for consumer products all over the Mediterranean, and contacts with neighbouring France informed and enhanced the emerging nation's cooking habits. Finally, Catalonia acted as a bridge between the food products that came from the New World and the rest of Europe.[15]

It is also in this respect that great interest in the study of Catalan cookery books dating back to the fourteenth century (such as the *Llibre del coc* / The Cook's Book by Mestre Robert and the anonymous *Llibre de Sent Soví* / Book of Sent Soví) was awakened. The latter, as the editor Joan Santanach attests, 'like any other gastronomic treatise, was seen as a practical text, a working tool at the service of cooks and, as they used it, they added to it, cut some of the recipes, and added refinements and further details on specific aspects of the dishes'. As such, it allowed Catalans to trace back 'features that are even today typical of Catalan cuisine: the *picada*[16] and the *sofregit*,[17] for example (the latter made with onion alone; tomatoes, like potatoes or peppers, not entering the Mediterranean diet until well after the discovery of the Americas)', turning it into 'a text that reflects a great swathe of the culinary tradition and the tastes of a whole period of history that we might describe as the dawn of Catalan cuisine'. Indeed, the recently discovered evidence of the international influence of these treatises has been used as irrefutable proof not only of cultural difference but of very early gastronomic sophistication.[18]

On the other hand, the *Renaixença*, the movement of cultural rebirth of the

---

[15] The summary is provided by Colman Andrews, 1998, p. 19. On p. 17 the same critic declares that 'In a sense, Rome made Catalonia; it *certainly* helped make Catalan gastronomy.'

[16] The *picada* is a compound condiment made with pounded garlic, parsley and a personal selection of nuts; it is added to the cooking dish at critical moments in the process.

[17] The *sofregit* is a starting cooking base made with browned onions in some cases and browned onions and tomatoes in others.

[18] *The Book of Sent Soví: Medieval Recipes from Catalonia* was published in English translation in 2008. Edited by Joan Santanach, the comments cited by this author are on pages 234, 11 and 234.

nineteenth century dealt with in Dominic Keown's chapter on Contemporary Culture, has been identified not only as the birth of Catalan collective consciousness but also as the moment of emergence of Catalan gastronomic modernity. In connection to this point, one further relevant aspect to be borne in mind across the whole cultural gamut is the role played by the cosmopolitan city of Barcelona, evinced here by the introduction of the first Italian restaurants into Spain right at the very beginning of the twentieth century. This has been regarded as key in identifying Catalonia as the only one of the Spanish gastronomic regions to have appropriated, reformed and developed Italian pasta and pizza as part of its own heritage. The point is noted by all experts and elucidated by Colman Andrews:

> Catalonia, just as it has a language, law, customs, its own history, and a political ideal, has a cuisine. There are regions, nationalities, peoples which have a special, characteristic dish without having a cuisine. Catalonia does have one, and it has something else besides: a great power to assimilate the dishes of other cuisines, like the French and the Italian, making them its own and modifying them according to its own style and taste.[19]

It is therefore not surprising to note how Catalan traditional cooking has usually been divided into two distinct sections depending on the type of fat they use, with olive oil being associated with the Mediterranean and lard as the European (inland and rural) aspect of the same, with the overall victory of oil over lard declared in recent years.

The other common practice in modern Catalan cookbooks has been that of using the basic sauces of the locality as the method of recognition of its traditional values. The sauces are: the *sofregit* (base sauce made of sautéed onion and tomato), the *samfaina* (base sauce made of sautéed onion, tomato and red peppers), the *picada* (mixture of crushed garlic, flat parsley, nuts and croutons usually added to finish off a dish) and the *allioli* (a mayonnaise-textured sauce made with crushed garlic and olive oil but with no egg), to which Narcís Comadira also adds the *romesco* (mixture of crushed roasted *nyora* peppers, almonds, garlic, oil and vinegar). However, their use as a means of classification may be misleading because it is common to find dishes that

---

[19] Andrews, 1998, p. xvii. Catalan confidence in their precocious cuisine is exemplified by Ferran Agulló's 1928 manual, *Llibre de la cuina catalana* /The Book of Catalan Cookery, which was so much in tune with the contemporary growth in nationalist sentiment that it has been regarded as 'the first book in which, Catalan cuisine is clearly and explicitly addressed as a national cuisine'. Fàbrega, 2007, p. 15.

start with a *sofregit* and are finished with a *picada*, and the *allioli* and the *romesco* can be used both as integral part of the cooking or as side sauces.[20]

In addition to this, in a world of mobility, global trade, ever-increasing offers of exotic produce in supermarkets and mushrooming exotic restaurants, opinions on what is genuine innovation or gastronomic pollution, as critics have indicated, tend to get polarized. What is more, the Catalan case is interesting when compared to other European countries in that, for many decades, global market forces were perceived as less of a danger than tourism, which came to be regarded as a gastronomically eroding force and a threat to real cooking. According to Luján, 'Catalan cooking's two worst enemies have been hurriedness (which has meant that old dishes have been abandoned not only in public establishments but also in family and private cooking) and tourism.' This he attributes to the fact that people in the tourist trade 'believe that those who travel to Catalonia, be it visitors from the rest of the Peninsula or from abroad, are not very interested in Catalan gastronomy'.[21]

What transpires from these observations is that, in spite of the deprivation of the post-Civil War years and the ruthless exploitation of dishes such as *paella* during the 1960s touristic boom, high levels of food awareness were maintained throughout the autochthonous Catalan population. In fact, the generalized appreciation of cooking, from the most simple dishes, such as the typical *pa amb tomata* (toasted crusty bread rubbed with garlic [optional] and tomato and seasoned with olive oil and salt) or *mongetes amb botifarra* (sautéed beans with sausage) to the most elaborated, such as the *pollastre amb escamarlans* (pot-roasted chicken with langoustines), the *vedella amb bolets* (casseroled veal with wild mushrooms) or the *peus de porc amb cargols* (pigs' trotters with snails) became a means of displaying not only the uniqueness of Catalan identity but the pride of being Catalan. This is also evinced by the title of Vázquez-Montalbán's manual of 1967 *L'art del menjar a Catalunya. Crònica de la resistència dels senyals d'identitat gastronòmica catalana/* The Art of Eating in Catalonia. Chronicle of the Resistance of the Features of Catalan Gastronomic Identity.[22]

---

[20] Comadira, 1997, p. 228.

[21] Luján, 2004, p. 11. Miguel Sen also blames the then minister of tourism of the 1960s, Manuel Fraga Iribarne, for creating a special tourist menu designed to promote the consumption of peach melba! Sen, 2007, p. 12.

[22] The first part of this book, with the title of 'Defence and Illustration of Catalan Cooking', is of particular interest as it covers a geographical distribution of products and tastes. The rest of the volume includes commentaries on bread, rice and pasta, herbs and stews, fish, meat, offal, beans and salt cod, and three special appendixes on mushroom

In the second edition of this book the author admitted that between its original publication and 1984 there had already been a considerable change for the better in terms of the quality of Catalan wine production. He was also prepared to dispute the success of homogenization by recognizing that the original cooking of the Costa Brava had managed to survive the repression in spite of having been severely threatened by the tourist industry, referring to how

> the miraculous rescue of the cooking of the coast and of the Empordà has taken place in spite of the growing conspiracy of the tourist industry prepared to squash everything that is gastronomically difficult to understand under two thousand metric tons of tourist menus for foreigners enslaved by low budgets, slimming diets, and the most savage illiteracy on the subject of the gastronomic culture of olive oil and lard.[23]

Indeed, Catalonia prides itself for being a country where the locals know how to eat; and this is important because it reaffirms the national unity of the collective. Roland Barthes has reflected pertinently on the issue, and we cite the following quotation in full given its relevance to our context.

> Food permits a person (...) to partake each day of the national past. In this case, this historical quality is obviously linked to food techniques (preparation and cooking). These have long roots, reaching back to the depth of the French past. They are, we are told, the repository of a whole experience, of the accumulated wisdom of our ancestors. French food is never supposed to be innovative, except when it rediscovers long-forgotten secrets. The historical theme, which was so often sounded in our advertising, mobilizes two different values: on the one hand, it implies an aristocratic tradition (dynasties of manufacturers, *moutarde du Roy*, the brandy of Napoleon); on the other hand, food frequently carries notions of representing the flavourful survival of an old, rural society that is itself highly idealized. In this manner, food brings the memory of the soil into our very contemporary life; hence the paradoxical association of gastronomy and industrialization in the form of canned 'gourmet dishes'. No doubt the myth of French cooking abroad (or as expressed to foreigners) strengthens this 'nostalgic' value of food considerably; but since the French themselves actively participate in this myth (especially when travelling), it is fair to say that through food the Frenchman experiences a certain national continuity. By

picking, wine and annual festivities (with special celebratory sweets), before moving on to the actual recipes in Part Two.

[23] Vázquez-Montalbán, 2004, p. 33.

way of a thousand detours, food permits him to insert himself daily into his own past and to believe in a certain culinary 'being' of France.[24]

The contemporary scene

As in the French case, the strong Catalan desire to strengthen and preserve traditional cooking has been triggered by the perceived threat of industrialized processes. And the Catalan response has been very similar to that of the Italian Slow Food movement, established in the Piedmont region in 1986 by a group of writers and chefs in reaction to the growing concern about the potential impact of McDonald's on Italy's food cultures, and formally launched as an international movement in 1989.

Slow Food argued for the general promotion of local food cultures and aimed to promulgate a new 'philosophy of taste' where the guiding principles should be 'conviviality and the right to taste and pleasure'. Other key objectives included disseminating and stimulating knowledge of 'material culture' (place of origin and production techniques), the preservation of agro-industrial heritage (biodiversity of crops, craft-based food production and traditions), and the protection of the historical, artistic and environmental heritage of traditional fare (cafés, cake shops, inns, craft workshops, etc.). In short, the movement sought to develop new forms of 'gastronomic associationalism' that link the cultural life of food to biodiverse production spaces. Even though there were no Catalan members in the Slow Food original committee and no big international events have been held there, many Catalan initiatives happen to coincide with those outlined in the Slow Food manifestos, and there are currently Slow Food centres in Balaguer, Barcelona, Falset, Manresa, Mollet del Vallès, Sitges and Tarragona.[25]

A surprising fact in this respect is that the success of celebrity chefs should also have been blamed for gastronomic problems since the 1990s. This negative attitude towards culinary stars had already been voiced by the remarkable writer Josep Pla, who claimed in *El que hem menjat*/ What We've Eaten (1981) that old family cookery was the only one worth preserving and continuing. Moreover, Manuel Vázquez-Montalbán also defended traditional cookery against undue sophistication in his *Contra los gourmets*/ Against Gourmets (2001), where he built on the definition of popular cooking as one based upon culinary models, very slow progress and a family and region-orientated character acting in opposition to 'clever' and 'experimental'

---

[24] Barthes, 1997, p. 24.
[25] For further information and for the source of the data on which this summary has been written, see www.slowfood.com

cookery. As such, the perceived threat seemed to come from *nouvelle cuisine*-style dishes with arty presentation and ludicrously expensive ingredients available to top chefs but not on offer in the open market.

According to Jaume Fàbrega, the intention behind these complaints was to encourage the recovery of a type of cooking made at home, characterized by 'the flavours that make up people's true taste' because for him – and countering alarmist voices – Catalan people still wanted to cook and eat well and, what was more, they wanted 'to keep faithful to the flavours of all times'.[26]

Nonetheless, the very notion of authenticity is in itself problematic, as may be seen with the reference to the distinguished critic Colman Andrews in his *Catalan Cuisine* volume where he announces his attempt 'to keep choices *authentic*', without employing unorthodox (or un-Catalan) ingredients or techniques in his representations of the great Catalan classics. However, he follows up this declaration of intent somewhat cryptically by reassuring the reader that, even though some of the recipes are strictly contemporary and may not be recognized by the traditionalists, they are 'no less Catalan, just because they belong to our own age'.[27]

Three-star Michelin chef Santi Santamaría underscores this hesitancy when he claims that 'during many years we have understood that cookery is culture, but our nation is not yet fully normalized if we constantly need to ask ourselves about the origin of our dishes'.[28] As is apparent from this lack of security, articulating any definition is evidently tricky these days given the transnationality of the global experience as evinced by the mobility of Catalan cultural tourists who, true to their international inclinations, are nowadays travelling all over the world. In this context, however, there is nothing which may be taken as straightforward. Peculiarly, for example, there is also an alternative tendency growing where *kitchen table tourism* is proving popular for *stay-at-home* travellers! To complicate matters further, the cookery programmes most liked by Catalans are not those using exotic recipes made with unfamiliar ingredients but those featuring their home produce being transformed into exquisite dishes by their own celebrity chefs. Paradoxically, then, the authenticity of Catalan cuisine and its relation to the collective experience is fraught with contradiction.

In fact, simultaneously to being prey to TV shows, a fairly wide section of contemporary Catalan tourism has recently been enticed away from their sofas to an ever-growing range of food-related activities and places of gastro-

---

[26] Fàbrega, 2004, pp. 7–8.
[27] Andrews, 1998, p. 9.
[28] Cited in Fàbrega, 2002, p. 6.

nomic interest. Cookery books, alimentary guides and specialized magazines abound, and in all cases the remit is similar: they promote local produce, stimulate the local economy and provide enjoyable outings.[29] And invariably, the Catalan card is heavily played, as can be seen in the title of Jaume Fàbrega's study of 2007, *Catalunya per sucar-hi pa: Guia comarcal d'atractius turístics, productes, plats, vins i festes gastronòmiques dels Països Catalans*/ Catalonia To Dip Your Bread In: a regional guide to tourist attractions, produce, dishes, wines and culinary festivals.

The author's intention in the compilation of this compendium was 'a desire to show, on the one hand, the gestation of this national cuisine from the middle ages onwards and, on the other, the hatching and forming of traditional Catalan cuisine (dishes, flavours and tastes that have survived until today) which took place during the second half of the nineteenth century'. It was at this time, Fàbrega argues, that those recipes transmitted through the oral tradition were finally recorded into books such as the anonymous *La cuynera catalana* of 1830. The originality of his approach, however, lies in going through each one of the Catalan regions, affording information about what to see, what local produce to buy, the authentic dishes of the region, the gastronomic calendar, the wines (with explanation of all the *Denominacions d'Origens* and their characteristics) and also the provision of a local recipe to try at home. Indeed, for many like him, 'the love of the land, the faithfulness to one's roots are also the love of its produce, its cuisine and the definition of national taste'.[30]

The internationalization of food

However, the issue is not only partial but complex for, in contrast to the falsity of international cooking, once generated by tourism or forays abroad, it is alleged that regional cuisine can be regarded as 'the corpus of recipes intimately linked not to a country or to an autonomous region, but to a specific county (*comarca* in Catalan), that is, to a *terroir*'. And, given that this tendency goes to their very origin, the simplicity and *primitivism* of these

---

[29] One example out of many is the case of the Girona newspaper *El Punt*, which issues a yearly, free 200-page guide to the region including a general introduction to Catalan cooking in Catalan, Spanish, French, English and German, featuring not only a large selection of restaurants but also a full calendar of gastronomic events, fairs, markets and other food and wine-related events.

[30] Fàbrega, 2007, pp. 7–9. It is worth noting how even today the language employed and sentiments expressed by Fàbrega are remarkably similar to those of the original nation-builders of the *Renaixença*.

products can become highly effective tools against the powers of globalized consumerism. In this respect, having identified their potential the *Generalitat*, the autonomous government, has taken the initiative and played a critical role. As Robert A. Davidson argues:

> Through the growing practice of officially 'denominating' areas and products as having a fundamental difference attached to their produce and practice, the Catalan government is engaging in a new relationship with the rural that, while directly connected to supranational practices of contemporary high end food marketing, also points to an awareness of new discourses regarding the civics and ethics of consumption.[31]

It was not until the 1980s that food consumption in Catalonia finally managed to shed its sinful connotations, and not until the 1990s that the beginnings, however murky, of an institutional policy of delimitation and protection of Catalan produce (more often than not linked to agricultural and farming subsidies) could be appreciated. This process was part of the Regularization of *Denominacions d'Origen* by the European Community, which started by addressing the needs of the wine industry and created, according to Warren Moran, a very clear example of regional politicization around food:

> *Appellations* function as a kind of trademark, allowing wine producers who satisfy certain production criteria to use a regional identity on their wines; for the customer, *appellations* signify certain standards of quality, often linked with artisanal principles of 'craftsmanship' in production. Within processes of globalisation geographical indications of provenance gain increasing currency (...) countering standardisation-through-internationalisation. Importantly, *appellations* mix natural environment of the region with the 'raw materials' (grapes) used and the skill involved in production and processing, thus ensuring a tie to place. Mutual publicity thus occurs – wines are famous for coming from a particular region, the region is renowned for its wines – making wine regions and vineyard tours popular with tourists.[32]

It is from this that Moran reaches the conclusion that the idea of 'distinctive local and regional products is embedded in some national and regional cultures' and thus, particular foods (cheeses are a good example), drinks and

---

[31] Davidson, 2007, p. 40. The subsequent quotation from this article is on the same page. For details about *Denominacions d'Origen*, see the corresponding section on the website of the Generalitat de Catalunya: www.gencat.cat

[32] Moran, 1993, p. 269. All other quotations from this work are on this page.

even whole cuisines, become attached to places. This is obvious in Catalonia where, as Davidson indicates, 'one may discern a compelling tension between local specificity and global market that reveals a new way of literally packaging the nation'. The practice is echoed in the lucid description of the contemporary scene by Pere Tàpias, who explains how 'Catalonia is a country where Sundays are taken up by two things: eating out and seeing Barça play. The bait of many villages has consisted of using one dish or a culinary product to promote its businesses and most attractive spots. This is a formula that works.'[33]

Indeed, this phenomenon falls totally in line with that described by Bell and Valentine for whom:

> As regions seek to market themselves while simultaneously protecting themselves from the homogenising forces of globalisation, regional identity becomes enshrined in bottles of wine or hunks of cheese. Questions of regional uniqueness are thus distilled to the iconic products of particular places.[34]

We can thus say that the idea of *appellation*-like geographical product indicators is one that has spread far beyond vineyards to become a common marketing strategy in contemporary food consumption and that almost any product that has some tie to place – no matter how 'invented' this may be – can be sold as embodying that place. To this extent one is tempted to ask not whether the chicken or the egg came first, but the cuisine and the nation. In this respect, when Davidson asks about the particular resonances of the *terroir* in the case of a stateless nation such as Catalonia, he is right in concluding that:

> In the absence of the real state apparatuses that permit total distinction (in the sense that 'total' equals recognized sovereignty as a separate political entity), the increased hold on the everyday that a formal connection with the *terroir* represents stands as a powerful tool for nation-building in both theoretical and practical terms.[35]

And indeed, the scale of the region is variously articulated through routine practices, including those of food consumption, which for Bell and Valentine foster regional pride or local patriotism and they do not necessarily have to

---

[33] Tàpias, 2006, p. 4.
[34] Bell & Valentine, 1997, p. 147. The quotation by Tàpias, 2006, is at p. 4.
[35] Davidson, 2007, pp. 4–6.

rely on public funding. However, that in turn can give distorted results, since it can encourage traditionalist cooking only because at locally-funded gastronomic events people do not expect innovation but rather a more conservative gastronomic sampling as one has to be faithful to the culinary style of the location.[36]

Another adverse result linked to this association has been the increasing use of boycotting as a consumer strategy instigated by some individual politicians whenever the relationship between Catalonia and the Spanish central government becomes strained. Given the close link between gastronomy and culture, the intention in these cases has not only been that of hurting the Catalan pocket but also that of denting Catalan regional pride or local patriotism. As Moran argues:

> Like community (and unlike the world city), the scale of the region sometimes faces the global defensively, seeing forces of globalisation as representing a threat to regional distinctiveness and specialism. (…) Part of this battle is over legislative restrictions from bodies such as the EU. (…) This in turn provokes defensive counter-strategies, whether that means offering vegetables up for adoption or trying to formalize the place-specificities of products, as in the case of wine regions.[37]

Michelin guide to Catalan cuisine

In connection to this issue, the birth of the gourmet culture has brought about a wide range of activities, celebrations, gastronomic fairs, talks, conventions, wine tours, tasting courses, cookery courses and competitions, etc. This global phenomenon has been described variously as 'Foodie-ism', 'food-snobbery' or, more extremely, 'gastro-porn', and regarded as being on a par with the fashion industry. But despite the pressures for what Barthes termed

---

[36] Besides the official apparatus there are also some private initiatives. The setting up of gastronomic establishments, as is the case of the Origen 99'9% group of restaurants in Barcelona and Tarragona, for example, which not only serve Catalan food but produce their own newsletter and members' club, exclusively destined to 'get to know, buy and eat Catalan cuisine products' (see www.origen99.com). Another interesting example can be found in *Descobrir Cuina*, 73, August 2007, pp. 63–9, which features a survey of ales under the title 'Catalan Beers: Drinks with Identity' by A. Fons, which includes beautifully nostalgic pictures and nicely written historical detail.

[37] Bell & Valentine, 1997, p. 205. The various campaigns for the boycott of Catalan goods, similar to a refusal to buy Scotch in view of the independence option favoured by the SNP, has become so pathetic that, were it not for its economic impact, one would find it amusing. For a few varied and paranoid views, see http://elboicot.iespana.es and www.boicot.org

as 'Ornamental food' and the influence of fashion and social position as determining consumer factors, modern living can easily go beyond the home design trend of open-plan kitchen-diners or living kitchens and into a cultural experience derived from the act of sharing specialized and meaningful foodstuffs. In this sense, it is reassuring to see how in Catalonia the emerging postmodern culinary culture (i.e. the mixing of local and global influences) manages to team up the ability to produce traditional dishes (often adapted to new health concerns) with a tentative exploration of the basics of 'new cookery' among the most ambitious amateurs.

In order to acquire this ability, however, access to celebrities and their secrets has been paramount. While on the one hand it can sometimes touch on the obsessive, like the description of cookbooks as 'gastro-porn' owing to the seductions of these lavishly photographed and appetising texts, other experts endorse such publications in the contemporary world as revealing artefacts of culture in the making. In fact, according to Vázquez-Montalbán, cooking lives in perpetual tension between tradition and innovation.

However, regional cooking represents an aversion towards the cultural penetration of efficiency-led, hurried cookery, that is, a reaction against the McDonaldization of Catalan society. While, from a political perspective, Giles Tremlett's explanation for a group of Catalan separatist protesters outside McDonald's on *Les Rambles* shouting ¡*Botifarra si!* ¡*Hamburguesa no!* in the 1970s was that 'If all they were worried about was Catalan sausages, the chances of *catalanismo* turning violent seemed slim,' from a gastronomic point of view the occurrence also confirms a strong awareness and use of the power of foodstuffs as both imperialist and revolutionary weapons.[38] The conflict arises, however, between those Catalan chefs who are seen as holding traditional and nutritional values and those who go for modern, experimental values, for, as Pere Tàpias says: 'with so much broadcasting about gestation and invention, little by little traditional cooking is getting pushed aside. Is it not possible to have peaceful coexistence of innovators and traditionalists? The answer is obviously not!'[39]

According to Miguel Sen, the phase of the documentation of traditional cookery and gastronomy undergone during the transition to Democracy was successful and therefore did not last very long; and, as a result, many

---

[38] The account of features such as 'gastro-porn' is taken from Smart, 1994. The tradition versus innovation antagonism described by Vázquez-Montalbán is cited by Pérez Escohotado, 2006, p. 7. The reflections on the demonstration outside McDonald's in Barcelona appear in Tremlett, 2006, p. 332.

[39] Tàpias, 2006, p. 16.

Catalans became subsequently distracted by the legacy of French *nouvelle cuisine* (with its desire for refinement and select products). This opened up the possibilities of a new type of cooking that rendered traditional Catalan cuisine obsolete, and the distance between cooking and gastronomy thus became increasingly greater for, as we know, cooking is about perfecting food and gastronomy is about perfecting cooking. It was from this point onwards that the new generation of chefs started to make its way into fame for, as Sen sees it, 'in the XXI Century the oracle cook will become part of the magazines' landscape and of the guides with suns and stars'. In the latest phase of Catalan cuisine and more specifically in the revolutionary cooking of celebrity chef Ferran Adrià, what emerges is a type of cooking that will place its emphasis on the theatricality of food and on the knowledge that we are in front of a unique spectacle.[40]

Adrià, who started out in 1983 as a head chef in *El Bulli* in Roses, on the Costa Brava, got his third Michelin rosette in 1994 and the St George's Cross – the highest accolade awarded for contribution to Catalan culture – in 2002. *El Bulli* was also voted by *Restaurant* magazine as the world's best place to dine for four years running (2006–9). For some – and certainly those in official circles – the concession of St George's Cross represented the recognition of cooking as an important means of Catalan cultural and social expression. His new style of cuisine, featuring manipulated ingredients (dry frozen or foamed up, for instance), produced dishes which, by the time they reached the table as 'consommé taggliatelli', 'tiny puffed quinoa grains in a cornet', 'parmesan and lemon crunchy asteroid balls', 'golden eggs' (a tiny scarab-sized, sweet button of exoskeleton, which when bitten releases a melting, warm yolk), 'mini parmesan ice-cream sandwiches' or 'trout egg tempura', were totally unrecognizable and thoroughly surprising.

However, these ground-breaking dishes generated so much controversy that in his book *El Bulli; 1994–1997*, Adrià not only felt the need to discard the terms 'molecular cooking', 'techno-emotional cuisine' or 'techno-cooking', so often applied to his creation, but to go so far as to redefine it as 'gastronomic deconstruction'. Likewise, he felt obliged to re-name the investigative process undertaken during the six winter months by his 50-strong team in their laboratory in Barcelona, as 'technique-concept cuisine'. What is more, together with Heston Blumenthal of *The Fat Duck*, Thomas Keller of *The French Laundry* and *Per Se*, and the writer Harold McGee, he put together a 'Statement on the "new cookery" ', trying to clarify

---

[40] Sen, 2007, pp. 15–37.

what they thought was a serious misunderstanding regarding their achievements. The co-signatories elaborated their declaration as follows:

> Three basic principles guide our cooking: excellence, openness, and integrity.
> Our cooking values tradition, builds on it and, along with tradition, is part of the ongoing evolution of our craft.
> We embrace innovation – new ingredients, techniques, appliances, information, and ideas whenever it can make a real contribution to our cooking.
> We believe that cooking can affect people in profound ways, and that a spirit of collaboration and sharing is essential to true progress in developing this potential.[41]

According to these gastronomes, their approach constituted not so much a new departure for world cookery but more of an update, which to some extent should have been expected as a consequence of the technological advances of the last decades. Indeed, as Bell and Valentine argue:

> One way to think the global and the home that might prove fruitful is by considering the impact of global technological transformations upon the domestic consumption of food. A whole history of food technology advances has impacted on home cooking and eating, from refrigerated transportation to the microwave, and from television cookery shows to supermarkets on the Internet. Many of these have facilitated the project of the self-through-food, bringing new devices to match (or make) new desires.[42]

However, public response to these chefs' new creations has tended to be much polarized and very emotional. This is not surprising because food, as Barthes reminds us, 'is not only a collection of products that can be used for statistical or nutrition studies. It is also, and at the same time, a system of communication, a body of images, a protocol of usages, situations, and behaviour.'[43]

Thus, given the cultural significance of this issue in terms of history and particularity in Catalonia, the otherwise laudable aims of the *new cookery* were sometimes met with hostility. As Sen argues, Adrià's innovations 'aroused the wrath of the kings of Taifas of Catalan cooking, who did not

---

[41] Adrià, Blumenthal, Keller & McGee, 2006, p. 1.
[42] Bell & Valentine, 1997, p. 202.
[43] Barthes, 1997, p. 21.

want to see over their frontiers the rise of the ambitious captain who, to cap it all, did not speak Catalan and cooked in the heart of the Empordà'.

Competition started to emerge in the wider Spanish context among Basque chef Juan Mari Arzak (of *Restaurante Arzak* in San Sebastian), Ferran Adrià (of *El Bulli* in Cala Monjoi, Roses) and Santi Santamaría (of *Can Fabes* in Sant Celoni) where the tandem Adrià–Arzak implicitly brought about the union of two autonomies with the greatest culinary potential and Santamaría was 'left as the count-duke of a culinary estate which was very important, traditional but emotionally not very original'.[44] This reaction was in direct response to the implied criticism made by the 'new cooks' when, elaborating on point number one on the opening page of their manifesto, they comment:

> In the past, cooks and their dishes were constrained by many factors: the limited availability of ingredients and ways of transforming them, limited understanding of cooking processes, and the necessarily narrow definitions and expectations embodied in local tradition. Today there are fewer constraints, and tremendous potential for the progress of our craft.[45]

Indeed, Adrià has insisted that 'my origins are in tradition, naturally, but my offerings belong to the world of innovation; and that means I follow my own path. It is about two worlds, two completely different realities,' and he is thus perfectly happy to produce bread and tomato sorbets, hydrogenated foamy soups and drinkable omelettes. However, the success of the more genuinely produce-based Santi Santamaría in Madrid and the opening of the market-oriented Carme Ruscalleda (of *Sant Pau* in Sant Pol de Mar)'s restaurant in Tokyo, seem to have started a public battle between the four Michelin three-star chefs.[46]

So it is not only Catalan traditional cooking that is threatened by globalization, but also high cuisine. In his book, *La cocina al desnudo/ The Kitchen Laid Bare*, Santamaría rails against what he calls the 'McDonaldization' of Michelin stars and asserts that a chef who uses chemical or synthetic products, made in a laboratory, is like an athlete who uses drugs. Likewise, the gourmet is reported as saying that 'Chefs should not legitimize forms of eating which are inconsistent with healthy dietary habits,' adding that some rivals were turning cookery into a 'media spectacle' but that 'to portray this as a debate about traditional versus modern cooking is a false contrast. It's

---

[44] Sen, 2007, p. 66 and p. 105.
[45] Adrià, Blumenthal, Keller & McGee, 2006, p. 1.
[46] The Adrià quotation appears in Escamilla, 2007, p. 14. Information about the chefs is gathered from the Michelin guide for Spain and Portugal, 2008.

really a debate about home-made versus industrial products, natural versus artificial. The public have the right to be informed about what they're eating.'[47]

What is more, for his part Santamaría claimed that cooks should not be preoccupied with creating sculptures or painting pictures with their work since 'a table is not an art gallery' and, in addition, that some chefs are offering a media spectacle far removed from the desire to offer a healthy meal, giving their patrons dishes that they themselves would not eat. However, criticism has also been levelled at Santamaría who has been accused of not producing traditional cooking as much as offering *nouvelle cuisine* with a few Catalan products thrown in. For her part, Ruscalleda explains her priorities by describing herself as employing 'a style of cooking that draws its main inspiration from the produce of the season and a reworking of the Catalan culinary tradition'.[48]

The fact is, however, as Sen has intimated, that it is precisely 'thanks to these celebrity chefs, Catalan cooking is in fashion in an international context'.[49] And this is a view shared by the director of the International Art Fair *Documenta* in Kassel, Roger M. Buergel, who invited Ferran Adrià to participate in the 2007 exhibition. On that occasion Adrià's presence caused debate not only because he did not travel to Kassel and his restaurant in Roses was named 'Pavilion G' of the exhibition, but because it was the first time a chef had been invited to join the cohort of artists of such a prestigious event. Adrià has been quick to emphasize the elevation of gastronomy in this respect: a point that might only have been expected from a nation that has produced some of the most outstanding exponents in the world of art and cuisine.

Indeed, his comments seem to recall, albeit tangentially, the spectacular *cri-de-guerre* 'Beauty will be edible or not at all' of his surrealist compatriot Salvador Dalí. 'In the past, there was no real dialogue between cookery and

---

[47] The references are taken from an article (without page reference) on the BBC news website on 27 July 2008, by Steve Kingstone. Here the author goes on to underline the uneasiness surrounding the polemic in his reflection that during 'our interview, it soon becomes clear that Mr Adrià resents the caricature of himself as a kind of Dr Frankenstein in a chef's hat'.

[48] Santamaría's words are cited in Catán, 2008, p. 1. The criticism against him is reported in Rivas, 2008, p. 1. And Ruscalleda's comments are on her website at www.ruscalleda.com. Sadly, Santamaría died unexpectedly on 16 February, 2011, at the young age of 53.

[49] Sen, 2007, p. 142. This is in agreement with Fàbrega for whom the second Golden Age of Catalan cuisine came in the 1990s with the new generation of chefs such as Santi Santamaría, Ferran Adrià, Carme Ruscalleda, Joan Roca and others. Fàbrega, 2002, p. 21.

other disciplines – like art, design, science and ecology, so what I've done is initiate that dialogue. But no one should ever dispute that I'm a chef.'[50] Perhaps surprisingly, given the force of this statement, Adrià shocked the gastronomic world in January 2010 by announcing that his restaurant would close for the seasons of 2012 and 2013. Despite the doubt that this declaration cast on the future of the institution, the chef was adamant that it would reopen albeit in the form of a trust: a type of experimental culinary academy or a '*Think Tank* of gastronomic creativity' as announced on their website.[51]

In conclusion, Catalonia is a nation well aware of the link between food and identity. The Catalans were among the first in Europe to write their recipes in cookery books and have ever since retained a discerning palate. They have a good knowledge of gastronomic history and have ensured that their traditional cuisine (once neglected and cheapened by tourism) has been returned to its former glory and reintroduced to restaurants of all categories in response to advancing consumerism and globalization. Not only that, but having recovered traditional recipes and promoted them through the media, they have incentivized the public to become even more discerning and willing to participate in culinary activities, all to the benefit of the local communities.

In tune with their desire for modernity, Catalans have been avid observers of gastronomic progress, and in recent years engaged with the debates of the new cookery alongside their enjoyment of exotic foreign meals without feeling that their own culinary culture is at stake. This is a healthy, varied, proud and mature food culture where, despite the battle between those in favour of tradition or experimentation, the protagonists have all achieved world fame. Of that, the Catalan nation feels justifiably proud.

---

[50] Kingstone, 2008. The same interviewer also relates: 'Two years ago I was at the Pompidou centre in Paris, and they had a huge wall displaying the creative process at El Bulli. It was faintly ridiculous but there is no doubt he's a big international star.'
[51] http://www.elbulli.com/docs201001/elBulliFundacion_en.pdf

Works Cited and Suggested Reading

Catalan gastronomy

Adrià, Ferran, Blumenthal, Heston, Keller, Thomas and McGee, Harold (10 December 2006) 'Statement on the "New Cookery"', *The Observer*: http://www.guardian.co.uk/uk/2006/dec/10/foodanddrink.obsfoodmonthly
——— www.elbulli.com
Andrews, Colman (1988) *Catalan Cuisine*. New York: Collier Books.
——— (2006) *Catalan Cuisine: Vivid Flavors from Spain's Mediterranean Coast*. Boston, MA: Harvard Common Press.
Catán, Thomas (21 May 2008) 'Santiago Santamaría Launches Tirade on Spain's Most-celebrated Chefs',
www.timesonline.co.uk/tol/news/world/europe/article3972596.ece
Comadira, Narcís (1997) *Fòrmules magistrals*. Barcelona: Empúries.
Davidson, Robert A. (2007) '*Terroir* and Catalonia', *Journal of Catalan Studies*, 10, pp. 39–53, www.anglo-catalan.org/jocs/10/articles.html
Davis, Irving (1999) *A Catalan Cookery Book: A Collection of Impossible Recipes*. Totnes: Prospect Books.
Escamilla, David (2007) 'Ferran Adrià. The Mediterranean Alchemist', *Barcelona de luxe*, 4, pp. 10–15.
Fàbrega, Jaume (2002) *El gust d'un poble. Els plats més famosos de la cuina catalana. De Verdaguer a Gaudí: el naixement d'una cuina*. Valls: Cossetània.
——— (2004) 'Pròleg', in Ribas Aguilera, R. (ed.), *Plats i secrets de l'Àvia Remei*. Valls: Cossetània Edicions, pp. 7–8.
——— (2007). *Catalunya per sucar-hi pa: Guia comarcal d'atractius turístics, productes, plats, vins i festes gastronòmiques dels Països Catalans*. Barcelona: Dux.
Fons, A. (2007) 'Cerveses catalanes: begudes amb identitat', *Descobrir Cuina*, 73, pp. 63–69.
Kingstone, Steve (27 July 2008) 'Catalonia's Culinary King Feels the Heat in Spain', http://news.bbc.co.uk/1/hi/world/europe/7523963.stm
Luján, Néstor and Perucho, Joan (1970) *El libro de la cocina española*. Barcelona: Danae.
——— (2004) 'Pròleg' in Vázquez-Montalbán, Manuel (2004) *L'art del menjar a Catalunya. El llibre roig de la identitat gastronòmica catalana*. Barcelona: Salsa Books, pp. 9–12.
Pérez Escohotado, Javier (2006) 'El pensamiento gastronómico de Manuel Vázquez-Montalbán', in *Crítica de la razón gastronómica*. Barcelona: Global Rhythm Press, pp. 91–114.
Pla, Josep (1981) *El que hem menjat*. Barcelona: Destino.
——— (2005) *Lo que hemos comido*. Barcelona: Destino (Spanish translation).
Rivas, Rosa (20 May 2008) 'Fogones en pie de guerra', *El País*,
www.elpais.com/articulo/Tendencias/Fogones/pie/guerra/elpepitdc/20080520elpepitdc_2/Tes
Roque, Maria Àngels (1993) 'El model català', in *Catalunya nació mediterrània*. Barcelona: Fundació Jaume I, pp. 42–96.

Ruscalleda, Carme, www.ruscalleda.com
Santamaría, Santi (2008) *La cocina al desnudo*. Madrid: Temas de Hoy.
—— www.canfabes.com
Santanach, Joan (ed.) (2008) *The Book of Sent Soví. Medieval Recipes from Catalonia*. Barcelona/Woodbridge: Barcino/Támesis.
Sen, Miguel (2007) *Luces y sombras del reinado de Ferran Adrià*. Barcelona: La Esfera de los libros.
Sevilla Ciordia, Patricia (14 June 2007) 'El director de la Documenta de Kassel niega que Adrià sea un mero "imán mediático" ', *La Vanguardia*, www.lavanguardia.es/premium/publica/publica?COMPID=51362145298 andID_PAGINA=22088andID_FORMATO=9andturbourl=false
Smart, Barry (1994) 'Digesting the Modern Diet: Gastro-porn, Fast Food and Panic Eating', in Tester, K. (ed.) *The Flâneur*. London: Routledge.
Tàpias, Pere (2006) *Taules i fogons. Un itinerari gastronòmic*. Valls: Cossetània.
Thrift, N. (1991) 'For a New Regional Geography 2', *Progress in Human Geography* 15, pp. 456–65.
Todolí, Vicent and Hamilton, Richard (eds) (2009) *Food for Thought. Thought for Food: A Reflection on the Creative Universe of Ferran Adrià*. Barcelona: Atcar.
Tremlett, Giles (2006) *The Ghosts of Spain: Travels Through a Country's Hidden Past*. London: Faber.
Vázquez-Montalbán, Manuel (1967) *L'art del menjar a Catalunya. El llibre roig de la identitat gastronòmica catalana*. Barcelona: Salsa Books.
—— (1986) *Tiempo para la mesa*. Barcelona: Difusora Internacional.
—— (1997) *La gula*. Barcelona: Lumen.
—— (1998) *Reflexiones de Robinsón ante un bacalao*. Madrid: Difusión Directa Édera.
—— (2001) *Contra los gourmets*. Barcelona: Mondadori.
—— (2005) *Las recetas de Carvalho*. Barcelona: Planeta.

Gastronomy: theory and topology

Barthes, Roland (1973) *Mythologies*. London: Paladin.
—— (1997) 'Toward a Psychosociology of Contemporary Food Consumption', in Counihan, C. and Van Esterik, P. (eds) *Food and Culture. A Reader*. London: Routledge, pp. 20–27.
Bell, David and Valentine, Gill (1997) *Consuming Geographies. We Are Where We Eat*. London: Routledge.
Lévi-Strauss, Claude (1997) 'The Culinary Triangle', in Counihan, C. and Van Esterik, P. (eds) *Food and Culture. A Reader*. London: Routledge, pp. 28–35.
Malinowski, Bronislav (1960) 'The Functional Theory', in *A Scientific Theory of Culture and Other Essays*. Oxford: Oxford University Press, pp. 149–176.
Moran, Warren (1993) 'Rural Space as Intellectual Property', *Political Geography*, 12, pp. 263–277.
Narayan, Uma (1995) 'Eating Cultures: Incorporation, Identity and Indian food', *Social Identities*, 1, pp. 63–86.
Tuan, Y. F. (1974) *Topophilia: A Study of Environmental Perception, Attitudes and Values*. Englewood Cliffs, NJ: Prentice-Hall.

International gastronomy

Brown, L. and Mussell, K. (eds) (1984) *Ethnic and Regional Foodways in the United States: The Performance of Group Identity*. Knoxville: University of Tennessee Press. The following chapters are from the same volume:
Gillespie, Angus K., 'A Wilderness in the Megalopolis: Foodways in the Pine Barrens of New Jersey', pp. 145–168; Kalcik, Susan, 'Ethnic Foodways in America: Symbol and the Performance of Identity', pp. 37–65; Raspa, Richard, 'Exotic Foods among Italian-Americans in Mormon Utah: Food as Nostalgic Enactment of Identity', pp. 185–194.

Hodgson, A. and Bruhn, C. (1993) 'Consumer Attitudes toward the Use of Geographical Product Descriptors as a Marketing Technique for Locally Grown or Manufactured Foods', *Journal of Food Quality*, 16, pp. 163–174.

Miele, Mara and Murdoch, Jonathan (2006) 'Slow Food', in Ritzer, George (ed.) *McDonaldization. The Reader*. London: Sage Publications, pp. 270–274.

Simmonds, Diane (1990) 'What Next? Fashion, Foodies and the Illusion of Freedom', in Thomlinson, A. (ed.) *Consumption, Identity and Style: Marketing, Meanings and the Packaging of Pleasure*. London: Routledge.

Thrift, N. (1991) 'For a New Regional Geography 2', *Progress in Human Geography*, 15, pp. 456–465.

Young, J. (1994) 'Kitchen Life', *Elle Decoration* 'Living Kitchen' supplement, pp. 4–5.

INDEX

ABC (Madrid newspaper), 137
Abella, Rafael, 193–4
Acció Olímpica, 147, 158
Adrià, Ferran, 3, 245–7, 249
Agamben, Giorgio, 114
Age d'or, L' (film), 25
agrarian reform, 80–1
Agulló, Ferran: *Llibre de la cuina catalana*, 235n
Alavedra, Joan, 173
Albéniz, Isaac, 169, 171
Albigensians *see* Cathars
Alcaraz, Jordi, 182
Alcover, Antoni-Maria, 129
Alfons III, King of Aragon, 61
Alfons V ('the Magnanimous'; Alfonso de Trastamara), King of Aragon, 62, 65, 124, 163
Alfonso X, King of Castile, 59
Alfonso XII, King of Spain, 73–5
Alfonso XIII, King of Spain: leaves Spain (1931), 79; as honorary president of RCD Espanyol, 152
Alghero (l'Alguer), Sardinia, 122
All Saints Day, 222
Almansa, Battle of (1707), 126
Almirall, Valentí, 18, 75
Almodis de la Marca, 51
Almodóvar, Pedro, 7, 200–1
Almohads, 59
Alvar, Manuel, 158
Amalric, Arnault, 55
Amic de les arts, L' (review), 25
anarchists, 74, 78, 104
Andalus, Al-, 41–2, 46

Andic, Isak, 114
Andorra: Catalan language in, 133, 139
Andrews, Colman, 234n, 235; *Catalan Cuisine*, 239
Àngels, Victòria dels, 177
Anido, Martinez, 78
Ansermet, Ernst, 174
anti-clericalism, 74n, 77, 82–3
Antonioni, Michelangelo, 20
Apartado de Correos (film), 185
Arabic language: in Iberia, 123–4
Aragon: united with Catalonia, 55, 122; and Muslim learning, 58; excluded from New World colonization, 124; court dissolved, 125
Aranda, Vicente, 186, 188, 196
Aribau, Bonaventura Carles, 5, 15–18, 128
Ariel (review), 26
Arnau, Count (legendary figure), 20
Arzak, Juan Mari, 247
Assemblea de Catalunya, 89, 92
Associació Catalana Contra la Contaminació Acústica, 112
Associació Catalana de Compositors, 179, 181–2
Associació de Música de Cámera, 175
Associació de Teixidors, 72
Associació Euternpense, 166
Associació Musical de Barcelona, 171
Associació Obrera de Concerts, 173
Associació Protectora de l'Ensenyança Catalana, 26, 129
Associació Wagneriana de Barcelona, 165

associacionisme, 143, 225
Asturias: miners' strike (1935), 81
Asturias-Leon, 42
ateneus (clubs), 212
Aulet, Jaume, 22n
Auric, Georges, 180
Autonomy, Statute of: (1932), 26, 82, 85, 130, 150; (1979), 34, 91–3; reformed (2006), 94–5
Avant-Garde, 23–5; in music, 179–83
Avenç, L' (artistic review), 19, 129
Avià (Berguedà), 227
Avignon: papal court at, 164
Aviñoa, Xosé, 164
Avui (newspaper), 187, 198
Aznar, José María, 94

Badia i Margarit, Antoni, 117
Baez, Joan, 32, 88
Bal i Gay, Jesús, 171, 175n
Balagué, Carles, 8, 87n, 193–5
Balaguer, Víctor, 168, 172
Balagueró, Jaume, 188
Balearic Isles, 121–2; Catalan language in, 134–5, 137
Balletbò-Coll, Marta, 188, 190, 201
Banda Municipal, 173
Barceló Torres, Carmen, 123
Bar-cel-ona (film), 189
Barcelona: qualities and character, 3, 7, 18, 22, 97–8, 109–10, 112–14; Cerdà plan (*Eixample*), 18–19, 100–2; as location for Picasso's 'Demoiselles d'Avignon', 24; in fiction, 28; and Charlemagne, 41–2; medieval schools, 46; sacked by Al-Mansur (985), 48; Floral Games, 60–1; municipal government (medieval), 60–1; decline (15th century), 65; industrialization and factories, 71; industrial unrest, 74, 78; falls to Franco, 84, 106; resistance to Francoist rule, 88; tram strike (1951), 88; architecture, 97, 102–3, 107, 109; class warfare in, 97, 103–4, 106; seafront development, 97, 111; urban renewal, 97–8; noise pollution, 98, 112; site and geography, 98–9; as tourist city, 98, 103, 109–12; as world metropolis, 98, 110, 188; relations with centralist Spain, 99–100; walls and boundaries, 99–100; revolts of 1842 and 1843, 100; International Exposition (1888), 102–3, 109, 146, 163, 165–6; International Exhibition (1929), 105, 109, 146, 173; in Spanish Civil War, 105–7; under Franco's dictatorship, 106; *Plan General Metropolitano* (1970s), 107; property speculation, 110–12; public services breakdowns, 110; separates from Frankish rule, 120; siege and recapture (1713–14), 126; Second Mediterranean Games (1955), 146; musical performances, 172, 176–7; as artistic centre, 188–9; depicted in films, 190–5, 198–200; Raval (red-light district), 190–1, 194; immigrants, 192; Carnival and festivals, 212–13, 216, 222;

Buildings, Institutions, etc.: *Ateneu Barcelonés*, 168, 217; *Carrer de Montcada*, 200; *Ciutadella*, 100, 102; *Conservatorio Superior Municipal*, 181; *Gran Teatre del Liceu*, 17, 165, 176–7; Montjuïc Castle, 105–6; *Passeig de Gràcia*, 101, 200; *La Patacada* (dance hall), 212; *La Pedrera*, 200; Picasso museum, 200; *Plaça Sant Jaume*, 207; *Sagrada Familia*, 108–9, 199; *Teatre de la Santa Creu*, 165; *Ateneu de Barcelona*, 168; *see also* FC Barcelona; Olympic Games (1992)
Barcelona, un mapa (film), 199, 201
Barnils, Ramon, 203

Barthes, Roland, 230, 237, 243
Bartolí Pau (composer), 171
Bartomeu, Josep, 179
Bases de Manresa, 75
Basque language, 118
Basques, 29, 143
Batista i Roca, Josep Maria, 144
Batllori, Miquel, 67
Baulenas, Lluís-Anton: *Amor idiota*, 199; *Anita no perd el tren*, 199
Belbel, Sergi, 34; *Carícies*, 34, 199; *Forasters*, 199; *Morir o no*, 199
Bell, David and Gill Valentine, 230–1, 233, 242, 246
Bellmunt, Francesc, 34, 37
Benach, Ernest, 147
Benet i Jornet, Josep Maria, 30; *Actrius*, 199; *Amic/Amat*, 199
Benguerel, Xavier, 182
Berenguer de Palou (troubadour), 50
Berenguer, Josep Lluís, 182
Berga: *Patum* (festival), 209–11, 215, 217–18, 221, 226
Berguedà (region), 223
Berlin: Olympic Games (1936), 145–6
Bermejo, Alberto, 199–200
Bernabéu, Santiago, 154
Betriu, Francesc, 186
Béziers: massacre (1209), 54
Biar: falls (1245), 56–7
Bigas Luna, J. J., 3, 35, 188; *Huevos de oro*, 34; *Jamón jamón*, 34; *La teta i la lluna*, 34–5, 37
Black, David, 136
Black Death, 60
Blancafort de Rosello, Manuel, 170, 176, 178–9
Blumenthal, Heston, 245
Boadella, Albert, 30
Bofill, Anna, 182
Bofill, Ricard, 3
Bohigas, Oriol, 107
Boix, Jaume, 194
Bonet, Maria de la la Mar, 33

Bonnassie, Pierre, 41
books: annual festival, 224
Boscà, Joan (Juan Boscán), 62
Bosch, General Milans del, 153
Bourbon dynasty: established in War of Spanish Succession, 13–14, 68, 126–7; restoration (1875), 73–4
'boy-scoutism' (*escoltisme*), 144
Brassens, Georges, 32
Brel, Jacques, 32
Brossa, Joan, 27–8, 181
Brühl, Daniel, 198
Buergel, Roger M., 248
Bullí, El, Roses (restaurant), 245, 249
Buñuel, Luis, 25, 27
Byron, George Gordon, 6th Baron, 16

Caballé, Montserrat, 3, 177
Cabezón, Antonio, 168
caganer (scatological figure), 222–3
Calders, Pere, 27–8, 31
Cambó, Francesc, 212
Camino, Jaime, 186, 188
Canadenca, La (electricity firm), 77
Cancionero Musical Popular Español, 168
Canigó, 45
cant dels ocells, El (film), 202n
cantautors, 32
Capellanus, Andreas: *De Amore*, 64
Caracremada (i.e. Ramon Vila Capdevila), 87
Carícies (film), 199–200
Carles, Agustí, 182
Carlists, 76; Wars, 71
Carmina Riuipullensia, 45
Carner, Josep, 23, 26, 172, 179, 181
Carnestoltes, King, 217
Carnival, 212, 216–18
Carolingians *see* Franks
Carreras, Josep, 3, 177
Carreras i Dagas, Joan, 168
Carreto, Martí, 154

Casals, Pau, 3, 163, 172–4, 182; *El pessebre*, 173
Casanova, Emili, 122
Casanovas, Josep Maria, 156, 181
Casas i Cerbó, Ramon, 19
casita blanca, La. La ciudad oculta (film), 87n, 193, 195
Casp, Compromise of (1412), 61, 67, 124–5
Castanya, Valentí, 159
castells, 207–9
Castile: supremacy, 124, 126–7
Castilian language, 62
Català i els Jocs Olímpics, El (collection), 157
Català, Victor (i.e. Caterina Albert), 30; *Solitud*, 20, 28
Catalan: as term, 10, 124–5
Catalan Athletics Federation, 151
Catalan language: proscribed and suppressed, 14n, 68, 106, 127, 130–1; revival as literary form (*Renaixença*), 15, 18, 128–9; emergence as official/literary language, 57–8, 62–3, 68; in Sardinia, 58; origins and development, 117–24; number and distribution of speakers, 120–2, 132–3; written, 122–3; literary decline, 125; north of Pyrenees, 125; effect of official Spanish on, 127; as popular oral language, 127; spelling and grammar standardized, 128–30; Dictionary, 129; in education, 129, 131–2, 134–5, 137, 139; as official language under Spanish Constitution, 131; and internet, 135–6; and effect of immigration, 138–9; future, 139–40; in sport, 155–8; broadcast, 156
Catalan Olympic Committee, 148
Catalan Rugby Federation, 150
Catalonia: cultural achievements, 2–6; disintegration, 3; medieval culture, 4, 67–9; post-Franco civil society, 13; proscribed and persecuted, 13–14, 68, 79; assimilated into Spain, 14; nationalist revival, 15–18; economic prosperity, 17; under Franco (1939–75), 26–7, 107, 130–1; militancy (1960s), 29; Carolingian Franks in, 41–4; land settlement, 44–5, 48, 80–1; territorial extent, 49, 52, 122; alliance with Aragon, 55; Federation (medieval), 58, 66; social-political decline (14th–15th centuries), 59–60, 65, 67; urbanization, 60; union with Castile (15th century), 62; civil war (1462–72), 67; industrialization, 71; political development (19th–20th centuries), 73–6; status and reforms in Second Spanish Republic, 79–81; in Spanish Civil War (1936–39), 82–4; occupied and ruled by Francoists, 85–6; resistance to Francoist rule, 87–9; Assembly formed (1971), 89; post-Autonomy elections and party politics, 90, 92–4; self-government re-established (1979–80), 90–1; parliament elected (1980), 91; Transition to democracy, 107, 215; name, 120; Spanish language in, 125; under Castilian rule (1715), 126–7; future, 137; immigration, 138–9, 225; representation as independent entity in sports, 147–51; national anthem, 214; as food trading area, 234
Catalunya Ràdio, 93, 132
Cathars (Albigensians): heresy and suppression, 53–5
Catholicism *see* Church (Catholic)
Centelles (Osona), 209
Centre de Promoció Cultura Popular i Tradicional Catalana (CPCPTC), 225–6
Centre Excursionista de Catalunya, 144
Centre Nacional Català (CNC), 75–6

Centre Nacionalista Republicà, 170
Cercle Manuel de Falla, 181
Cerdà, Àngel, 181
Cerdà, Idelfons, 18–19, 100–1
Cerdanya, 125
Cervantes Saavedra, Miguel, 65
Cervelló, Jordi, 182
Cervera, 127
Charlemagne, Emperor of the West, 41, 44, 118, 120
Charles III, King of Spain, 126–7
Charles V, Holy Roman Emperor, 122
Charles, Archduke of Austria, 13
Charles Martel, Frankish ruler, 120
Chausson, Ernest, 166, 171
chefs, 244–8; *see also* gastronomy
Chien andalou, Le (film), 25
choral singing and choirs, 17, 166–7, 212
Christ Pantocrator (painting subject), 47
Christmas, 222–3
Chronicles (medieval), 59
Church (Catholic): and anti-clericalism, 74n, 77, 82–3; under Franco, 86, 88; and festivals, 211, 213–14, 216–18, 220, 223; calendar, 223; *see also* Papacy
churches: founded, 45–6
Cicle Històric del Quartet de Corda, 172
cinema: Barcelona School, 2, 8, 37, 185–6; Spanish, 7; under Franco, 33; Catalan, 185–7, 189–90; and documentary films, 190–7; feature films, 197–201; experimental, 202–3
Cingolani, Stefano, 63
Cirlot, Juan Eduardo, 181
ciutadans honrats, 60–1
ciutat cremada, La (film), 33, 186, 189
Clarà, Josep, 158
class (social): and industrialization, 71–3; conflict in Barcelona, 97, 103–4

Clavé, Josep Anselm, 17, 166–7, 173, 182, 212
Club 49, 27, 181
Club Femení i d'Esports, 144
cobla (wind band), 163, 207–8
Coixet, Isabel, 8, 37, 188, 190, 202–3
Coll, Julio, 180
Colon, Germà, 119
Comadira, Narcís, 29, 235
Comediants, Els (performance group), 31, 35, 108, 215
Comellas, Joan, 181
Comisiones Obreras (CCOO), 88
Comissió Coordinadora de Forces Polítiques de Catalunya, 89
Comitè Català pro-Esport Popular, 145
Comitè Olímpic de Catalunya (COC), 151
Comitè Organitzador Olímpic de Barcelona-92 (COOB), 158
Companys, Lluís, 80, 146, 195
Companys, procés a Catalunya (film), 33, 189, 195
Compositors Independents de Catalunya, 177–8
Condor Legion (German), 84
Confederació Nacional del Treball (CNT), 23, 76–8, 80, 82–3, 104
Congrés de Cultura Catalana (1975–7), 131, 146
Congrés de les Societats Obreres de la Regió Espanyola (1870), 73
Conjunt Català de Música Contemporània, 179
Conservatives (political), 73, 76
Consistori de Barcelona, 60–1
Constantinople: falls (1453), 67
Construcción, En (film), 190–3
Convergència i Unió (CiU), 91–4
cookery books, 234, 240
cooking *see* gastronomy
Cop de Poma (musical project), 181
Corbeil, Treaty of (1258), 55, 58
Corella, Roís de, 124

Coronel Macià (film), 187
Corpus Christi (festival), 211, 213, 216–18, 220, 223
Corsica, 122
Costa Brava. Family Album (film), 190, 201
Coubertin, Pierre, Baron de, 145, 157, 160–1
courtly love, 48, 50–1
Crickboom, Matthieu, 166, 171–2
Crusades, 68
Cuba: crisis (1898), 75; music, 180
Cunillé, Lluïsa: *Barcelona, un mapa*, 199, 201
Curial e Güelfa (anon.), 124
cuynera catalana, La (cookbook), 15

D'Ací i D'Allà (sporting series), 155–6
Dagoll-Dagom (performance group), 31
Dalí, Salvador, 3, 25, 248
dance, 16
Danse Macabre, 60
Dante no es únicamente severo (film), 186
Dau al 7 (review), 27
Davidson, Robert A., 7, 36, 189, 241–2
Davies, C. (ed.): *Companion to Hispanic Studies*, 1n
De nens (film), 197
decadència, 14 & n
Declaration of Linguistic Rights, 158
Decroly, Jean-Ovide, 129
Delegación Nacional de Deportes, 154
Delgado, Maria, David George and Lourdes Orozco (eds): *Catalan Theatre 1975–2006: Politics, Identity and Performance*, 7
Democratic Sexennium, 72
Denominacions d'Origen (EU), 241
Dent, Edward, 174
Desclot, Bernat: Chronicle, 59, 123
Descobrir Cuina (journal), 243n
Deutsches Filminstitut, Frankfurt, 187
Dhuoda, Countess of Barcelona, 51

Di Stéfano, Alfredo, 153–4
Diada de Catalunya (festival), 223
Dies d'agost (film), 190, 202–3
diet, 231
d'Indy, Vincent, 166, 171
Direcció General de Política Lingüística, 158
Ditirambo (film), 186
Domènech i Muntaner, Lluís, 102–3, 169
Dominican Order, 54
Duran, Lluís, 144
Dylan, Bob, 32, 88

Ebro, Battle of the (1938), 84
Eiximenis, Francesc: *Le Crestià*, 62–5, 123
El 9 Esportiu, 156
Elionor, Queen of Aragon, 68
Emma (daughter of Count Guifred I of Barcelona), 51
Encina, Juan del, 168
England: national representation in football, 148–9
Ermegarda de Narbona, 51
Ermessenda of Carcassonne, 46, 51
Escarré, Abbot, 195
Escola Municipal de Música, 172, 179
Esplader, Anton M., 112
Espriu, Salvador, 35, 210; *Cementiri de Sinera*, 27; *Pell de brau*, 29
Esquerra Republicana de Catalunya (ERC), 79–81, 83, 89, 92, 94, 144
Esteva, Jacinto, 186
Estudis de Música Contemporánea, 179
ETA, 29, 88
Eucharistic Congress *see* International Eucharistic Congress
European Charter for Regional or Minority Languages, 133, 137
European Fund for Economic Cohesion, 192
European Union, 109, 189, 192; regulations, 241, 243

Euskal Herria, 2
excursionisme, 143–4, 150

Fabra, Pompeu, 77, 129
Fàbrega, Jaume, 239; *Catalunya per sucar-hi pa*, 240
Facerias, Josep Lluís, 87, 193–5
Falla, Manuel de, 173, 181
falles, 209
Fata Morgana (film), 186, 196
Faura i Pujol, Neus, 156
FC Barcelona ('Barça'): status, 3, 8, 149–50, 153–4; closed down for anti-Spanish sentiments, 105, 130, 153; founded, 143, 152; and Catalan identity, 151–3; successes and celebrity, 151–2; broadcast matches, 157; literature on, 159; agreement with UNESCO, 161; public events, 225
Federació d'Entitats Excursionistes, 150
Federació de Treballadors de la Regió Espanyola (FTRE), 74
Federació Regional Espanyola, 73
feminism, 21; *see also* women
Ferdinand (Ferran II; 'the Catholic'), King of Aragon, 62, 67, 124
Ferran I (Fernando) de Trastamara, King of Aragon, 61, 125
Ferrandis, Antonio, 196
Ferrater, Gabriel, 29
Ferré, Léo, 33
Festa de la Fil·loxera, 221
Festa de la Mercè, 212, 226
Festa del Roser, 211
Festa de Sant Jordi, 224
Festcat (annual summer school), 225
festivals: traditional, 9, 207–9, 215; origins, 209–10; history and development, 210–14; politicization, 212–13, 223–4; revivals and reinventions, 215–16, 221, 225–6; support and organizations for, 215; symbolism, 215; conduct and style, 216–21; local significance, 219–20; attended by celebrities, 220; as romantic meeting places, 220; and food, 223; and holidays, 224; modern management, 226–7; social importance, 226–7
feudalism, 48–50, 55, 67; and festivals, 210
Ficció (film), 190, 203
fiction: Catalan, 27–30
Fiesta del Trabajo, 223
film *see* cinema
Fletxa, Mateu, 164
Floral Games, 60–3
Foix, Josep Vicenç, 25, 26, 176
folk music, 10, 32
folksong, 164, 167
Foment del Treball Nacional, 74
food *see* gastronomy
Food of Love (film), 199–201
football, 149–50, 159; *see also* FC Barcelona
Forn, Josep Maria, 33, 187–9, 195
Fòrum Universal de les Cultures (2004), 225
France: musical influence, 164
Franco, General Francisco: and homogenization of Spain, 14; dictatorship, 26, 29, 85–8, 106–7, 130; death, 33–4, 87, 89, 107; suppresses Asturian miners' strike, 81; in Spanish Civil War, 82, 84, 130; opposition to, 88–9; dislikes foreign words, 156; depicted in films, 193–7; and Eva Perón, 194; adapts festivals, 213, 217, 223–4; restores saints' days, 223; and food in unitary nation, 231–2
Franja d'Aragó, 133
Franks (Carolingians), 41–4, 120
Fraternidad, La, 166
Freinet, Célestin, 129
Frente Popular, 81
Friendly Societies, 73

Frigola, Bonaventura, 166
Front d'Esquerres de Catalunya, 81
Front Català d'Ordre, 81
Front Nacional de Catalunya (FNC), 89
Fruicions (journal), 173
Füfner, Jindřich, 145
Fura dels Baus, La (performance group), 31, 35, 108
Fuster, Joan: *Literatura catalana contemporània*, 36

Galicia, 2
Gamper, Joan (*born* Hans), 143, 152
Garcia Morante, Manuel, 182
Garcia Robles, José, 166–7
Gasser, Lluís, 182
gastronomy: Catalan, 2, 229, 232–9, 243, 248–9; regional, 230–2; international and local, 240–3; *see also* chefs
Gaudí, Antoni: celebrity, 3, 102, 109; style, 19; Barcelona buildings, 97, 102, 108, 199
Gay, Cesc, 188, 190, 203
Gehry, Frank, 109
Generalitat, 80–3, 90–3, 95, 130, 150, 157, 189, 226
George, David and John London, 31
Gerhard, Roberto: genius and compositions, 3, 175–6; as Avant-Garde composer, 25, 27, 171; exile, 163, 174; influence, 178–9; *Ariel* (ballet), 174, 176
Gesta comitum Barcinonensium, 55
Gies, David: *Cambridge Companion to Modern Spanish Culture*, 1
Gil, Rafael, 180
Gimferrer, Pere, 29
Gimpera, Teresa, 196
Girona, 41
Gironès, Josep, 155
Gloriosa (1868 revolution), 72–3
Goded Lloris, General Manuel, 82
Godfroi de Bouillon, 68

Good Bye, Lenin (film), 198
Graham, Helen and Jo Libanyi: *Spanish Cultural Studies: An Introduction*, 1–4
Granados, Enrique, 169, 171, 175, 177
Great Britain: national representation in sports, 148–9
Greece: areas in Catalan federation, 122
Guadalupe, decree of (1486), 67
Gual, Adrià, 175
Güell, Baró de, 146
Guerín, José Luis, 8, 37, 188, 190–4
Guerra Dolça (festival), 218
Guerrero, Pedro, 168
Guilhem, Count of Toulouse, 42
Guimerà, Àngel, 18, 21; *Cel i mar*, 31; *Terra baixa!*, 21
Guinjoan, Joan, 182
Guinovart, Carles, 182
Guthrie, Woody, 32

Haelffter, Rodolfo, 175n
Haget, Henri, 158
Halla-aho, Hilla, 119
Hannibal, 118
Heraldo de Madrid (newspaper), 150
heresy: medieval, 53
Hereu, Jordi, 113
Hispania Schola Musica Sacra, 168
Home dels Nassos, L', 218
Homilies d'Organyà, 118
Homs, Joaquim, 25, 174, 176, 178–9
Horta d'Oriola, 122
Huerga, Manuel, 197–8
humanism, 65
Humanitat, La (newspaper), 144

Ibarz, Alexander, 5, 10, 16, 120, 123, 163, 168
Ibsen, Henrik, 20
Iniciativa per a Catalunya Verds (ICV), 94
Institut d'Estudis Catalans (IEC), 21–2, 77, 88, 129, 131

International Amateur Rugby Federation, 150
International Biennial of Sportsmen in Art, Third, 160
International Eucharistic Congress, Barcelona (1952), 193–4, 213
International Mountaineering and Climbing Federation, 150
International Musicological Society (ISM), 3rd Conference, Barcelona (1936), 173
International Olympic Committee (IOC), 148
International Society for Contemporary Music (ISCM), 172–4, 180
International Workers' Association, 73
internet: and Catalan language, 135–6
IRA (Irish Republican Army), 29
Ireland: literary culture, 5; identity, 16, 19
Isabel, Queen of Castile, 62, 124
Isamendi, Isasi, 180
Isarn, Guitard: *Greuges*, 118
Isil (village), Pallars Sobirà, 209
Italy: food and cuisine, 235, 238

Janés, Josep, 178
Jaume I, King of Aragon, 55–8, 99, 122–3
Jaume III, King of Majorca, 123
Jaume, Count of Urgell, 61, 124
Joan I, King of Aragon, 64, 164
Jocs Florals (poetic festival), 16, 128, 168
Joglars, Els (performance group), 30–2
Johnson, Louise, 8, 88, 225
Johnson, Samuel, 13
Jones, R.O., 9
Jordà, Joaquim, 186, 188, 195–7
Jordan, Barry and Rikki Morgan-Tamosunas (eds): *Contemporary Spanish Cultural Studies*, 1
Juan Carlos I, King of Spain, 89
Juana la Loca, Queen of Castile, 124

Junoy, Josep Maria, 175

Kassel: International Art Fair *Documenta* (2007), 248
Keller, Thomas, 245
Keown, Dominic, 102, 128, 143, 165, 235
Kingtone, Steve, 248n, 249n
Knighton, Tessa, 6, 17, 25

labour movement: beginnings, 73–4; in 20th century, 77–8; *see also* trade unions
Lacuesta, Isaki, 202n
Lamadrid, Marqués de, 146
Lamote de Grignon, Joan, 172–4, 177–8
Land and Freedom (film), 83n
Lapeyra, Josep (composer), 171
Lasarte, Ainaud de: *El Llibre Negre de Catalunya*, 99n
Latin language: and development of Catalan, 117–19, 123
learning and education: medieval, 59
Leavitt, David: *The Page Turner*, 199
Leges Palatinae (Majorca), 123
Lent, 223
Lerroux, Alejandro, 76, 81
Lévi-Strauss, Claude, 229
Lewis, Archibald, 42
Ley de Reforma Politica (LRP), 90
Ley Orgánica de Armonización del Proceso Autonómico (LOAPA), 92–3
Leyenda del tiempo, La (film), 202n
Liberals (political), 72–3, 76
Liceu theatre *see* Barcelona: Gran Teatre del Liceu
Lincoln Centre, New York: 'Film in Catalunya. 1906–2006', 185–6
'Literary History of Spain' series, 9
Llach, Lluís, 33
Llagostera, Ferran, 189
Llanas, Albert, 182
Lleida, 59, 84

Llibre de Sent Soví (anon.; ed. Joan Santanach), 234
Lliga Regionalista (political party), 18, 21, 22n, 76, 77, 79–81, 212
Llobet Gràcia, Llorenç, 185
Llull, Ramon, 57–8, 123
Llúria, Roger de, 152
Loach, Ken, 83n
Louis I (the Pious), King of the Franks, 42, 99, 120
Lowe, Sid, 154
Luján, Néstor, 180, 236; *El Libro de la cocina española* (with Juan Perucho), 232

McDonald's (food chain), 238, 244, 247
McGee, Harold, 245
Macià, Francesc, 80
Maeterlinck, Maurice, 20
Malinowski, Bronislaw, 229
Mallorca: conquered (1229), 56–7
mals usos (regime), 67
Mancomunitat, 77, 79, 130
Mango (Barcelona company), 113–14
Manichaeanism, 53
Manifiesto de los 2.300 (1981), 137
Manifiesto en defensa de la lengua común (2008), 137
Manolos, Los (musical group), 35
Manresa (city), 226
Manresa, Laia, 196
Mansur, Al-, 48
Maquis: oppose Francoist rule, 86–7
Maragall, Joan: 'El Cant de la senyera', 167; *Cant espiritual*, 180; *Visions*, 20
Marca Hispanica, 42
Marçal, Maria Mercè, 30
March, Ausiàs, 62, 65, 124
Marquet, Félix, 185
Marshall, Frank, 175
Martí I, King of Aragon, 61, 68, 124
Martí, Josep, 7, 32n
Martí, Sadurní, 63

Martí i Pol, Miquel, 29
Martí-Olivella, Jaume, 7, 33, 36
Martínez Figuerola, Àlex, 182
Martorell, Joanot, 65; *Tirant lo Blanc*, 65–6, 124
Masana, Antonio, 195
Massó, Enric, 107
Medieval Culture, 4, 41–70
Mediterranean Games, Second (1955), 146
Mediterrània (trade fair), 226
Memorial de Greuges, 75
Mendoza Lassalle, César de, 178
Menorca, 126
Mercury, Freddie, 177
Merino, Imma, 191
Messiaen, Olivier, 180–1
Mestres Quadreny, Josep Maria, 181–2
Metge, Bernat, 64–5, 123; *Lo Somni*, 62, 64
Michelin guide (Spain and Portugal), 243, 245, 247
Mieres (Garrotxa region), 227
Millet, Lluís, 166–7, 170, 172
Miralles, Enric, 109
Miró, Joan: genius, 3; style, 25; and ballet *Ariel*, 176; and Mestres Quadreny, 181
Modernisme, 18–21, 97, 101–2; in music, 169–72
Moix, Terenci, 30, 200
Mola, General Emilio, 82
Moll, Francesc de B., 129
Mompou, Frederic, 174–80
monasteries, 45–6, 48, 120
Moncada, Jesús, 202
Mones com la Becky (film), 188, 195–7
Moniz, Egas, 195–6
Montaliu, Manuel de, 170
Montessori, Maria, 129
Montfort, Simon de, 54–5
Montilla, José, 95
Montllor, Ovidi, 33

Montsalvatge, Xavier, 172, 176–7, 179–80
Montserrat monastery, 46, 88; Enthronement of the Virgin (1947), 214
Monzó, Quim, 34; *El perquè de tot plegat!*, 34, 198
Moore, Roger, 201
Moore, Thomas, 5, 11, 16
Moors (Muslims): in Spain, 41–2, 44, 48, 120; in Valencia, 56–8; learning and technical expertise, 58–9; in Barcelona, 99; defeated by Charles Martel (732), 120
Morales, Cristóbal de, 168
Moran, Josep, 119
Moran, Josep and Joan Anton Rabella, 117
Moran, Warren, 241, 243
Morera, Enric, 166, 170–2, 182; *El Comte Arnau*, 168, 171
Moret, Joaquim, 118
Mossarabic language, 123
Mossos d'Esquadra, 93
Motte-Lacroix, Ferdinand, 177
Movimiento Ibérico de Liberación (MIL), 197
Mundo, El (newspaper), 137
Munt, Silvia, 186
Muntaner's Chronicle (1320s), 59, 123
Muret, Battle of (1213), 55
music: Catalan, 6; and nationalist revival, 17; international influences, 163–5; avant-garde, 179–83; and literature, 182
Muslims: immigrants, 218; *see also* Moors
Mussolini, Benito, 85

Naples, 65, 122, 163
Narayan, Uma, 230
nationalism: European revival, 16–17
Navarro, Arias, 89
Nicholson, Jack, 200

Nicolau, Antoni, 166
Nietzsche, Friedrich, 20
Nin i Serra, Joan Antoni, 167–8
nobility: feudal, 48–9; and burgher class, 60; *see also* class (social)
Nogués, Xavier, 172
Nonell, Isidre, 19
Normes de Castelló, 129
Northern Ireland, 29, 33
Noucentisme, 21–3, 34; in music, 169, 172
Nous Directors Catalans (group), 189
nouvelle cuisine, 245
Nova Cançó, 1, 29, 32, 88, 131
Noyes, Dorothy, 8, 16, 35
Nueva Planta, Decree of (1715), 68, 126
Nuix, Jep, 182
Núria, Statute of (1931), 80

Obra del Cançoner Popular de Catalunya, 167
Ocaña, retrat intermitent (film), 186
Occitan (language), 51, 57, 62, 125
Oliba, Count of Berga and Ripoll, 46
Oliver, Maria Antònia, 30
Oller, Narcís, 18, 23, 119
Olympic Games: Barcelona (1992), 8, 31–2, 35–6, 97, 107–9, 145–7, 157–8, 189, 207, 225, 277; Berlin (1936), 145–6; national representation, 148; Cultural Olympiad, 160–1
Òmnium Cultural, 88, 131, 158
Once, El (magazine), 159
opera, 165, 168, 171–2
Opus Dei, 88
orchestras, 172–4, 178
Ordinacions de la Casa Real, 123
Orfeó Barcelonès, 166
Orfeó Català, 166–7, 169, 171
orgia, L' (film), 34
orienteering, 147
Oriola (Orihuela), 122

Orquestra de l'Associació d'Amics de la Música, 172
Orquestra Filharmònica, 174, 178
Orquestra Municipal, 174
Orquestra Pau Casals, 173
Orquestra Sinfònica de Barcelona, 172–3
Ors, Eugeni d', 22
Orwell, George: *Homage to Catalonia*, 83n, 106
Oset, Àngel, 195

Padrós, David, 182
Pahissa, Jaume, 163, 172, 174–6; *La princesa Margarida*, 175
País, El (newspaper), 157
Palau de la Música, 169
Palestra (sporting organization), 144
Pàmias, Joan Antoni, 177
Pan's Labyrinth (film), 87n
Papacy: and heresy, 53–4; and Jaume I, 56; and Pere I's acquisition of Sicily, 58; *see also* Church (Catholic)
Parc de la Ciutadella (film), 196
Parcerisas, Francesc, 29
Partal, Vicenç, 136
Partido Democrático, 72
Partido Popular (PP), 94–5, 134, 137, 197
Partido Socialista Obrero Español (PSOE), 74, 90, 92–3
Partit dels Socialistes Catalunya (PSC), 91–2
Partit Obrer d'Unificació Marxista (POUM), 83
Partit Republicà Democràtic i Federal (PRDF), 72
Partit Republicà Radical (PRR), 76
Partit Socialista Unificat de Catalunya (PSUC), 83, 88–9, 92
Passenger, The (film), 200
Patum see Berga
Peace and Truce of God, 46, 50
Pedrell, Felip, 167–72, 175–6; *La Celestina*, 168; *Els Pirineus*, 165, 168; *Por nuestra música*, 168; *L'ultimo Abenzaraggio*, 167
Pedrolo, Manuel de, 28
Pei, I.M., 109
Pen Club: international conference (Barcelona, 1935), 26
Peña, Richard, 186
Pere I, King of Aragon, 55, 58
Pere III, King of Aragon (II of Barcelona), 59, 123
Pere IV, King of Aragon (III of Barcelona; 'el Cerimoniós'), 59, 61
Peret (flamenco singer), 35
performing arts *see* theatre
Perón, Eva, 194
perquè de tot plegat, El (film), 198
Perucho, Joan (novelist), 29–30
Perucho, Juan (gastronome), 232
Petronilla, Countess, 55
Philip V, King of Spain (*earlier* duc d'Anjou), 13, 26, 126, 127
Phonos (sound laboratory), 181–2
phylloxera: and wine festival, 221
Pi i Margall, Francesc, 17, 72
Pi de la Serra, Francesc, 33
Picasso, Pablo, 19; museum, 200; 'Les Demoiselles d'Avignon', 23–4
Pinto, João Maria, 196–7
Pla, Josep: *El que hem menjat*, 238
plaça del Diamant, La (film), 186, 198
Plan de Estabilización (1959), 131
Plataforma Pro-Seleccions Esportives Catalanes, 148
Poble català, El (journal), 170
Poesia (review), 26
poetry, 22–4, 26–7, 29
Poitiers, Battle of (732), 41, 120
Polley, Sarah, 202
Ponç, Joan, 181
Pons, Josep Sebastià, 172
Pons, Ventura, 8, 34, 186, 188, 190, 198–201
Popular Front, 82

Porcel, Baltasar, 30
Porchet, Adrián, 165
Portabella, Pere, 188
poster art, 159–60
Poveda, Miquel, 35
Prat de la Riba, Enric, 18, 21–2, 77, 129–30, 210; *La nacionalitat catalana*, 21
Prim, Josep Maria, 180
Primo de Rivera, Miguel: dictatorship, 21, 26, 76, 78, 104–5, 130, 146; and *excursionisme*, 143; outlaws *sardana*, 213
Publicitat, La (newspaper), 144
Pueyo, Salvador, 182
Puig Antig, Salvador, 197
Puig i Cadalfach, Josep, 102
Puig de Cebolla, 56
Pujol, Francesc, 172–3, 198n, 201n
Pujol, Jordi, 91–2
Punt, El (newspaper), 240n
Puyana, Rafael, 181
Pyrenees: in medieval times, 41–2; iron mining, 45
Pyrenees, Treaty of the (1659), 125

Quart, Pere (Joan Oliver), 27
Quartet Renaixement, 172
Queipo de Llano, General Gonzalo, 82

Rabella, Joan Anton *see* Moran, Josep and Joan Anton Rabella
Ràdio Associació de Catalunya, 156
Ràdio Barcelona, 156–7
Ràdio Catalana, 156
Raduà, Josep Maria, 148–9
Raimon (musician), 33, 210
Rambla, La (newspaper), 144, 150
Ramon Berenguer I, Count, 49
Ramon Berenguer IV, Count, 55
RCD Espanyol (football club), 152, 154
Real Cédula (1768), 127
Real Madrid (football club), 153–4
Recha, Marc, 8, 37, 188, 190, 202–3

Renaixença, La, 15–18, 69, 72, 103, 128, 143, 165, 169, 207–8, 234
Renau, Josep, 159
Resina, Joan Ramon, 107
Restaurant (magazine), 245
restaurants, 235; *see also* chefs; gastronomy
Revista Musical Catalana, 167–8
Reyes, Fernando, 182
Riba, Carles, 23, 26, 35
Ribas, Antoni, 33, 186, 189
Riera, Carme, 30
Ripoll, 45–6
Riquer, Martí de, 123
Robbins, Tim, 202
Robert, Mestre: *Llibre del coc*, 234
Rodoreda, Mercè, 30; *Plaça del Diamant*, 28–9, 37, 186
Rodriguez Zapatero, José Luis, 94
Roger, Miquel, 182
Roig, Jaume, 65
Roig, Montserrat, 30
Roís de Corella, Joanot, 65
Roland (legendary hero), 41
Romance languages, 117–19
Romanesque style, 45–7
Romans: found Barcelona (Barcino), 99; in Iberia, 118; Empire collapses (476), 120
Romanticism, 15, 72
Roselló, Joan, 119
Roser i Puig, Montserrat, 8
Rosselló: annexed by France, 125
Rovira Beleta, Francisco, 185
rugby football, 150–1
Ruiz-Pipó, Antonio, 181
Rumba catalana (dance), 35
Ruscalleda, Carme, 247–8
Rusiñol, Santiago, 20, 171; *L'auca del senyor Esteve*, 20, 217

Sabater brothers (*maquis*), 87
Saïd (film), 190
St Sylvester's Day, 218

Salazar, Adolfo, 175n
Salvà, Bernat, 187
Salvador, Juli, 185
Salvador Puig Antich (film), 197–8
Salvador, Santiago, 104
Salvador Duch, J., 152
Salvat-Papasseit, Joan, 24–5, 28, 179
Samaranch, Juan Antonio, 107, 146
Samitier, Josep, 153
Samper, Baltasar, 175, 178
San Sebastian, Pact of (1930), 79
Sánchez-Juan, Sebastià, 179
Sánchez Piñol, Albert: *Pandora al Congo*, 36; *Pell freda*, 36
sanctuaries, 219–20
Sanjurjo, General José, 82
Sant Climent de Taüll (church), 46
Sant Cugat del Vallès (monastery), 120
Sant Fèlix d'Urgell, 46
Sant Jaume de Queralbs (church), 46
Sant Joan (Midsummer night), 209–10, 222
Sant Joan de les Abadesses, 46, 51
Sant Jordi, Jordi de, 124
Sant Pere de Rodes (monastery), 46, 120
Sant Sadurní d'Anoia, 221
Santa Llúcia (fair), 223
Santa Maria de Ripoll (monastery), 46, 120
Santamaría, Santi, 239, 247–8; *La cocina al desnudo*, 247
Santanach, Joan, 234
Santos, Mateo, 185
sardana (dance), 16, 163, 171, 207–8, 212–13
Sardinia, 58, 122
Sarsanedas, Jordi, 29
Sastre, Ramón, 179
Sau, Statute of (1979), 91, 95
sauces (culinary), 235
Schneider, Maria, 200
scholasticism, 65
Scipio, 118

Scotland: identity, 15, 19
Scott, Sir Walter, 15
Secció Filològica, 129
Secretari General de l'Esport, 158
Seeger, Pete, 32, 88
Segrelles, Josep, 159
Segura i Mas, Antoni and Elisenda Barbé i Pou, 6, 17, 103, 212
Sen, Miguel, 232, 244–6
Septimania, 42–4
Serra, Albert, 202n
Serra, Rosa, 158
Serrallonga (17th-century bandit), 20
Serrano Bedoya, General Francisco, 73
Serrat, Joan Manuel, 33
Shelley, Percy Bysshe, 16
Sicily: in Catalan Federation, 58, 122
Siguan, Miquel, 128
Sindicato Español Universitario (SEU), 88
Sindicats Lliures, 78, 104
Sitges, 217
Slow Food, 238
Smith, Andrew, 98, 108, 112
Sociedad Española de Football, 152
Societat Catalana de Concerts, 166, 171
Societat Coral Barcino, 166
Societat del Born, 212
Societat Filharmònica, 166, 171, 173
Societats Euterpenses, 17
Sofcatalà (organization), 136
Solé Tura, Jordi and Eliseo Aja, 130
Soler, Llorenç, 190
Solidaritat Catalana, 76, 129
Solidaritat Obrera, 76
Sontag, Susan, 197
Soriano, Carmen, 155
Souvenir (film), 190, 200
Spain: cultural achievements, 2–3; loses overseas colonies, 17–18, 21, 75; war with USA (1898), 18, 21, 75; absolutism ends (1833), 71; military coup (1923), 78; elections (1936),

81–2; under Franco, 85–9; excluded, then admitted to United Nations, 87; Stabilization Plan (1959), 87; monarchy re-established (1969), 89; post-Franco political development, 89–91; membership of European Union, 109, 189; attitude to status of Catalan language, 137; national sporting teams, 147–8; cinema, 186; official holidays, 224; cuisine, 232–3

Spanish Civil War (1936–39), 82–5, 105–6, 130, 153, 174

Spanish language: linguistic frontier with Catalan, 122; in Catalonia, 125, 127

Spanish Republic, First (1873–74), 17, 72–3

Spanish Republic, Second (1931–39), 26, 79, 130

Spanish Succession, War of (1714), 13–14, 68, 72, 99; effect on Catalan language, 124–6

sport: in Catalonia, 8, 155; outdoor, 143–4; organizations, 144; and national representation, 148–9; and language, 155–8; and culture, 158–61; *see also* FC Barcelona; Olympic Games

Sport (magazine), 157

Strauss, Richard, 173

Stravinsky, Igor, 174

strikes (industrial unrest), 77–8

Strubell, Miquel, 6, 15, 57, 163

Suárez, Adolfo, 89–91

Suárez, Gonzalo, 186

submarí, a les estovalles, Un (film), 189–90

Sunyol i Garriga, Josep, 153

surrealism, 25

swimming: representative teams, 149

Sylvester II, Pope (Gerbert of Aurilhac), 46

Tancament de Caixes, 75

Tàpias, Pere, 242, 244

Tàpies, Antoni, 27, 181

Tarantos, Los (film), 185

Tarradellas, Josep, 91

Tavani, Giuseppe, 44, 61

Taverna-Bech, Francesc, 182

Teixidor, Jordi, 30

Tejero, Colonel Antonio, 33, 92

TERMCAT (language centre), 155, 158

Terradelles, Domènec: *La Merope*, 176

Terry, Arthur, 4–5, 20–1, 30; *Companion to Catalan Literature*, 14n

theatre (and performing arts): in Catalonia, 6–7; scholarly studies of, 10; under Franco, 27, 30–1

Thrift, N., 230

Tokyo: Ruscalleda's restaurant, 247

Toldrà, Eduard, 172, 175, 177

Torrent, Ferran: *La vida abisma*, 199

Toulouse: Floral Games (*Consistori de Tolosa*), 60

tourism: in Barcelona, 98, 103, 109–12; effect on local cuisine, 236–7, 239

Tours, Third Council of (813), 118

trade unions: legalized, 73; power, 104

Tragic Week (July 1909), 23, 76–7, 104, 186, 213

Trastamara dynasty, 62, 65, 67–8

Tremlett, Giles, 244

Tribunal Constitucional, 93

Tricicle, El (theatre group), 32, 35

Trinca, La (musical group), 33

Tripartit (coalition government), 94–5

troubadours, 47–8, 50–4, 60–1

Trueta, Josep, 3

TV3, 93, 132

Twain, Mark, 140

Tyrs, Miroslav, 145

UNESCO, 226

Unió Catalanista (UC), 75–6

Unió Regionalista (UR), 75–6

Unión de Centro Democrático (UCD), 90, 93
Unión General de Trabajadores (UGT), 74
Unión Patriótica, 78
United Nations: admits Spain, 87
United States of America: war with Spain (1898), 18, 21, 75; Civil Rights movement, 32–3, 88
Universal Exhibition (1888) *see* Barcelona: International Exposition
Usatges de Barcelona (legal code, 1173), 49–50
Utrecht, Treaty of (1713), 126
Uzcudún, Paulino, 155

Valencia: captured (1238), 56–7; cultural advance, 65, 124; settlement, 123; language, 124–5, 134–5, 137, 139; under Castilian rule, 126
Valéry, Paul: *Cimitière marin*, 27
Valls, Manuel, 181
Valls (Tarragona), 16, 207, 223
Vallverdú, Francesc, 29
Vanguardia, La (newspaper), 157
Vatican Council, Second, 88
Vázquez-Montalbán, Manuel: *L'art de menjar a Catalunya*, 233, 236–7; *Contra los gourmets*, 238
Vela, Leonor, 131
Venice International Film Festival (2007), 186
Ventura, Pep, 16
Verdaguer, Jacint, 18, 128, 181; *L'Atlàntida*, 166; *Canigó*, 174
Vergés, Rosa, 190, 200
Veu de Catalunya, La (newspaper), 22, 76, 128, 155

Vic: early school, 46
Victoria, Tomás Luis de, 168
Vida en sombras (film), 185
vida secreta de las palabras, La (film), 190, 202–3
vieja memoria, La (film), 186
Vilanova i la Geltrú, 218, 227
Vilarubias, Felio A., 194
Villar, Àngel María, 147
Villaronga, Agustí, 188
Vinalopó Mitjà, 122
Viñes, Ricardo, 177
Visigoths, 41–2, 51, 99
Vives, Amadeu, 166
Vives, Vicens, 216

Wagner, Richard, 165, 170
Weavers, The (US group), 32–3
Webern, Anton, 174, 176
wine, 237, 240
women: as writers, 28–30; status in medieval Catalonia, 51; national football teams, 149; in sports, 150–1; *see also* feminism
Workers' Olympics, 145–6
Wotowicz, Boleslaw, 174
Wright, Roger, 117, 119, 123

Xàtiva: falls (1244), 56
Xirau, Ramon, 29
Xut! (newspaper), 155, 159

Yepes, Narciso, 181
Ysaÿe, Eugène, 171

Zabaleta, Nicanor, 181
Zamora, Ricardo, 153 (Madrid newspaper), 137